PEACH BOY RIVERSIDE

7

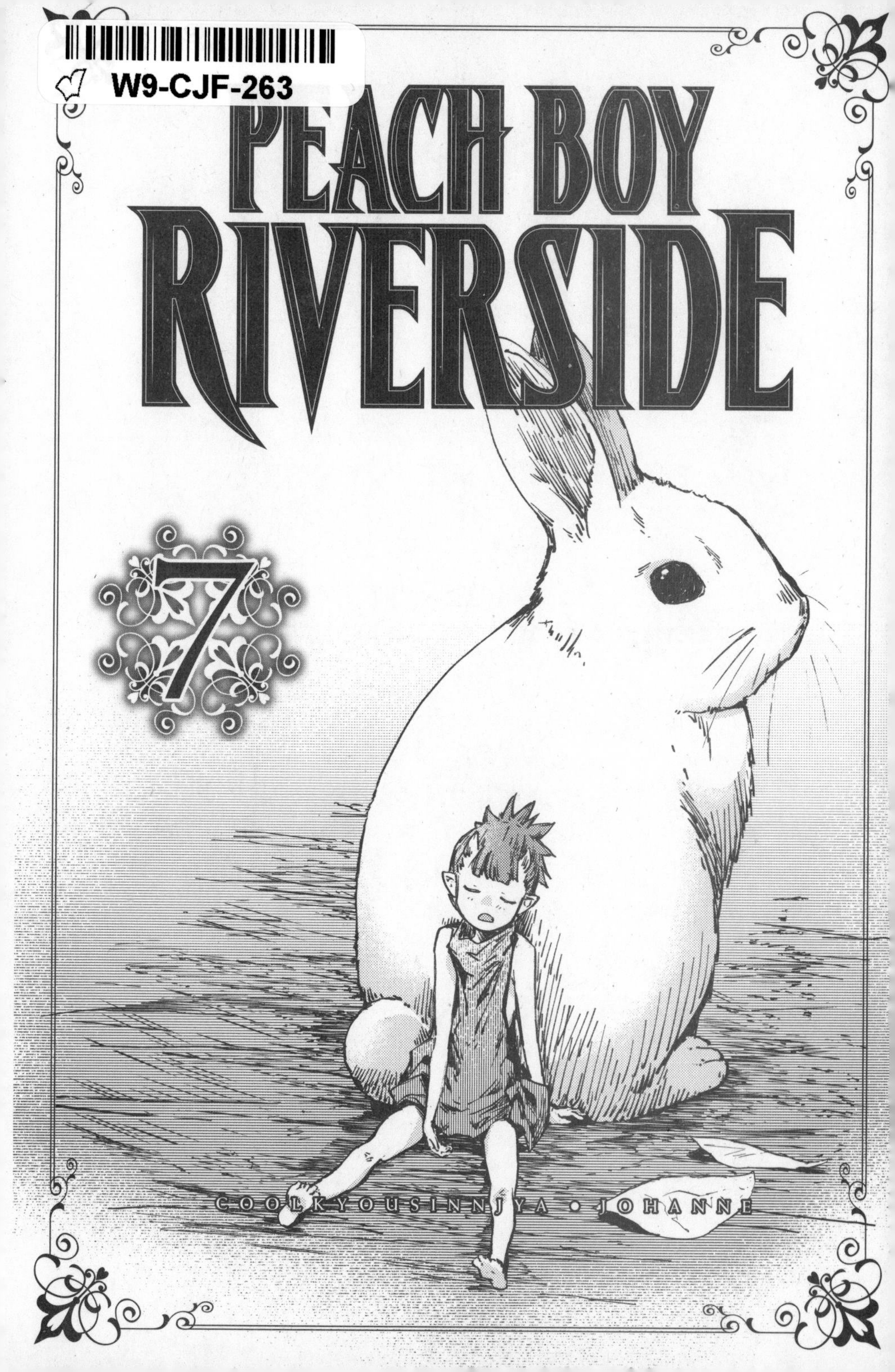

COOLKYOUSINNJYA • JOHANNE

CONTENTS

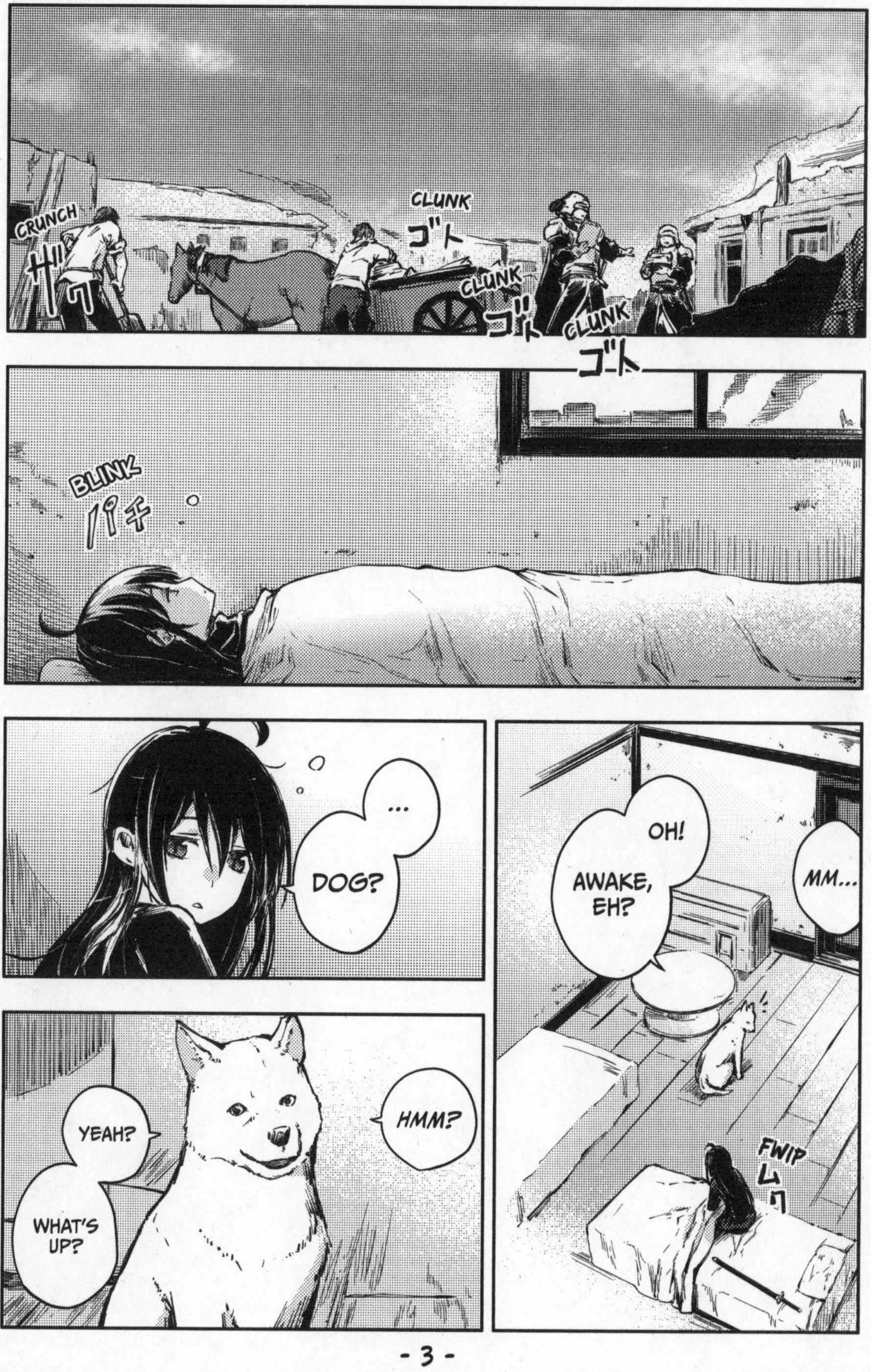
CLUNK
ゴト
CLUNK
ゴト
CLUNK
ゴト
CRUNCH
ザク
BLINK
パチ
MM...
OH!
AWAKE, EH?
FWIP
ムク
...
DOG?
HMM?
YEAH?
WHAT'S UP?

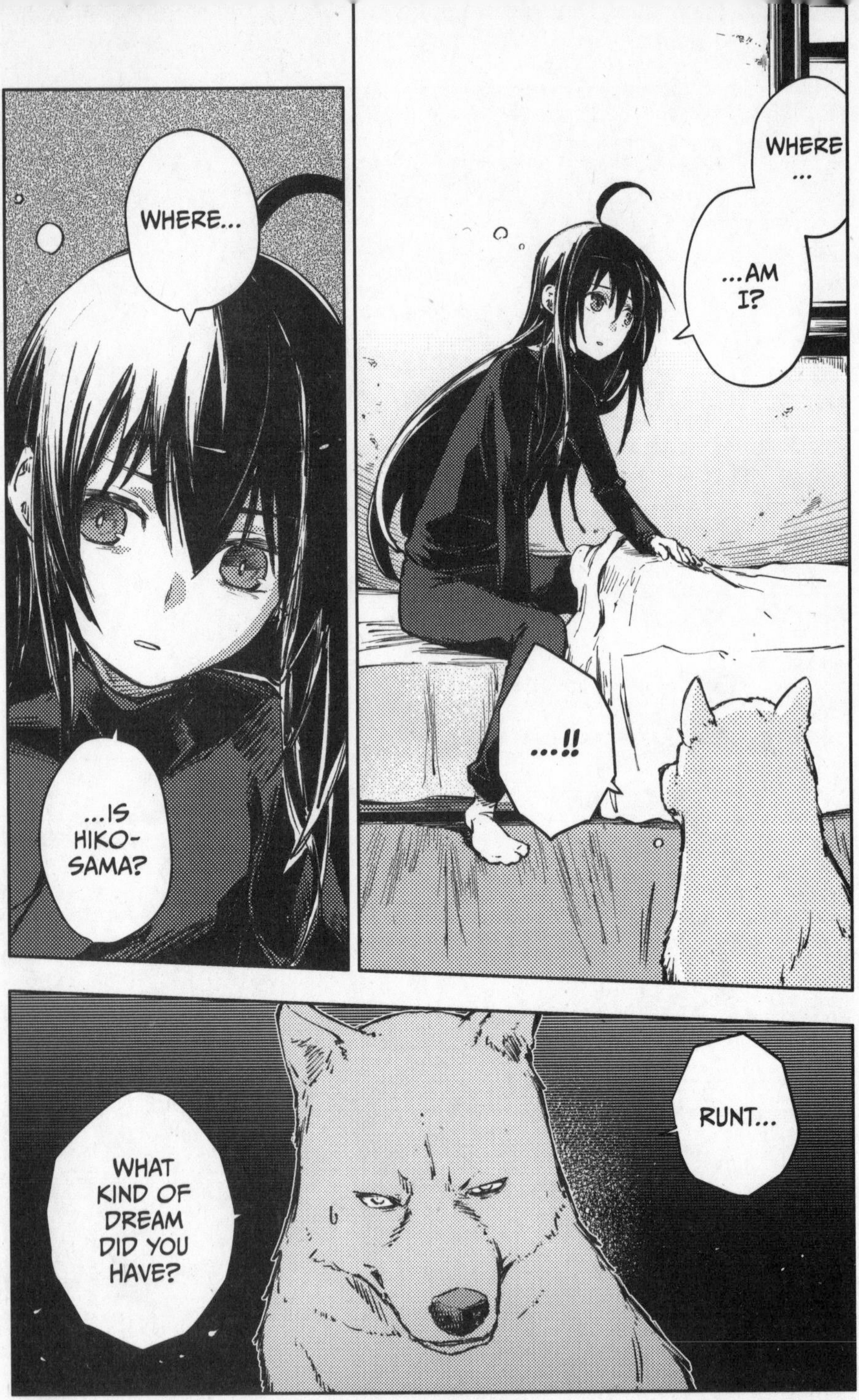
WHERE ...
...AM I?
...!!
WHERE...
...IS HIKO-SAMA?
RUNT...
WHAT KIND OF DREAM DID YOU HAVE?

CHAPTER 24: "MIKOTO" AND THE PAST

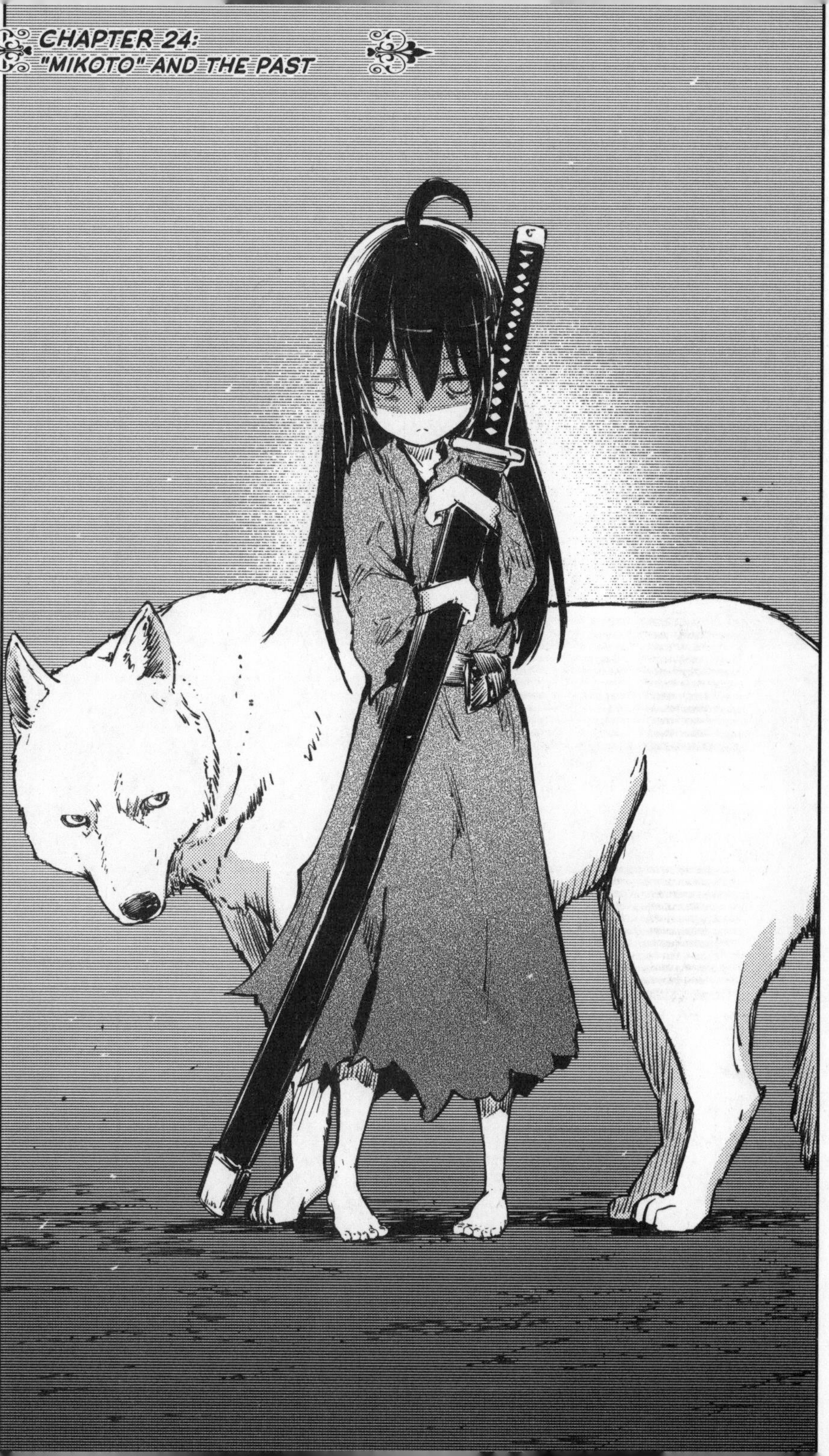

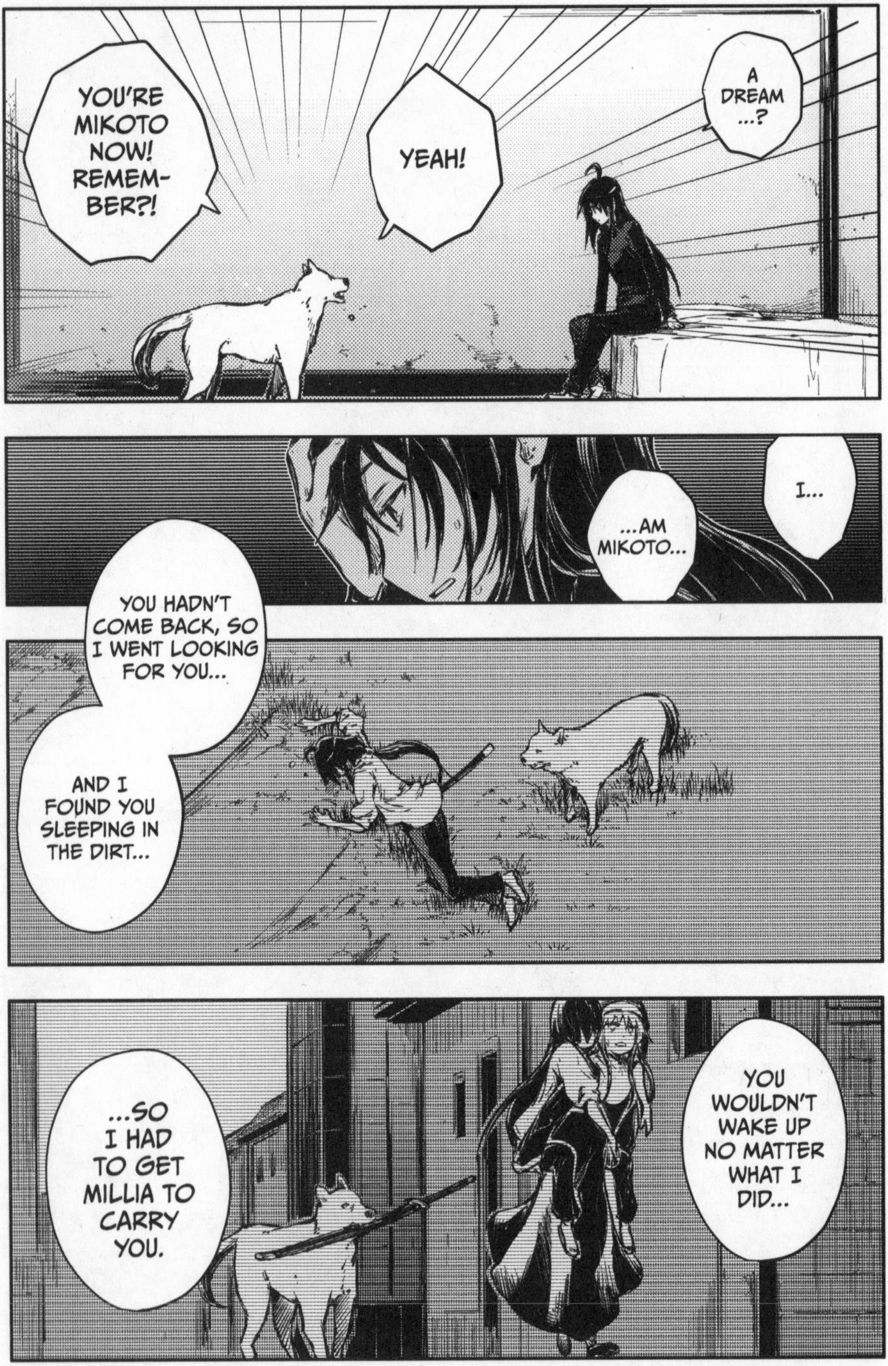
A DREAM ...?
YEAH!
YOU'RE MIKOTO NOW! REMEMBER?!
I...
...AM MIKOTO...
YOU HADN'T COME BACK, SO I WENT LOOKING FOR YOU...
AND I FOUND YOU SLEEPING IN THE DIRT...
YOU WOULDN'T WAKE UP NO MATTER WHAT I DID...
...SO I HAD TO GET MILLIA TO CARRY YOU.

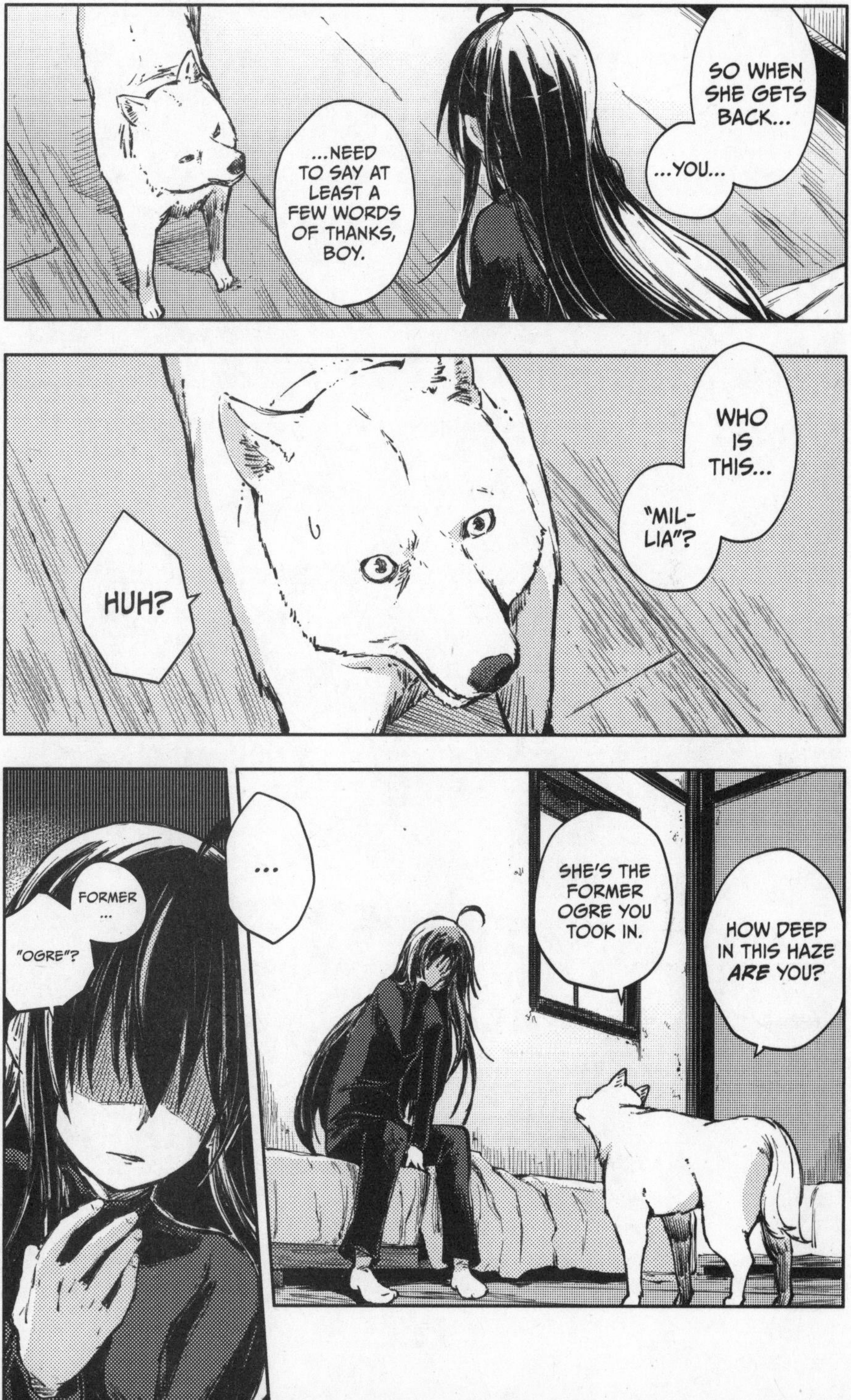
SO WHEN SHE GETS BACK...
...YOU...
...NEED TO SAY AT LEAST A FEW WORDS OF THANKS, BOY.
WHO IS THIS...
"MIL-LIA"?
HUH?
HOW DEEP IN THIS HAZE *ARE* YOU?
SHE'S THE FORMER OGRE YOU TOOK IN.
...
FORMER ...
"OGRE"?

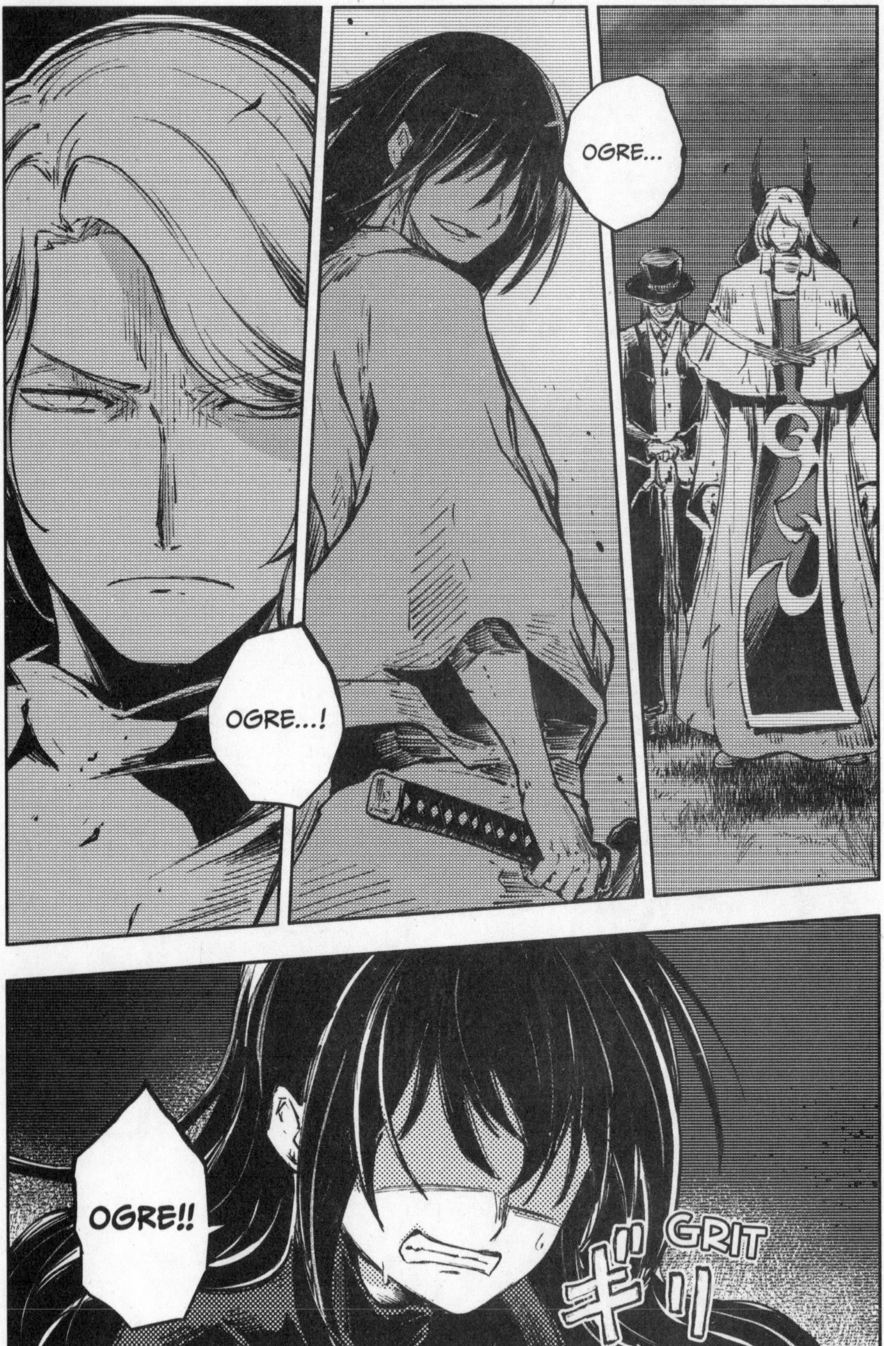
OGRE...
OGRE...!
OGRE!!
ギリ GRIT

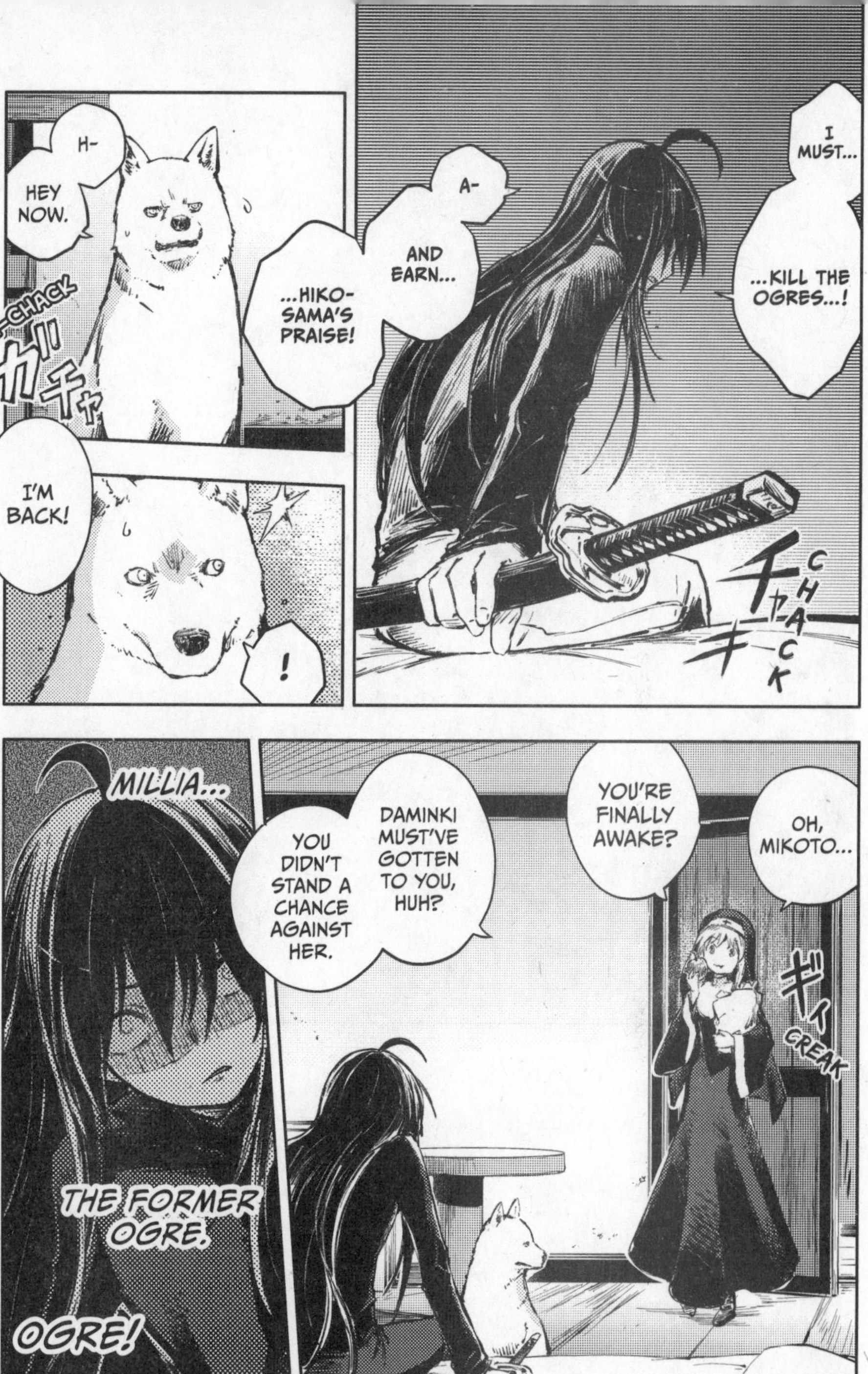
I MUST...
...KILL THE OGRES...!
A-
AND EARN...
...HIKO-SAMA'S PRAISE!
CHACK
H-
HEY NOW.
KA-CHACK
I'M BACK!
!
OH, MIKOTO...
YOU'RE FINALLY AWAKE?
DAMINKI MUST'VE GOTTEN TO YOU, HUH?
YOU DIDN'T STAND A CHANCE AGAINST HER.
CREAK
MILLIA...
THE FORMER OGRE.
OGRE!

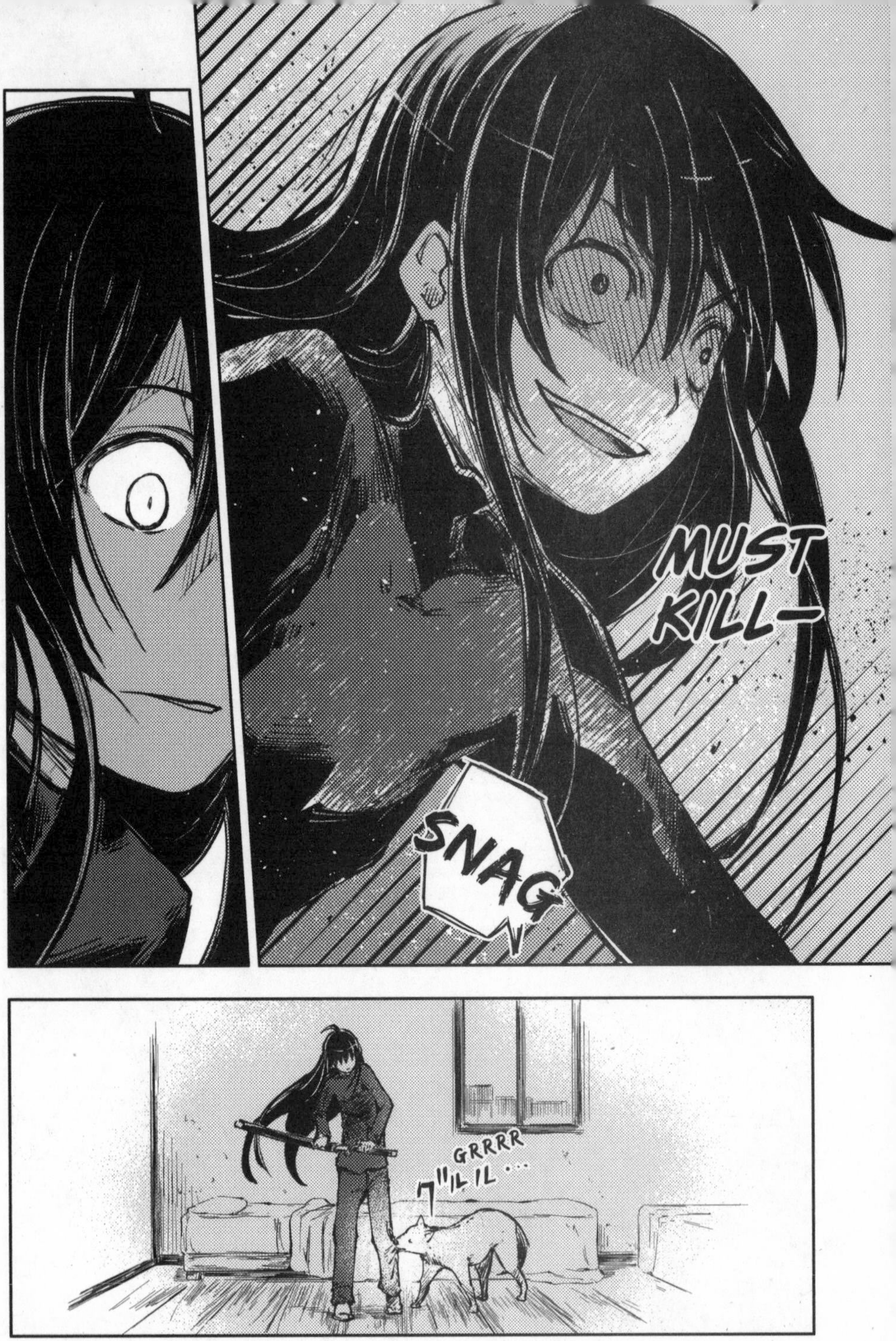
MUST KILL—
SNAG
GRRRR
グルル...

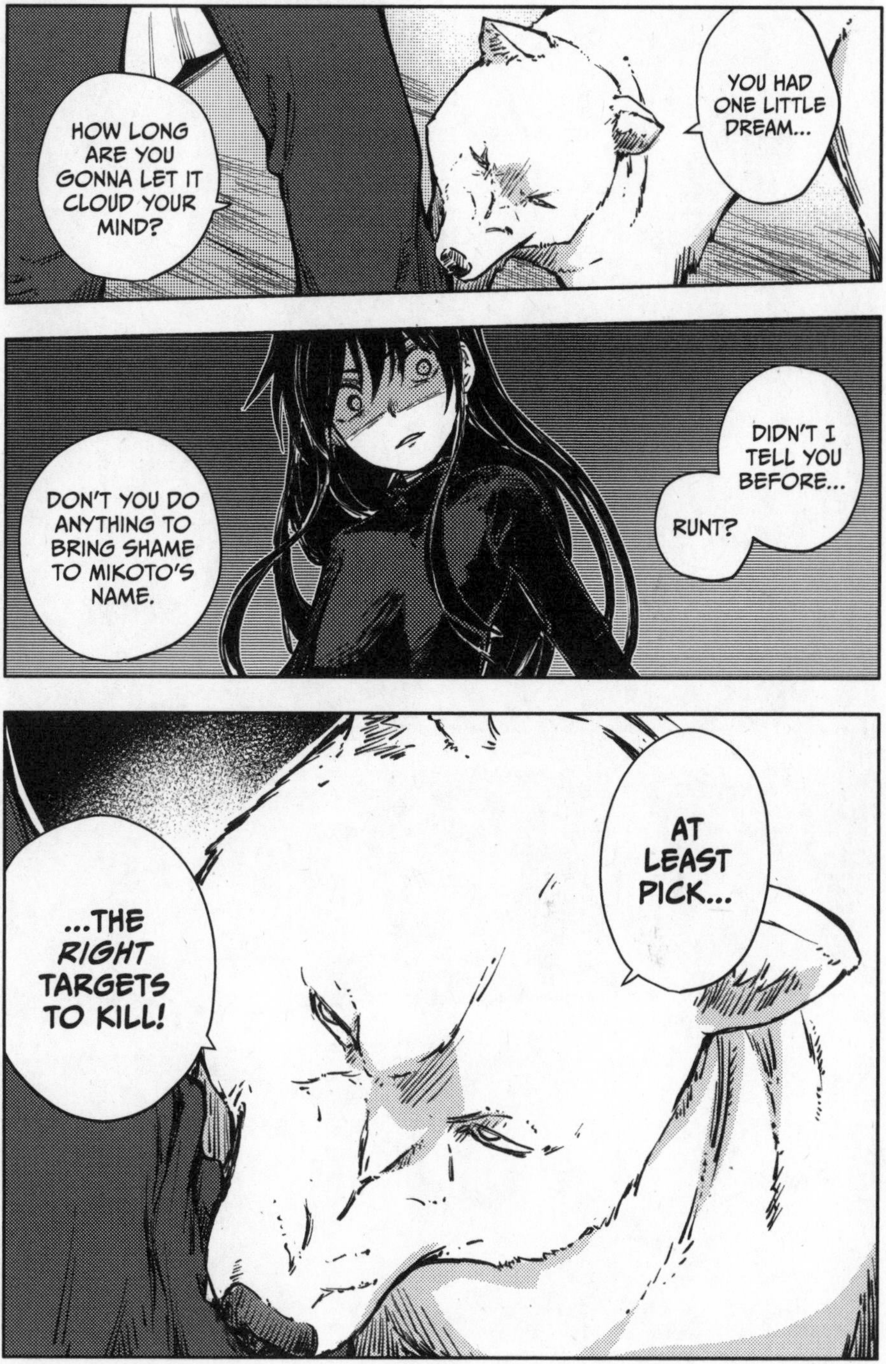
YOU HAD ONE LITTLE DREAM...
HOW LONG ARE YOU GONNA LET IT CLOUD YOUR MIND?
DIDN'T I TELL YOU BEFORE...
RUNT?
DON'T YOU DO ANYTHING TO BRING SHAME TO MIKOTO'S NAME.
AT LEAST PICK...
...THE *RIGHT* TARGETS TO KILL!

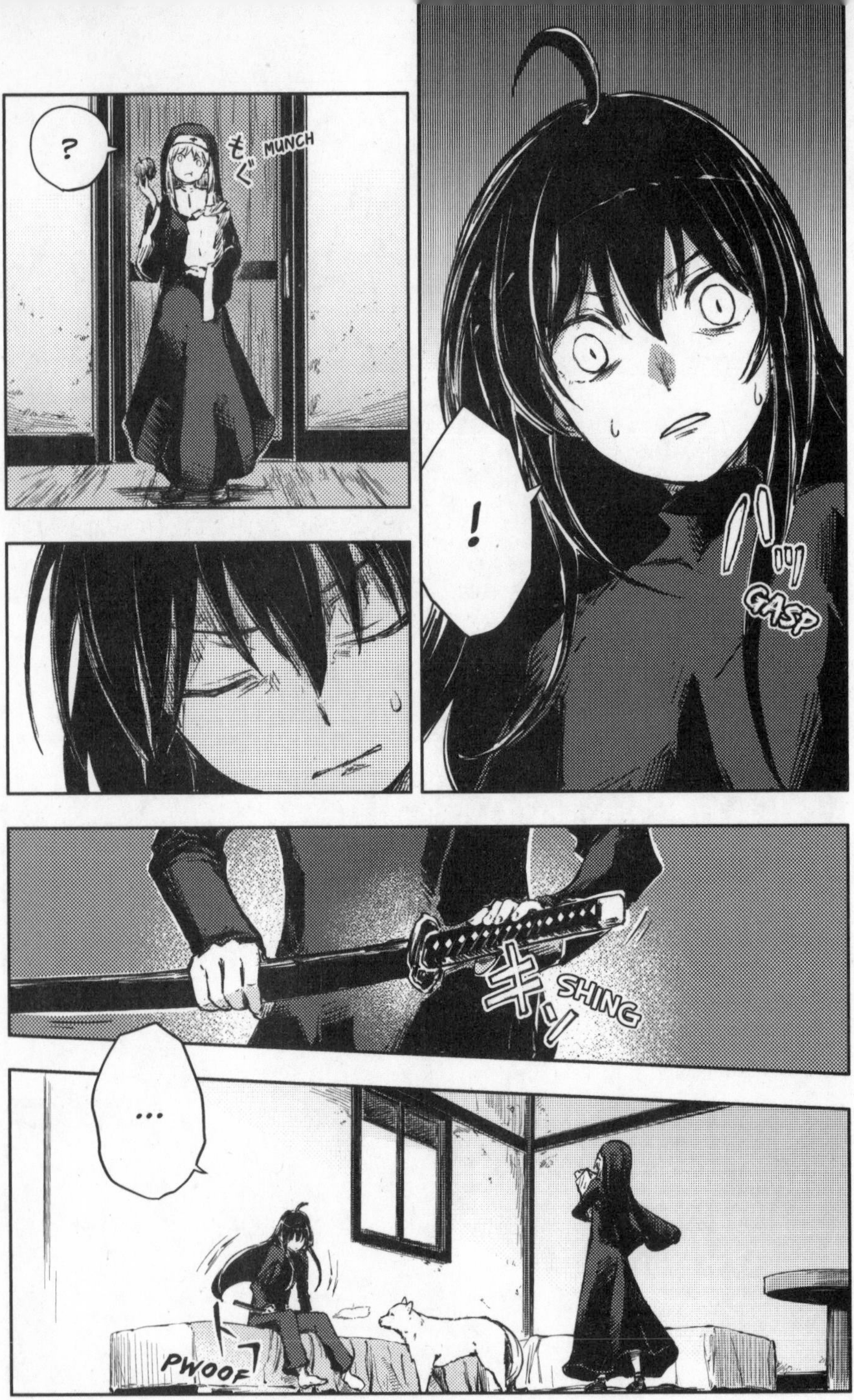
!
GASP
?
もぐ MUNCH
SHING
...
PWOOF

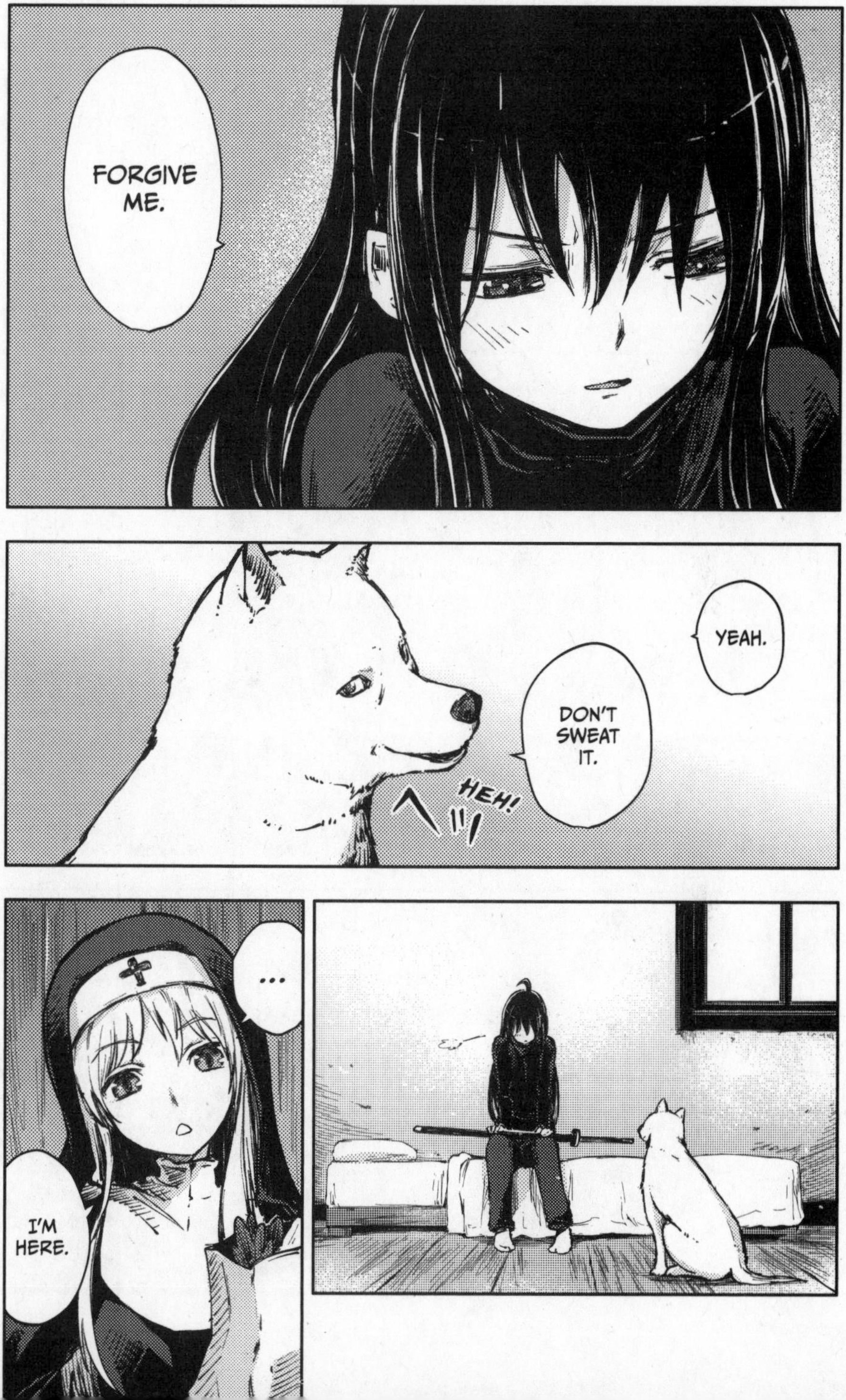
FORGIVE ME.
YEAH.
DON'T SWEAT IT.
HEH!
...
I'M HERE.

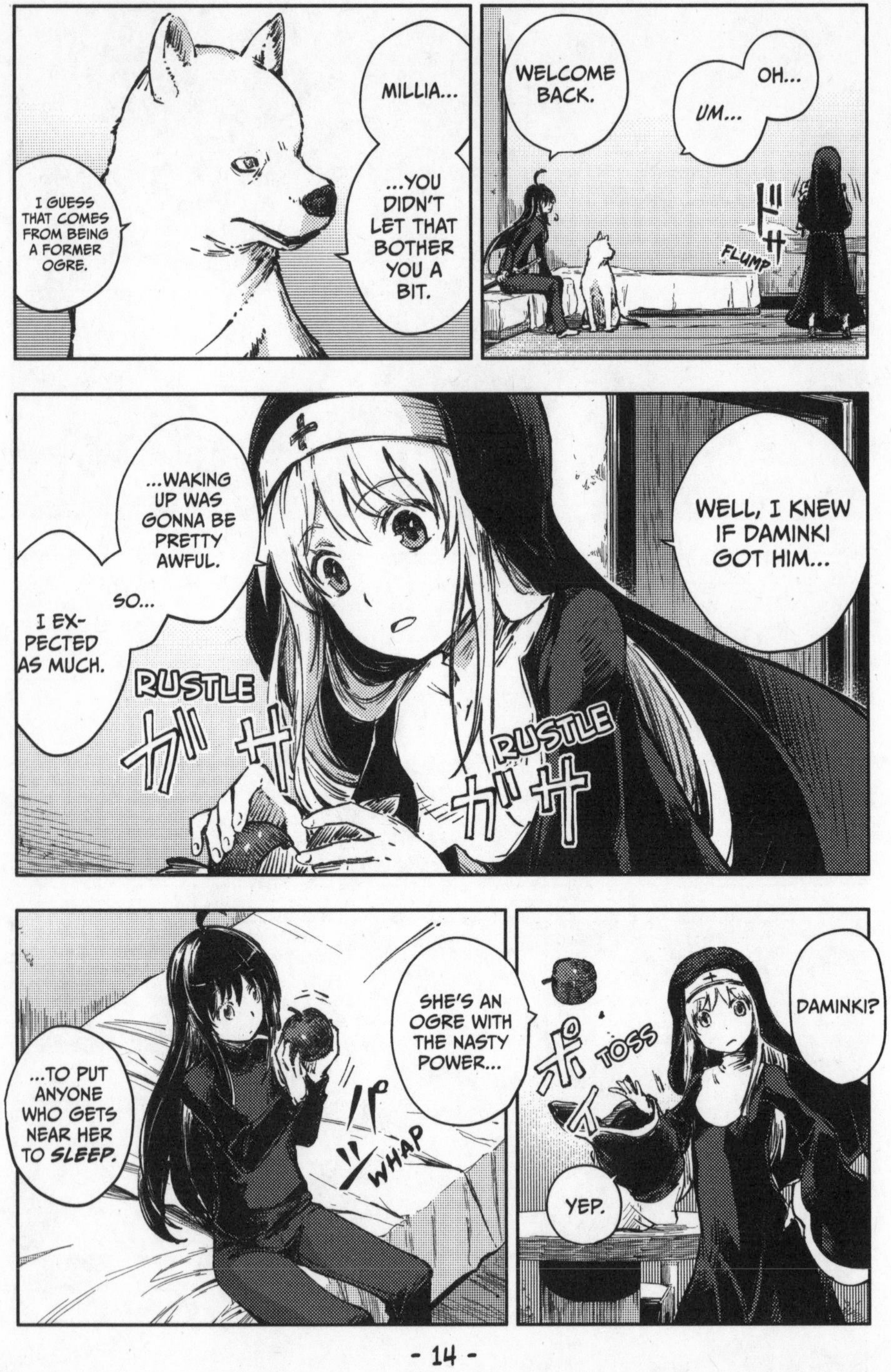
OH...
UM...
WELCOME BACK.
ドサ
FLUMP
MILLIA...
...YOU DIDN'T LET THAT BOTHER YOU A BIT.
I GUESS THAT COMES FROM BEING A FORMER OGRE.
WELL, I KNEW IF DAMINKI GOT HIM...
...WAKING UP WAS GONNA BE PRETTY AWFUL.
SO...
I EX-PECTED AS MUCH.
ガサ
RUSTLE
ガサ
RUSTLE
DAMINKI?
ポイ
TOSS
YEP.
SHE'S AN OGRE WITH THE NASTY POWER...
パ
WHAP
...TO PUT ANYONE WHO GETS NEAR HER TO *SLEEP*.

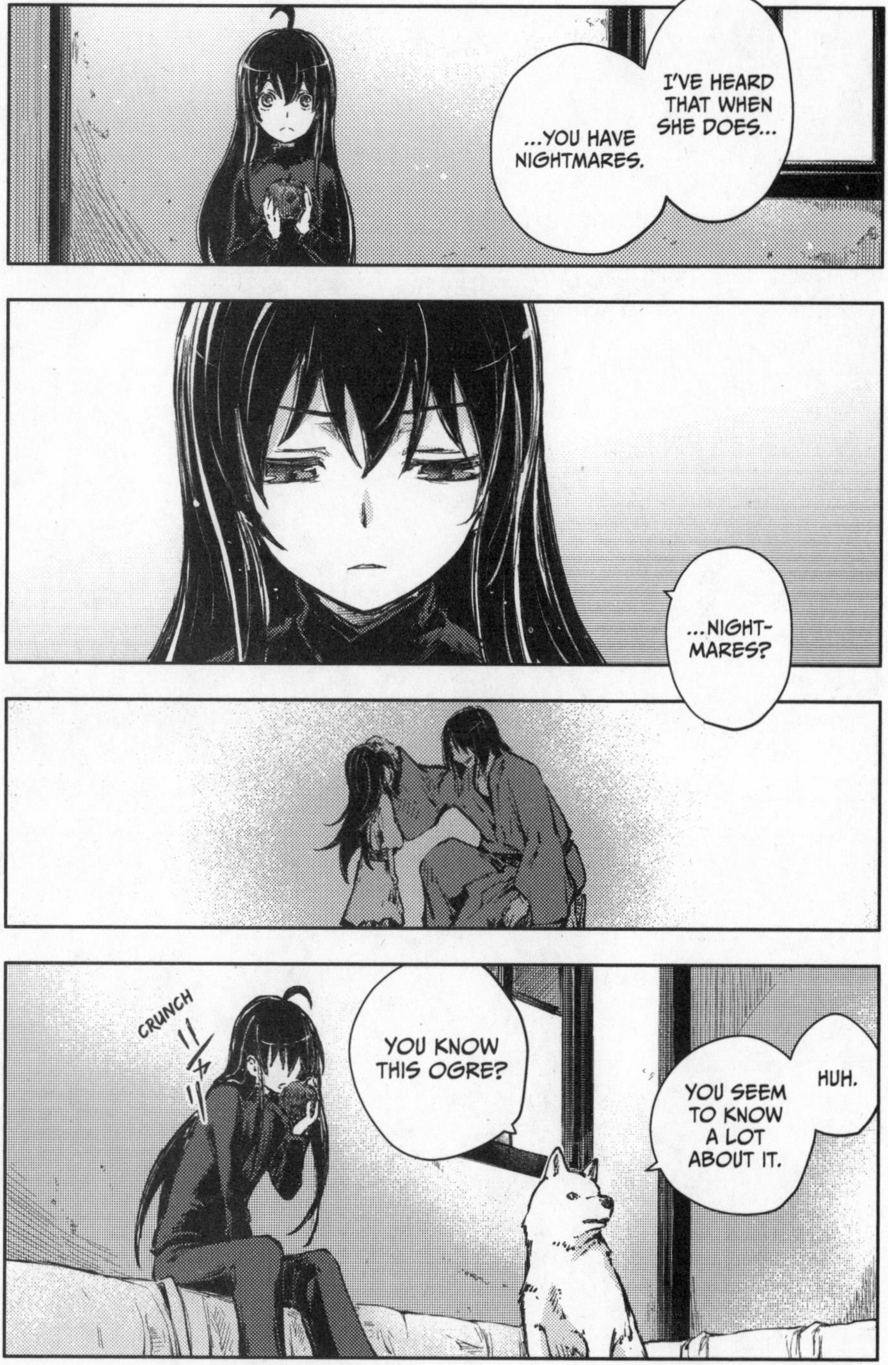
I'VE HEARD THAT WHEN SHE DOES...
...YOU HAVE NIGHTMARES.
...NIGHT-MARES?
HUH.
YOU SEEM TO KNOW A LOT ABOUT IT.
YOU KNOW THIS OGRE?
CRUNCH

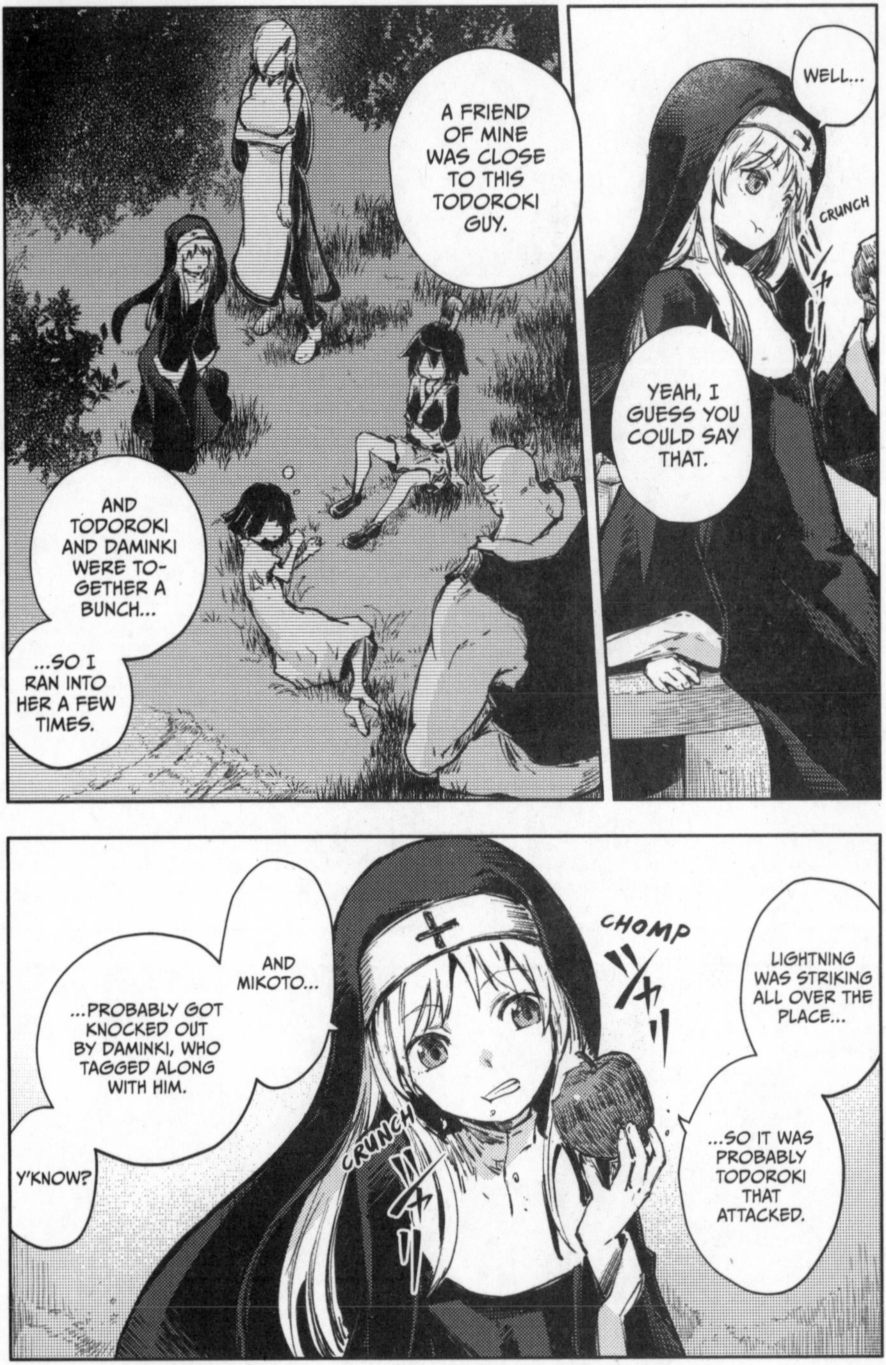
WELL...
CRUNCH
YEAH, I GUESS YOU COULD SAY THAT.
A FRIEND OF MINE WAS CLOSE TO THIS TODOROKI GUY.
AND TODOROKI AND DAMINKI WERE TO-GETHER A BUNCH...
...SO I RAN INTO HER A FEW TIMES.
LIGHTNING WAS STRIKING ALL OVER THE PLACE...
CHOMP
...SO IT WAS PROBABLY TODOROKI THAT ATTACKED.
AND MIKOTO...
...PROBABLY GOT KNOCKED OUT BY DAMINKI, WHO TAGGED ALONG WITH HIM.
CRUNCH
Y'KNOW?

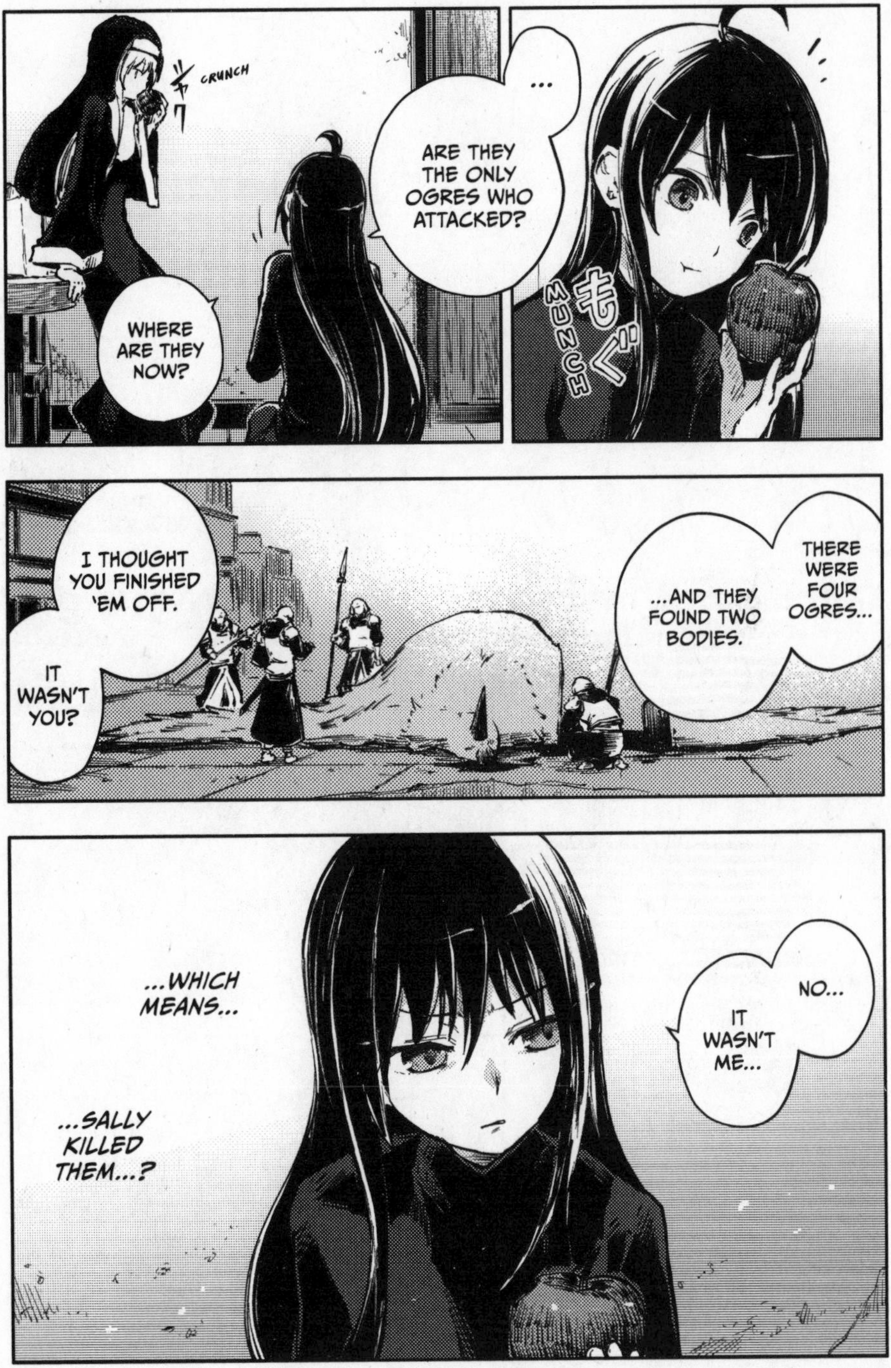
もぐ
MUNCH
...
ARE THEY THE ONLY OGRES WHO ATTACKED?
CRUNCH
WHERE ARE THEY NOW?
THERE WERE FOUR OGRES...
...AND THEY FOUND TWO BODIES.
I THOUGHT YOU FINISHED 'EM OFF.
IT WASN'T YOU?
NO...
IT WASN'T ME...
...WHICH MEANS...
...SALLY KILLED THEM...?

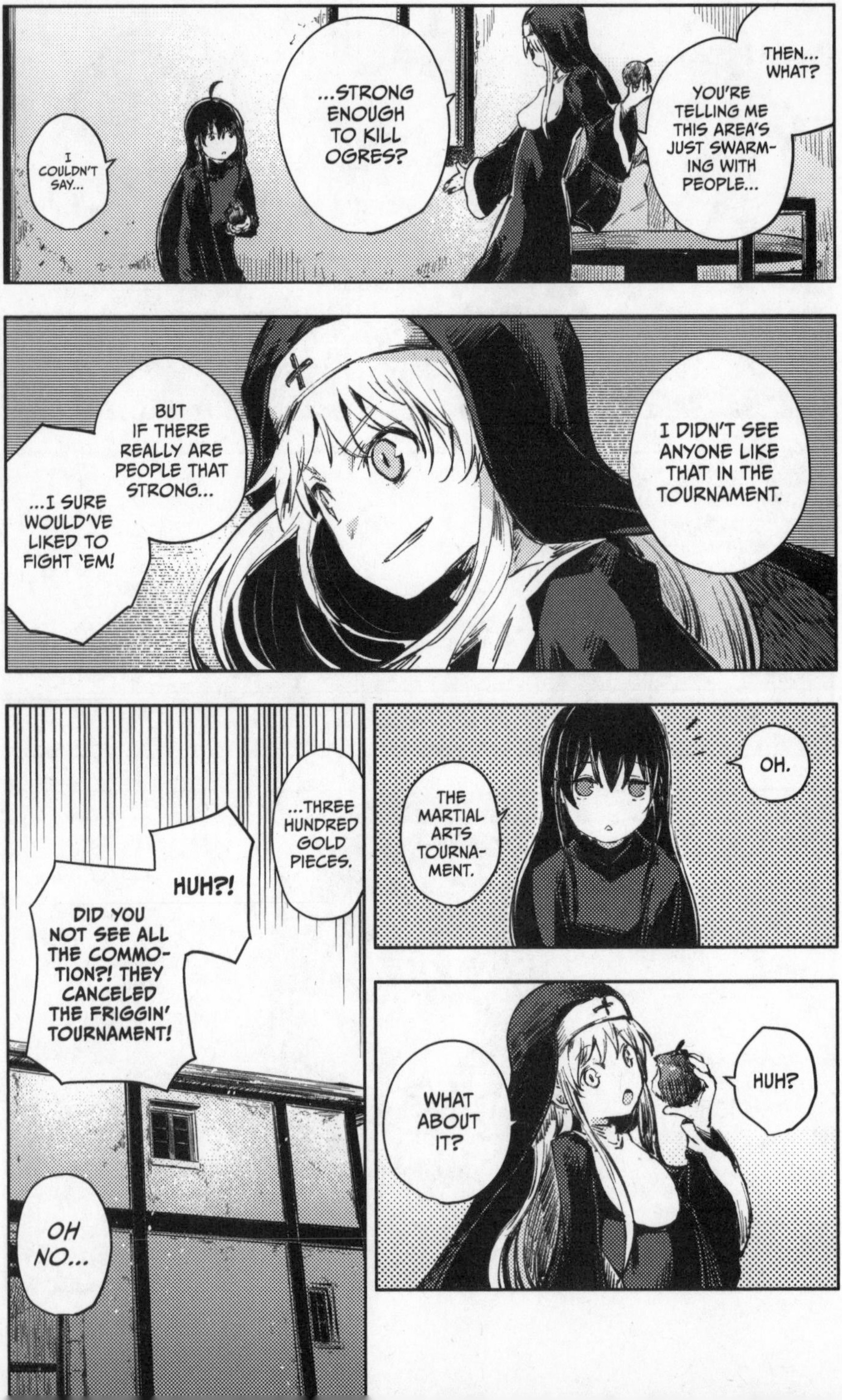
THEN... WHAT?
YOU'RE TELLING ME THIS AREA'S JUST SWARMING WITH PEOPLE...
...STRONG ENOUGH TO KILL OGRES?
I COULDN'T SAY...
I DIDN'T SEE ANYONE LIKE THAT IN THE TOURNAMENT.
BUT IF THERE REALLY ARE PEOPLE THAT STRONG...
...I SURE WOULD'VE LIKED TO FIGHT 'EM!
OH.
THE MARTIAL ARTS TOURNAMENT.
HUH?
WHAT ABOUT IT?
...THREE HUNDRED GOLD PIECES.
HUH?!
DID YOU NOT SEE ALL THE COMMOTION?! THEY CANCELED THE FRIGGIN' TOURNAMENT!
OH NO...

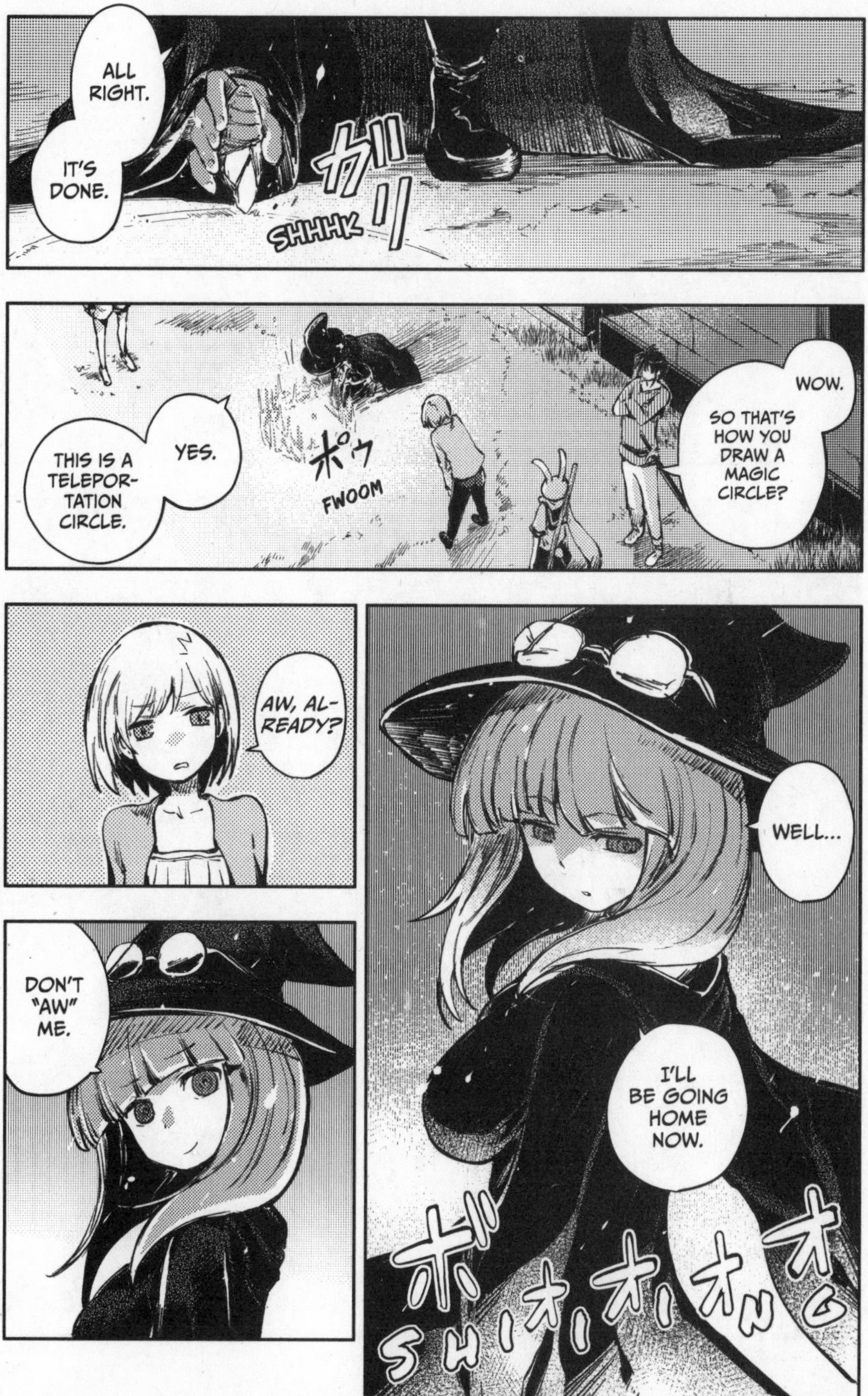
ALL RIGHT.
IT'S DONE.
ガリ
SHHHK
WOW.
SO THAT'S HOW YOU DRAW A MAGIC CIRCLE?
ポウ
FWOOM
YES.
THIS IS A TELEPORTATION CIRCLE.
WELL...
I'LL BE GOING HOME NOW.
ボォォォオ
SHIIING
AW, AL-READY?
DON'T "AW" ME.

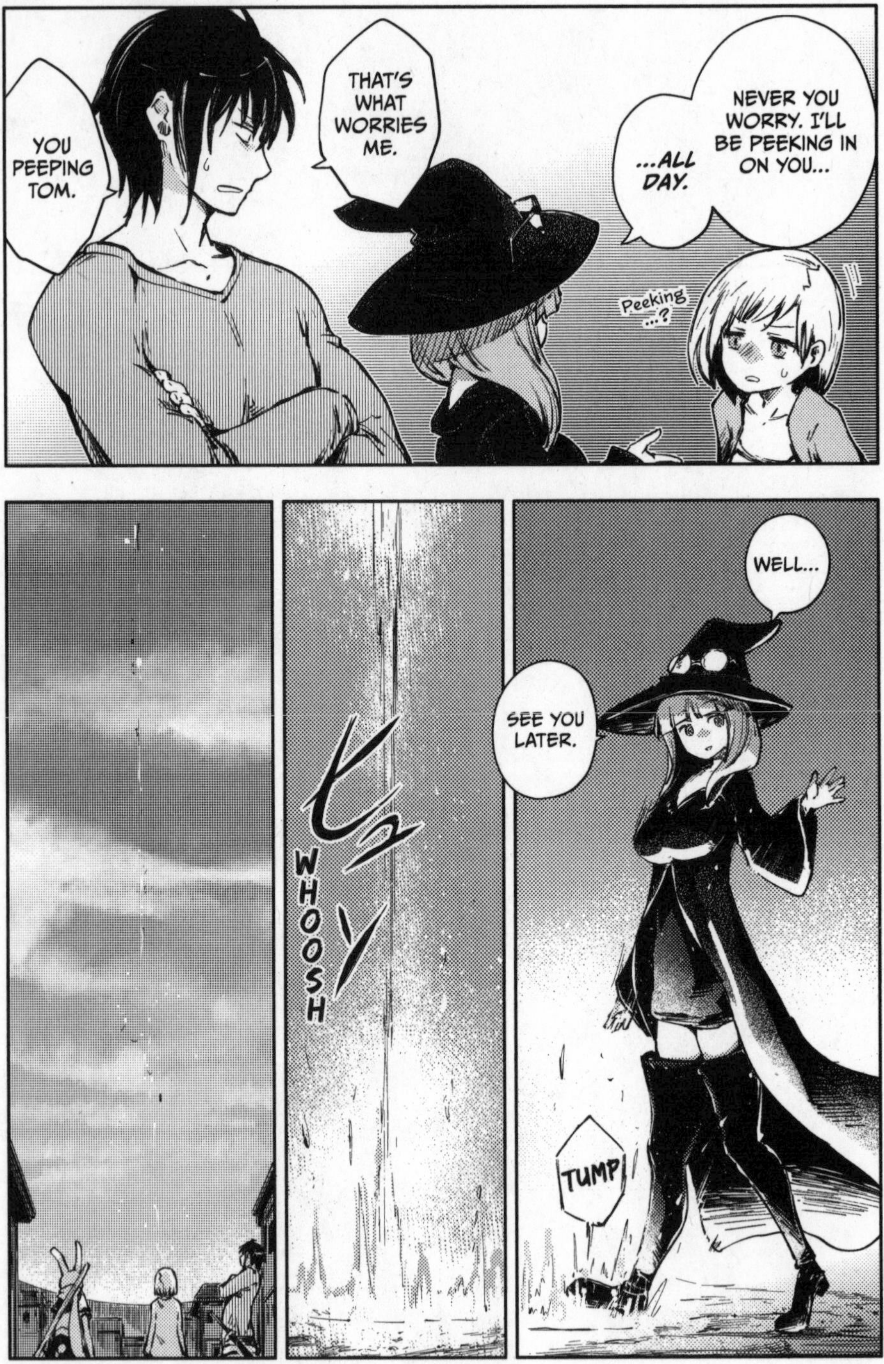
NEVER YOU WORRY. I'LL BE PEEKING IN ON YOU...
...ALL DAY.
Peeking ...?
THAT'S WHAT WORRIES ME.
YOU PEEPING TOM.
WELL...
SEE YOU LATER.
TUMP
WHOOSH

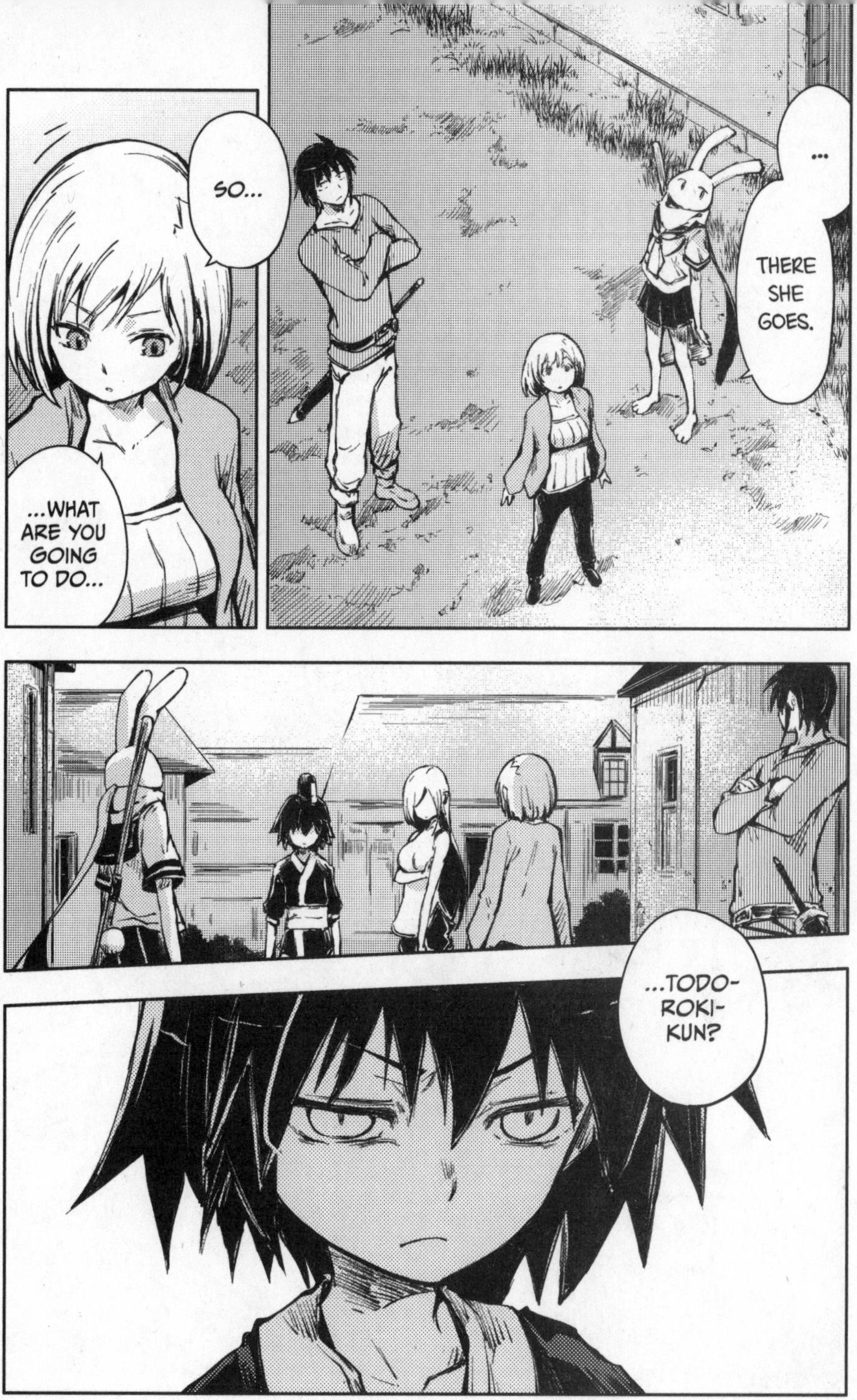
...
THERE SHE GOES.
SO...
...WHAT ARE YOU GOING TO DO...
...TODO-ROKI-KUN?

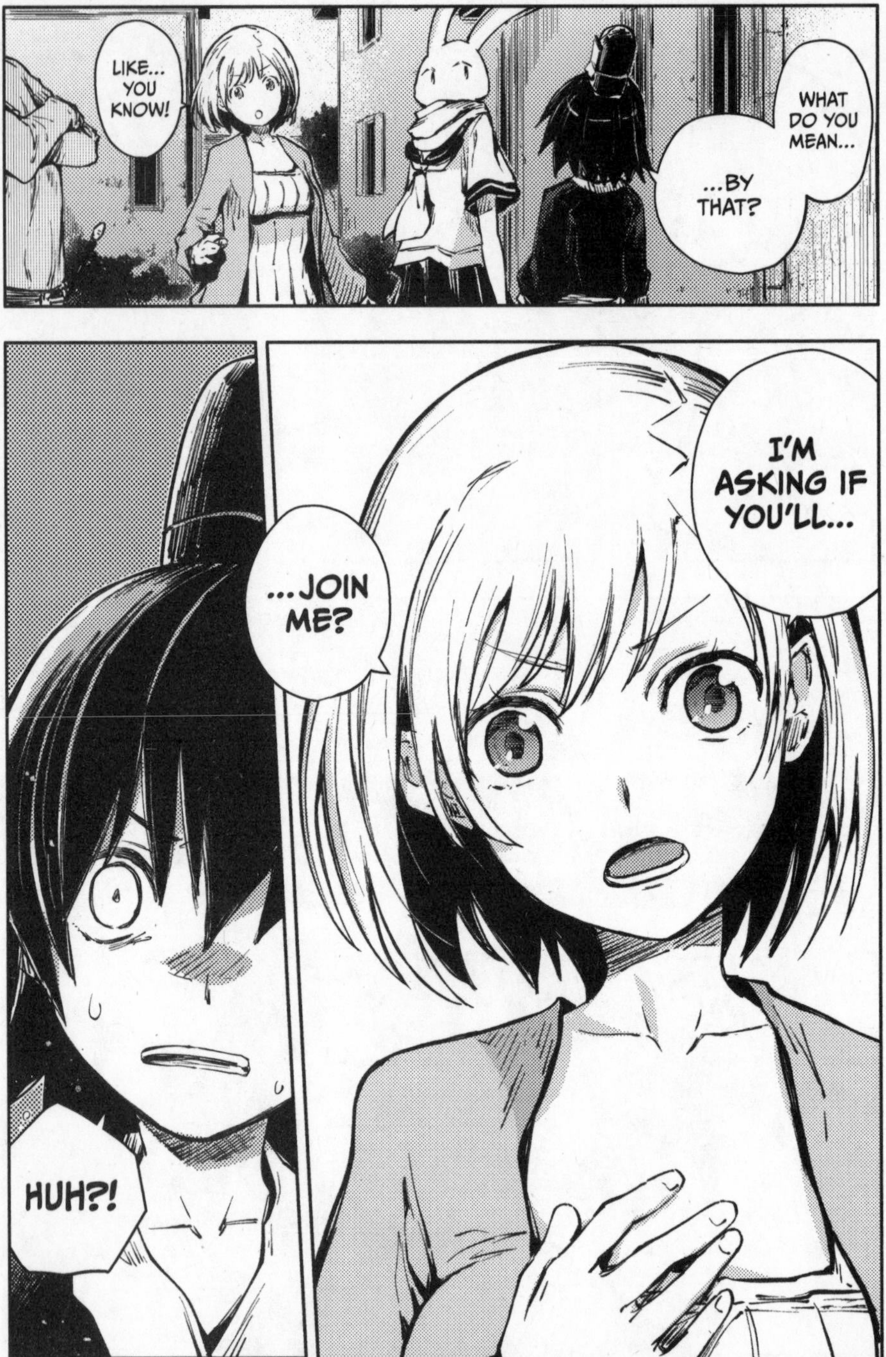
WHAT DO YOU MEAN...
...BY THAT?
LIKE... YOU KNOW!
I'M ASKING IF YOU'LL...
...JOIN ME?
HUH?!

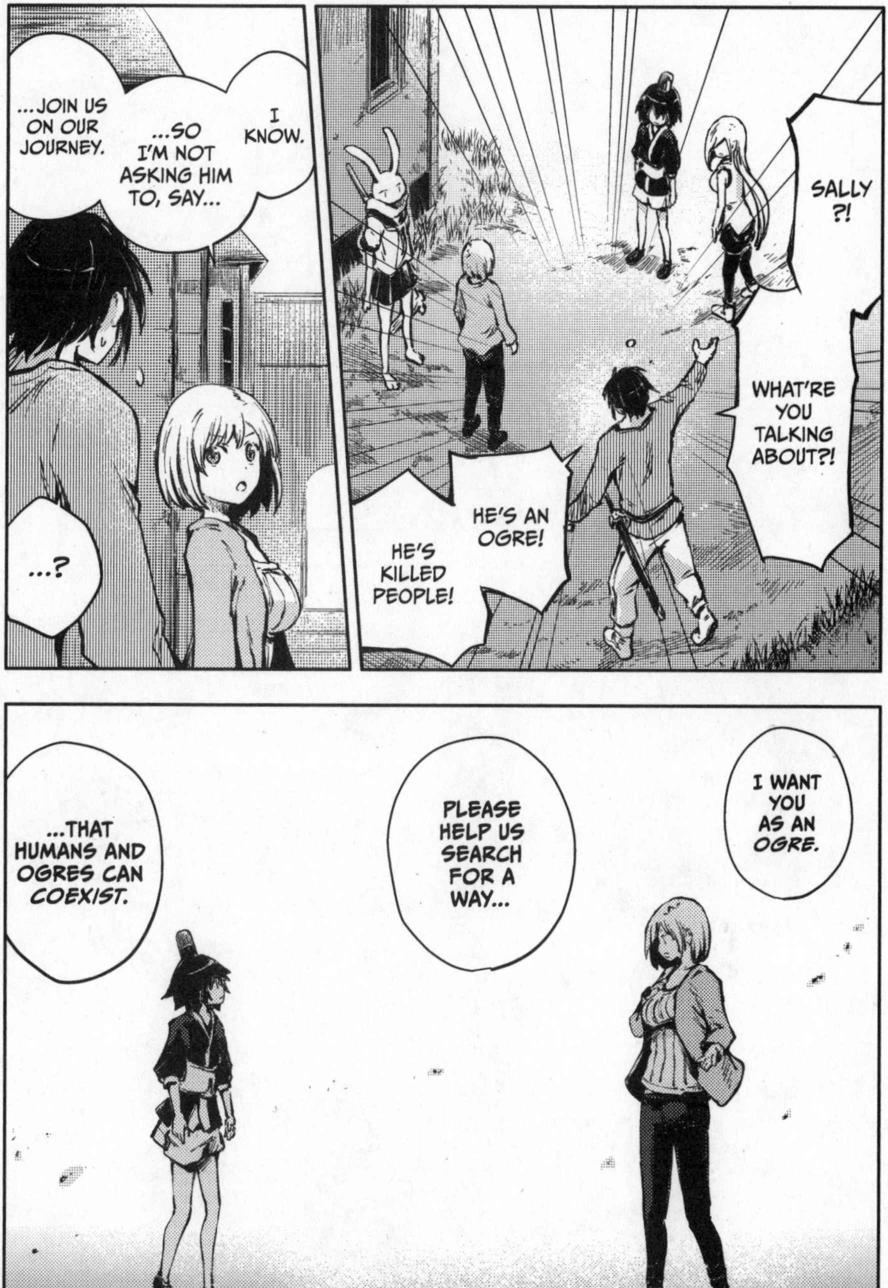
SALLY ?!
WHAT'RE YOU TALKING ABOUT?!
HE'S AN OGRE!
HE'S KILLED PEOPLE!
I KNOW.
...SO I'M NOT ASKING HIM TO, SAY...
...JOIN US ON OUR JOURNEY.
...?
I WANT YOU AS AN OGRE.
PLEASE HELP US SEARCH FOR A WAY...
...THAT HUMANS AND OGRES CAN COEXIST.

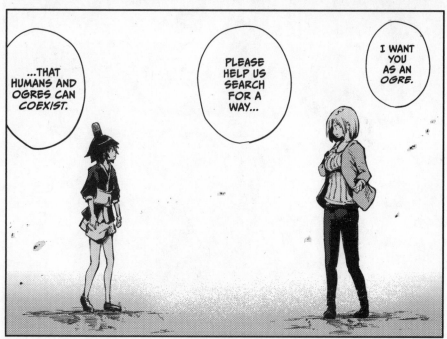

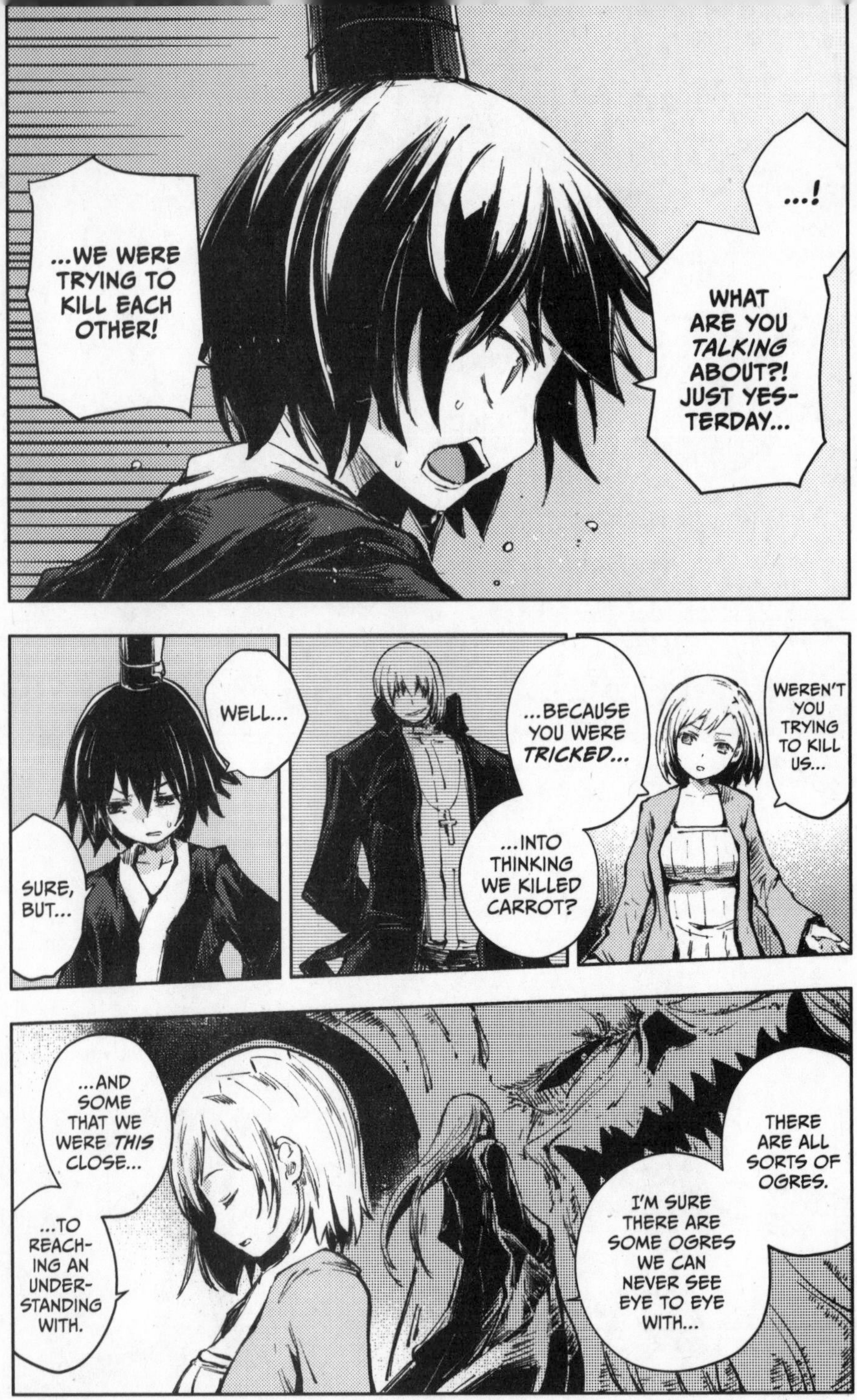
...!
WHAT ARE YOU *TALKING* ABOUT?! JUST YES-TERDAY...
...WE WERE TRYING TO KILL EACH OTHER!
WEREN'T YOU TRYING TO KILL US...
...BECAUSE YOU WERE *TRICKED*...
...INTO THINKING WE KILLED CARROT?
WELL...
SURE, BUT...
THERE ARE ALL SORTS OF OGRES.
I'M SURE THERE ARE SOME OGRES WE CAN NEVER SEE EYE TO EYE WITH...
...AND SOME THAT WE WERE *THIS* CLOSE...
...TO REACHING AN UNDER-STANDING WITH.

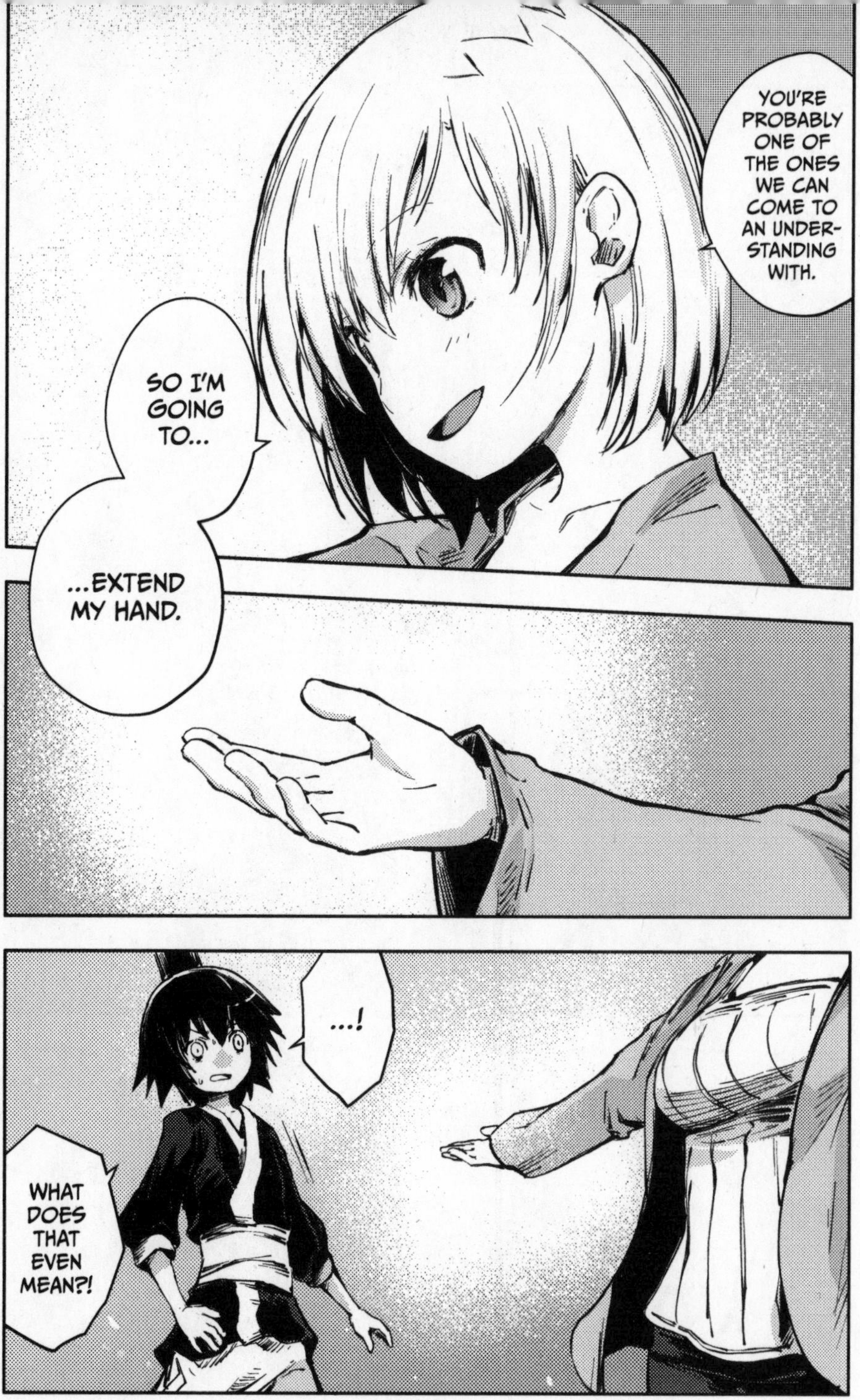
YOU'RE PROBABLY ONE OF THE ONES WE CAN COME TO AN UNDER-STANDING WITH.
SO I'M GOING TO...
...EXTEND MY HAND.
...!
WHAT DOES THAT EVEN MEAN?!

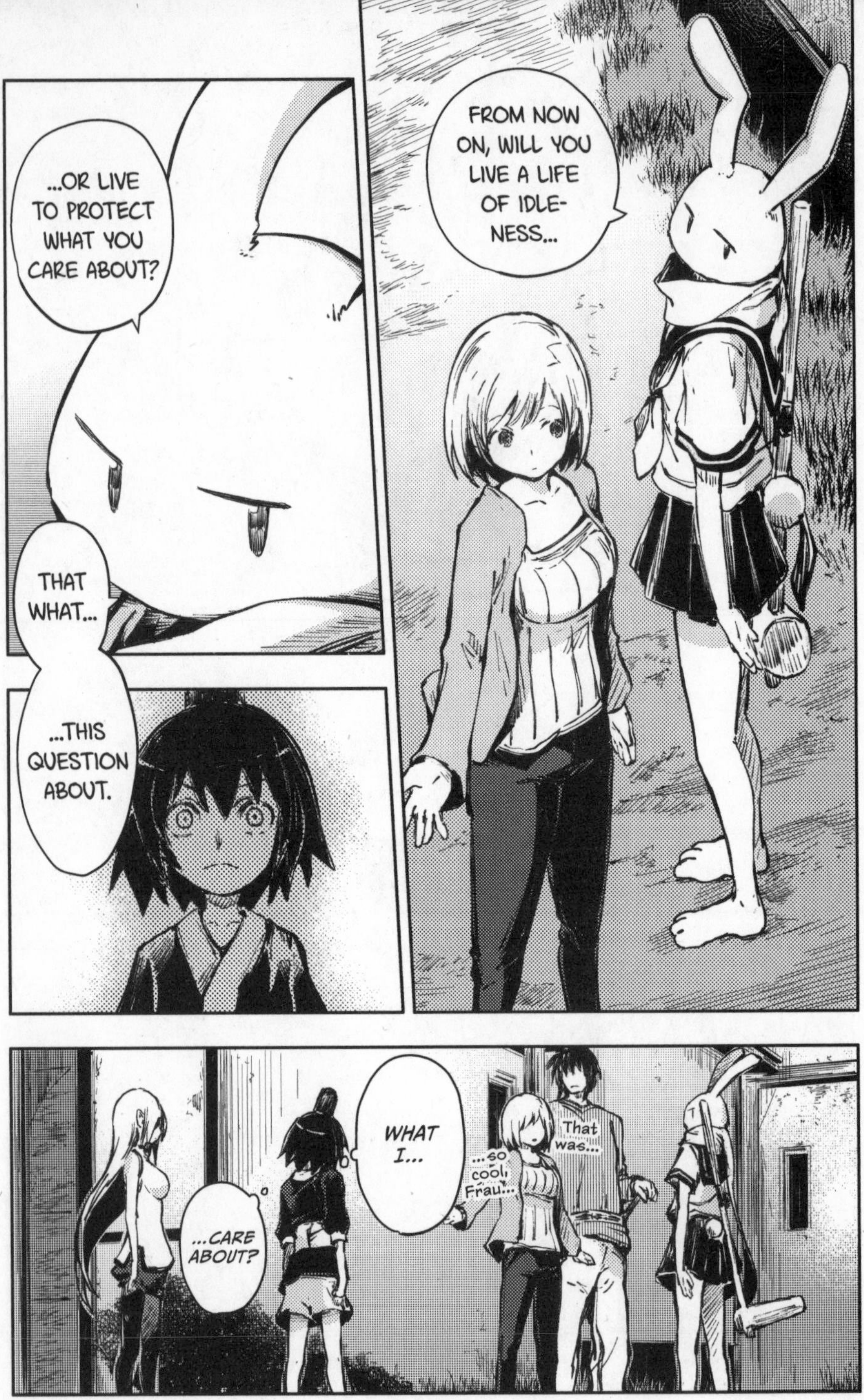
FROM NOW ON, WILL YOU LIVE A LIFE OF IDLE-NESS...
...OR LIVE TO PROTECT WHAT YOU CARE ABOUT?
THAT WHAT...
...THIS QUESTION ABOUT.
That was...
...so cool, Frau...
WHAT I...
...CARE ABOUT?

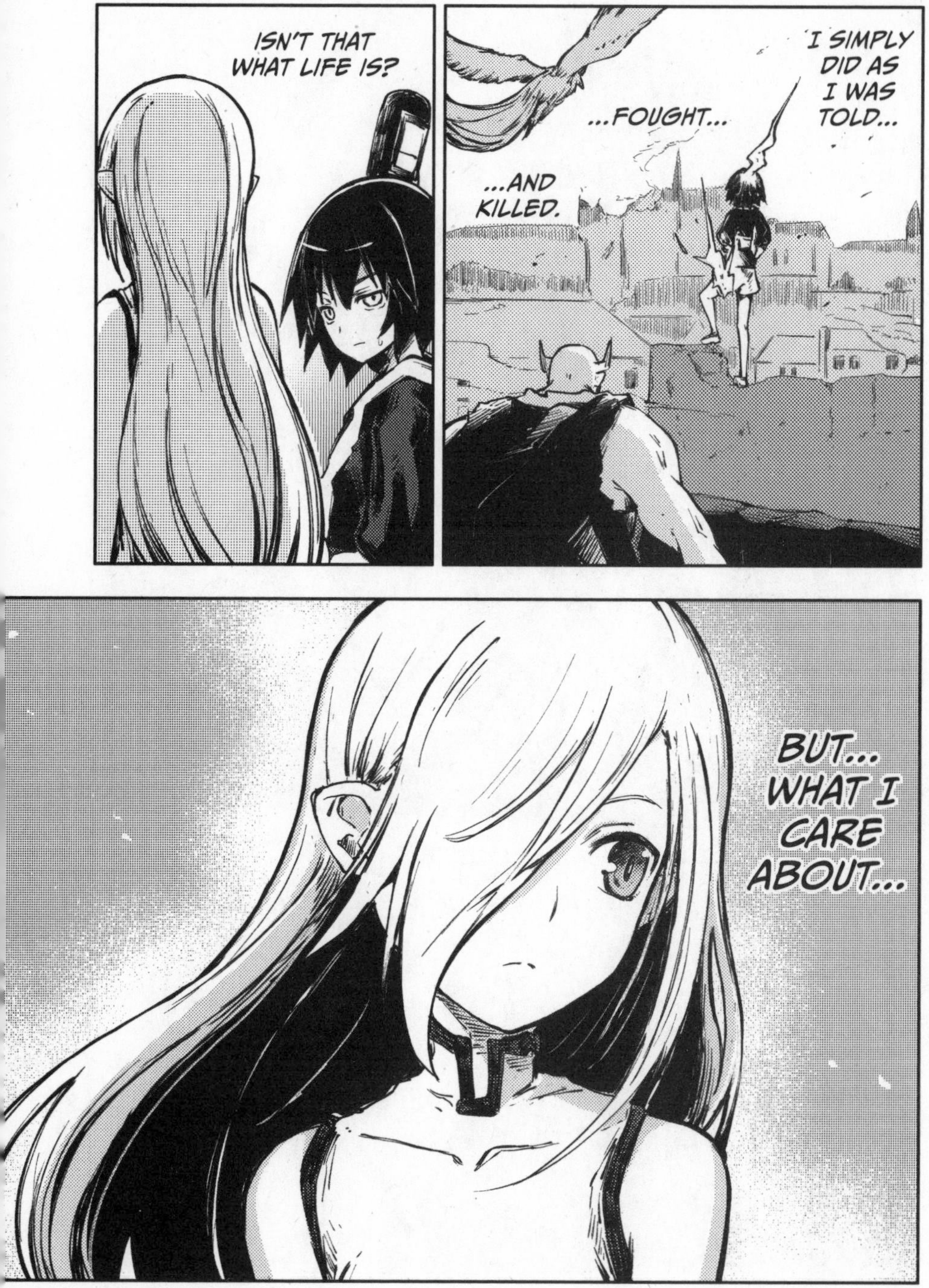
I SIMPLY DID AS I WAS TOLD...
...FOUGHT...
...AND KILLED.
ISN'T THAT WHAT LIFE IS?
BUT... WHAT I CARE ABOUT...

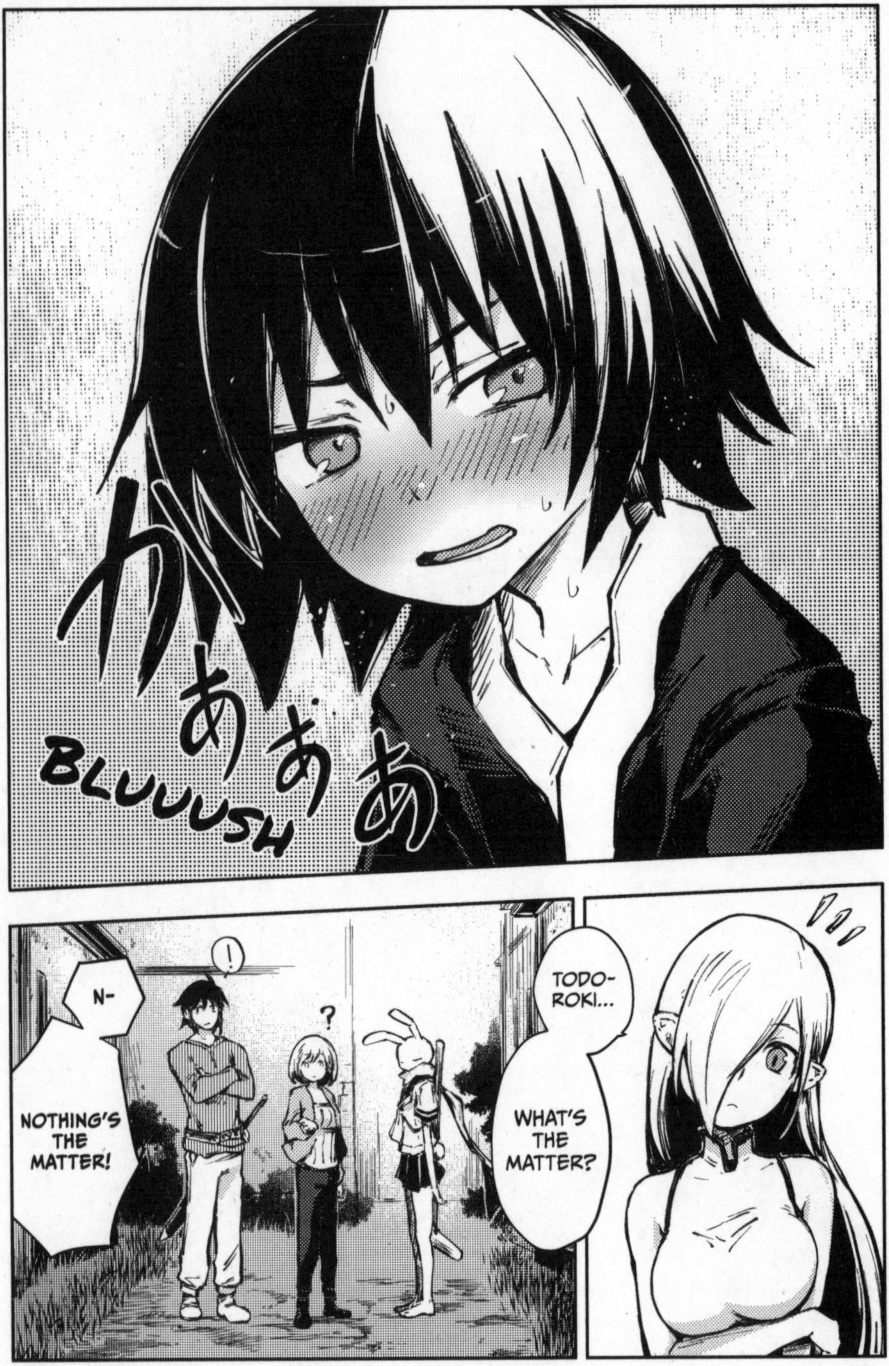
かあああ
BLUUUSH
TODO-ROKI...
WHAT'S THE MATTER?
!
?
N-
NOTHING'S THE MATTER!

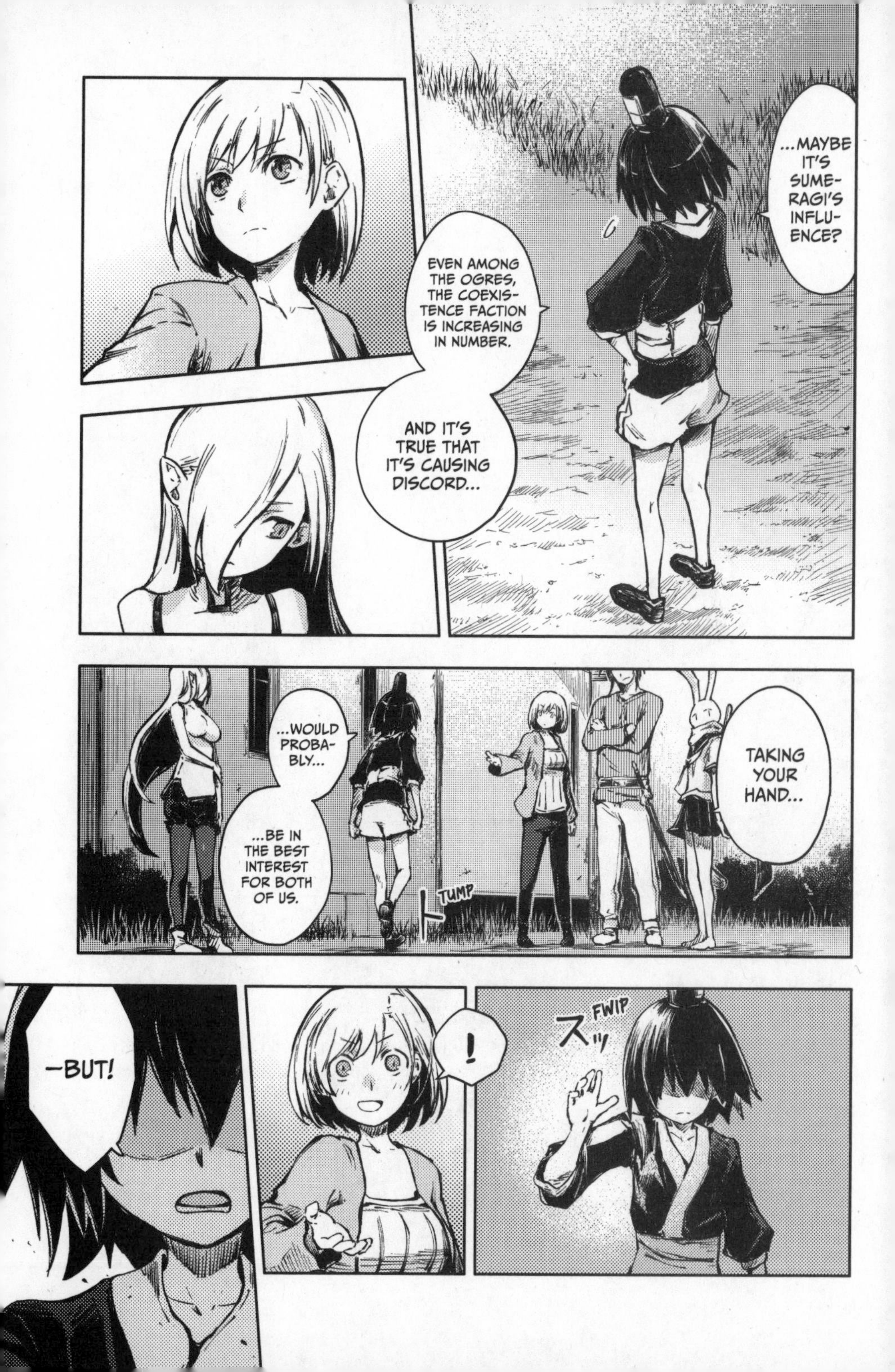

...MAYBE IT'S SUMERAGI'S INFLUENCE?
EVEN AMONG THE OGRES, THE COEXISTENCE FACTION IS INCREASING IN NUMBER.
AND IT'S TRUE THAT IT'S CAUSING DISCORD...
TAKING YOUR HAND...
...WOULD PROBABLY...
...BE IN THE BEST INTEREST FOR BOTH OF US.
ト TUMP
スッ FWIP
!
—BUT!

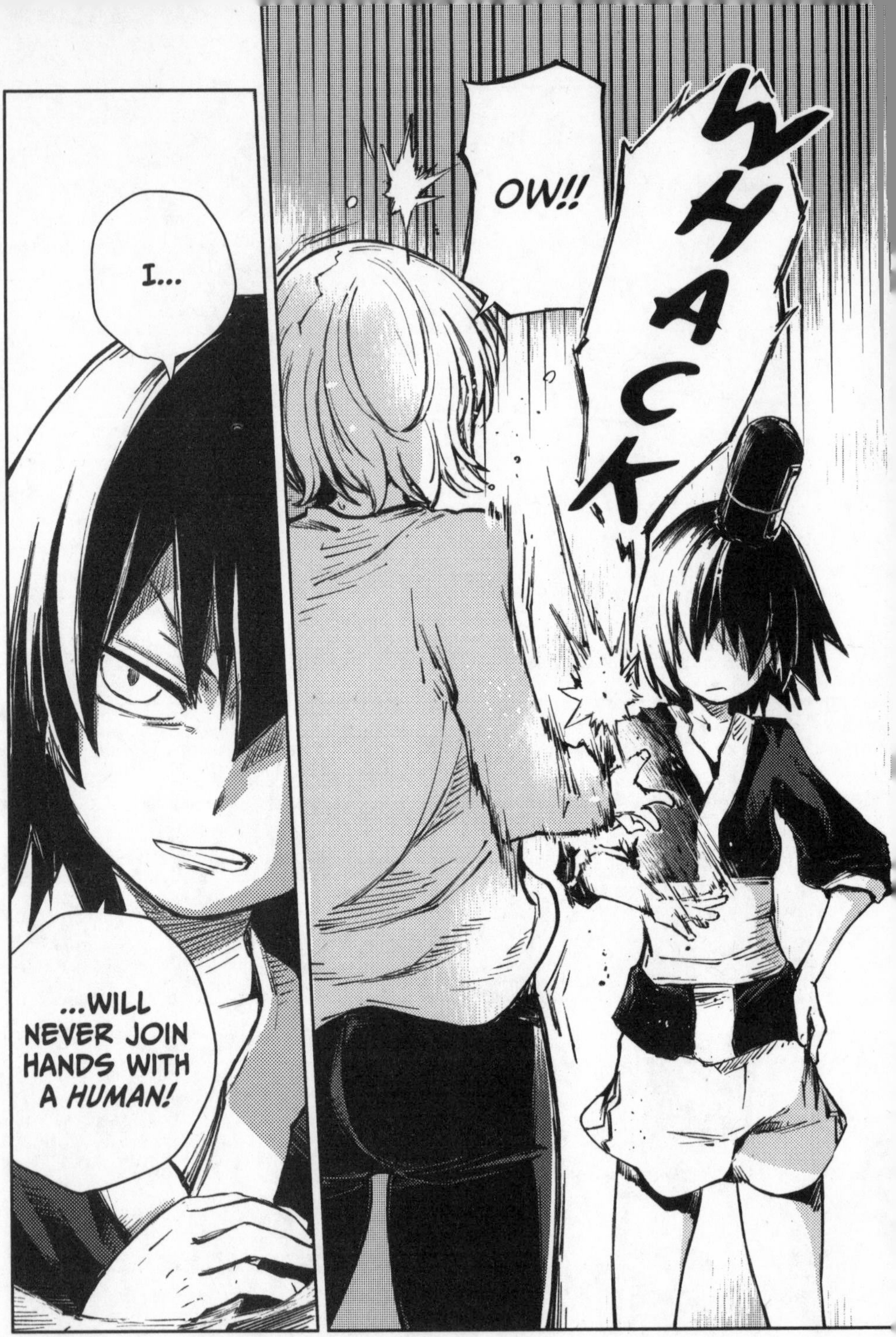
WHACK
OW!!
I...
...WILL NEVER JOIN HANDS WITH A HUMAN!

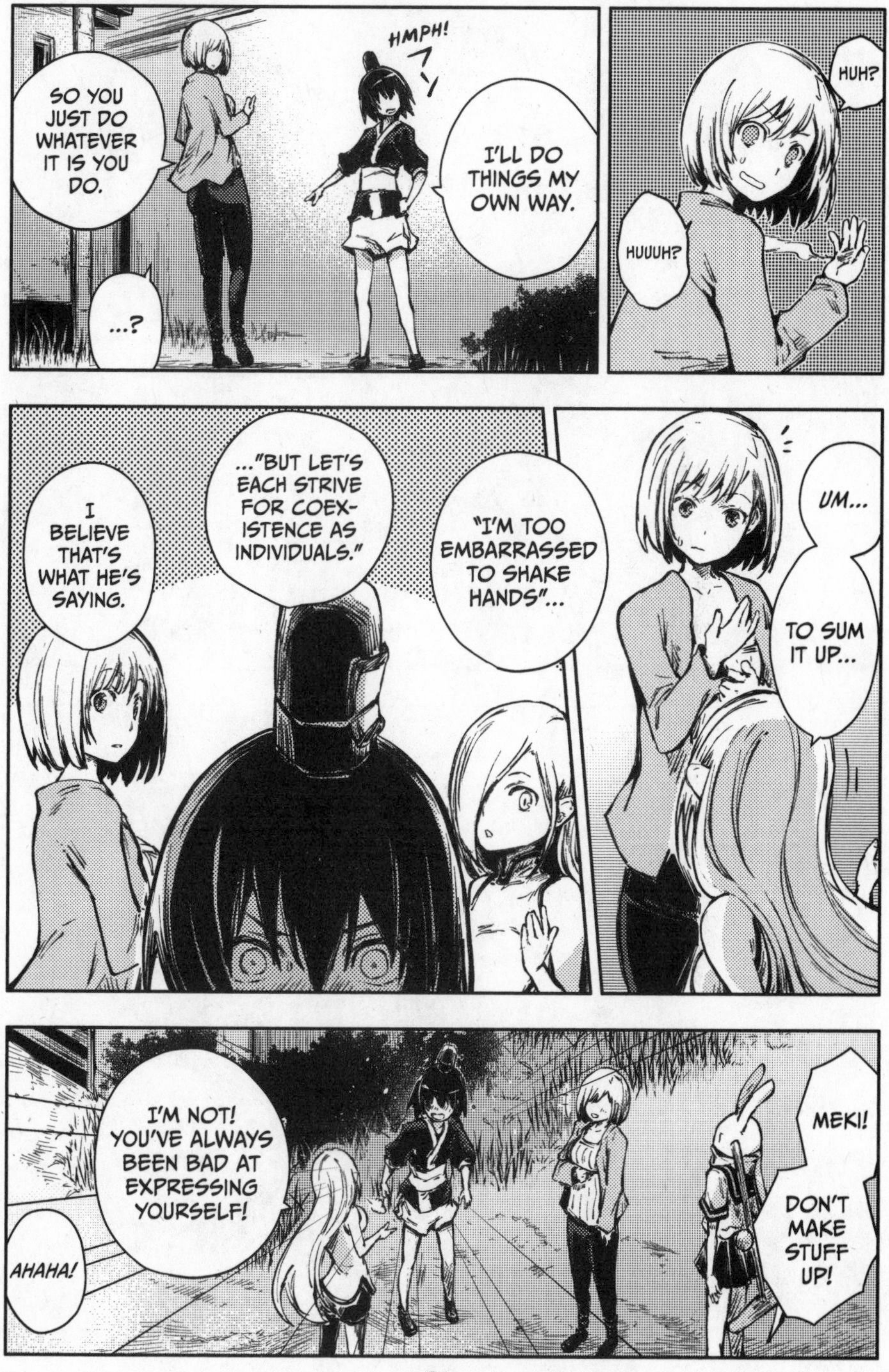
HUH?
HUUUH?
HMPH!
I'LL DO THINGS MY OWN WAY.
SO YOU JUST DO WHATEVER IT IS YOU DO.
...?
UM...
TO SUM IT UP...
"I'M TOO EMBARRASSED TO SHAKE HANDS"...
..."BUT LET'S EACH STRIVE FOR COEXISTENCE AS INDIVIDUALS."
I BELIEVE THAT'S WHAT HE'S SAYING.
MEKI!
DON'T MAKE STUFF UP!
I'M NOT! YOU'VE ALWAYS BEEN BAD AT EXPRESSING YOURSELF!
AHAHA!

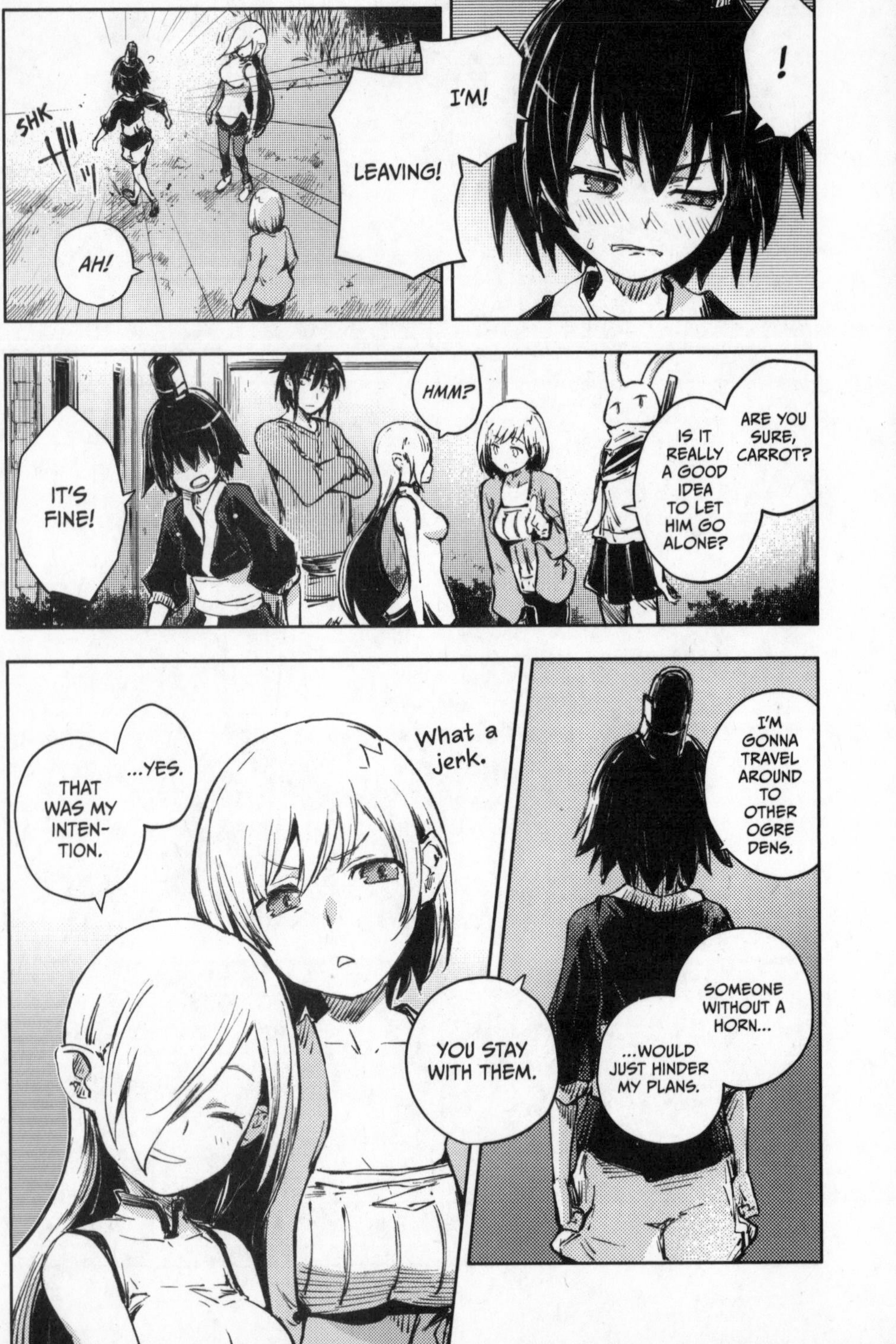
!
I'M! LEAVING!
SHK
AH!
ARE YOU SURE, CARROT? IS IT REALLY A GOOD IDEA TO LET HIM GO ALONE?
HMM?
IT'S FINE!
I'M GONNA TRAVEL AROUND TO OTHER OGRE DENS.
SOMEONE WITHOUT A HORN...
...WOULD JUST HINDER MY PLANS.
What a jerk.
...YES. THAT WAS MY INTEN-TION.
YOU STAY WITH THEM.

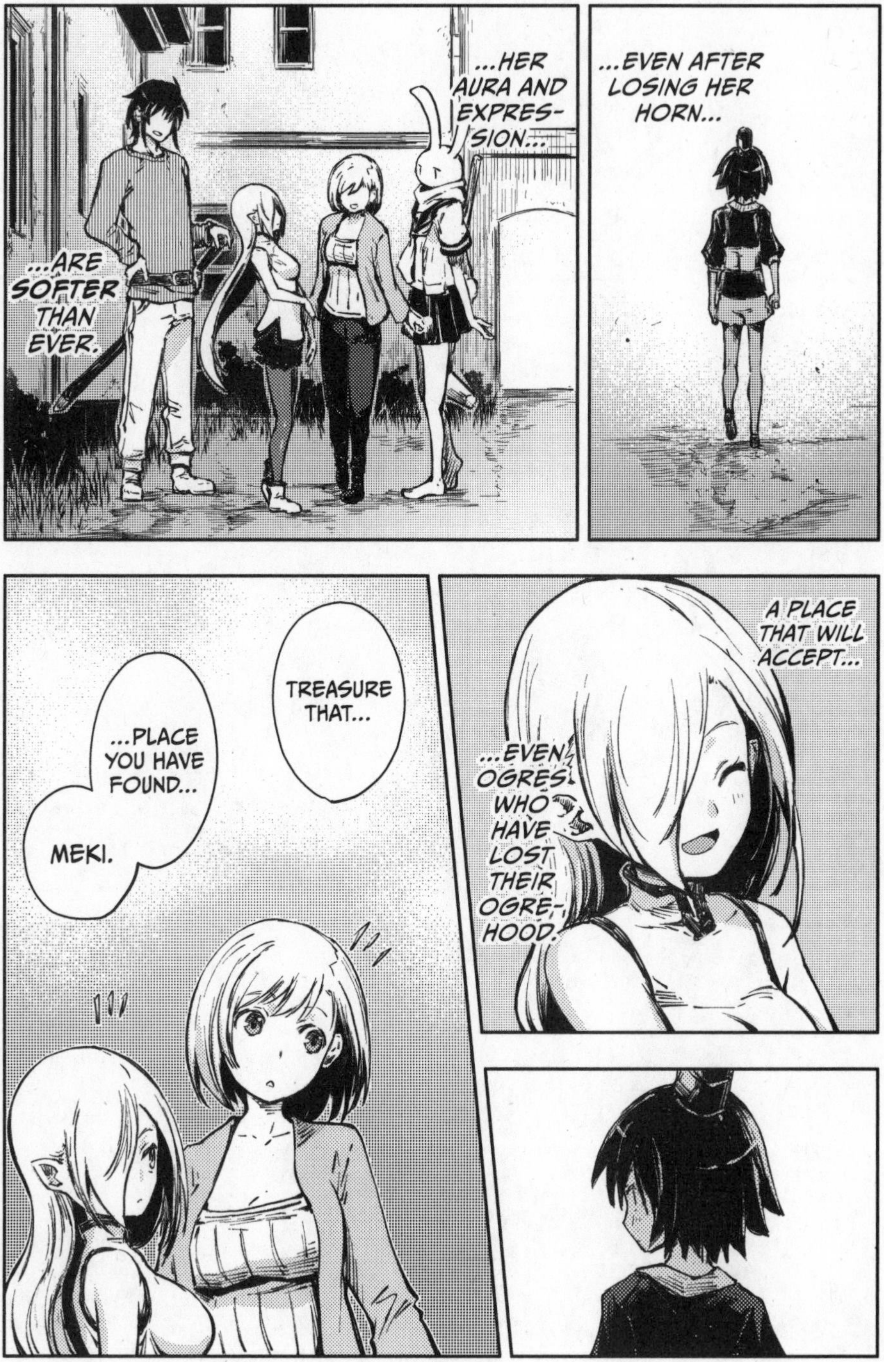
...EVEN AFTER LOSING HER HORN...
...HER AURA AND EXPRES-SION...
...ARE SOFTER THAN EVER.
A PLACE THAT WILL ACCEPT...
...EVEN OGRES WHO HAVE LOST THEIR OGRE-HOOD.
TREASURE THAT...
...PLACE YOU HAVE FOUND...
MEKI.

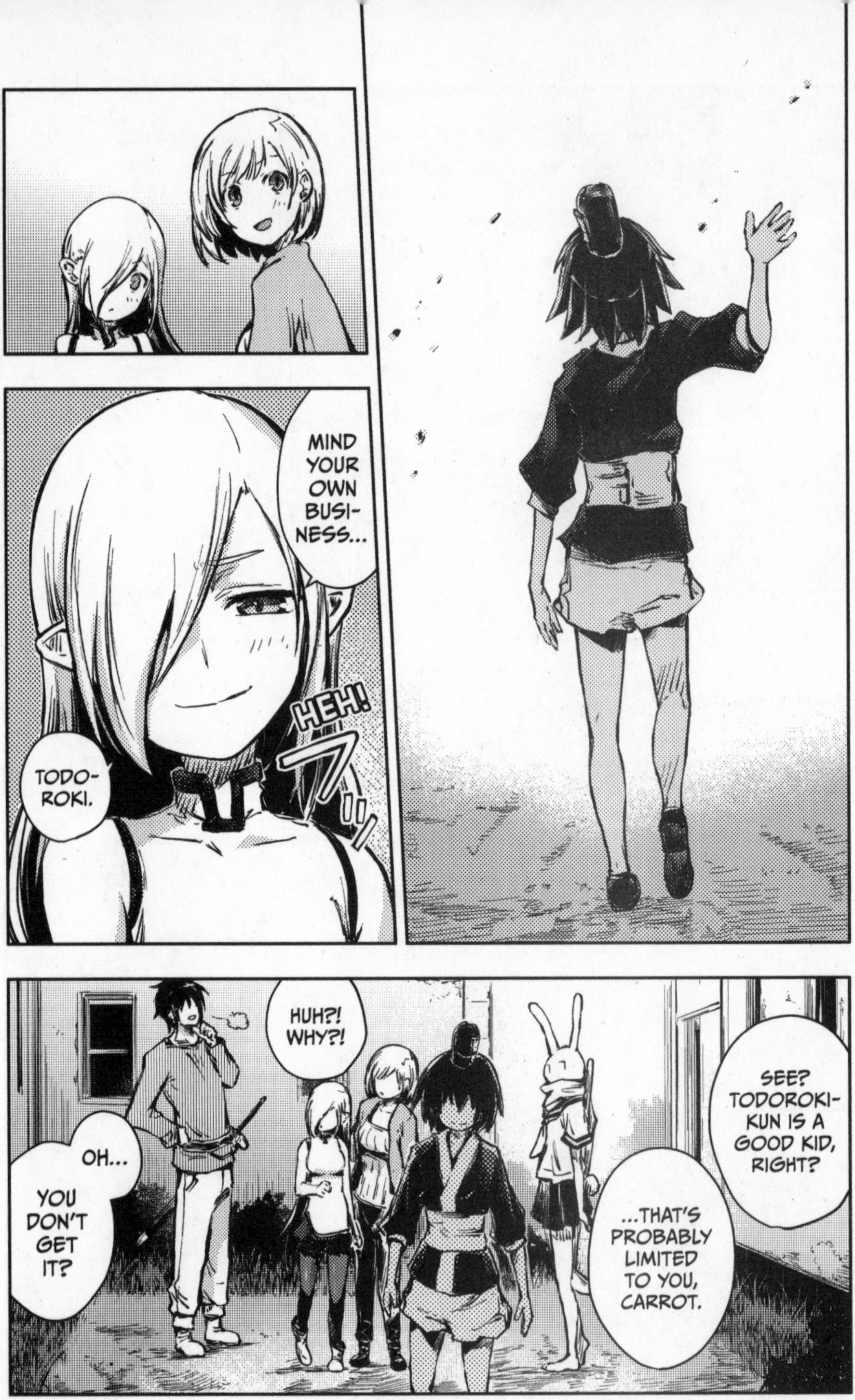
MIND YOUR OWN BUSI-NESS...
HEH!
TODO-ROKI.
SEE? TODOROKI-KUN IS A GOOD KID, RIGHT?
...THAT'S PROBABLY LIMITED TO YOU, CARROT.
HUH?! WHY?!
OH...
YOU DON'T GET IT?

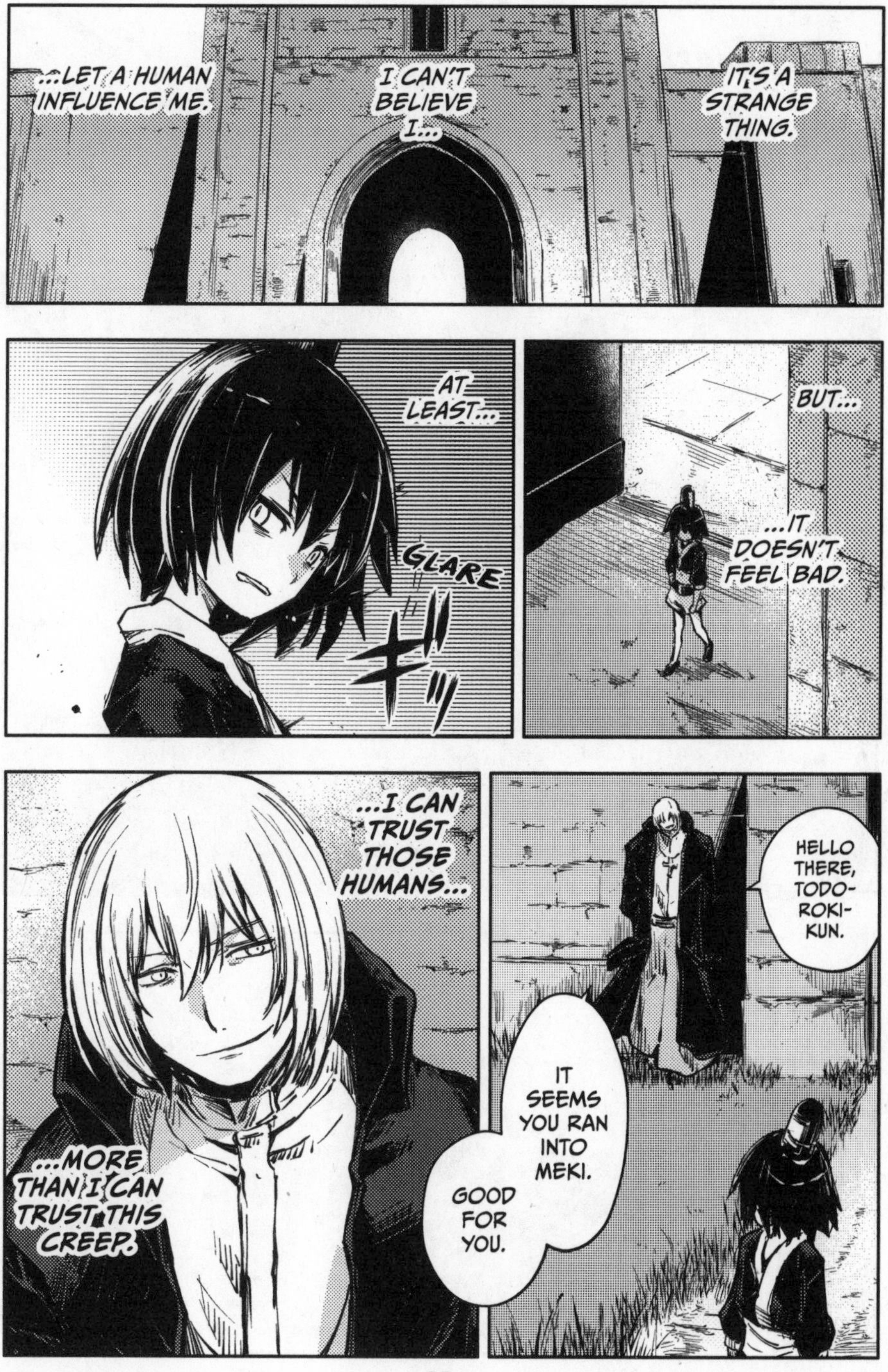
IT'S A STRANGE THING.
I CAN'T BELIEVE I...
...LET A HUMAN INFLUENCE ME.
BUT...
...IT DOESN'T FEEL BAD.
AT LEAST...
GLARE
HELLO THERE, TODOROKI-KUN.
IT SEEMS YOU RAN INTO MEKI.
GOOD FOR YOU.
...I CAN TRUST THOSE HUMANS...
...MORE THAN I CAN TRUST THIS CREEP.

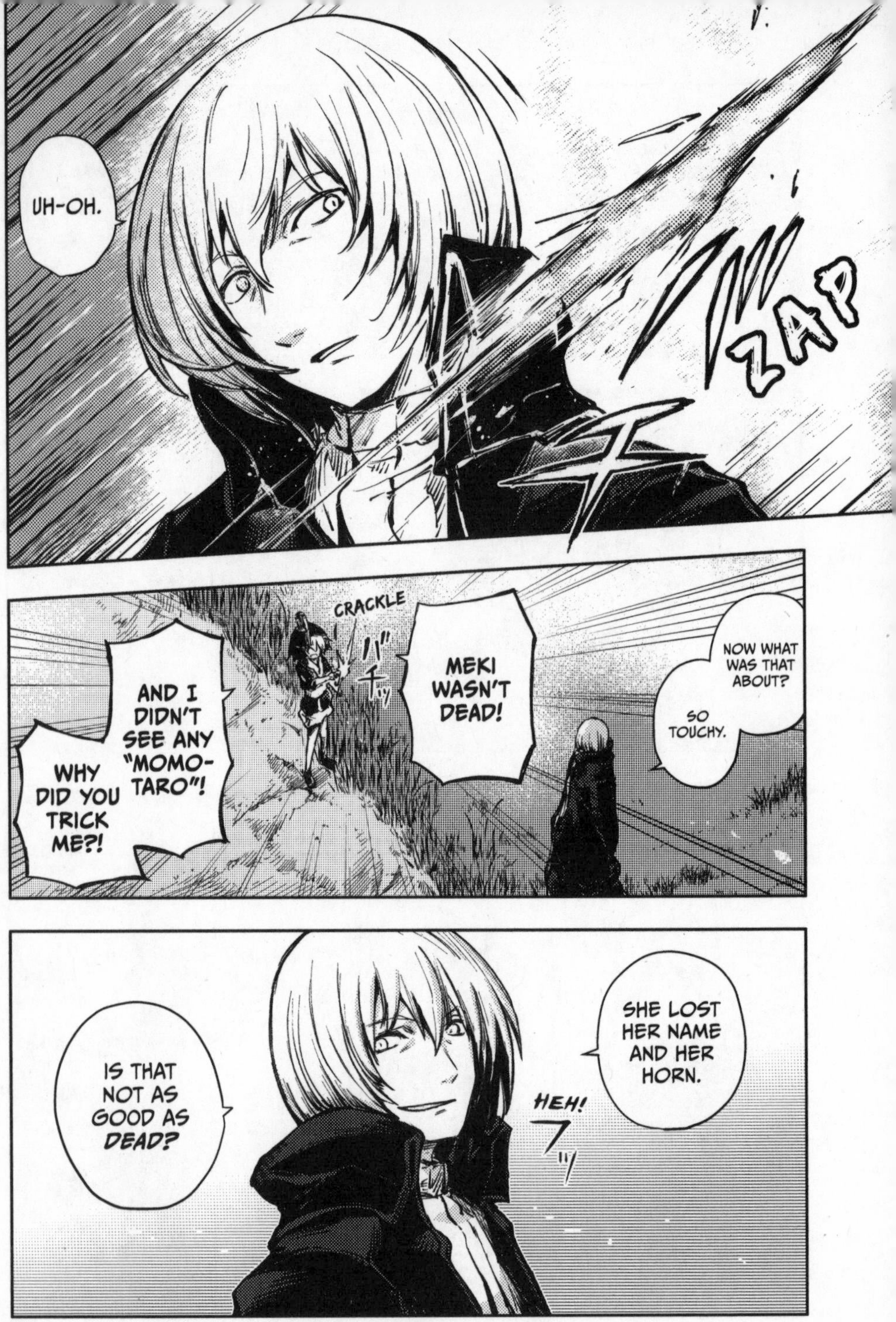
UH-OH.
ZAP
NOW WHAT WAS THAT ABOUT?
SO TOUCHY.
MEKI WASN'T DEAD!
CRACKLE
バチッ
AND I DIDN'T SEE ANY "MOMO-TARO"!
WHY DID YOU TRICK ME?!
SHE LOST HER NAME AND HER HORN.
HEH!
フッ
IS THAT NOT AS GOOD AS DEAD?

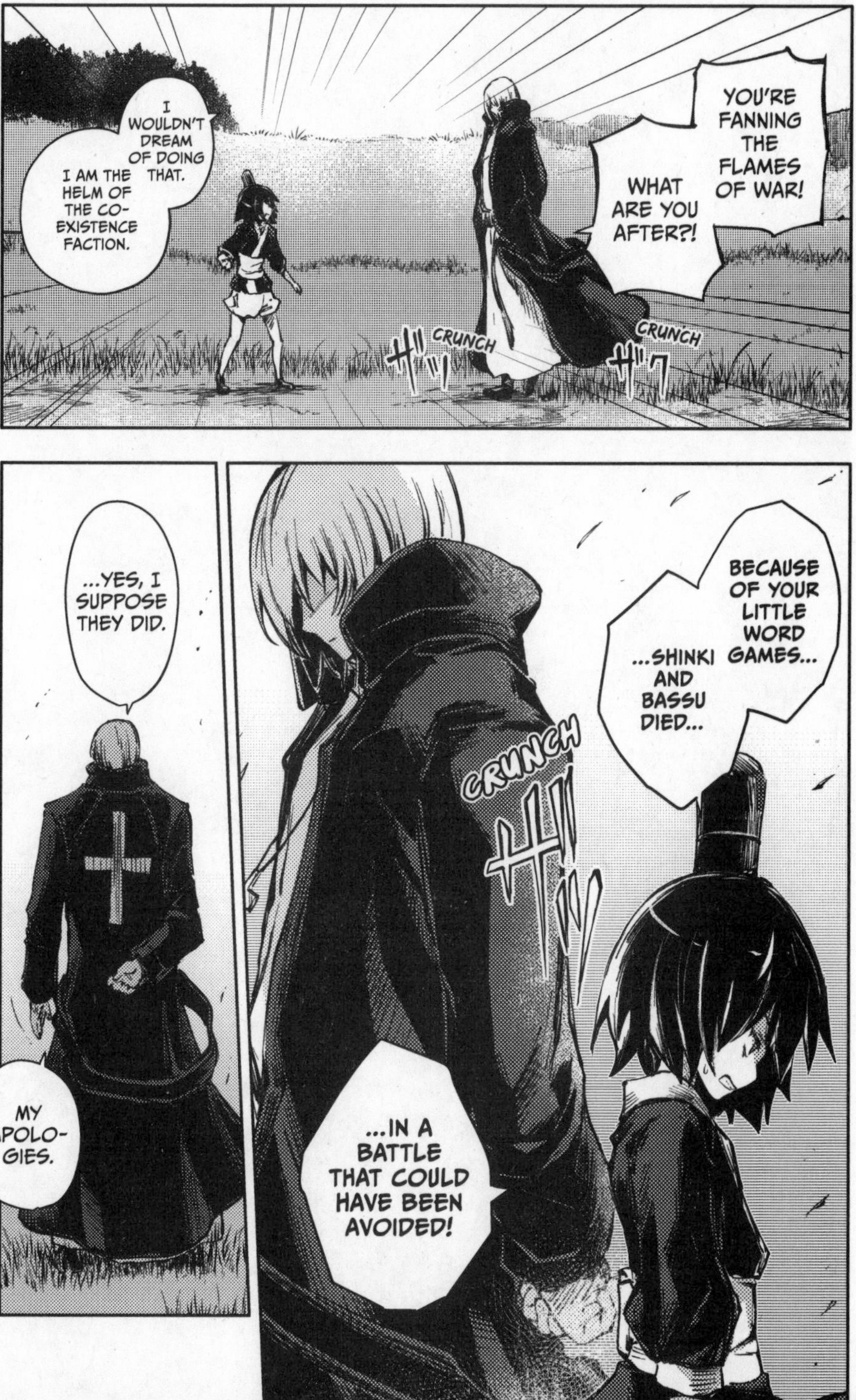
YOU'RE FANNING THE FLAMES OF WAR!
WHAT ARE YOU AFTER?!
I WOULDN'T DREAM OF DOING THAT.
I AM THE HELM OF THE CO-EXISTENCE FACTION.
CRUNCH
CRUNCH
BECAUSE OF YOUR LITTLE WORD GAMES...
...SHINKI AND BASSU DIED...
CRUNCH
...IN A BATTLE THAT COULD HAVE BEEN AVOIDED!
...YES, I SUPPOSE THEY DID.
MY APOLOGIES.

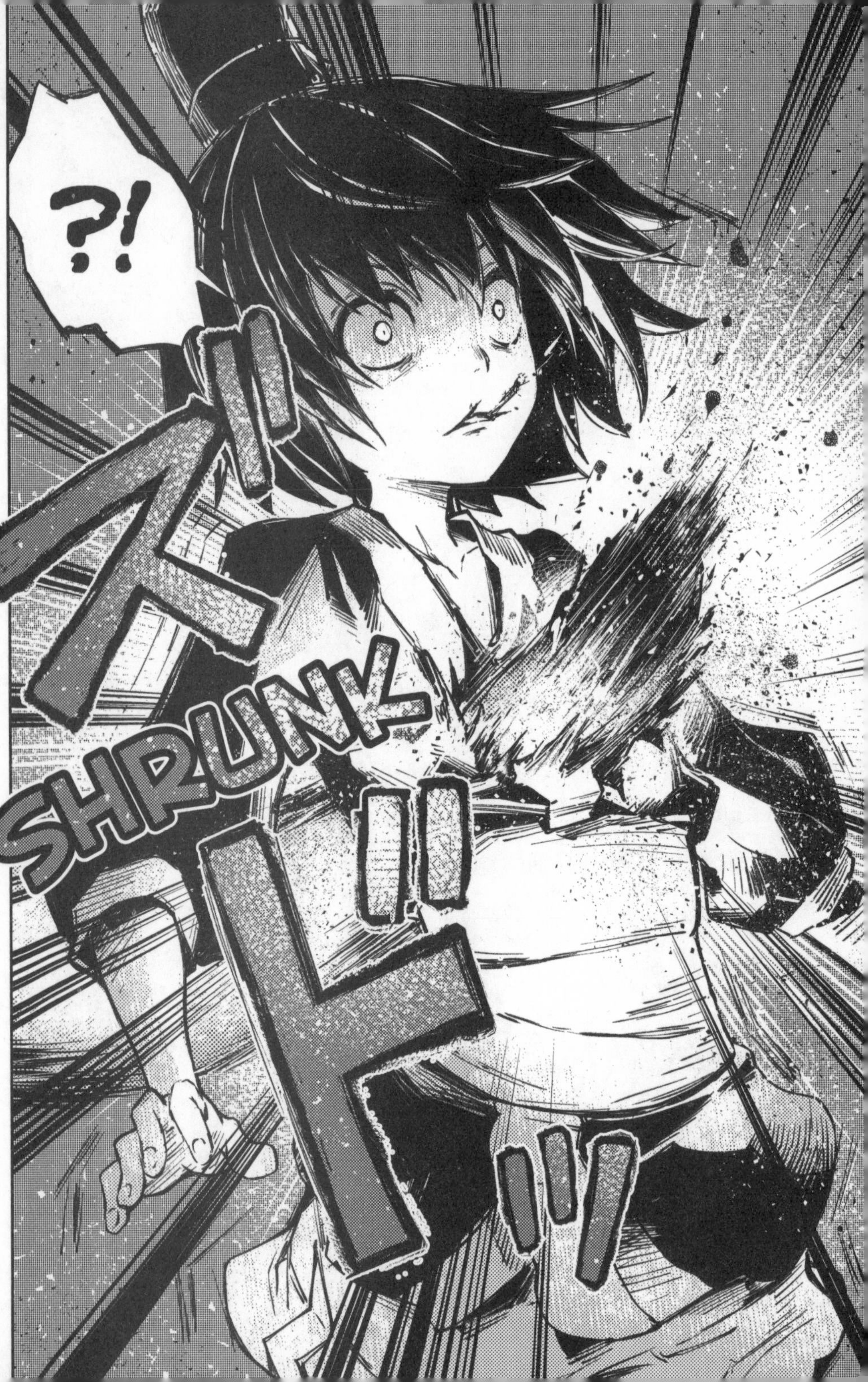
?!
SHRUNK

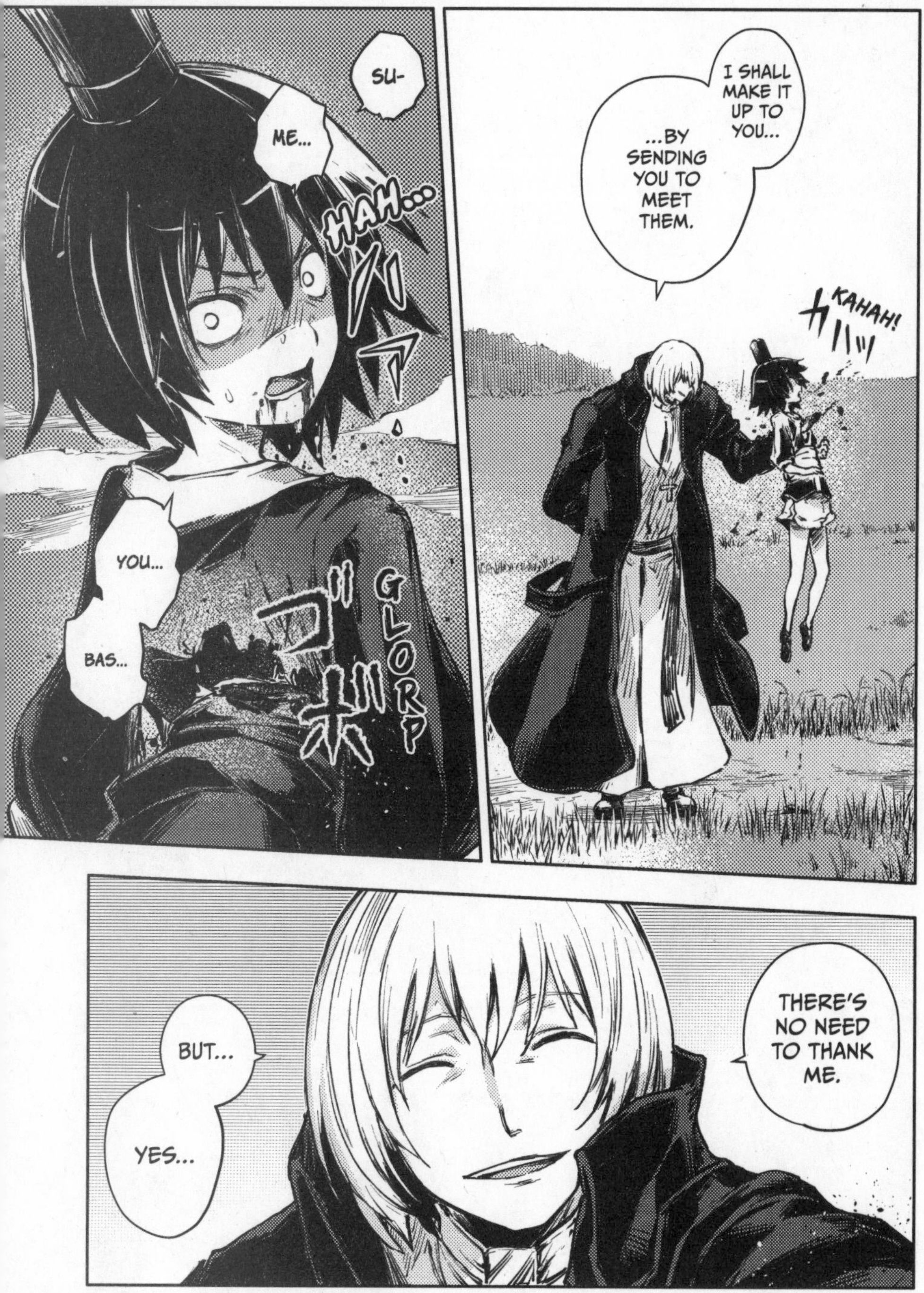
I SHALL MAKE IT UP TO YOU...
...BY SENDING YOU TO MEET THEM.
KAHAH!
SU-
ME...
HAH...
YOU...
BAS...
GLORP
THERE'S NO NEED TO THANK ME.
BUT...
YES...

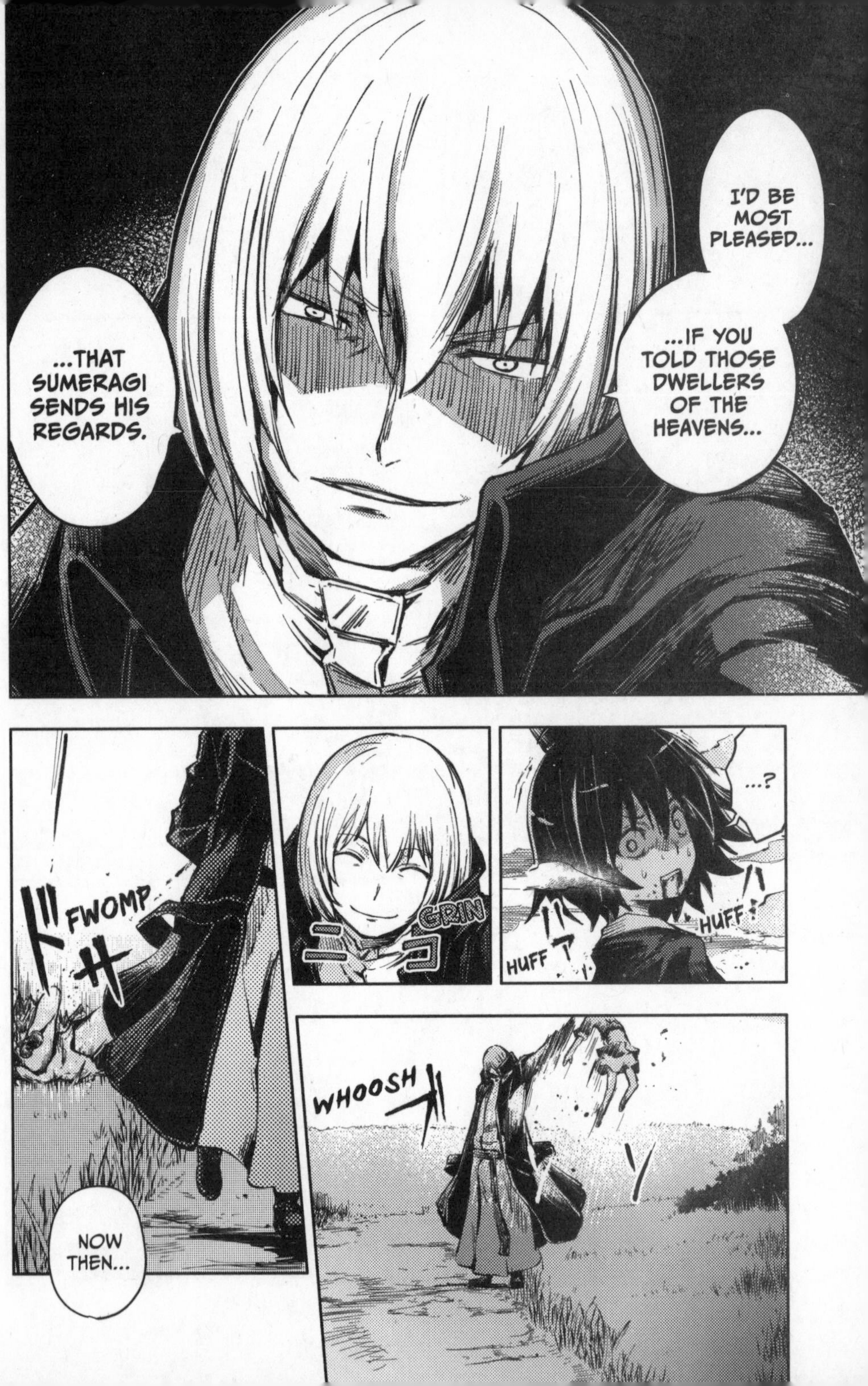
I'D BE MOST PLEASED...
...IF YOU TOLD THOSE DWELLERS OF THE HEAVENS...
...THAT SUMERAGI SENDS HIS REGARDS.
...?
HUFF
HUFF
GRIN
WHOOSH
FWOMP
NOW THEN...

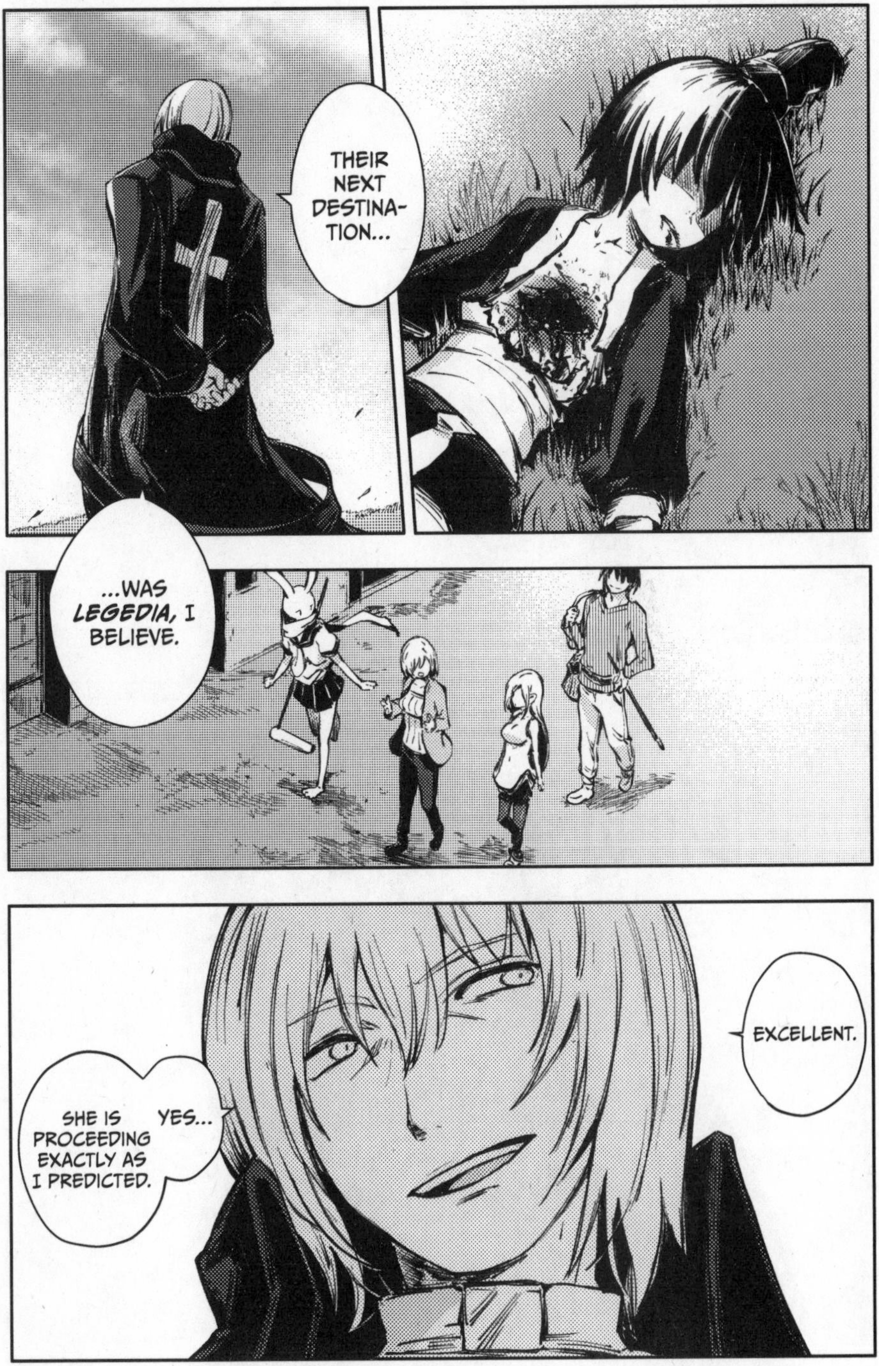
THEIR NEXT DESTINATION...
...WAS LEGEDIA, I BELIEVE.
EXCELLENT.
YES... SHE IS PROCEEDING EXACTLY AS I PREDICTED.

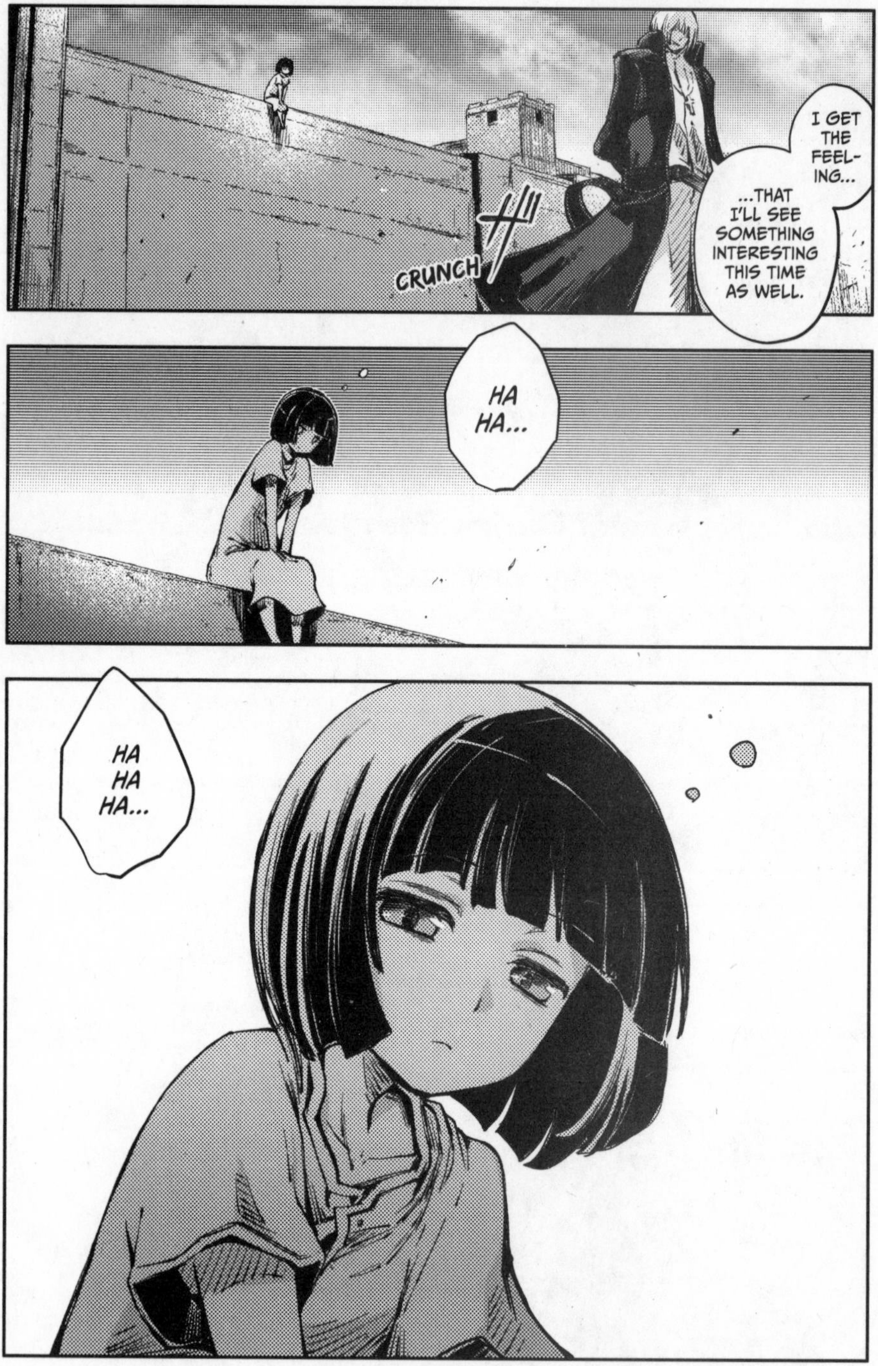
I GET THE FEEL-ING...
...THAT I'LL SEE SOMETHING INTERESTING THIS TIME AS WELL.
CRUNCH
HA HA...
HA HA HA...

I'll keep an eye on you in the bath and when you're using the bathroom as well, since people tend to let their guards down then.
No, you don't have to do that.
You *really* don't have to do that.

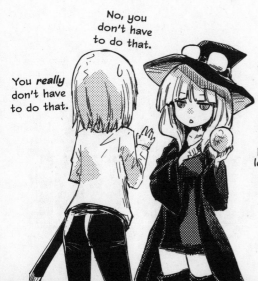

PEACH BOY
RIVERSIDE

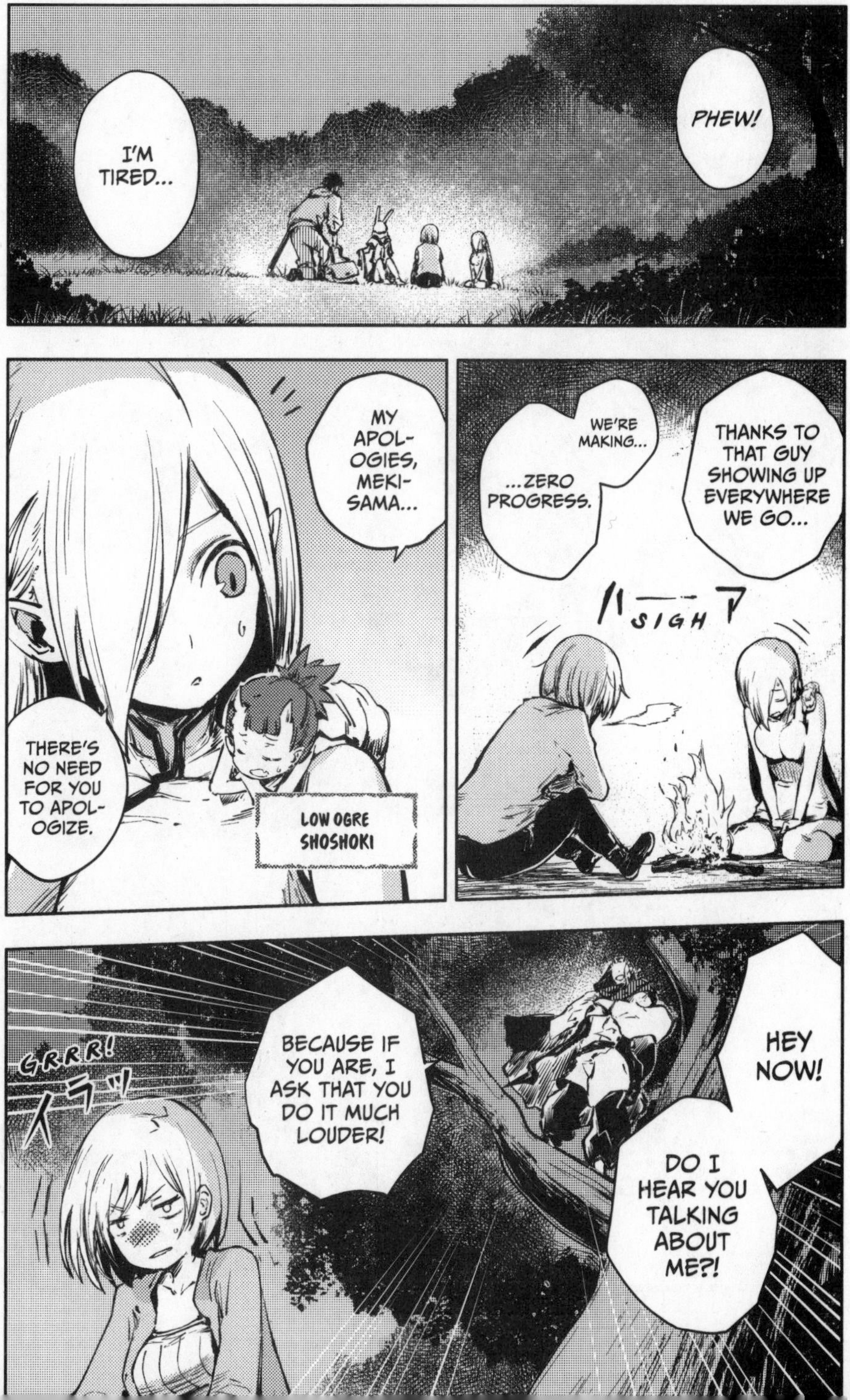
PHEW!
I'M TIRED...
THANKS TO THAT GUY SHOWING UP EVERYWHERE WE GO...
WE'RE MAKING...
...ZERO PROGRESS.
SIGH
MY APOL-OGIES, MEKI-SAMA...
THERE'S NO NEED FOR YOU TO APOL-OGIZE.
LOW OGRE SHOSHOKI
HEY NOW!
DO I HEAR YOU TALKING ABOUT ME?!
BECAUSE IF YOU ARE, I ASK THAT YOU DO IT MUCH LOUDER!
GRRR!
イラッ

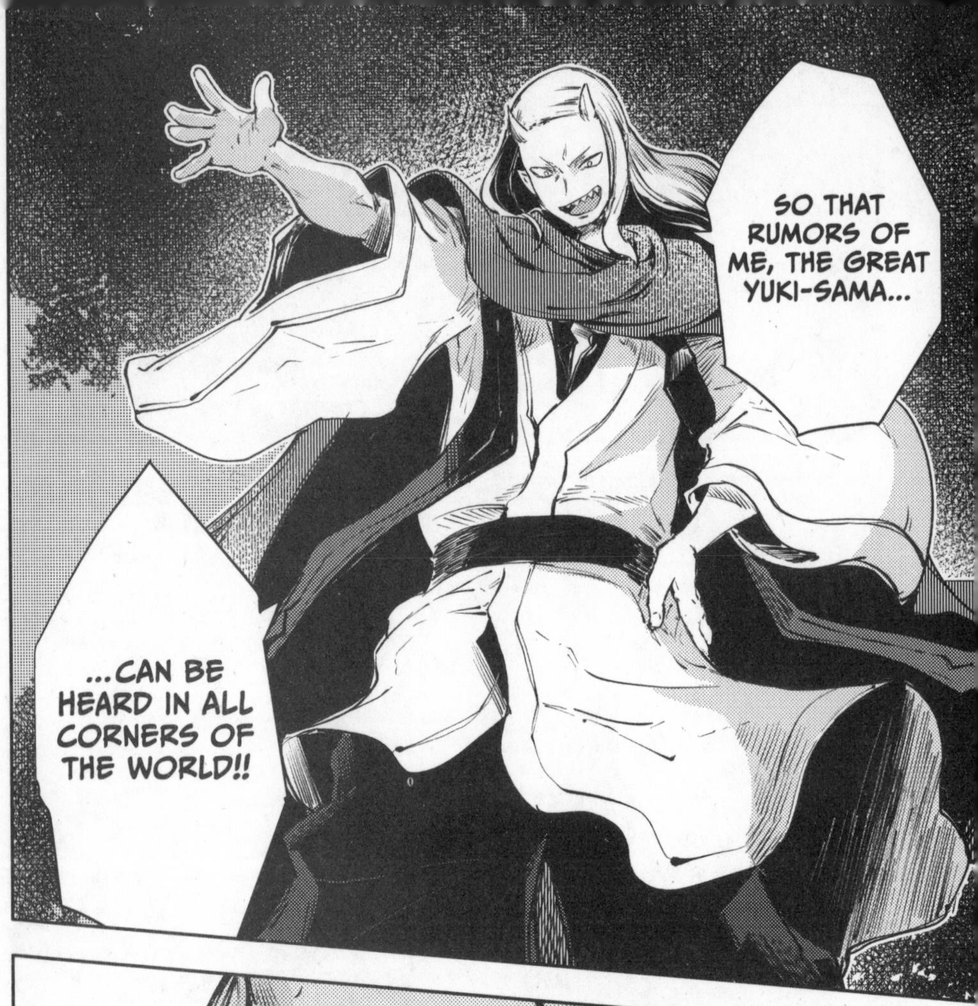
SO THAT RUMORS OF ME, THE GREAT YUKI-SAMA...
...CAN BE HEARD IN ALL CORNERS OF THE WORLD!!
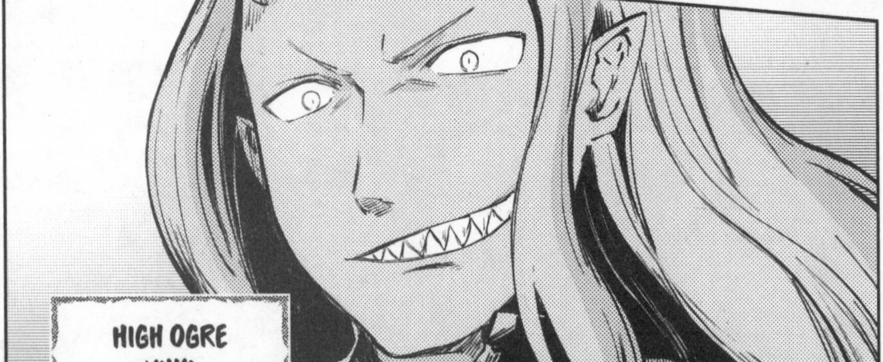
HIGH OGRE YUKI

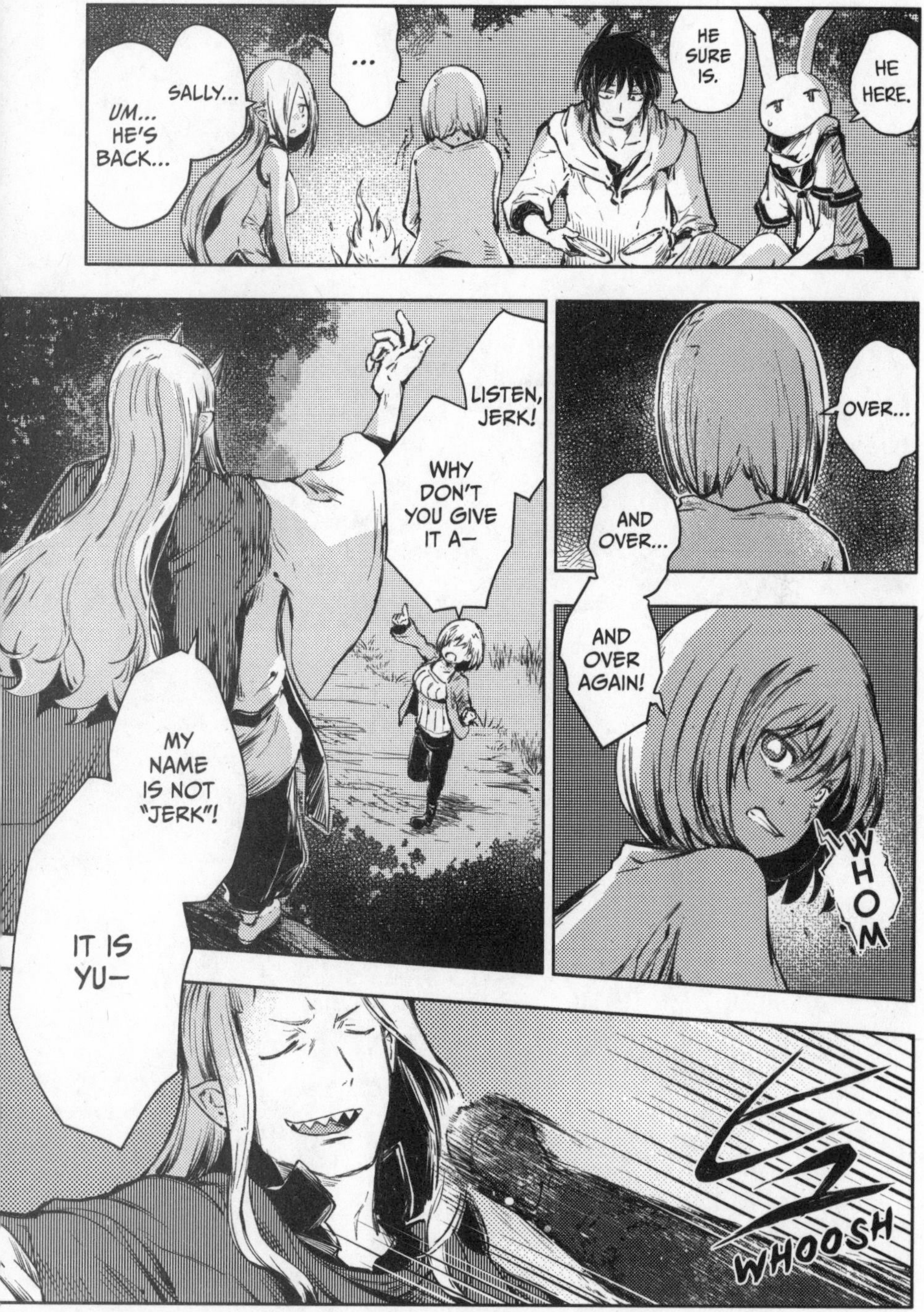
HE HERE.
HE SURE IS.
...
SALLY... UM... HE'S BACK...
OVER...
AND OVER...
AND OVER AGAIN!
WHOM
LISTEN, JERK!
WHY DON'T YOU GIVE IT A—
MY NAME IS NOT "JERK"!
IT IS YU—
WHOOSH

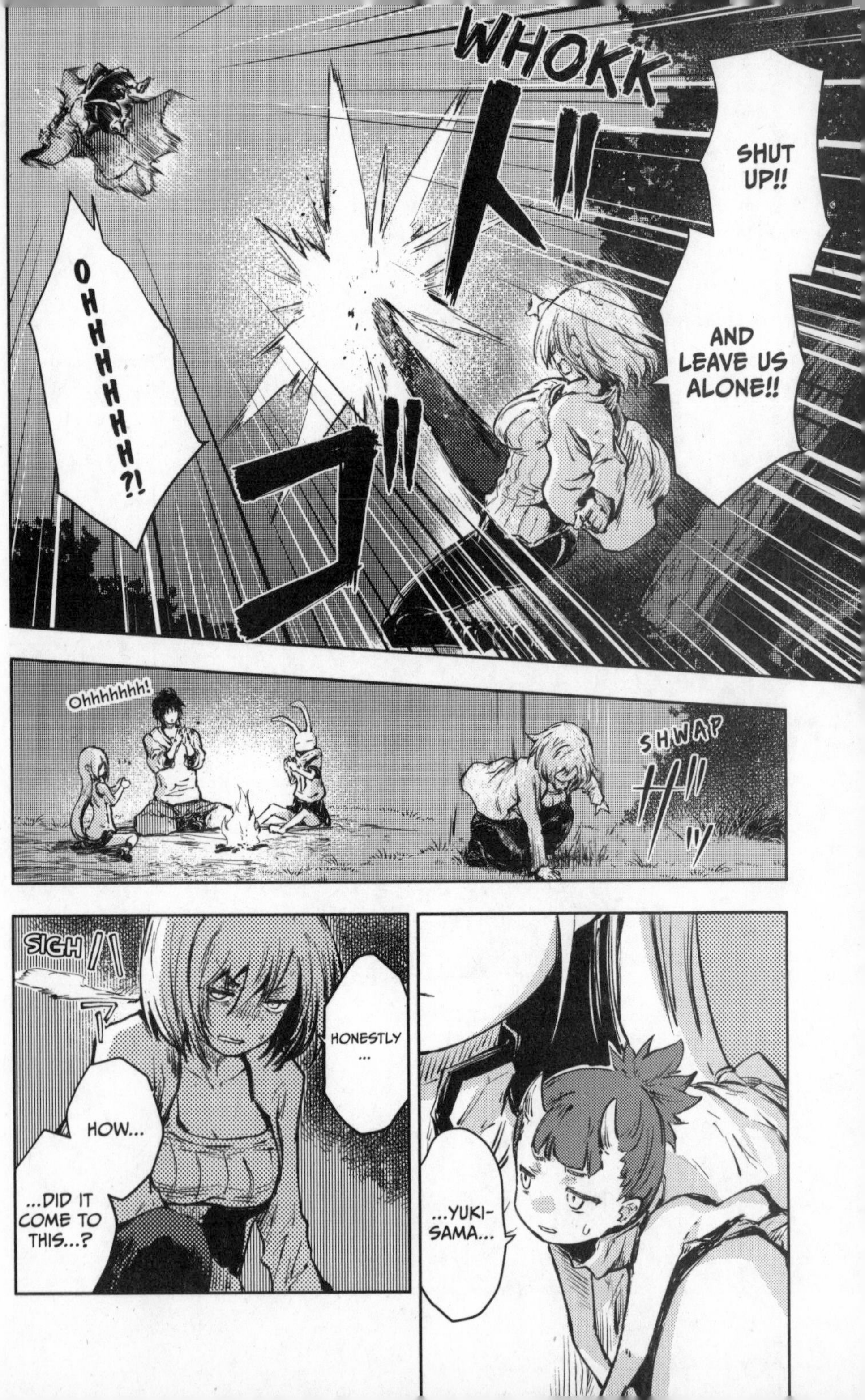
WHOKK
SHUT UP!!
AND LEAVE US ALONE!!
OHHHHHHH?!
SHWAP
Ohhhhhhh!
...YUKI-SAMA...
SIGH
HONESTLY ...
HOW...
...DID IT COME TO THIS...?

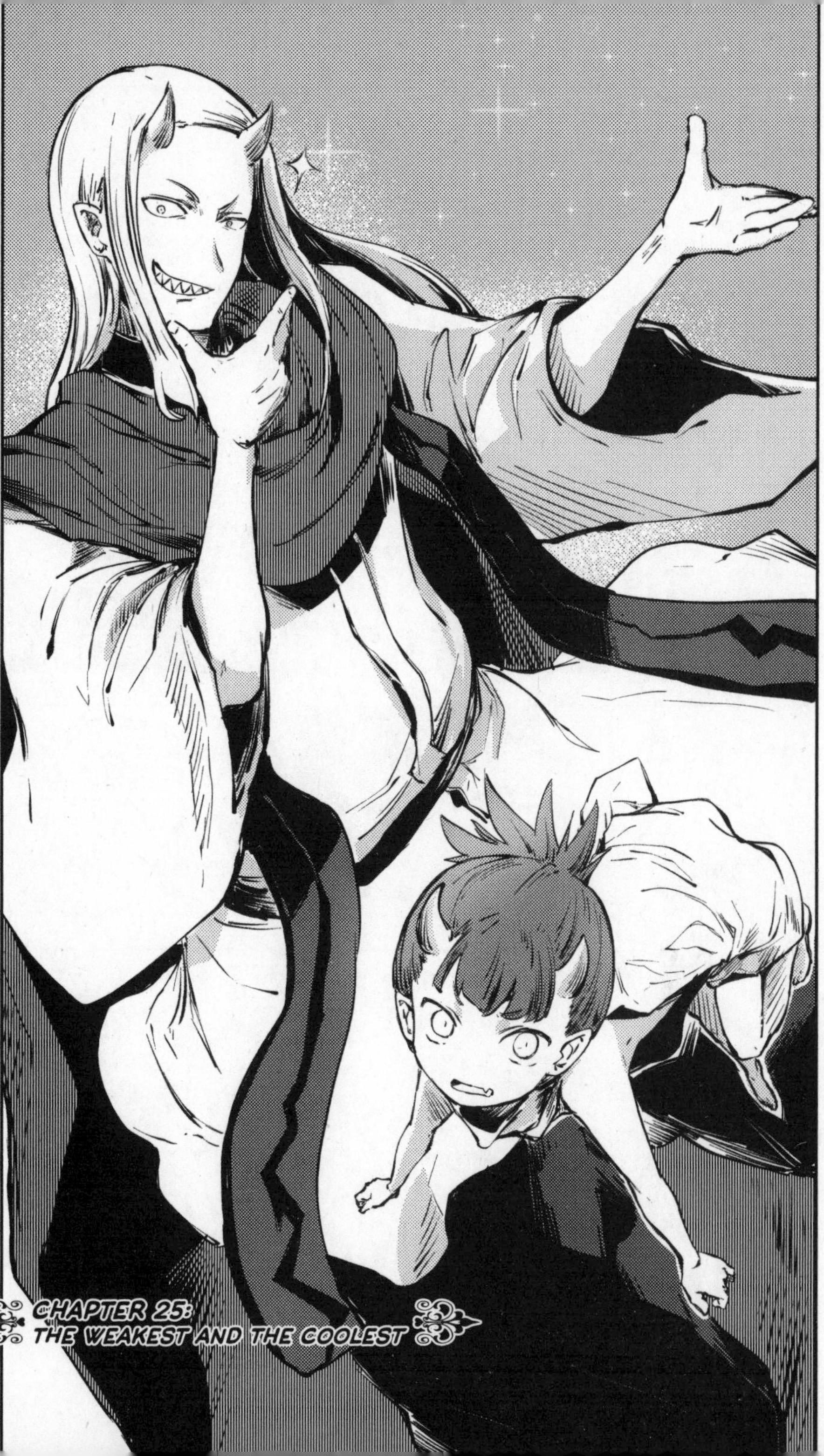
CHAPTER 25:
THE WEAKEST AND THE COOLEST

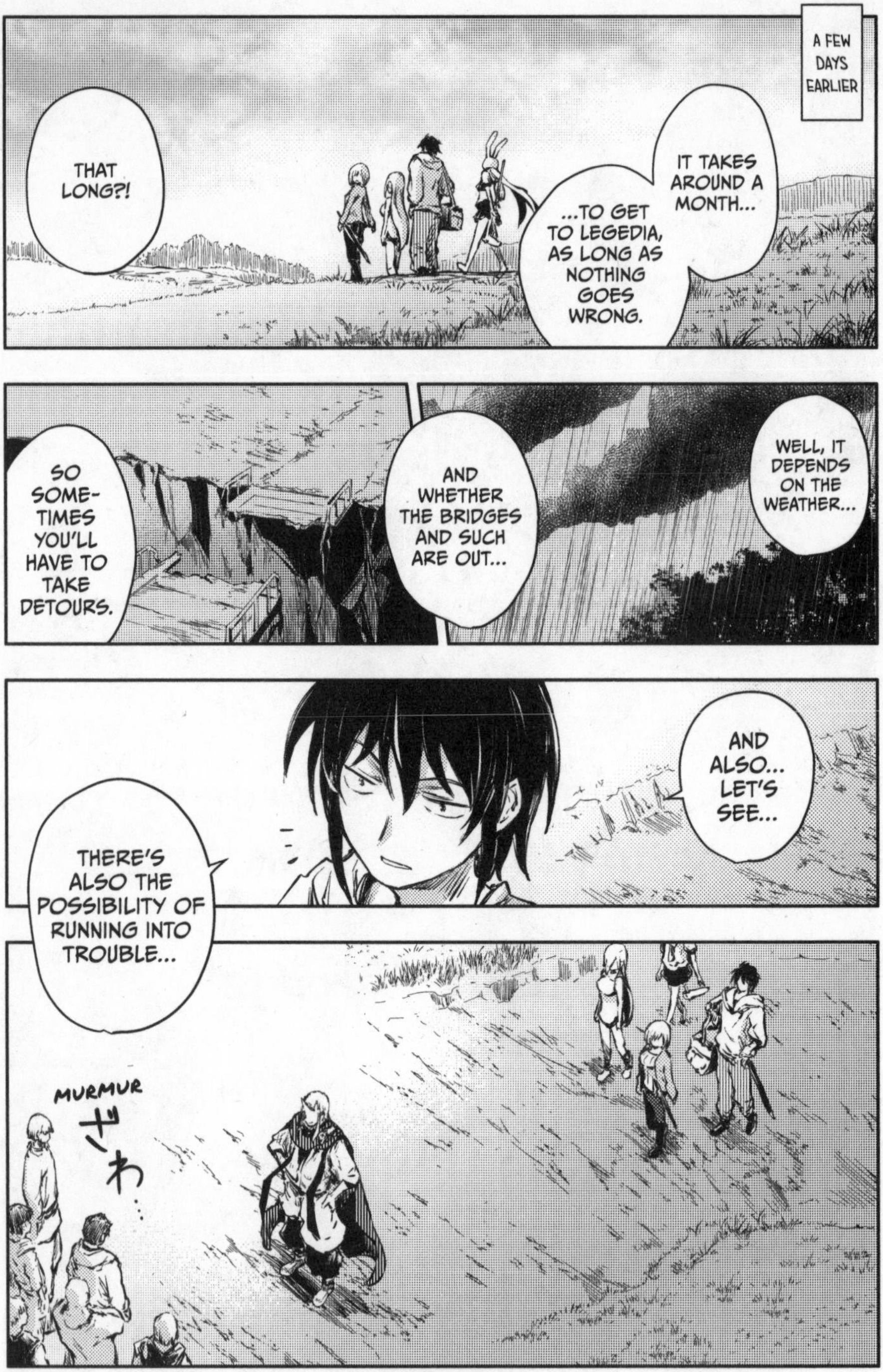
A FEW DAYS EARLIER
IT TAKES AROUND A MONTH...
...TO GET TO LEGEDIA, AS LONG AS NOTHING GOES WRONG.
THAT LONG?!
WELL, IT DEPENDS ON THE WEATHER...
AND WHETHER THE BRIDGES AND SUCH ARE OUT...
SO SOME-TIMES YOU'LL HAVE TO TAKE DETOURS.
AND ALSO... LET'S SEE...
THERE'S ALSO THE POSSIBILITY OF RUNNING INTO TROUBLE...
MURMUR
ざわ…

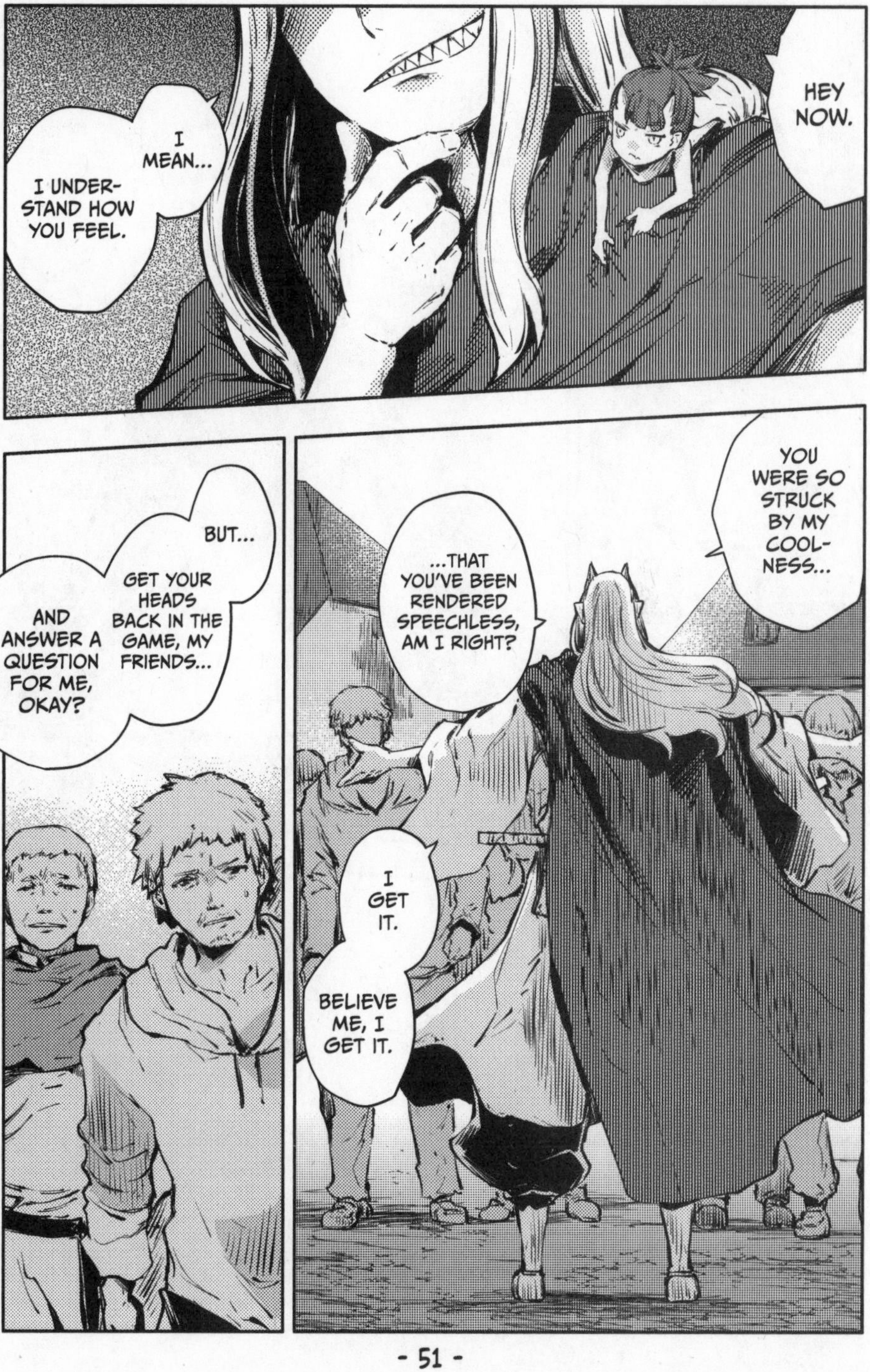
HEY NOW.
I MEAN...
I UNDER-STAND HOW YOU FEEL.
YOU WERE SO STRUCK BY MY COOL-NESS...
...THAT YOU'VE BEEN RENDERED SPEECHLESS, AM I RIGHT?
I GET IT.
BELIEVE ME, I GET IT.
BUT...
GET YOUR HEADS BACK IN THE GAME, MY FRIENDS...
AND ANSWER A QUESTION FOR ME, OKAY?

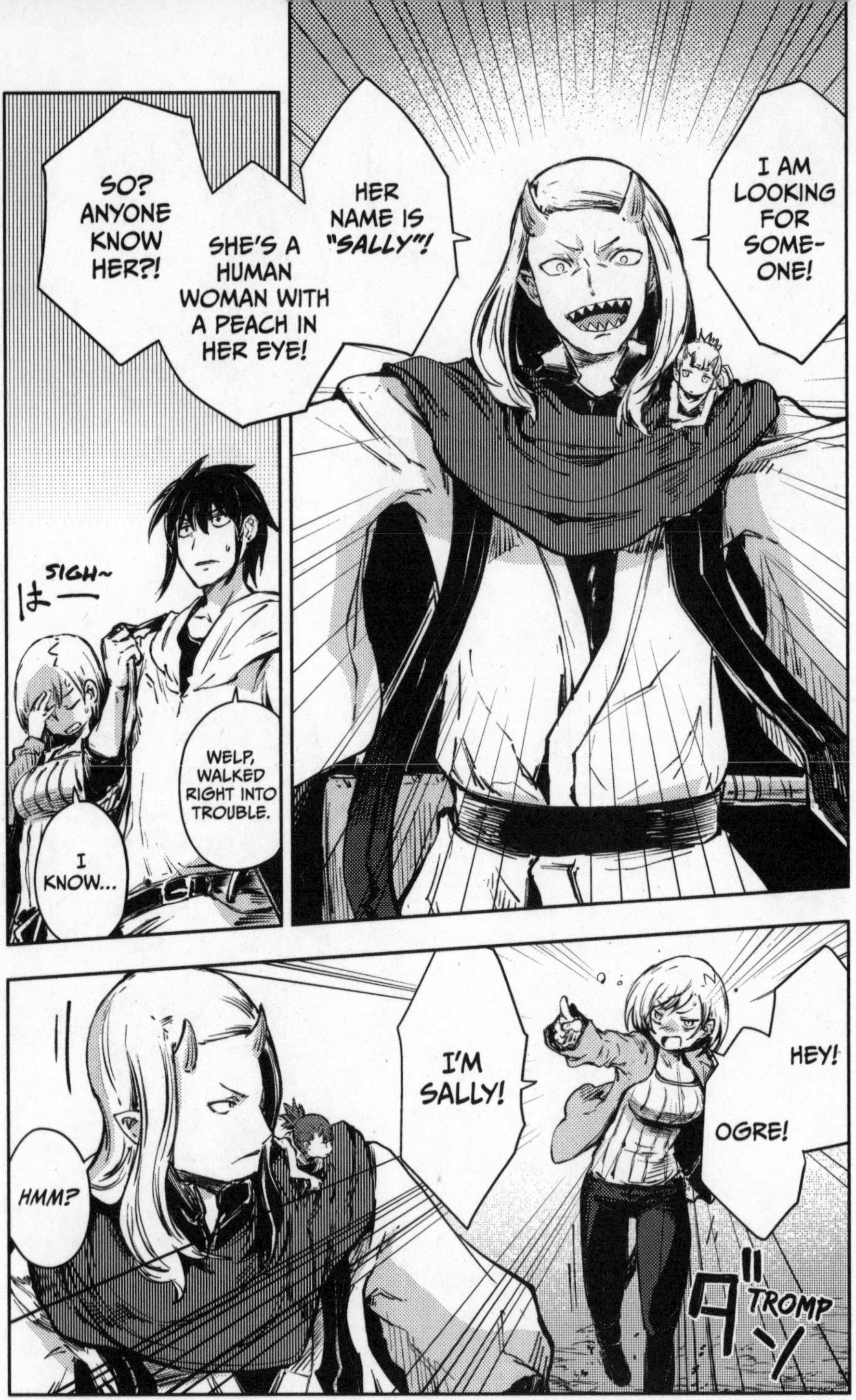
I AM LOOKING FOR SOME-ONE!
HER NAME IS "SALLY"!
SHE'S A HUMAN WOMAN WITH A PEACH IN HER EYE!
SO? ANYONE KNOW HER?!
は一 SIGH~
WELP, WALKED RIGHT INTO TROUBLE.
I KNOW...
HEY!
OGRE!
I'M SALLY!
ダン TROMP
HMM?

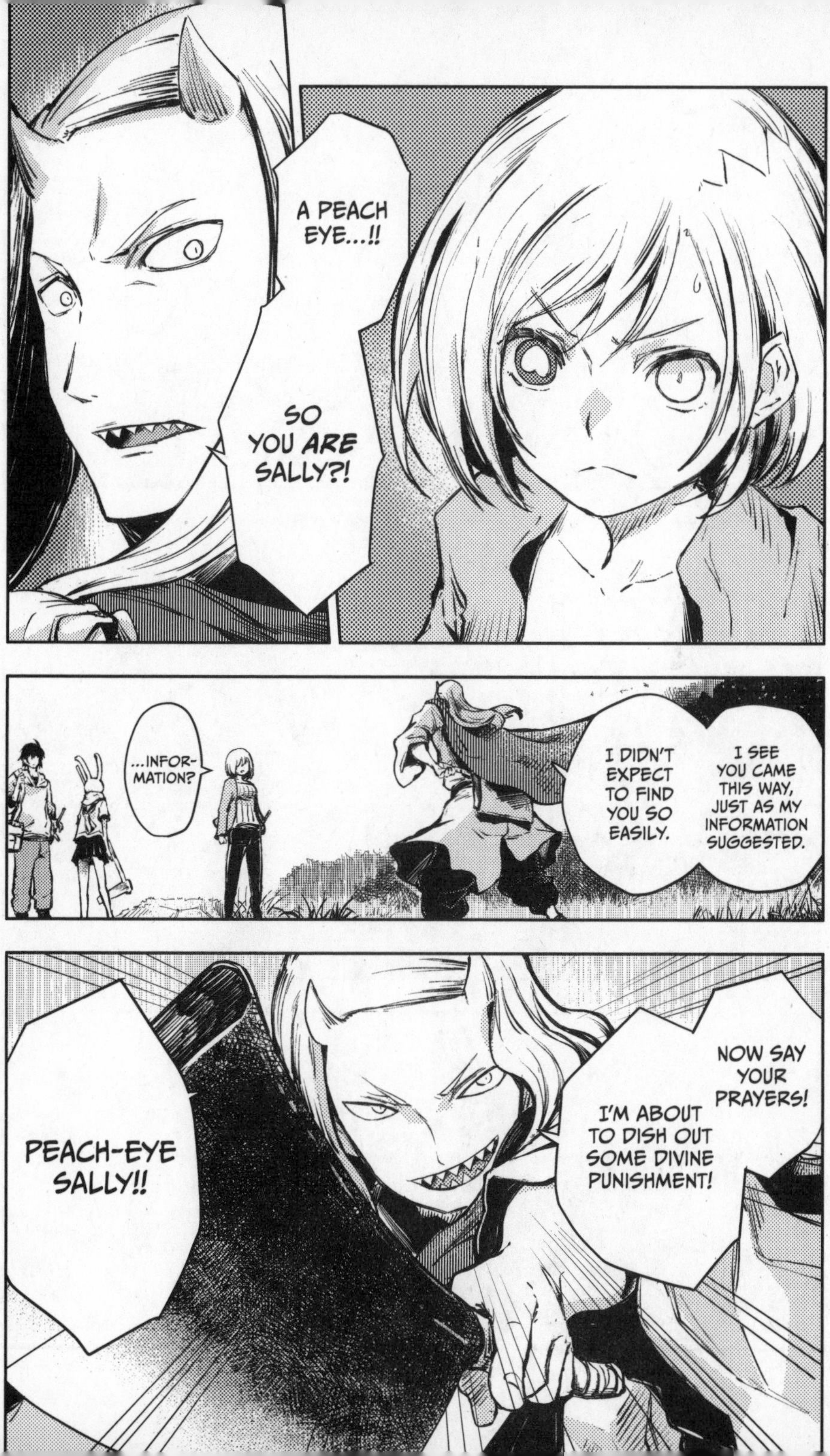
A PEACH EYE...!!
SO YOU ARE SALLY?!
I SEE YOU CAME THIS WAY, JUST AS MY INFORMATION SUGGESTED.
I DIDN'T EXPECT TO FIND YOU SO EASILY.
...INFOR-MATION?
NOW SAY YOUR PRAYERS!
I'M ABOUT TO DISH OUT SOME DIVINE PUNISHMENT!
PEACH-EYE SALLY!!

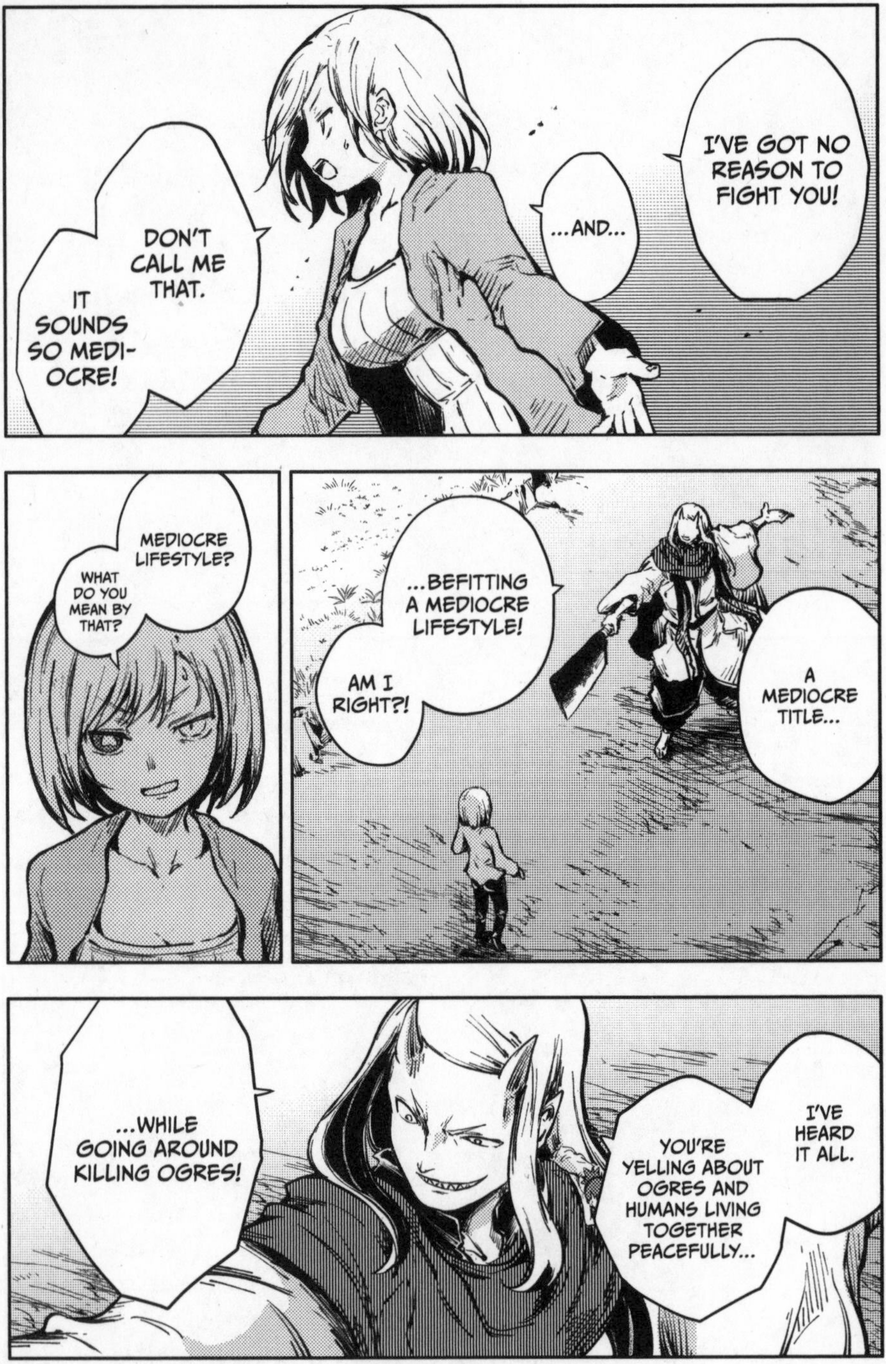
I'VE GOT NO REASON TO FIGHT YOU!
...AND...
DON'T CALL ME THAT.
IT SOUNDS SO MEDI-OCRE!
A MEDIOCRE TITLE...
...BEFITTING A MEDIOCRE LIFESTYLE!
AM I RIGHT?!
MEDIOCRE LIFESTYLE?
WHAT DO YOU MEAN BY THAT?
I'VE HEARD IT ALL.
YOU'RE YELLING ABOUT OGRES AND HUMANS LIVING TOGETHER PEACEFULLY...
...WHILE GOING AROUND KILLING OGRES!

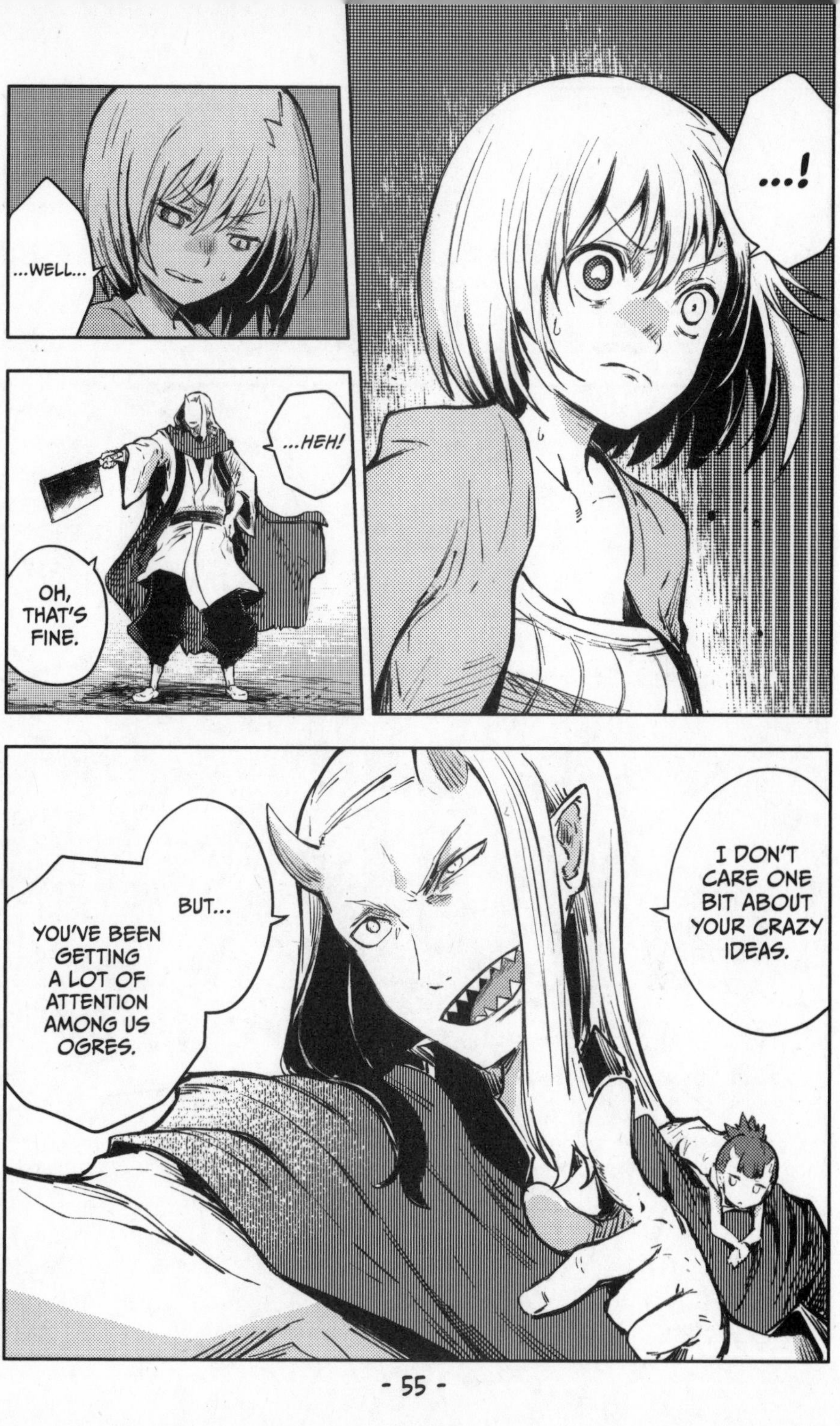
...!
...WELL...
...HEH!
OH, THAT'S FINE.
I DON'T CARE ONE BIT ABOUT YOUR CRAZY IDEAS.
BUT...
YOU'VE BEEN GETTING A LOT OF ATTENTION AMONG US OGRES.

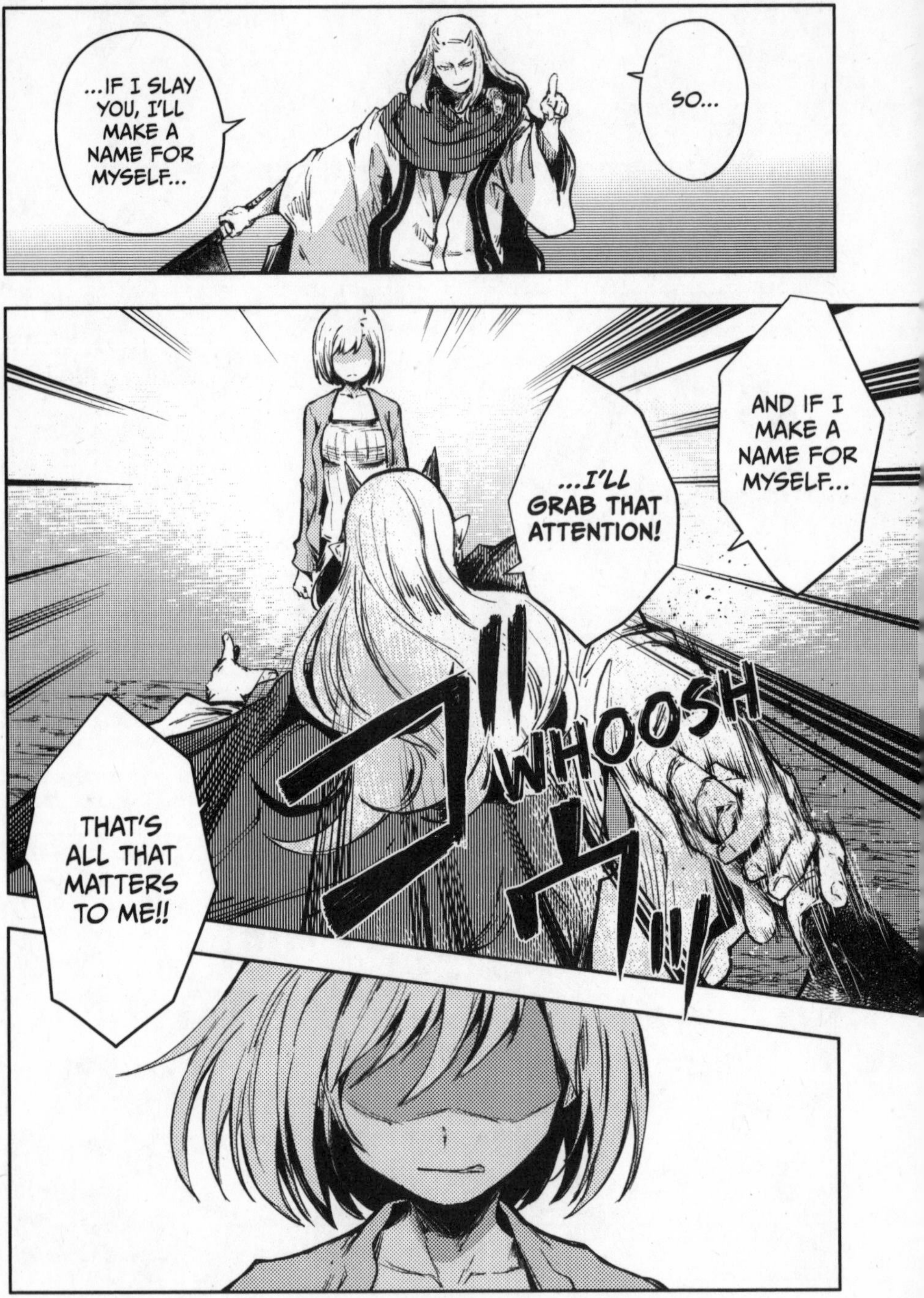
SO...
...IF I SLAY YOU, I'LL MAKE A NAME FOR MYSELF...
AND IF I MAKE A NAME FOR MYSELF...
...I'LL GRAB THAT ATTENTION!
WHOOSH
THAT'S ALL THAT MATTERS TO ME!!

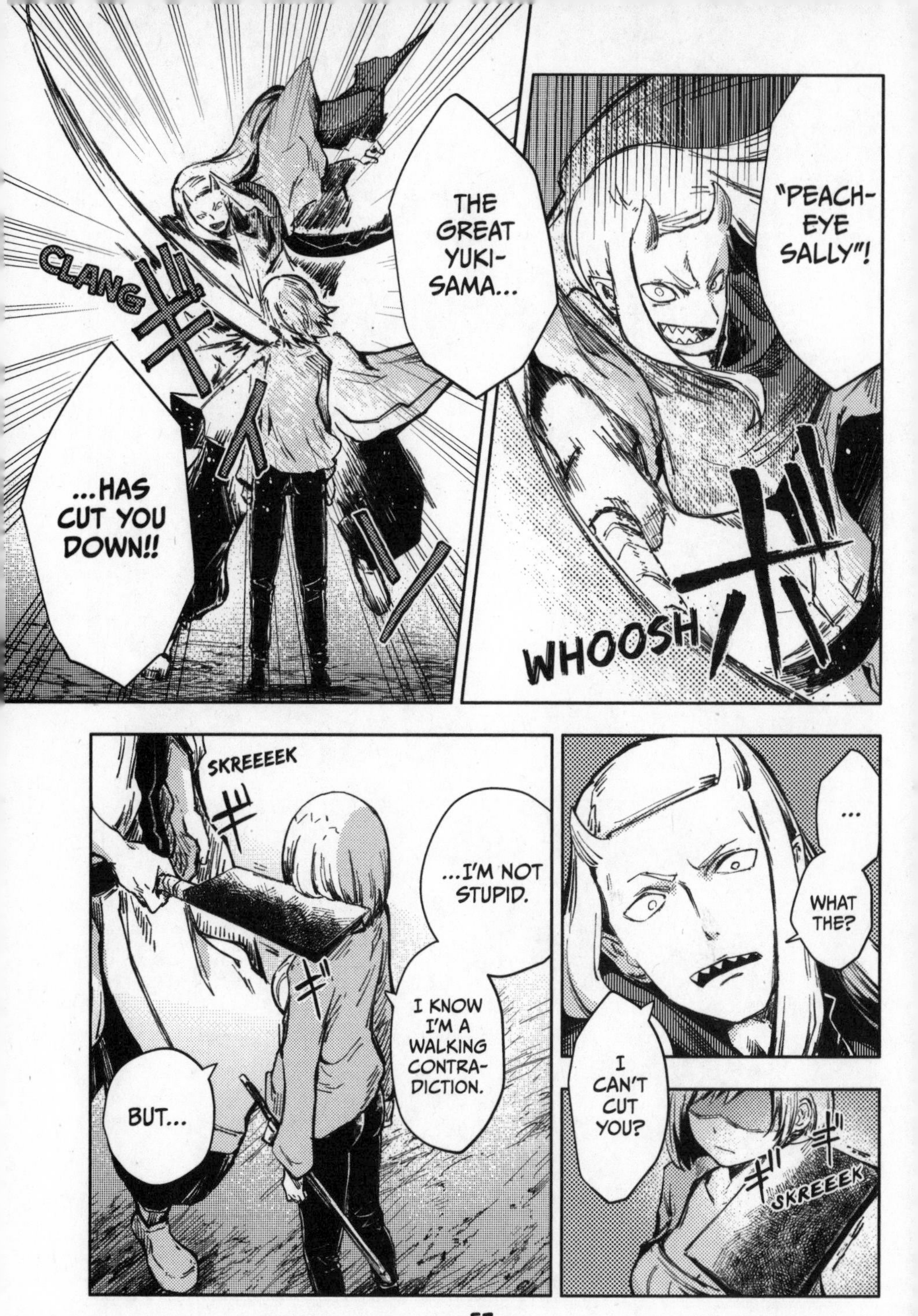
"PEACH-EYE SALLY"!
WHOOSH
THE GREAT YUKI-SAMA...
CLANG
...HAS CUT YOU DOWN!!
...
WHAT THE?
I CAN'T CUT YOU?
SKREEEK
SKREEEEK
...I'M NOT STUPID.
I KNOW I'M A WALKING CONTRA-DICTION.
BUT...

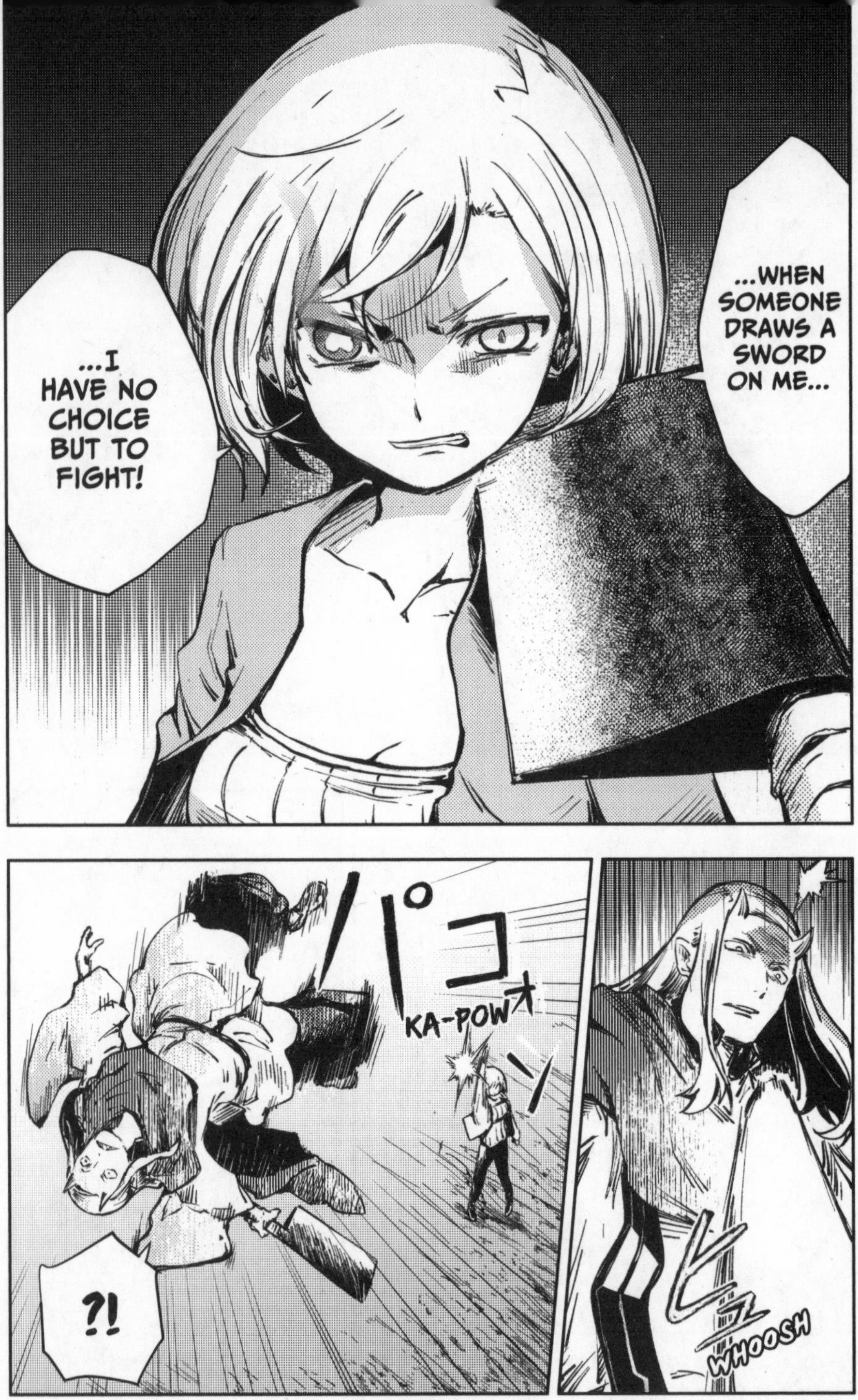
...WHEN SOMEONE DRAWS A SWORD ON ME...
...I HAVE NO CHOICE BUT TO FIGHT!
WHOOSH
パコ
KA-POW
?!

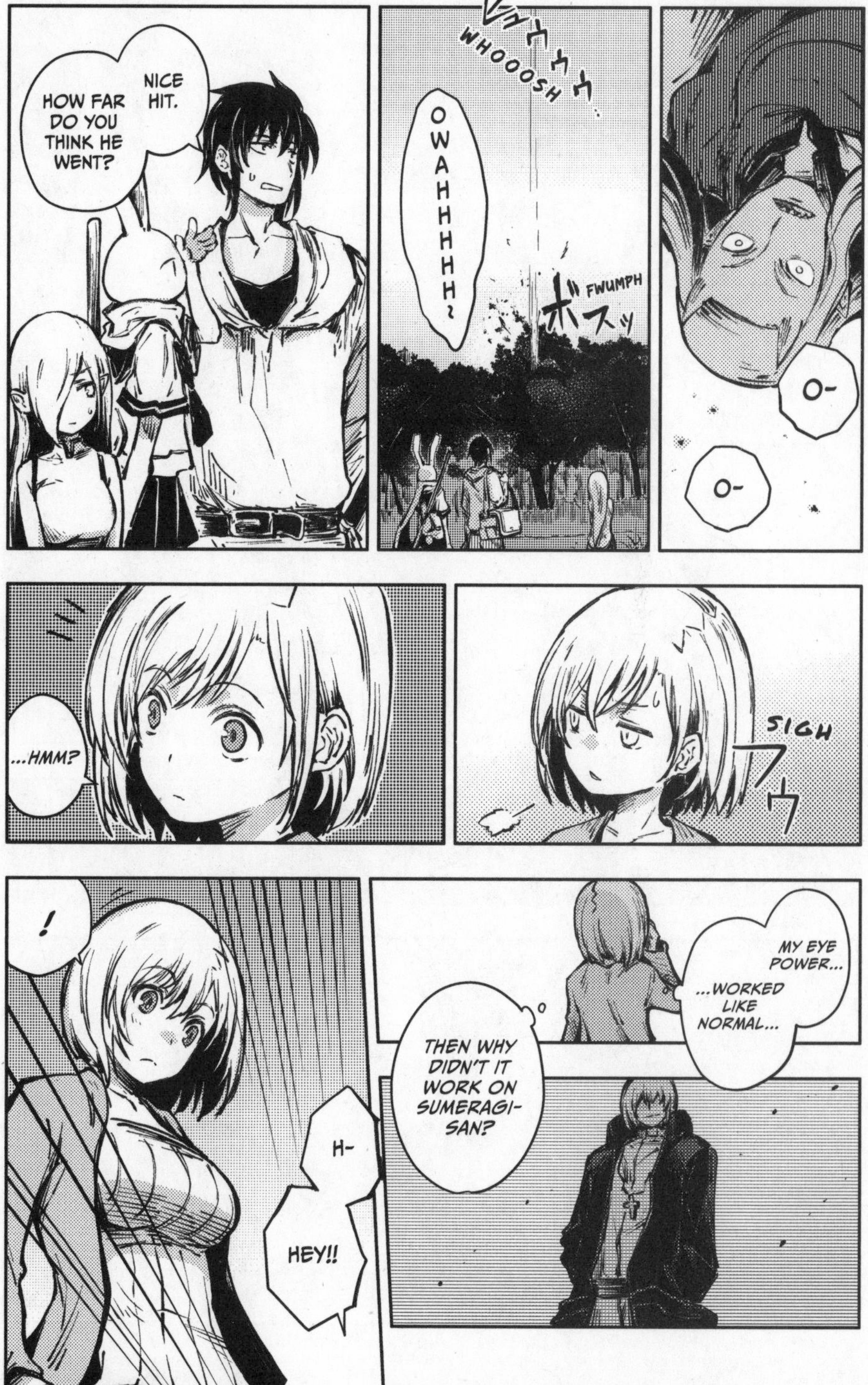
O-
O-
WHOOOOSH
OWAHHHHH~
FWUMPH
ボスッ
NICE HIT.
HOW FAR DO YOU THINK HE WENT?
SIGH
フウ
...HMM?
MY EYE POWER...
...WORKED LIKE NORMAL...
THEN WHY DIDN'T IT WORK ON SUMERAGI-SAN?
!
H-
HEY!!

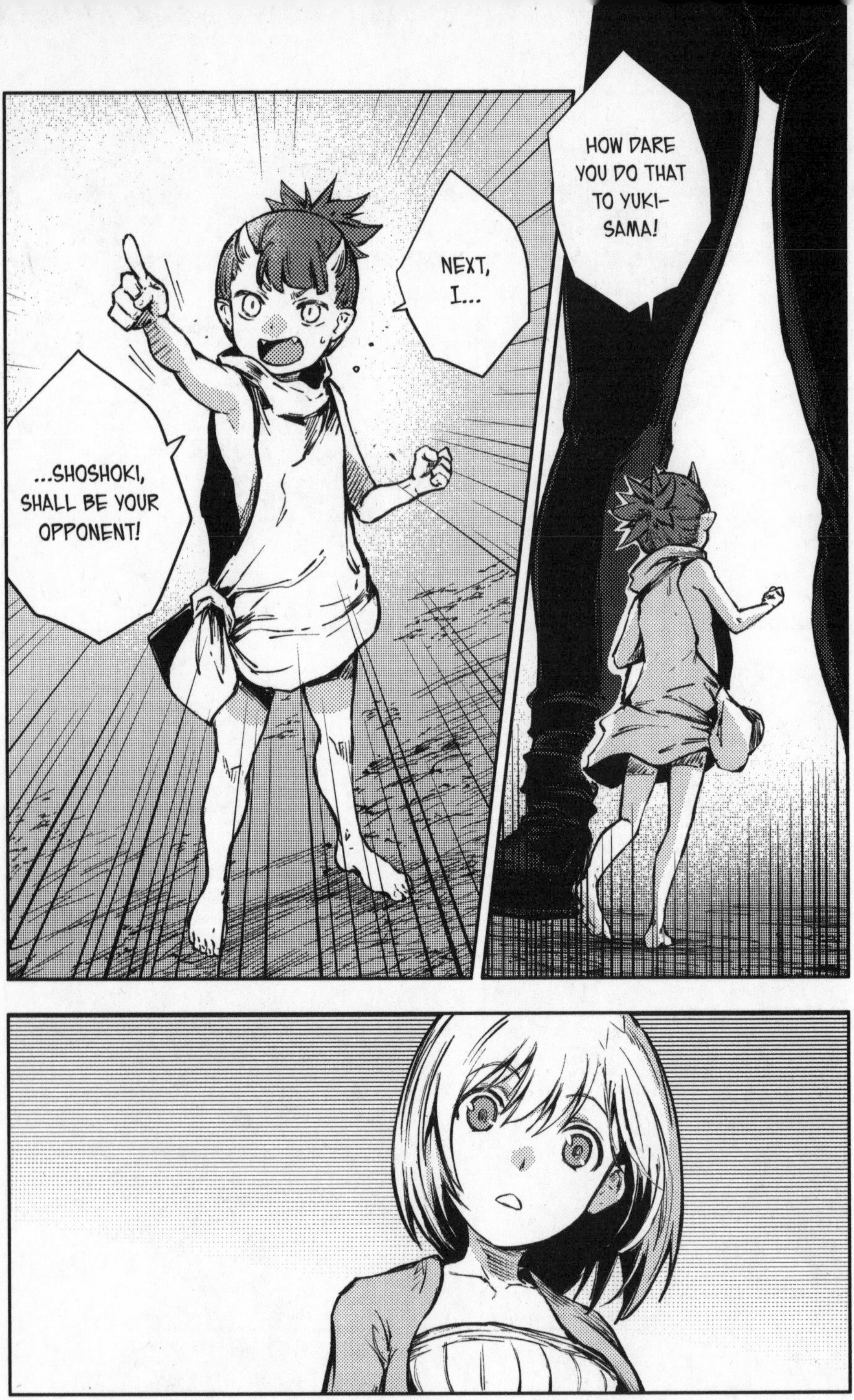
HOW DARE YOU DO THAT TO YUKI-SAMA!
NEXT, I...
...SHOSHOKI, SHALL BE YOUR OPPONENT!

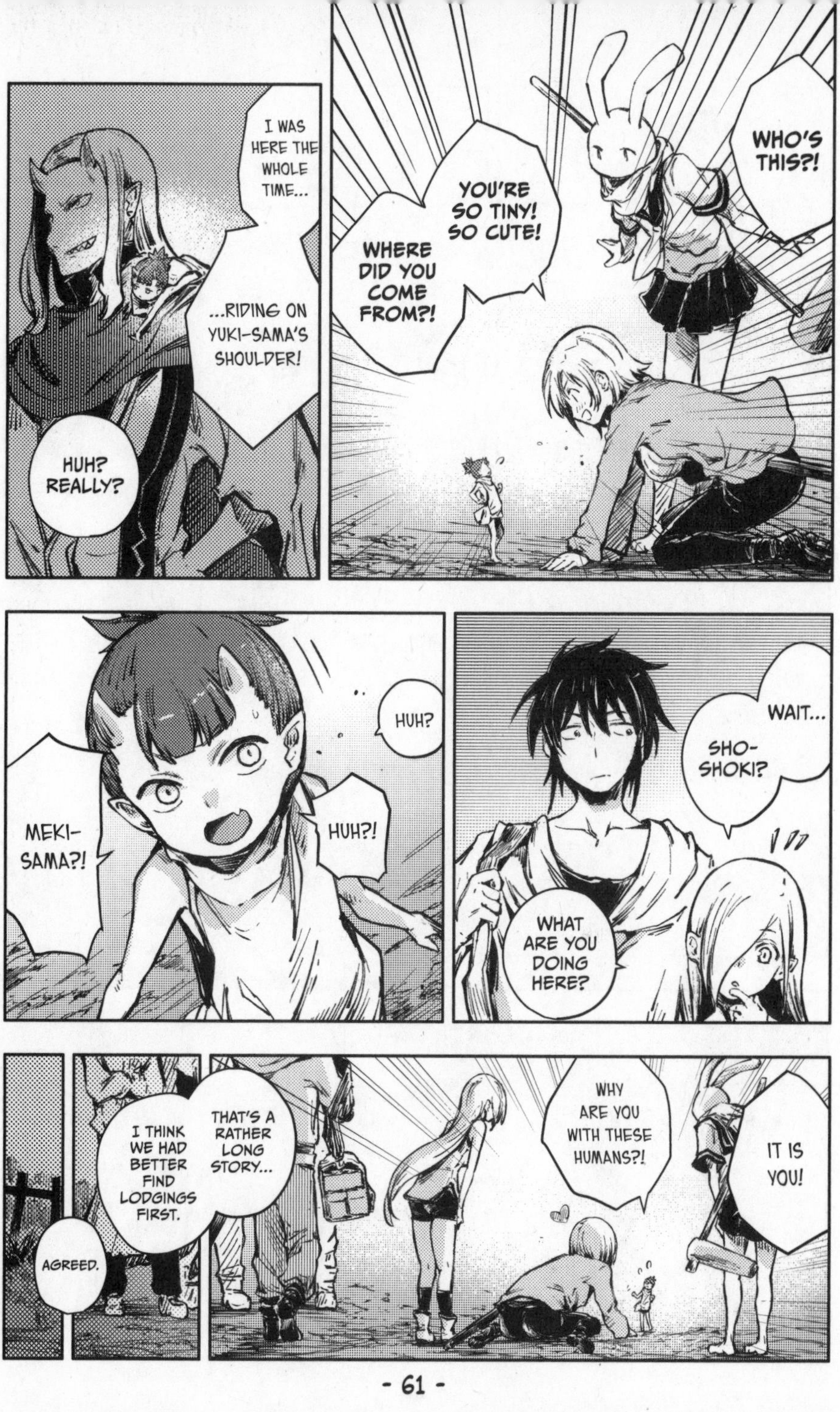
WHO'S THIS?!
YOU'RE SO TINY! SO CUTE!
WHERE DID YOU COME FROM?!
I WAS HERE THE WHOLE TIME...
...RIDING ON YUKI-SAMA'S SHOULDER!
HUH? REALLY?
WAIT... SHO-SHOKI?
WHAT ARE YOU DOING HERE?
HUH?
HUH?!
MEKI-SAMA?!
IT IS YOU!
WHY ARE YOU WITH THESE HUMANS?!
THAT'S A RATHER LONG STORY...
I THINK WE HAD BETTER FIND LODGINGS FIRST.
AGREED.

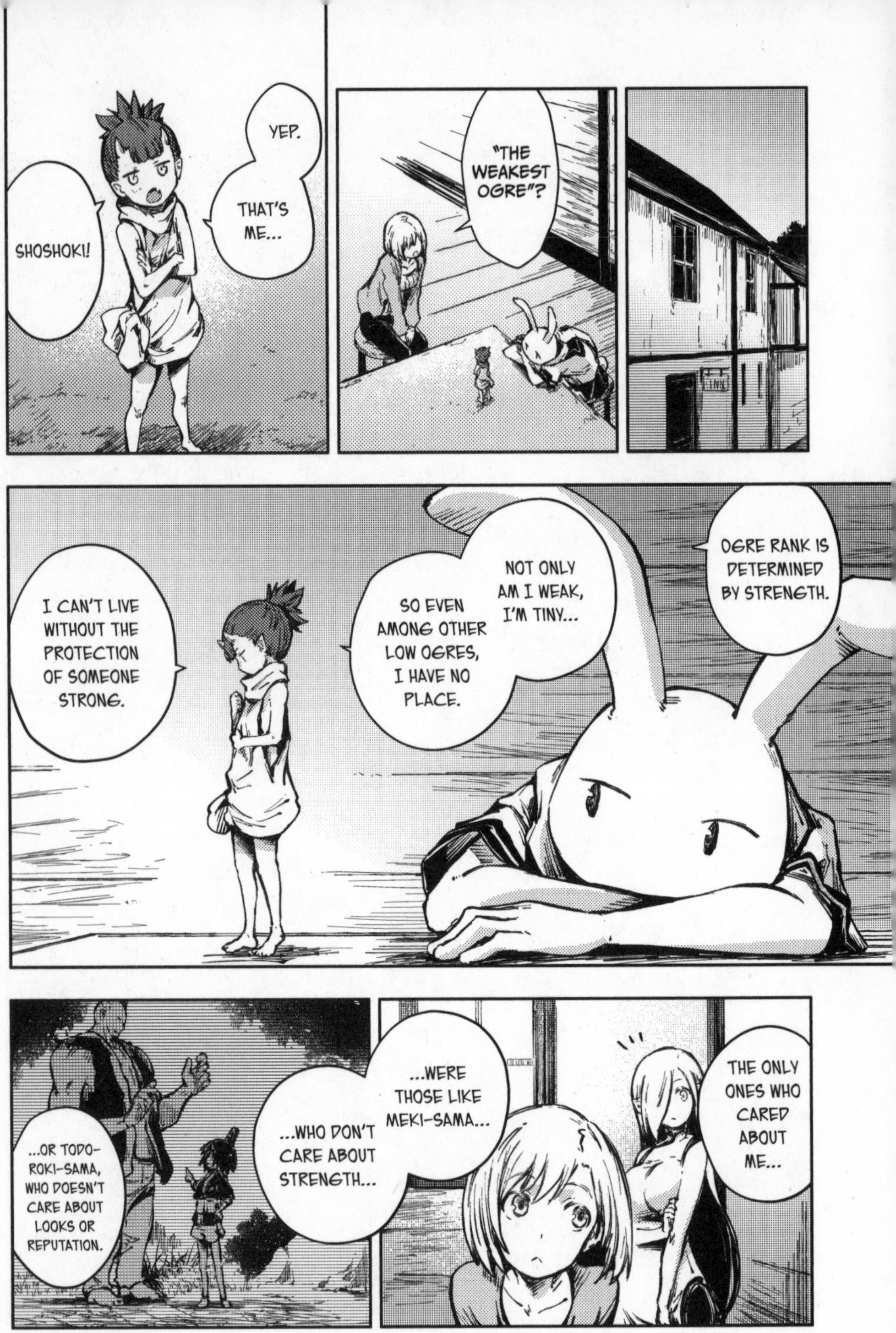
INN
"THE WEAKEST OGRE"?
YEP.
THAT'S ME...
SHOSHOKI!
OGRE RANK IS DETERMINED BY STRENGTH.
NOT ONLY AM I WEAK, I'M TINY...
SO EVEN AMONG OTHER LOW OGRES, I HAVE NO PLACE.
I CAN'T LIVE WITHOUT THE PROTECTION OF SOMEONE STRONG.
THE ONLY ONES WHO CARED ABOUT ME...
...WERE THOSE LIKE MEKI-SAMA...
...WHO DON'T CARE ABOUT STRENGTH...
...OR TODO-ROKI-SAMA, WHO DOESN'T CARE ABOUT LOOKS OR REPUTATION.

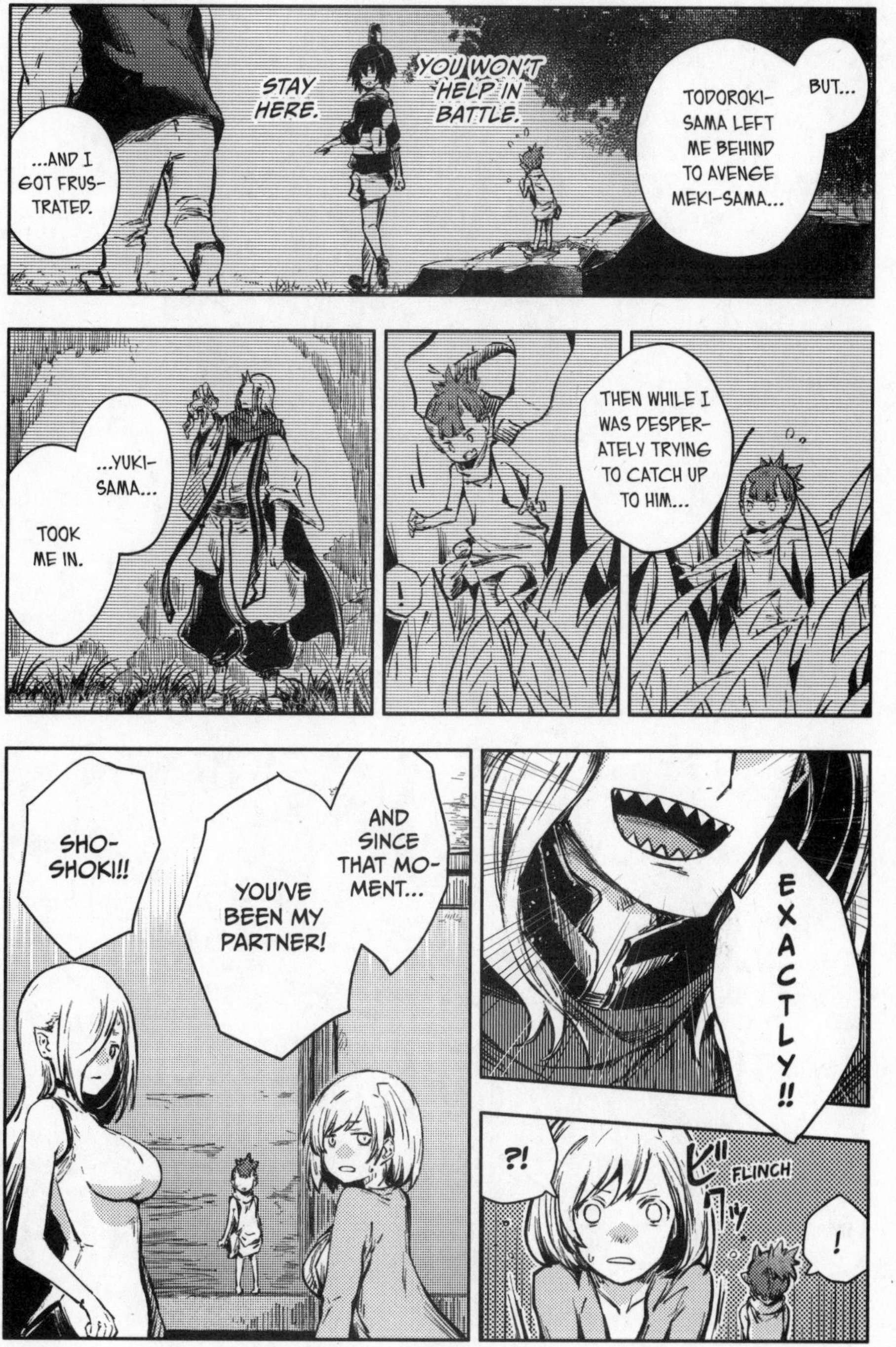
BUT...
TODOROKI-SAMA LEFT ME BEHIND TO AVENGE MEKI-SAMA...
YOU WON'T HELP IN BATTLE.
STAY HERE.
...AND I GOT FRUS-TRATED.
THEN WHILE I WAS DESPER-ATELY TRYING TO CATCH UP TO HIM...
!
...YUKI-SAMA...
TOOK ME IN.
EXACTLY!!
ビクッ
FLINCH
?!
!
AND SINCE THAT MO-MENT...
YOU'VE BEEN MY PARTNER!
SHO-SHOKI!!

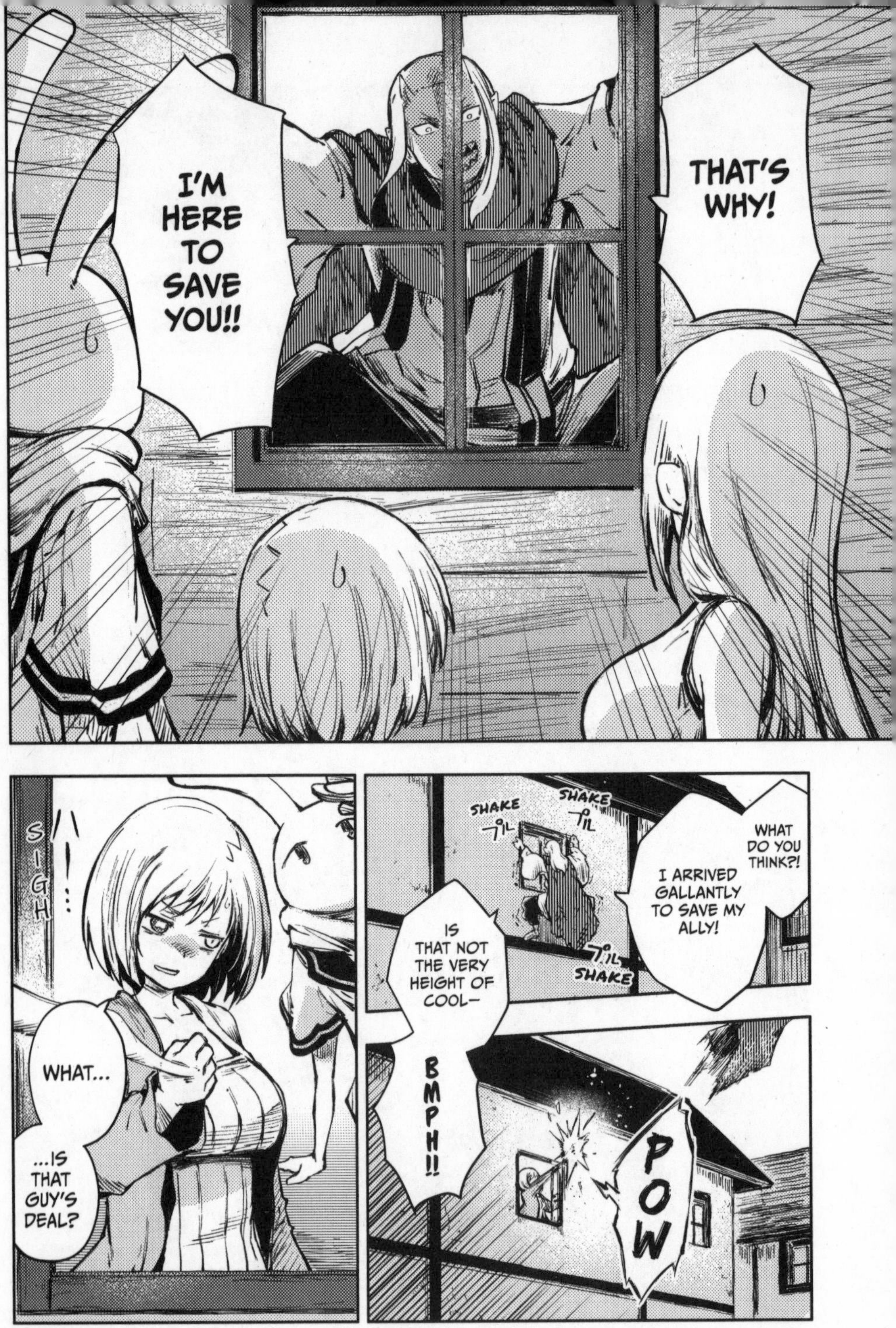
THAT'S WHY!
I'M HERE TO SAVE YOU!!
SHAKE
SHAKE
WHAT DO YOU THINK?!
I ARRIVED GALLANTLY TO SAVE MY ALLY!
SHAKE
IS THAT NOT THE VERY HEIGHT OF COOL—
BMPH!!
POW
SIGH...
WHAT...
...IS THAT GUY'S DEAL?

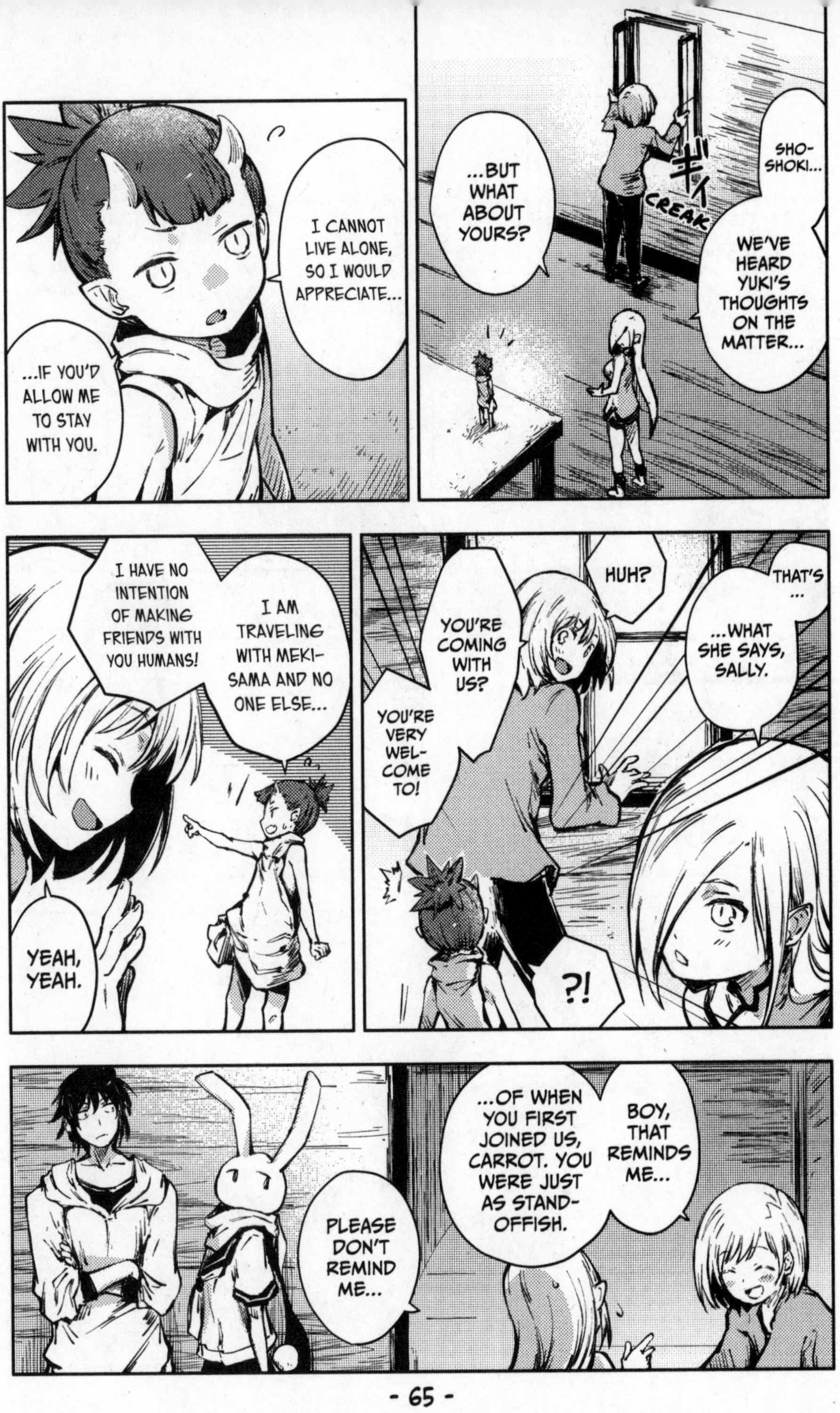
SHO-SHOKI...
WE'VE HEARD YUKI'S THOUGHTS ON THE MATTER...
ギイ
CREAK
...BUT WHAT ABOUT YOURS?
I CANNOT LIVE ALONE, SO I WOULD APPRECIATE...
...IF YOU'D ALLOW ME TO STAY WITH YOU.
THAT'S ...
...WHAT SHE SAYS, SALLY.
HUH?
YOU'RE COMING WITH US?
YOU'RE VERY WEL-COME TO!
?!
I AM TRAVELING WITH MEKI-SAMA AND NO ONE ELSE...
I HAVE NO INTENTION OF MAKING FRIENDS WITH YOU HUMANS!
YEAH, YEAH.
BOY, THAT REMINDS ME...
...OF WHEN YOU FIRST JOINED US, CARROT. YOU WERE JUST AS STAND-OFFISH.
PLEASE DON'T REMIND ME...

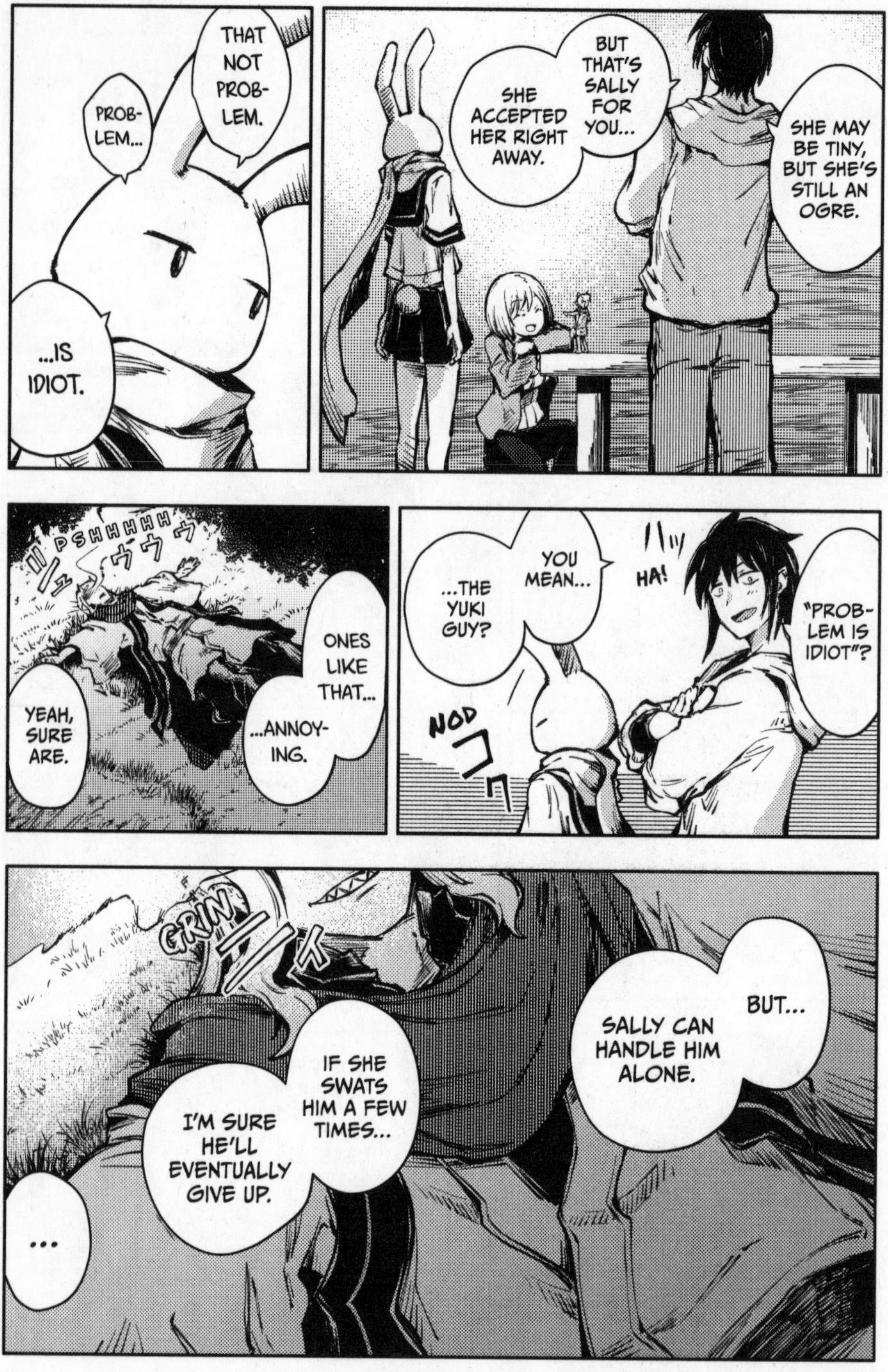
SHE MAY BE TINY, BUT SHE'S STILL AN OGRE.
BUT THAT'S SALLY FOR YOU...
SHE ACCEPTED HER RIGHT AWAY.
THAT NOT PROB-LEM.
PROB-LEM...
...IS IDIOT.
"PROB-LEM IS IDIOT"?
HA!
YOU MEAN...
...THE YUKI GUY?
NOD
PSHHHHHH
ONES LIKE THAT...
...ANNOY-ING.
YEAH, SURE ARE.
BUT...
SALLY CAN HANDLE HIM ALONE.
GRIN
IF SHE SWATS HIM A FEW TIMES...
I'M SURE HE'LL EVENTUALLY GIVE UP.
...

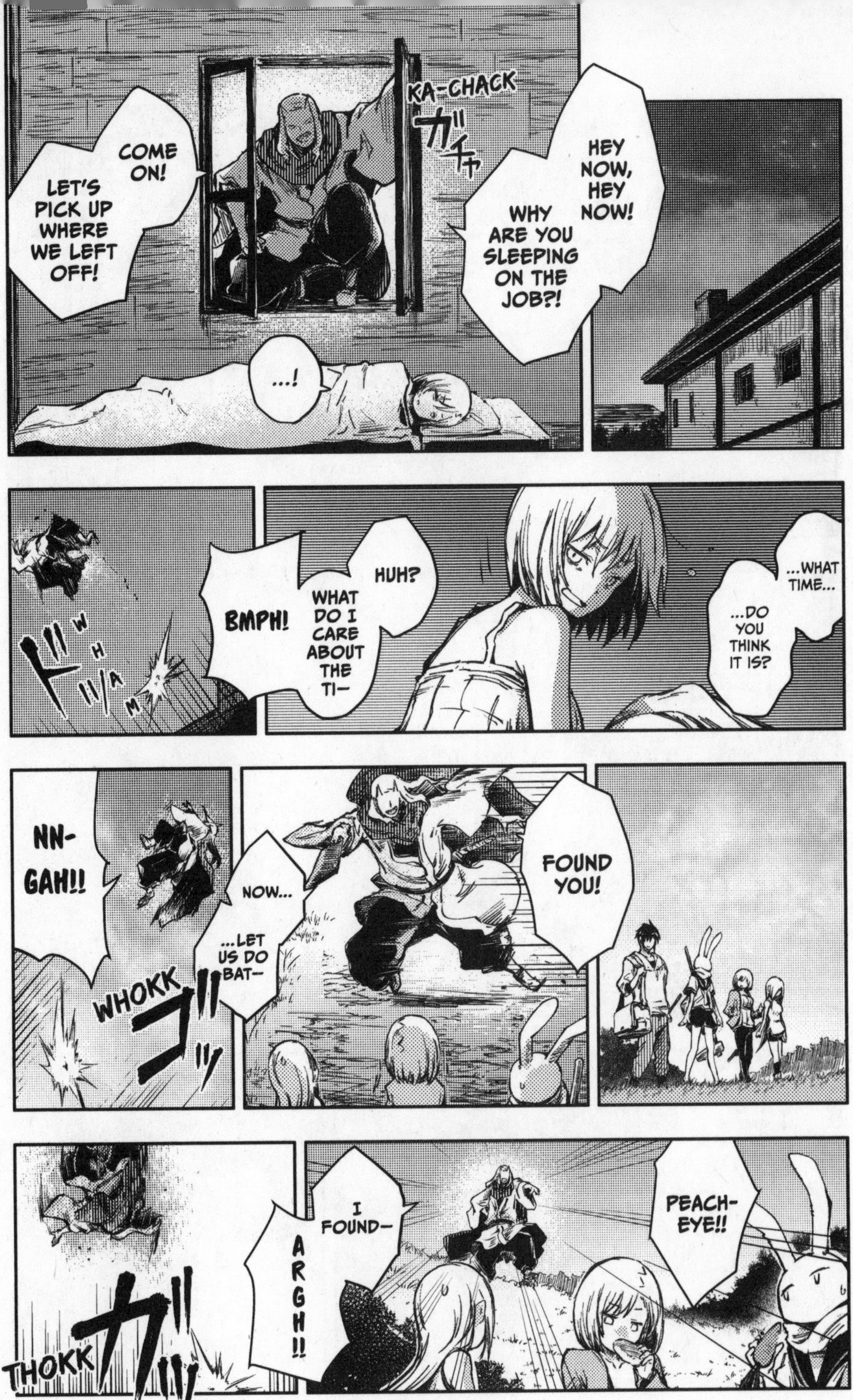
HEY NOW, HEY NOW!
WHY ARE YOU SLEEPING ON THE JOB?!
KA-CHACK ガチャ
COME ON!
LET'S PICK UP WHERE WE LEFT OFF!
...!
...WHAT TIME...
...DO YOU THINK IT IS?
HUH?
WHAT DO I CARE ABOUT THE TI—
BMPH!
WHAM ド
FOUND YOU!
NOW...
...LET US DO BAT—
NN-GAH!!
WHOKK ゴッ
PEACH-EYE!!
I FOUND—
ARGH!!
THOKK ガッ

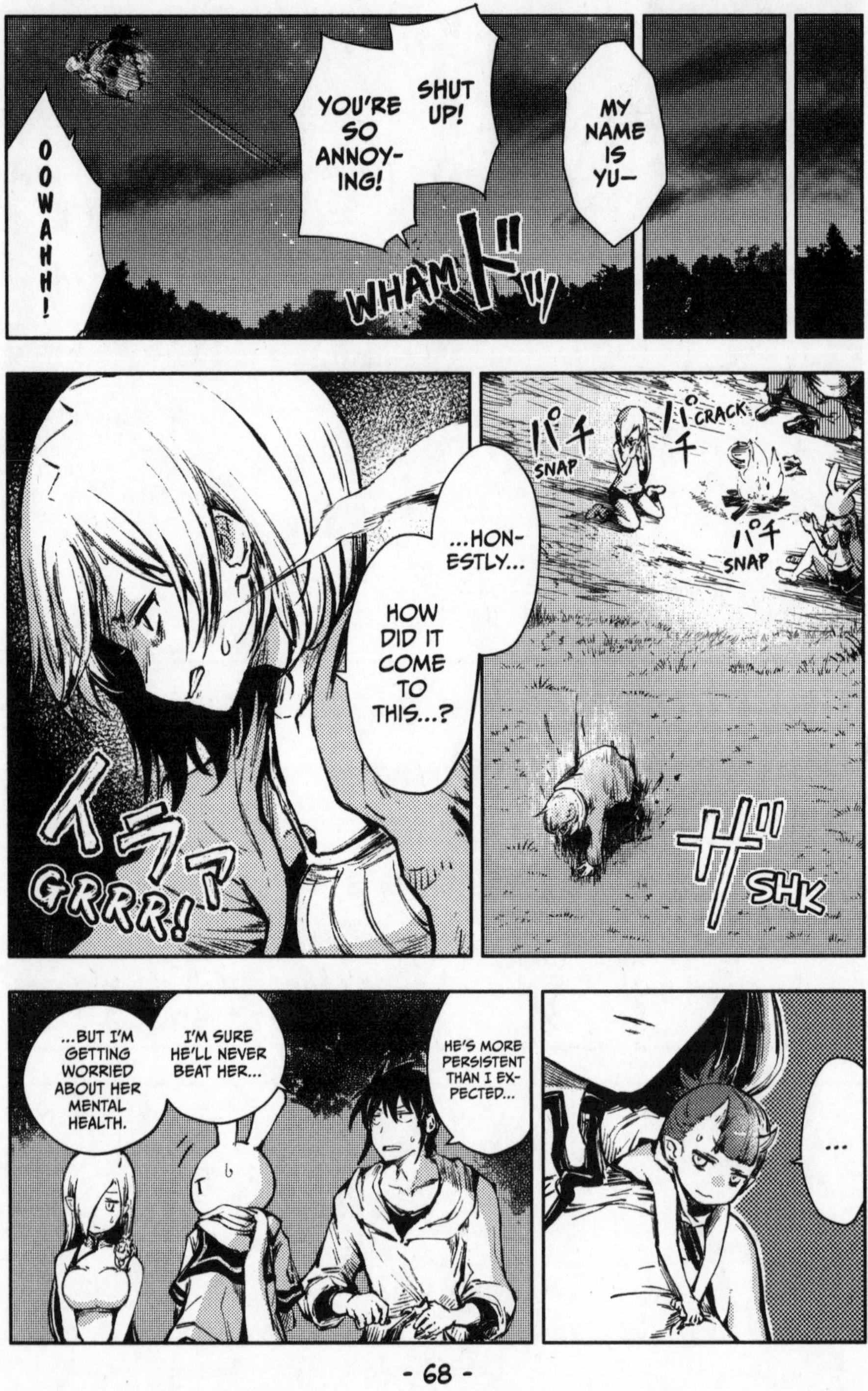
MY NAME IS YU—
SHUT UP!
YOU'RE SO ANNOY-ING!
WHAM ドッ
OOWAHH!
パチ CRACK
パチ SNAP
パチ SNAP
ザ SHK
...HON-ESTLY...
HOW DID IT COME TO THIS...?
イラァ GRRRR!
...
HE'S MORE PERSISTENT THAN I EX-PECTED...
I'M SURE HE'LL NEVER BEAT HER...
...BUT I'M GETTING WORRIED ABOUT HER MENTAL HEALTH.

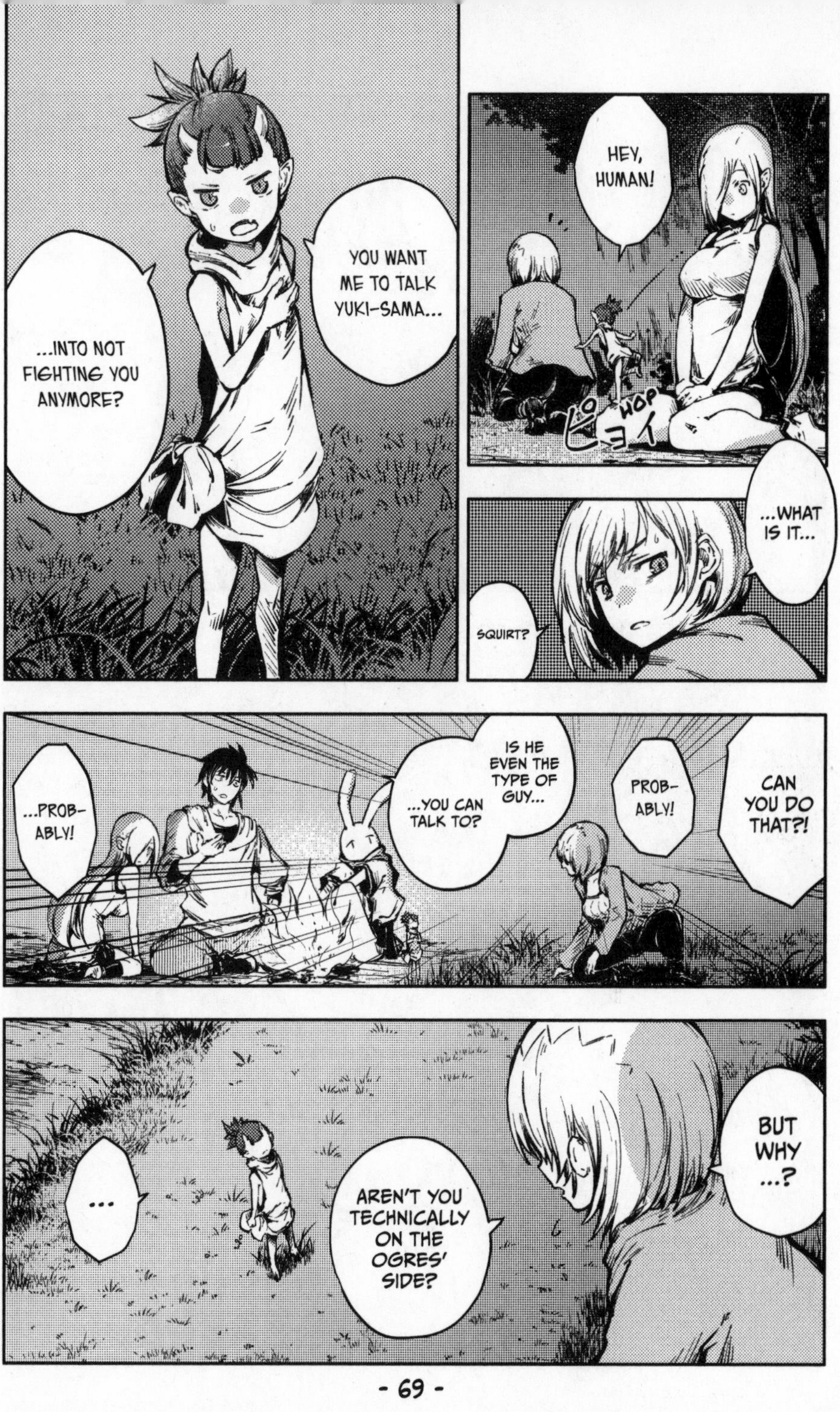
HEY, HUMAN!
HOP
ピョイ
...WHAT IS IT...
SQUIRT?
YOU WANT ME TO TALK YUKI-SAMA...
...INTO NOT FIGHTING YOU ANYMORE?
CAN YOU DO THAT?!
PROB-ABLY!
IS HE EVEN THE TYPE OF GUY...
...YOU CAN TALK TO?
...PROB-ABLY!
BUT WHY ...?
AREN'T YOU TECHNICALLY ON THE OGRES' SIDE?
...

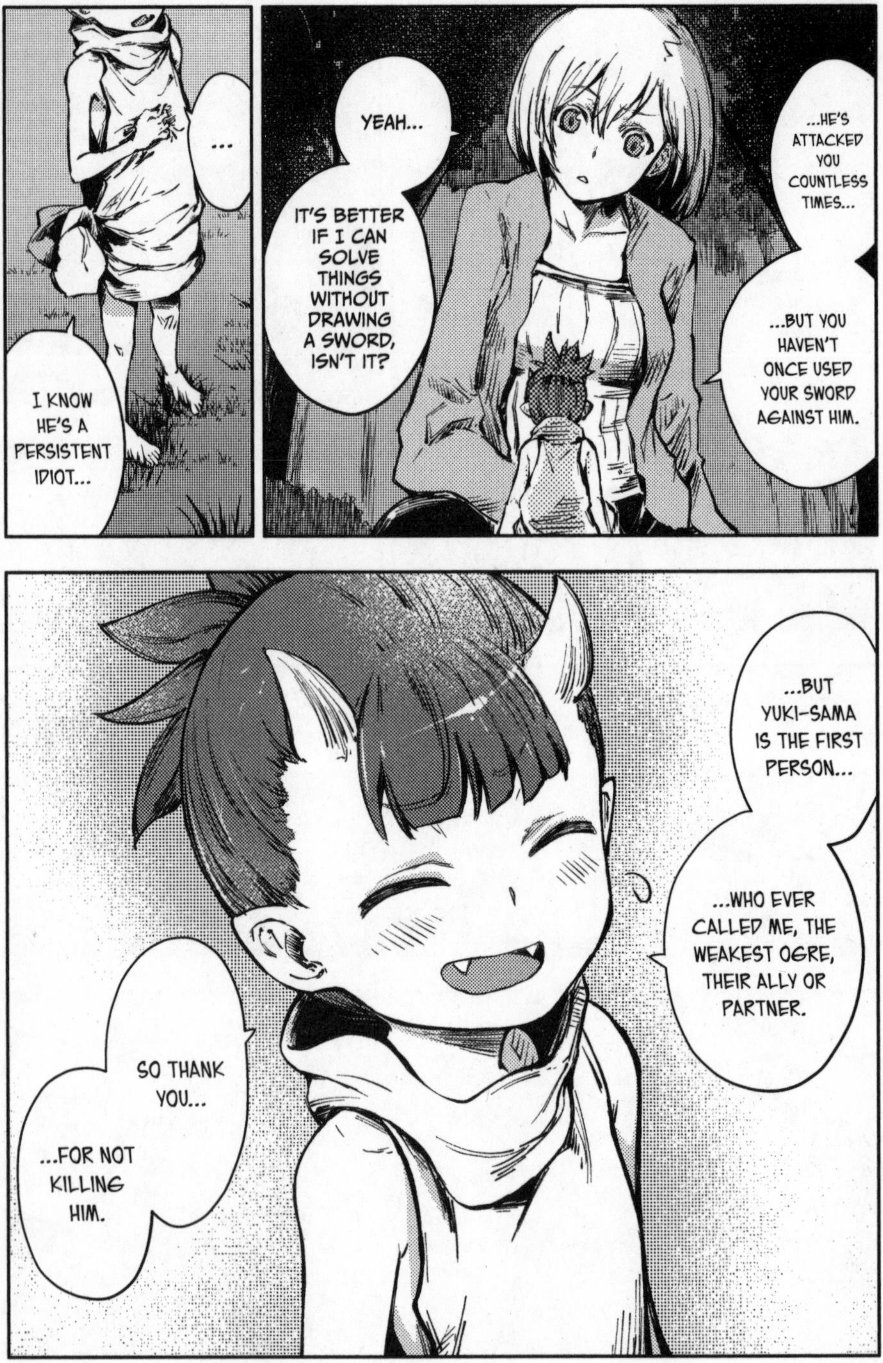
...HE'S ATTACKED YOU COUNTLESS TIMES...
...BUT YOU HAVEN'T ONCE USED YOUR SWORD AGAINST HIM.
YEAH...
IT'S BETTER IF I CAN SOLVE THINGS WITHOUT DRAWING A SWORD, ISN'T IT?
...
I KNOW HE'S A PERSISTENT IDIOT...
...BUT YUKI-SAMA IS THE FIRST PERSON...
...WHO EVER CALLED ME, THE WEAKEST OGRE, THEIR ALLY OR PARTNER.
SO THANK YOU...
...FOR NOT KILLING HIM.

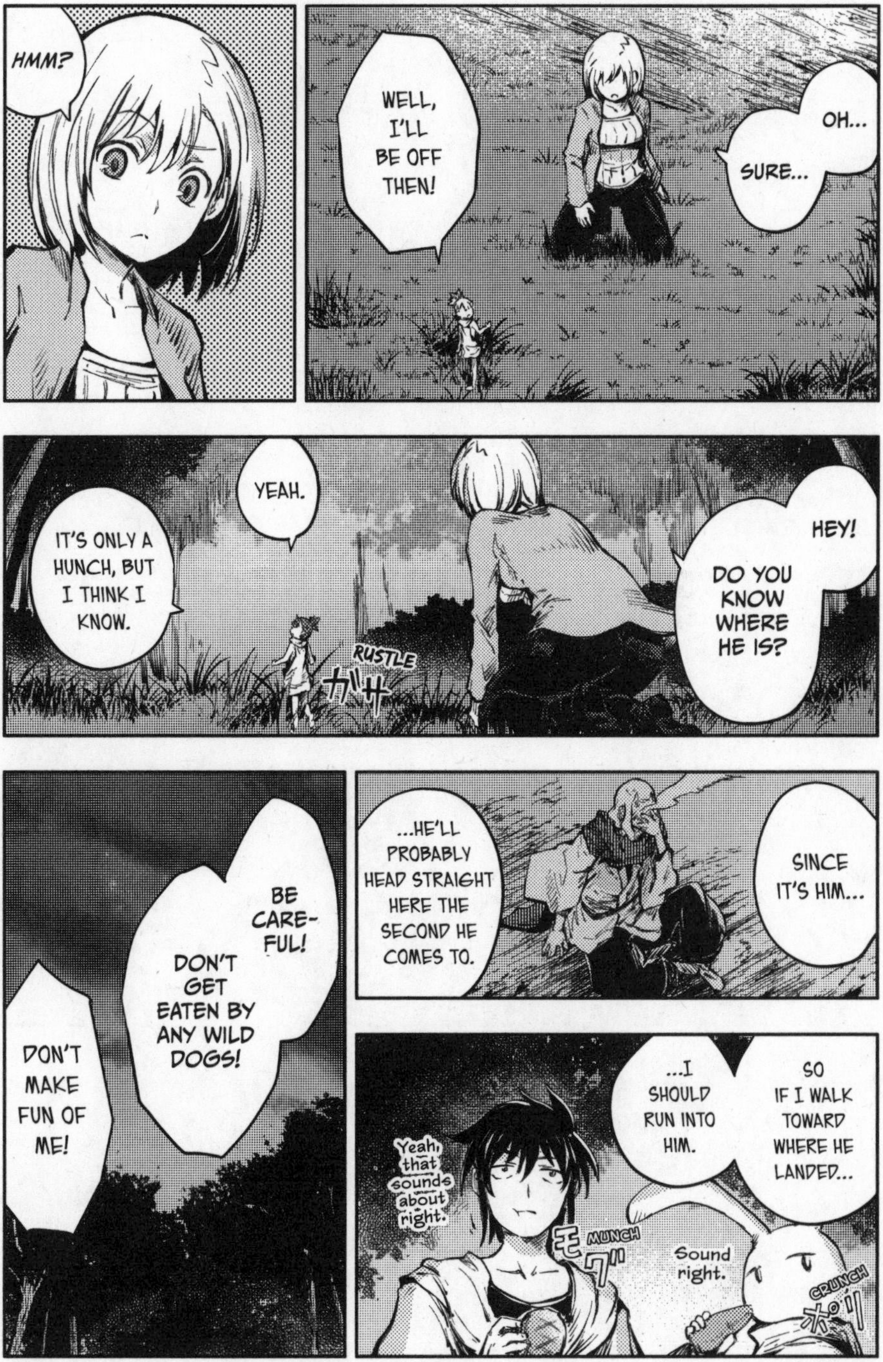
OH... SURE...
WELL, I'LL BE OFF THEN!
HMM?
HEY! DO YOU KNOW WHERE HE IS?
YEAH.
IT'S ONLY A HUNCH, BUT I THINK I KNOW.
RUSTLE
ガサ
SINCE IT'S HIM...
...HE'LL PROBABLY HEAD STRAIGHT HERE THE SECOND HE COMES TO.
SO IF I WALK TOWARD WHERE HE LANDED...
...I SHOULD RUN INTO HIM.
CRUNCH
ポリ
Sound right.
MUNCH
モグ
Yeah, that sounds about right.
BE CARE-FUL!
DON'T GET EATEN BY ANY WILD DOGS!
DON'T MAKE FUN OF ME!

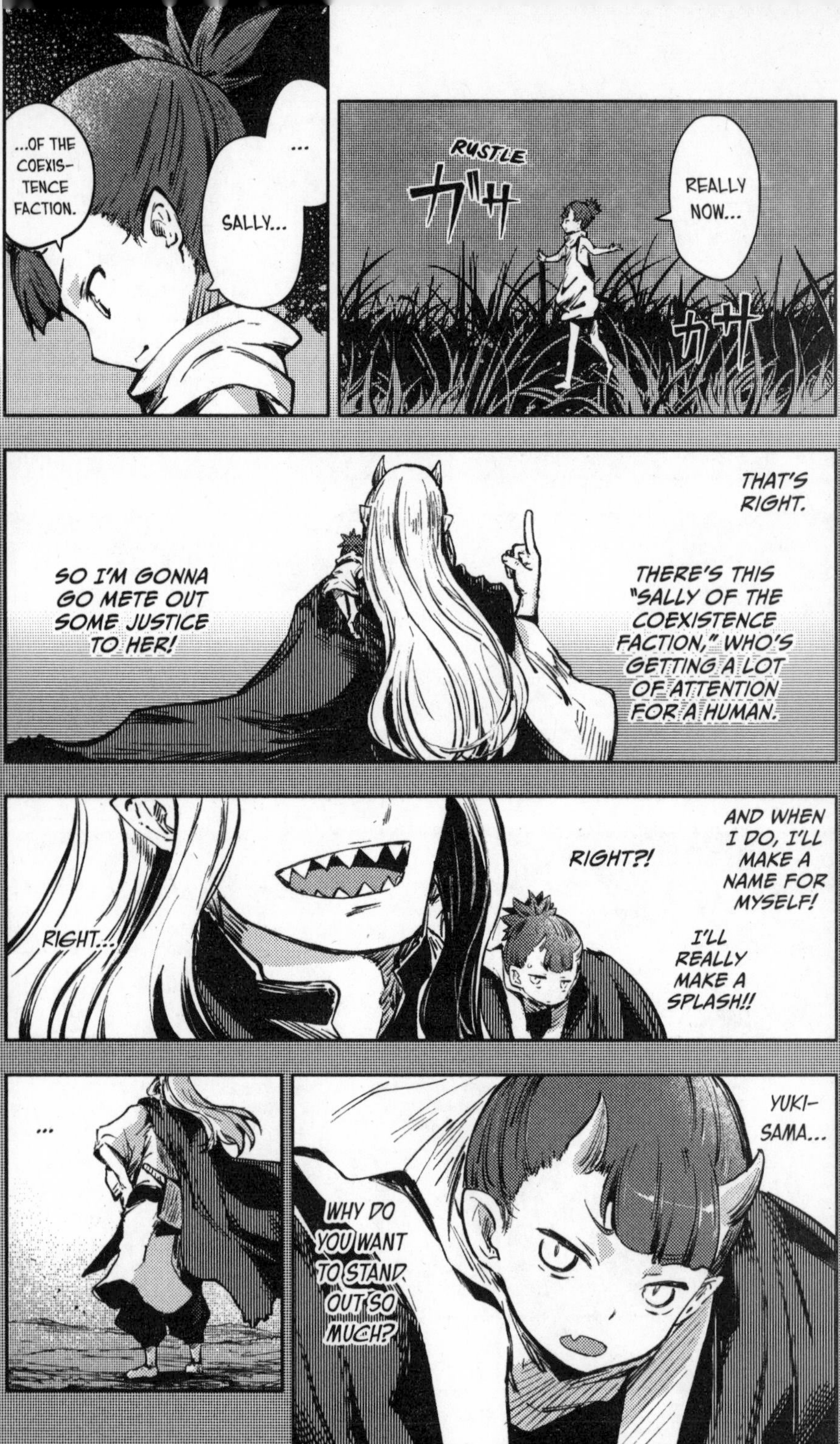
RUSTLE
ガサ
REALLY NOW...
カサ
...
SALLY...
...OF THE COEXISTENCE FACTION.
THAT'S RIGHT.
THERE'S THIS "SALLY OF THE COEXISTENCE FACTION," WHO'S GETTING A LOT OF ATTENTION FOR A HUMAN.
SO I'M GONNA GO METE OUT SOME JUSTICE TO HER!
AND WHEN I DO, I'LL MAKE A NAME FOR MYSELF!
I'LL REALLY MAKE A SPLASH!!
RIGHT?!
RIGHT...
YUKI-SAMA...
WHY DO YOU WANT TO STAND OUT SO MUCH?
...

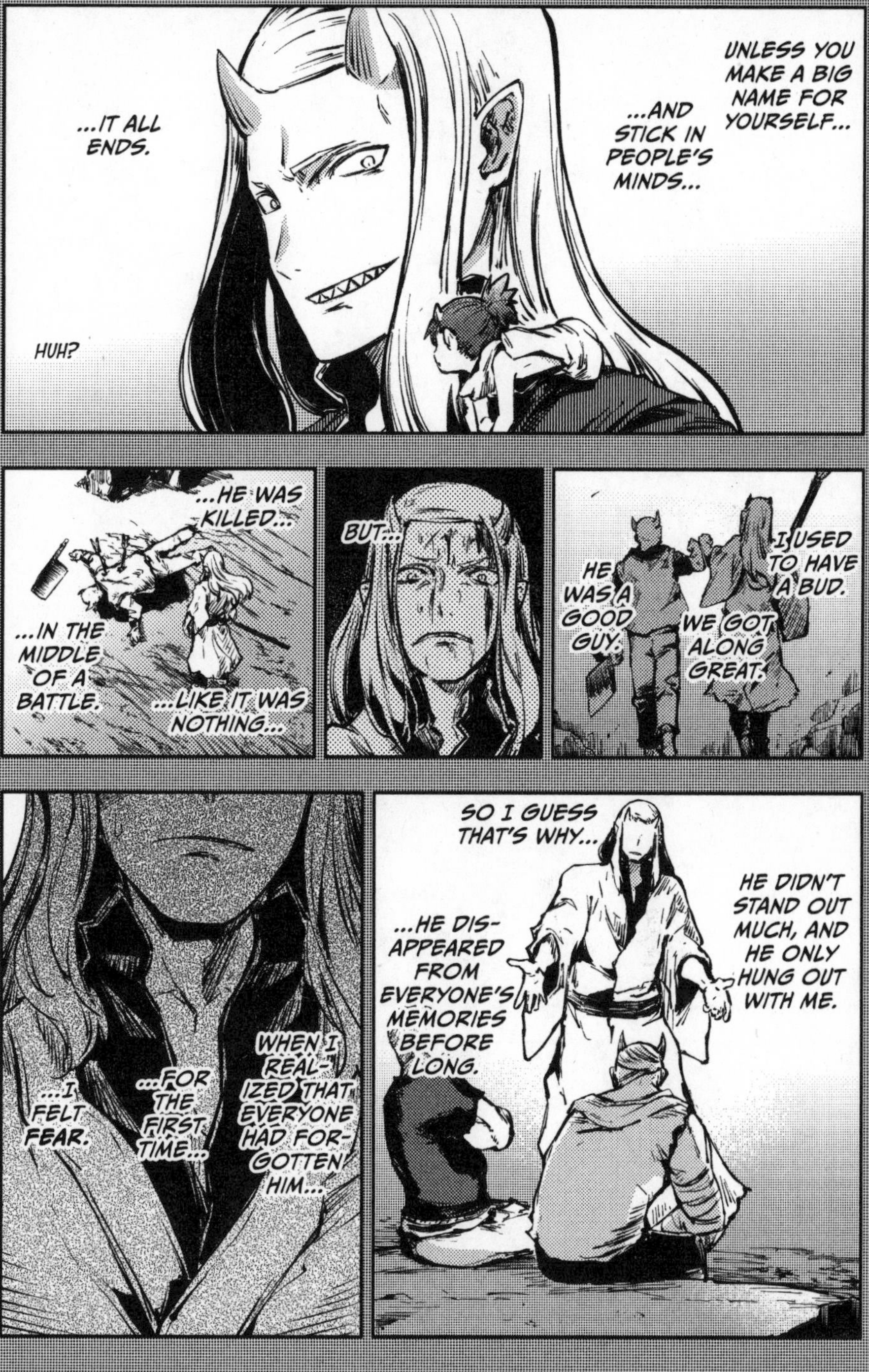
UNLESS YOU MAKE A BIG NAME FOR YOURSELF...
...AND STICK IN PEOPLE'S MINDS...
...IT ALL ENDS.
HUH?
I USED TO HAVE A BUD.
WE GOT ALONG GREAT.
HE WAS A GOOD GUY.
BUT...
...HE WAS KILLED...
...LIKE IT WAS NOTHING...
...IN THE MIDDLE OF A BATTLE.
HE DIDN'T STAND OUT MUCH, AND HE ONLY HUNG OUT WITH ME.
SO I GUESS THAT'S WHY...
...HE DIS-APPEARED FROM EVERYONE'S MEMORIES BEFORE LONG.
WHEN I REAL-IZED THAT EVERYONE HAD FOR-GOTTEN HIM...
...FOR THE FIRST TIME...
...I FELT FEAR.

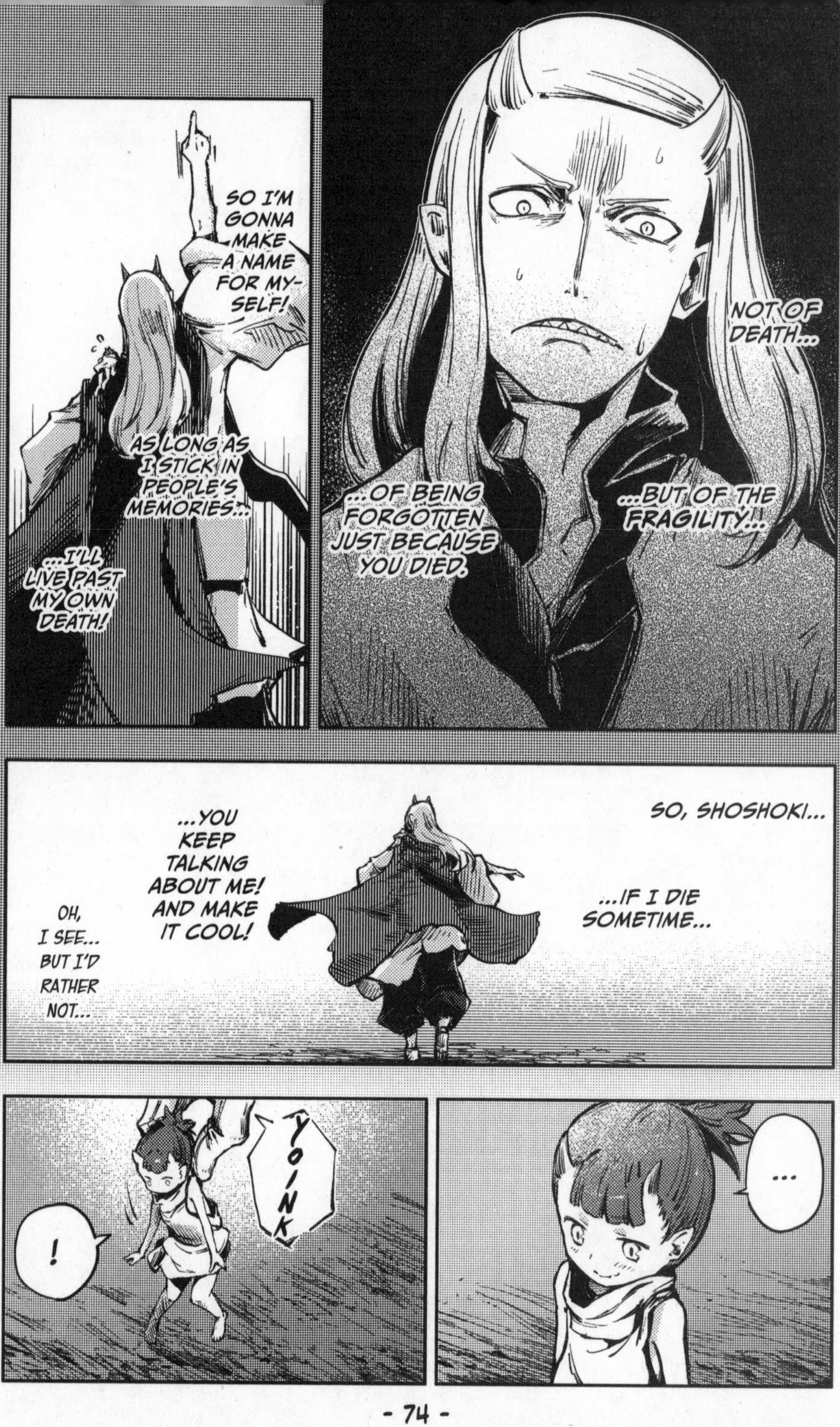
NOT OF DEATH...
...BUT OF THE FRAGILITY...
...OF BEING FORGOTTEN JUST BECAUSE YOU DIED.
SO I'M GONNA MAKE A NAME FOR MY-SELF!
AS LONG AS I STICK IN PEOPLE'S MEMORIES...
...I'LL LIVE PAST MY OWN DEATH!
SO, SHOSHOKI...
...IF I DIE SOMETIME...
...YOU KEEP TALKING ABOUT ME! AND MAKE IT COOL!
OH, I SEE... BUT I'D RATHER NOT...
...
YOINK
!

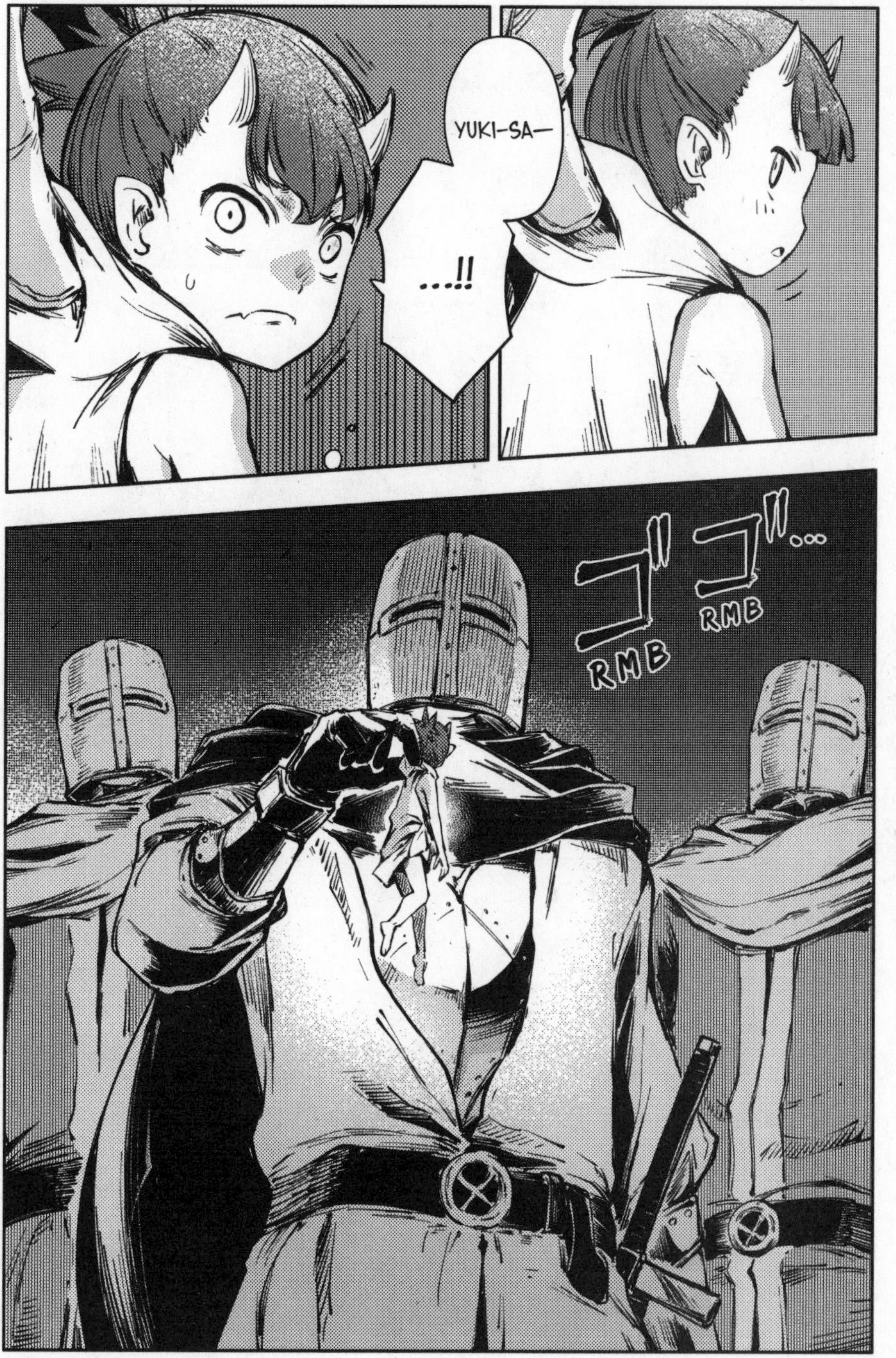
YUKI-SA—
...!!
ゴ゛...
RMB
ゴ゛
RMB

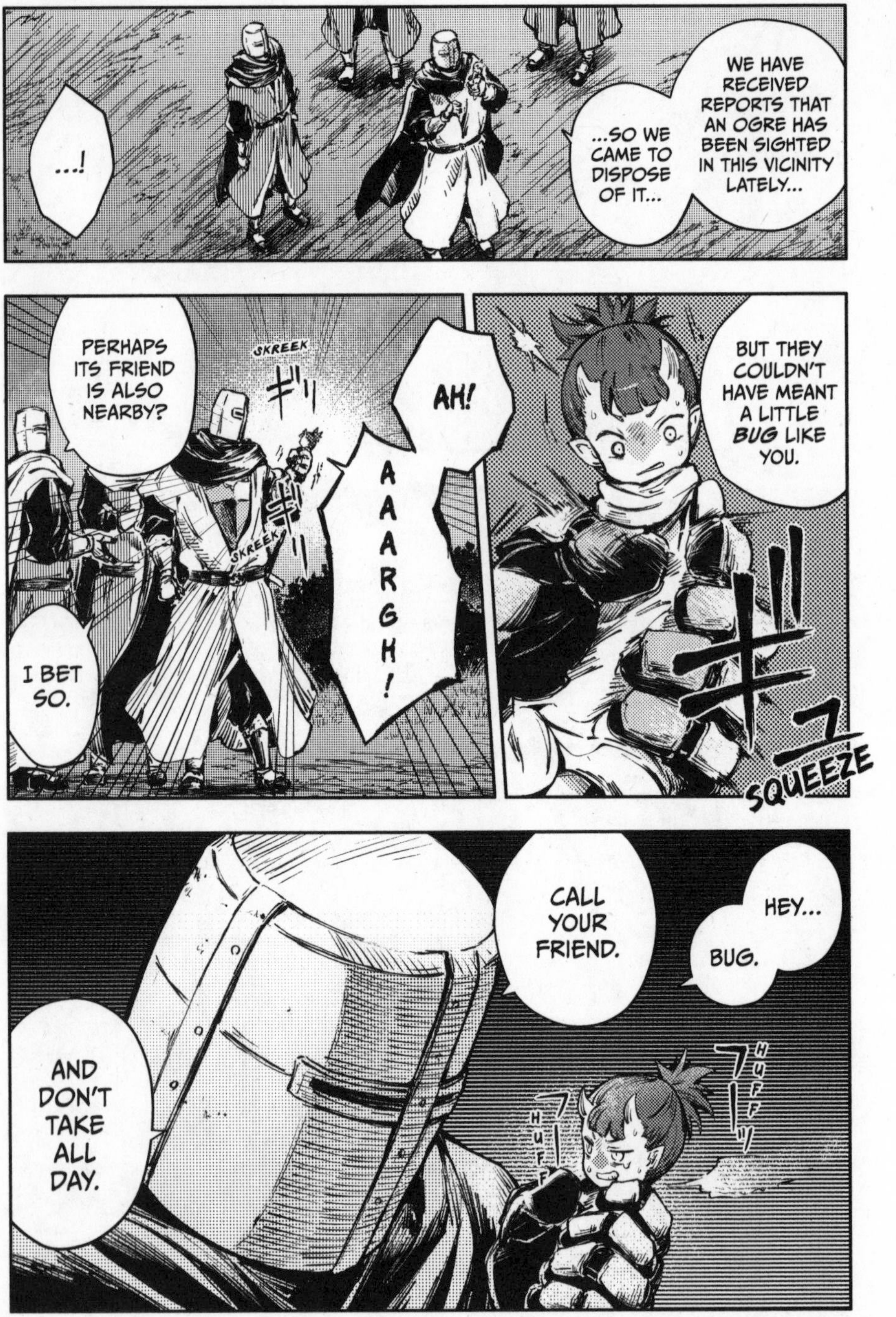
WE HAVE RECEIVED REPORTS THAT AN OGRE HAS BEEN SIGHTED IN THIS VICINITY LATELY...
...SO WE CAME TO DISPOSE OF IT...
...!
BUT THEY COULDN'T HAVE MEANT A LITTLE *BUG* LIKE YOU.
SQUEEZE
AH!
SKREEK
PERHAPS ITS FRIEND IS ALSO NEARBY?
AAAARGH!
SKREEK
I BET SO.
HEY...
BUG.
CALL YOUR FRIEND.
AND DON'T TAKE ALL DAY.
HUFF
HUFF

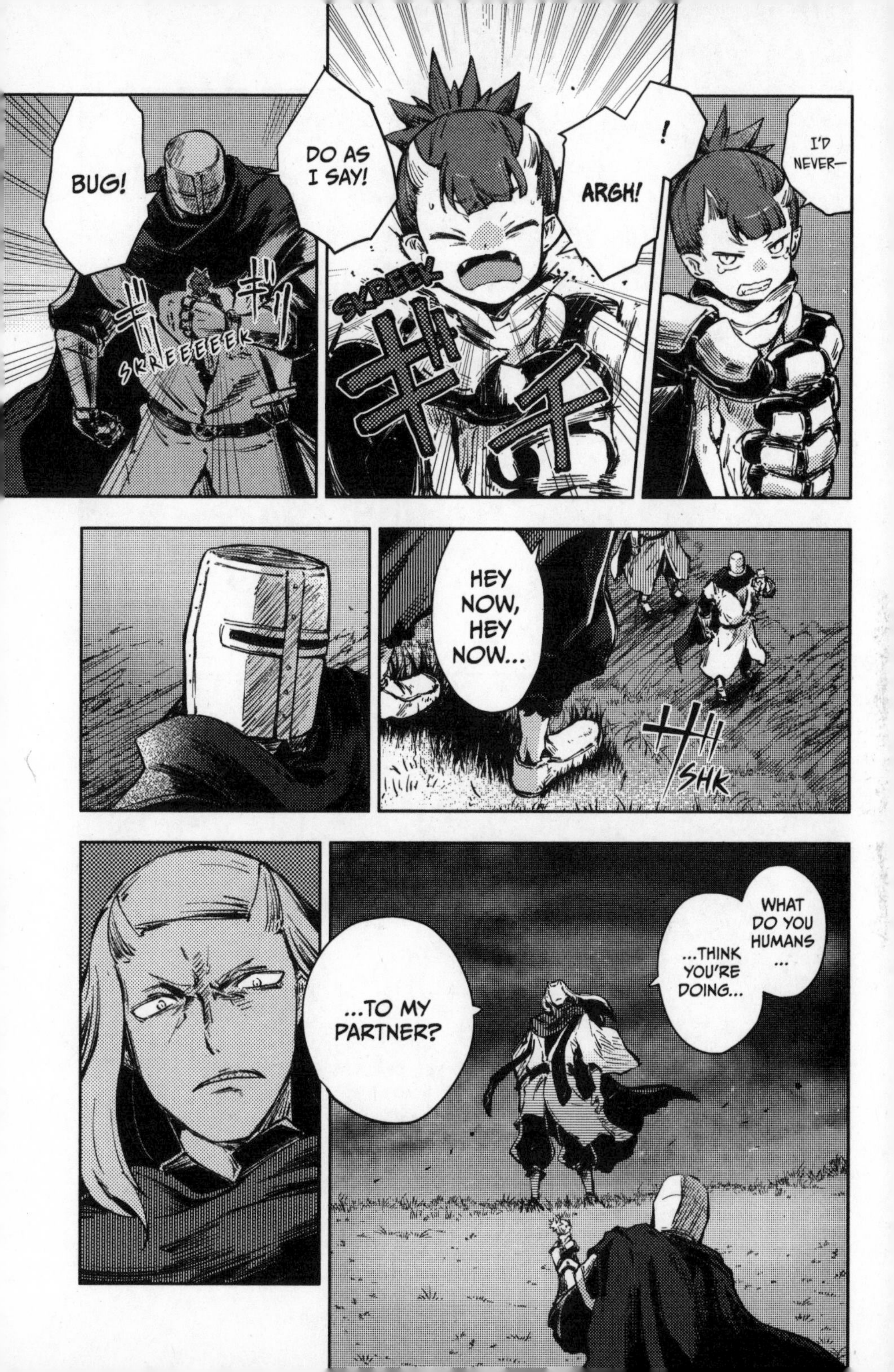
I'D NEVER—
!
ARGH!
DO AS I SAY!
SKREEEK
ギギ
BUG!
ギギ
SKREEEEEEK
HEY NOW, HEY NOW...
SHK
WHAT DO YOU HUMANS ...
...THINK YOU'RE DOING...
...TO MY PARTNER?

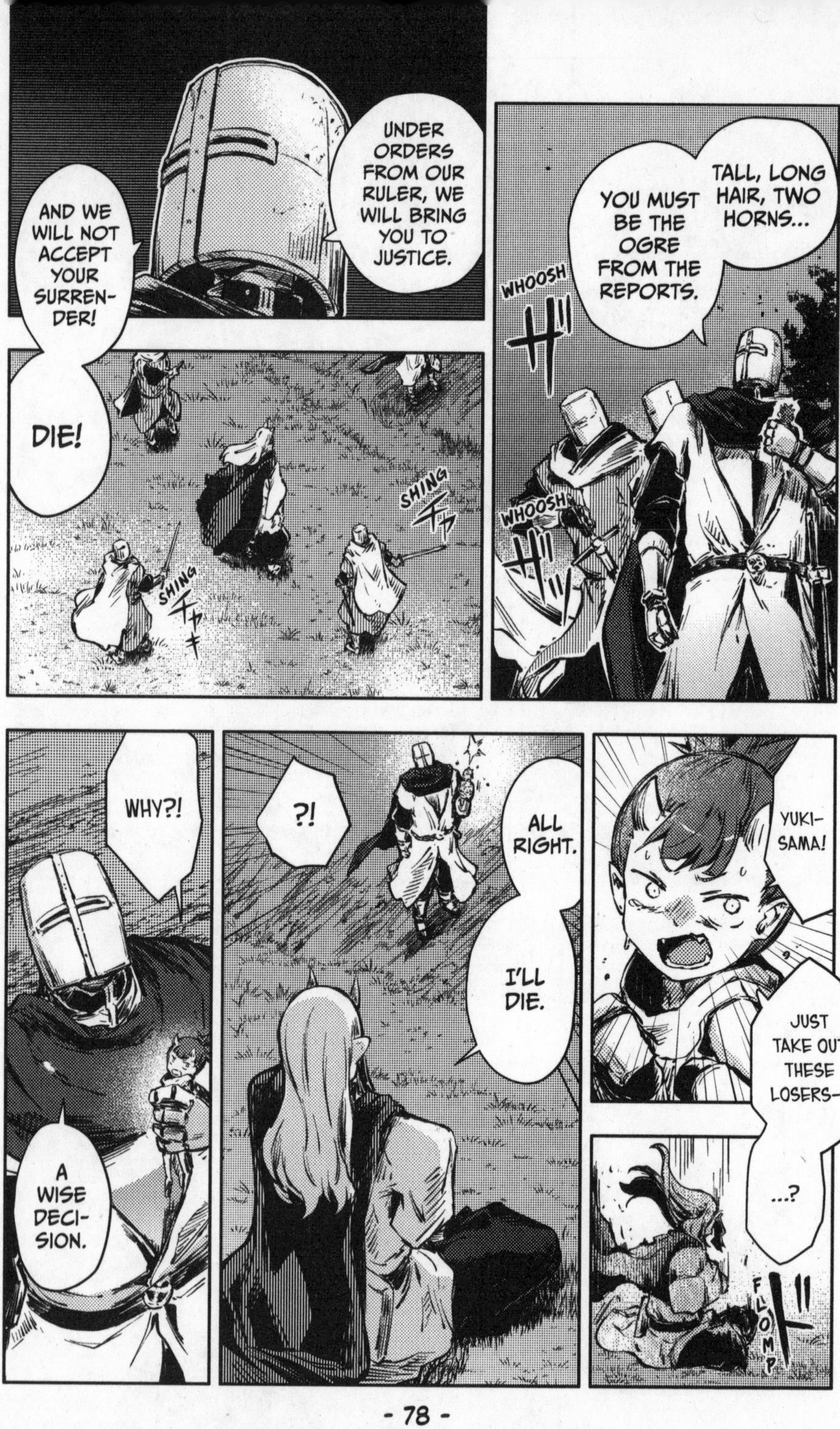
WHOOSH ザッ
TALL, LONG HAIR, TWO HORNS...
YOU MUST BE THE OGRE FROM THE REPORTS.
WHOOSH ザッ
UNDER ORDERS FROM OUR RULER, WE WILL BRING YOU TO JUSTICE.
AND WE WILL NOT ACCEPT YOUR SURREN-DER!
DIE!
SHING チャ
SHING チャキ
YUKI-SAMA!
JUST TAKE OUT THESE LOSERS—
...?
FLOMP ドッ
ALL RIGHT.
?!
I'LL DIE.
WHY?!
A WISE DECI-SION.

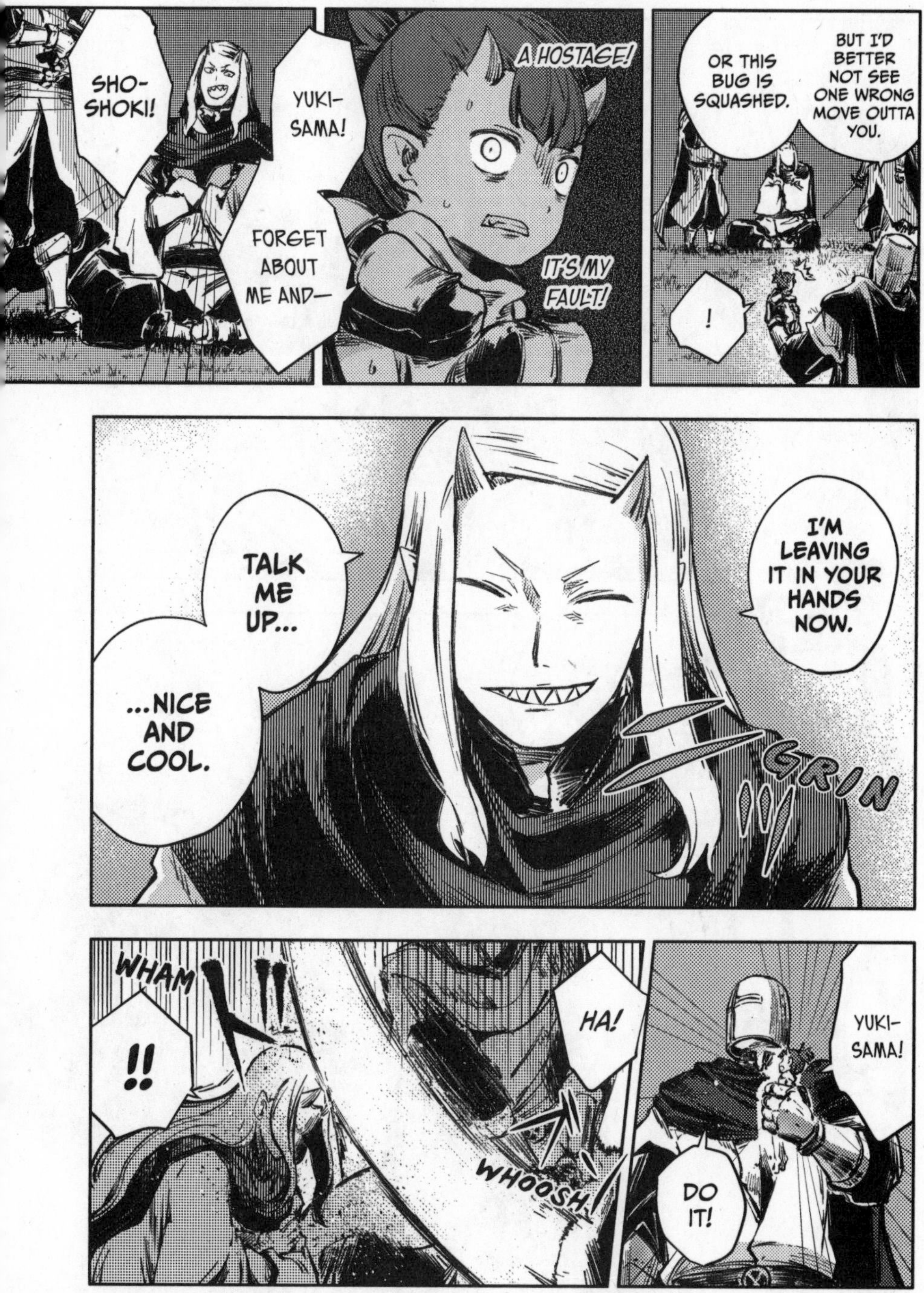
BUT I'D BETTER NOT SEE ONE WRONG MOVE OUTTA YOU.
OR THIS BUG IS SQUASHED.
!
A HOSTAGE!
IT'S MY FAULT!
YUKI-SAMA!
FORGET ABOUT ME AND—
SHO-SHOKI!
I'M LEAVING IT IN YOUR HANDS NOW.
GRIN
TALK ME UP...
...NICE AND COOL.
YUKI-SAMA!
DO IT!
HA!
WHOOSH
WHAM
!!

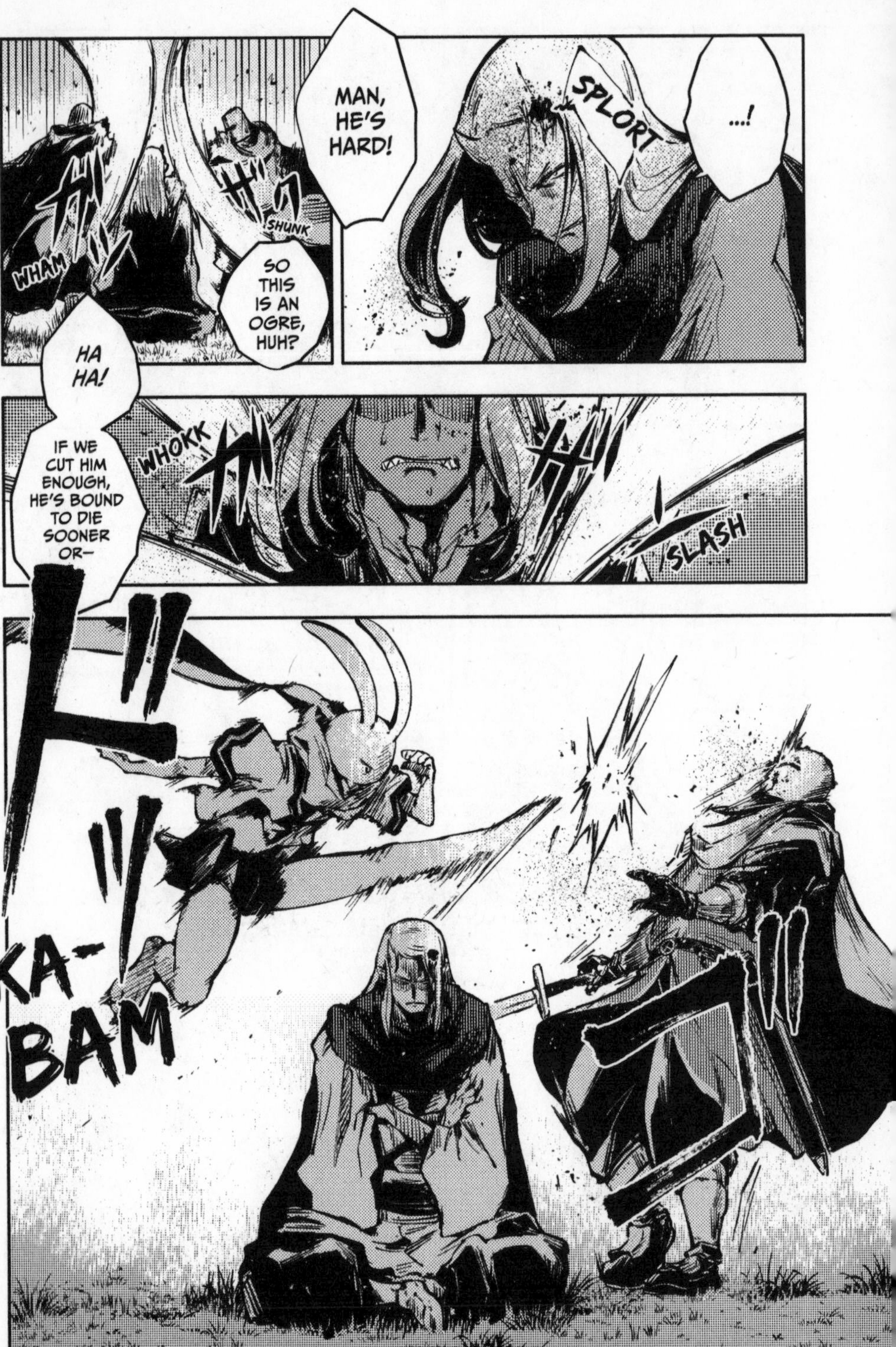
SPLORT
...!
MAN, HE'S HARD!
SHUNK
WHAM
SO THIS IS AN OGRE, HUH?
HA HA!
IF WE CUT HIM ENOUGH, HE'S BOUND TO DIE SOONER OR—
SLASH
WHOKK
KA-BAM

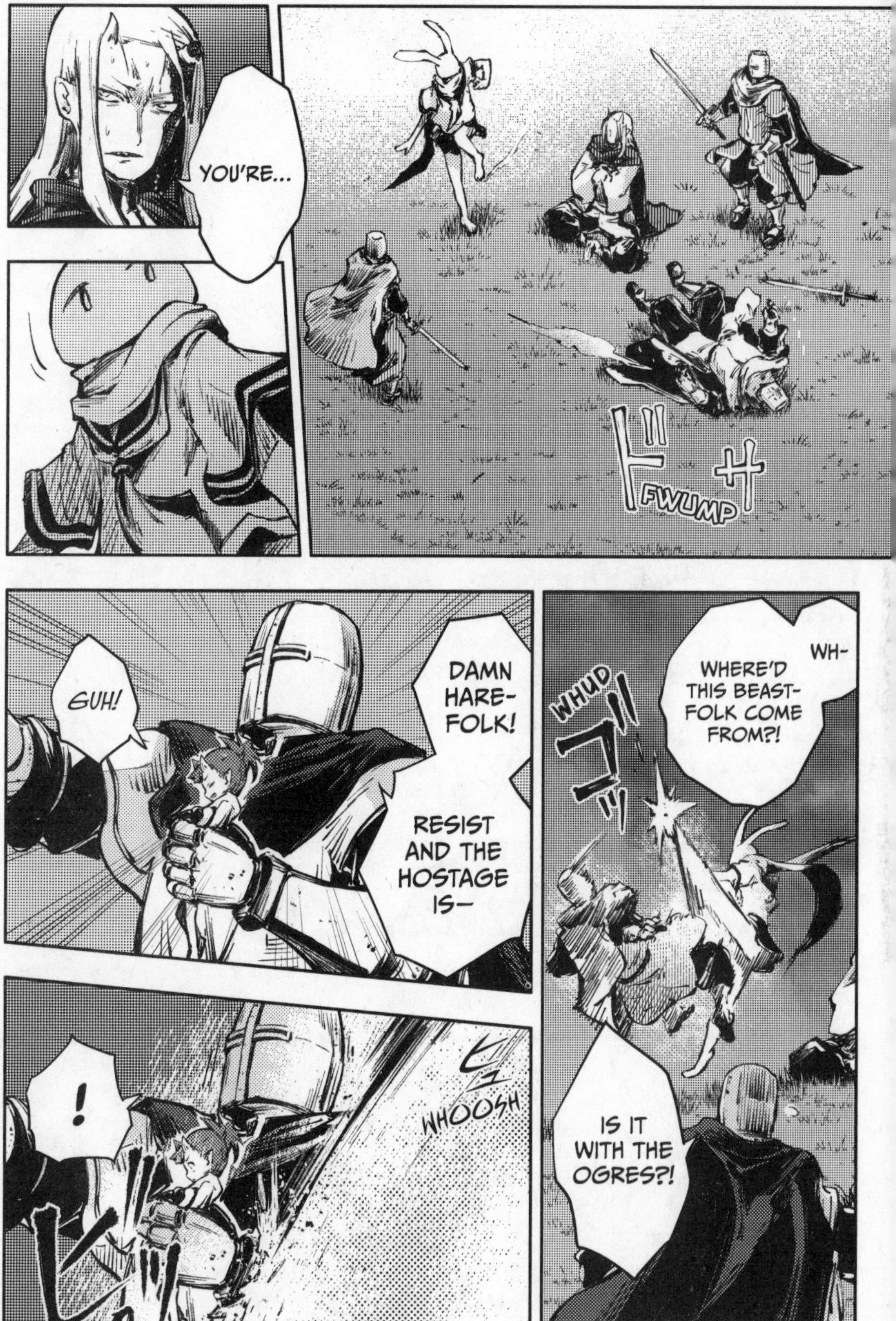
FWUMP
YOU'RE...
WH-
WHERE'D THIS BEAST-FOLK COME FROM?!
WHUD
IS IT WITH THE OGRES?!
DAMN HARE-FOLK!
RESIST AND THE HOSTAGE IS—
GUH!
WHOOSH
!
SHRIP

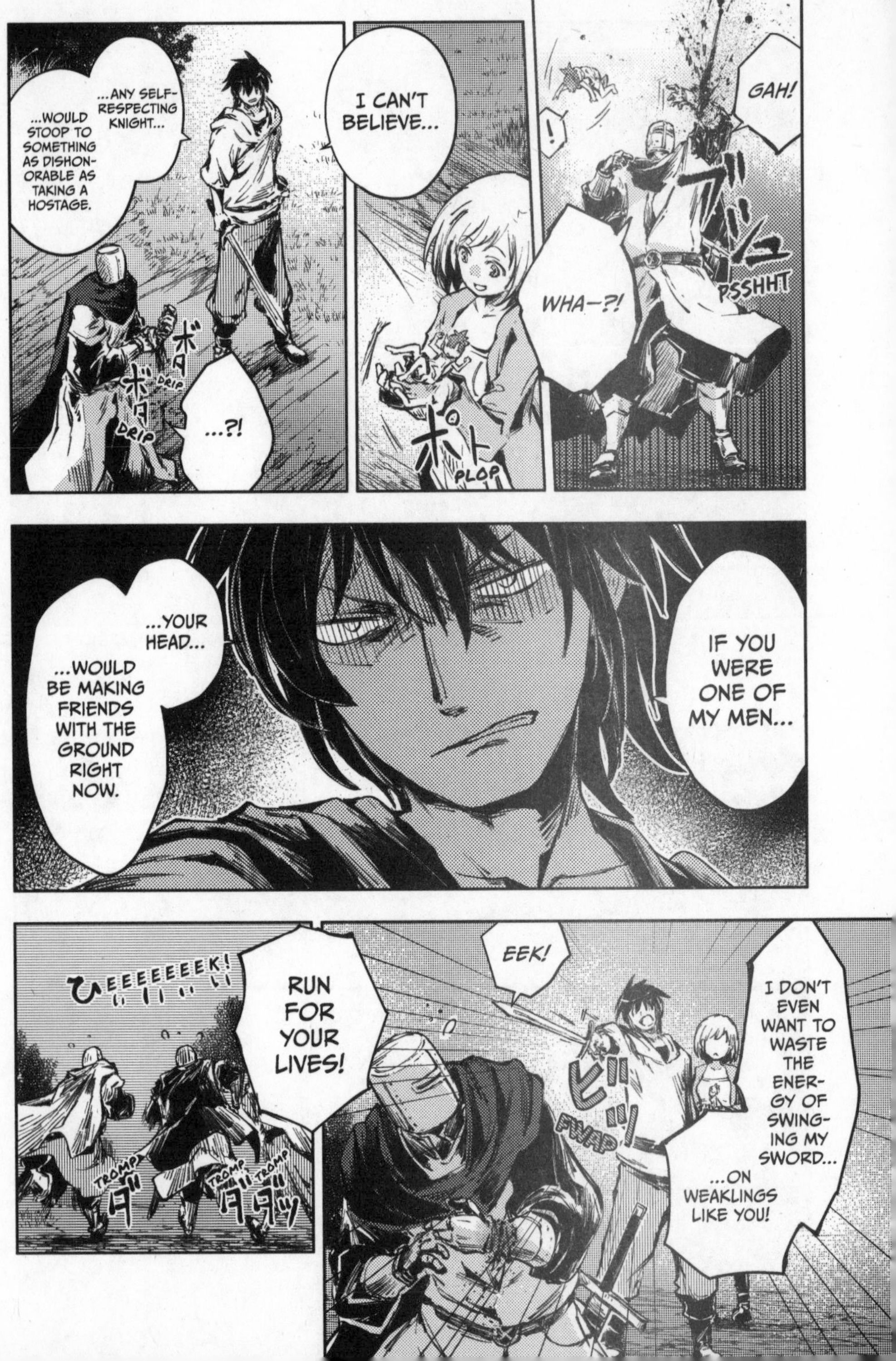
GAH!
PSSHHT
WHA—?!
I CAN'T BELIEVE...
PLOP
...ANY SELF-RESPECTING KNIGHT...
...WOULD STOOP TO SOMETHING AS DISHONORABLE AS TAKING A HOSTAGE.
DRIP
DRIP
...?!
IF YOU WERE ONE OF MY MEN...
...YOUR HEAD...
...WOULD BE MAKING FRIENDS WITH THE GROUND RIGHT NOW.
I DON'T EVEN WANT TO WASTE THE ENERGY OF SWINGING MY SWORD...
...ON WEAKLINGS LIKE YOU!
EEK!
FWAP
RUN FOR YOUR LIVES!
EEEEEEEEK!
TROMP
TROMP
TROMP

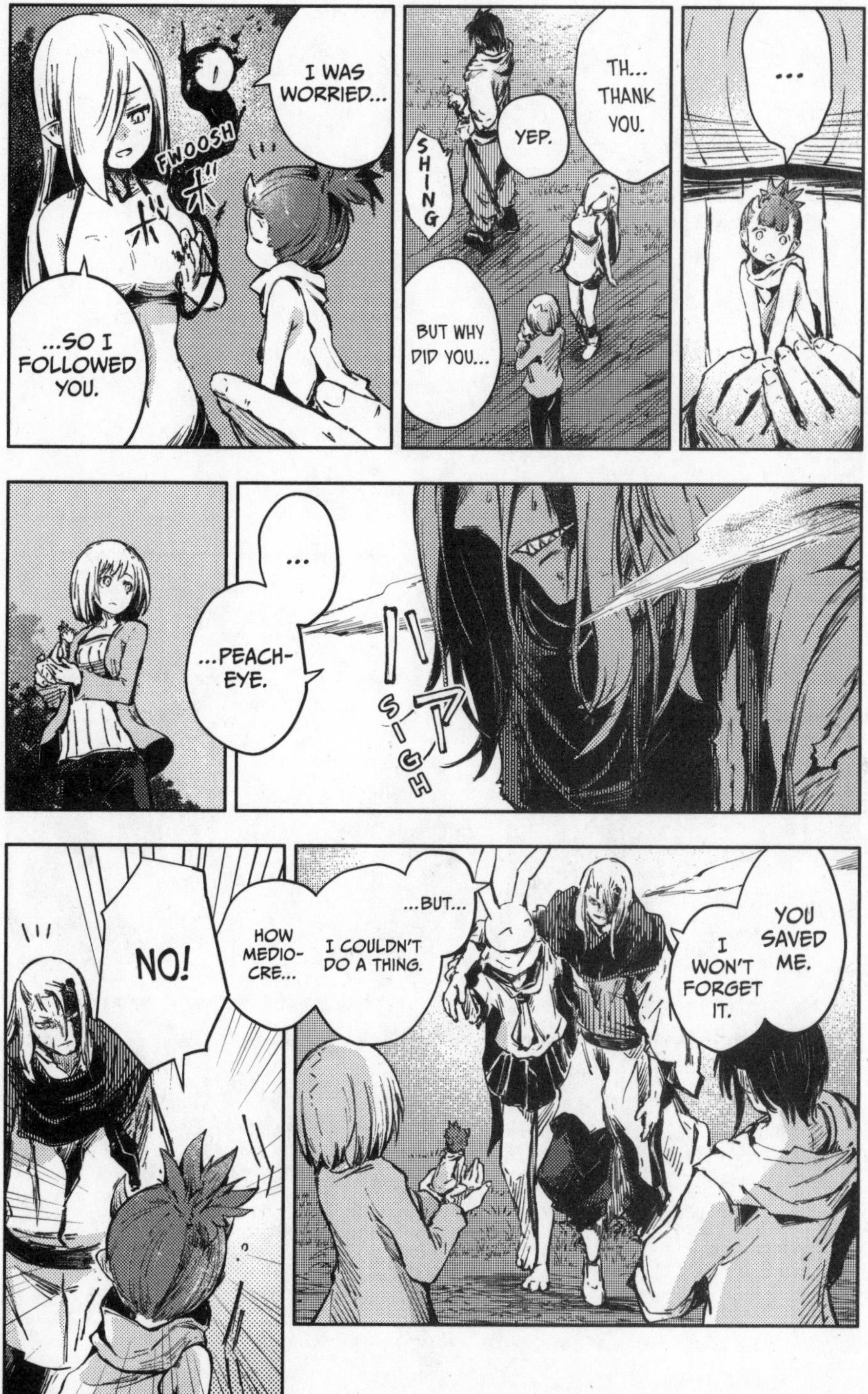
...
TH... THANK YOU.
YEP.
SHING
BUT WHY DID YOU...
I WAS WORRIED...
FWOOSH
...SO I FOLLOWED YOU.
...
...PEACH-EYE.
SIGH
YOU SAVED ME.
I WON'T FORGET IT.
...BUT...
I COULDN'T DO A THING.
HOW MEDIO-CRE...
NO!

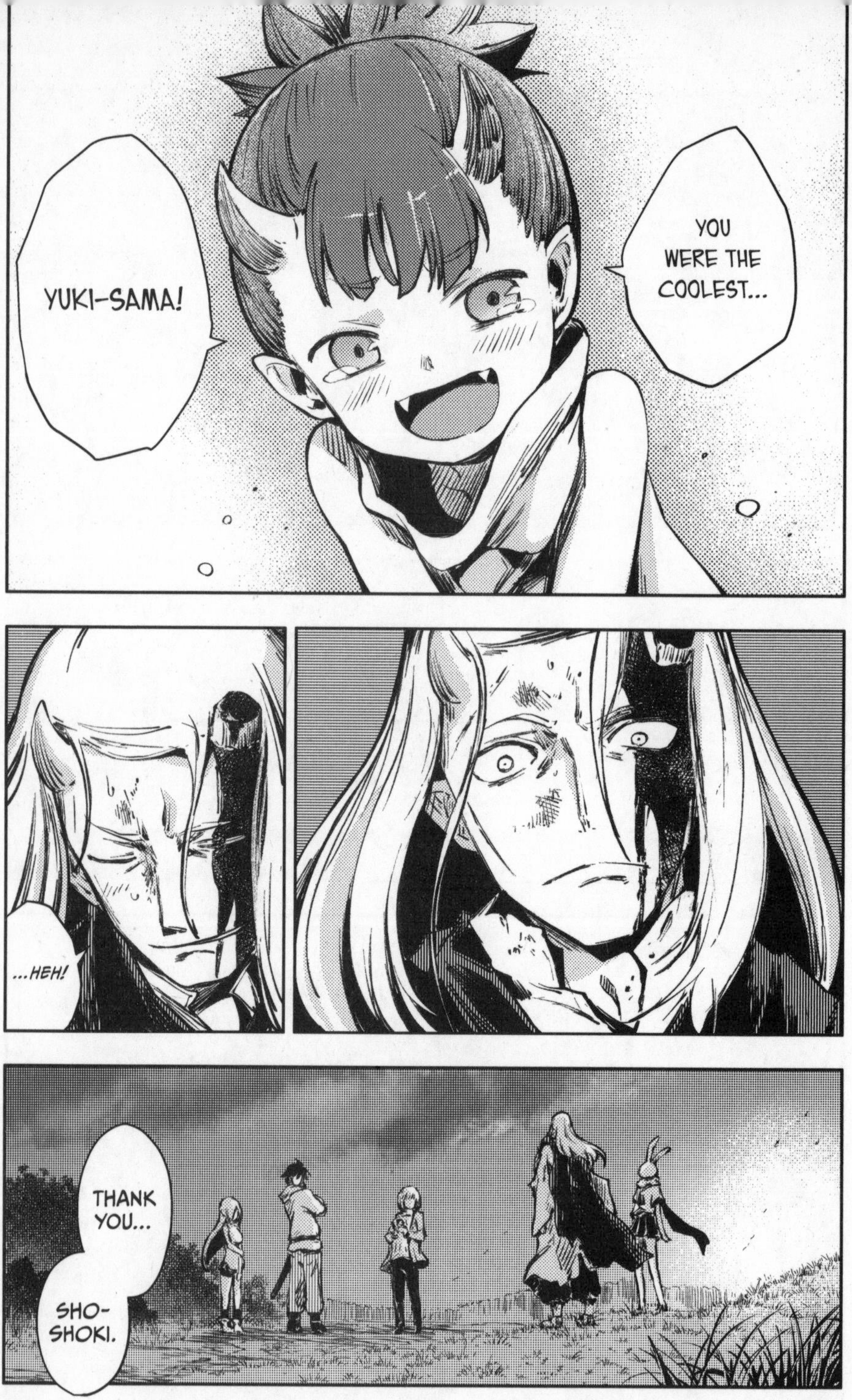
YOU WERE THE COOLEST...
YUKI-SAMA!
...HEH!
THANK YOU...
SHO-SHOKI.

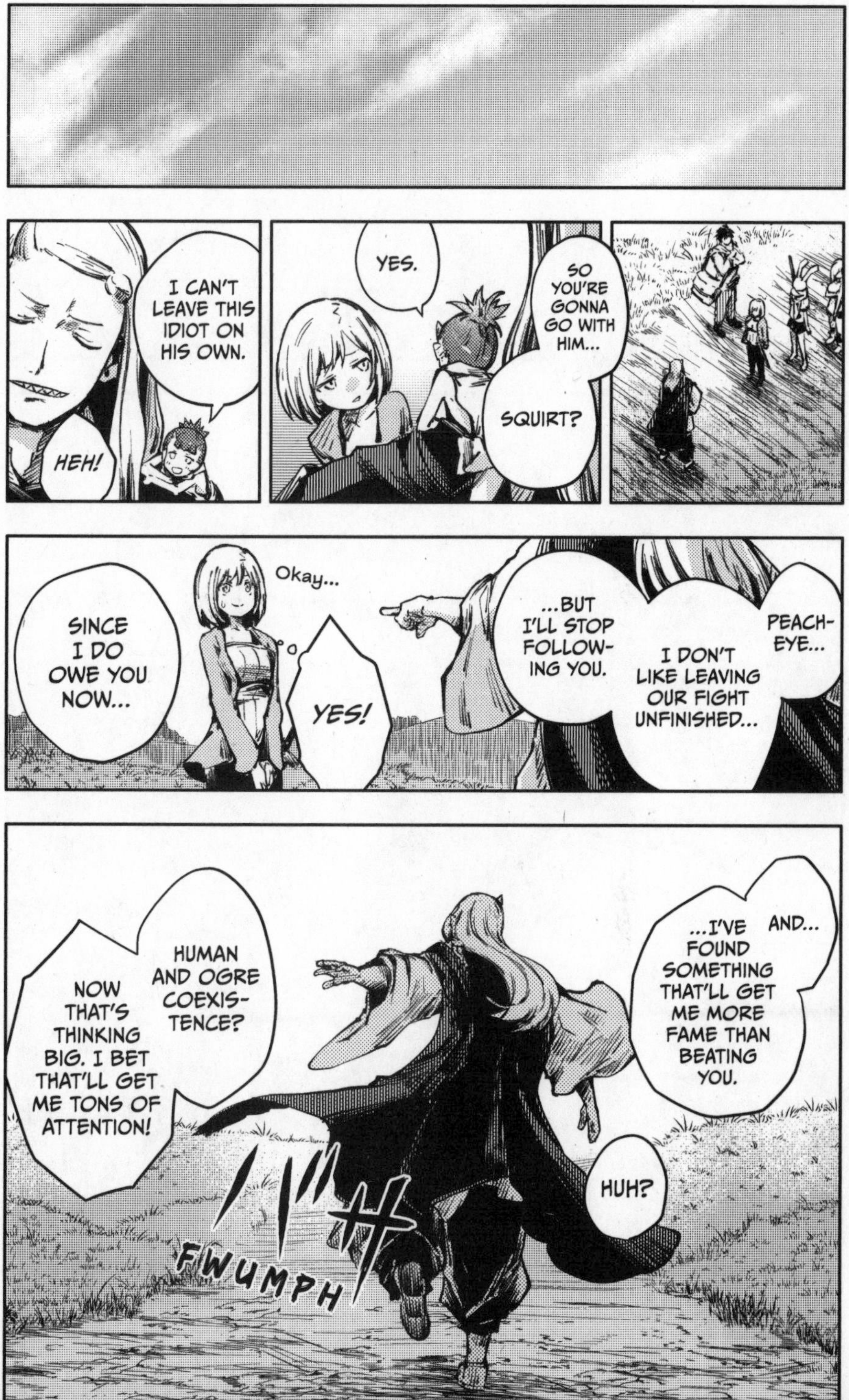

SO YOU'RE GONNA GO WITH HIM...
SQUIRT?
YES.
I CAN'T LEAVE THIS IDIOT ON HIS OWN.
HEH!
PEACH-EYE...
I DON'T LIKE LEAVING OUR FIGHT UNFINISHED...
...BUT I'LL STOP FOLLOWING YOU.
YES!
Okay...
SINCE I DO OWE YOU NOW...
AND...
...I'VE FOUND SOMETHING THAT'LL GET ME MORE FAME THAN BEATING YOU.
HUH?
HUMAN AND OGRE COEXISTENCE?
NOW THAT'S THINKING BIG. I BET THAT'LL GET ME TONS OF ATTENTION!
FWUMPH

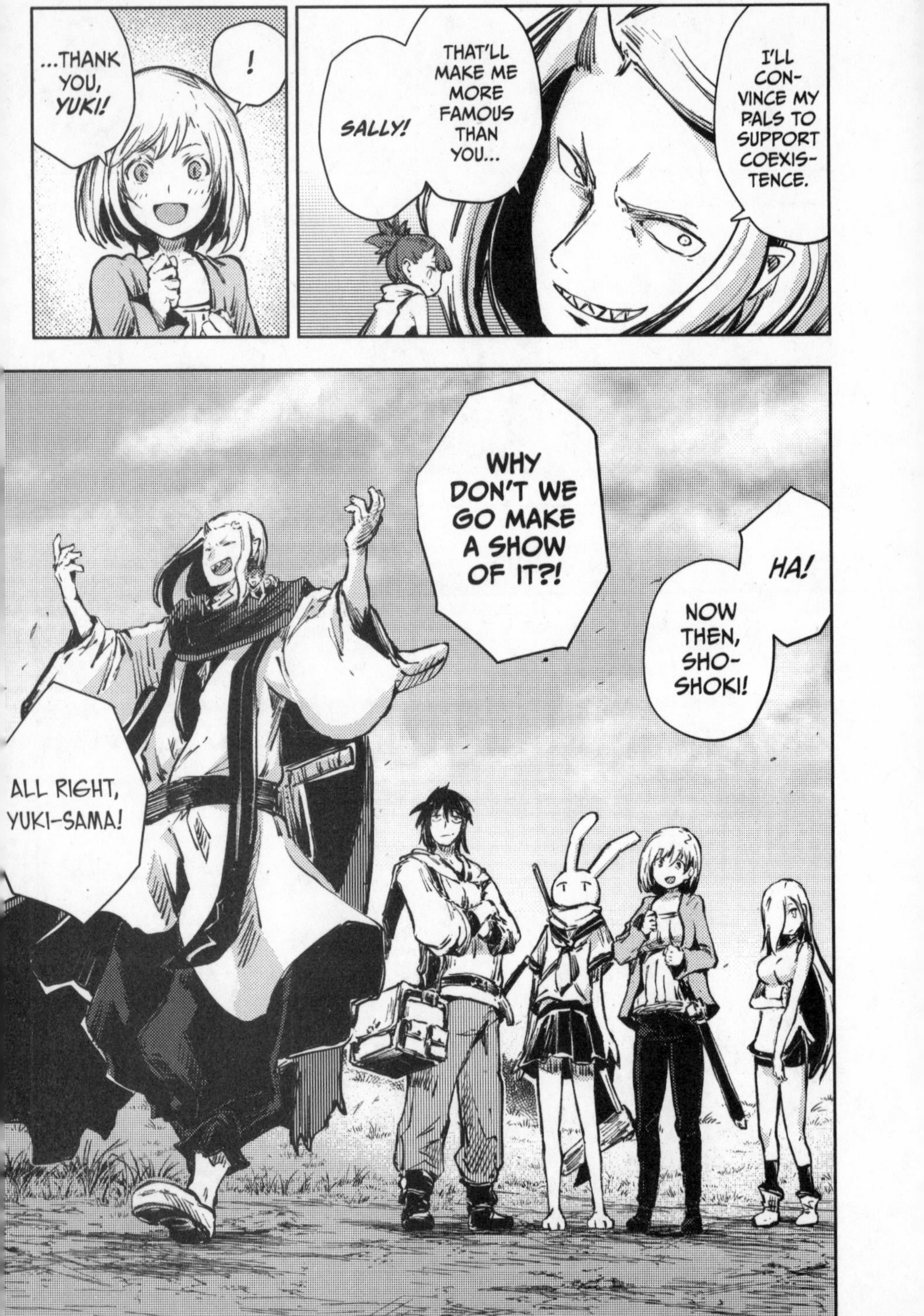
I'LL CON-VINCE MY PALS TO SUPPORT COEXIS-TENCE.
THAT'LL MAKE ME MORE FAMOUS THAN YOU...
SALLY!
!
...THANK YOU, YUKI!
HA!
NOW THEN, SHO-SHOKI!
WHY DON'T WE GO MAKE A SHOW OF IT?!
ALL RIGHT, YUKI-SAMA!

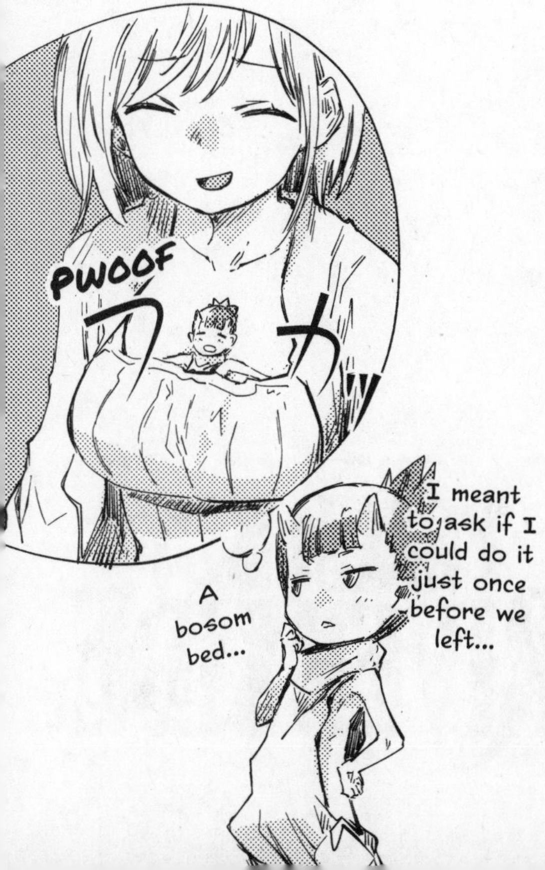
PWOOF
I meant to ask if I could do it just once before we left...
A bosom bed...

PEACH BOY
RIVERSIDE

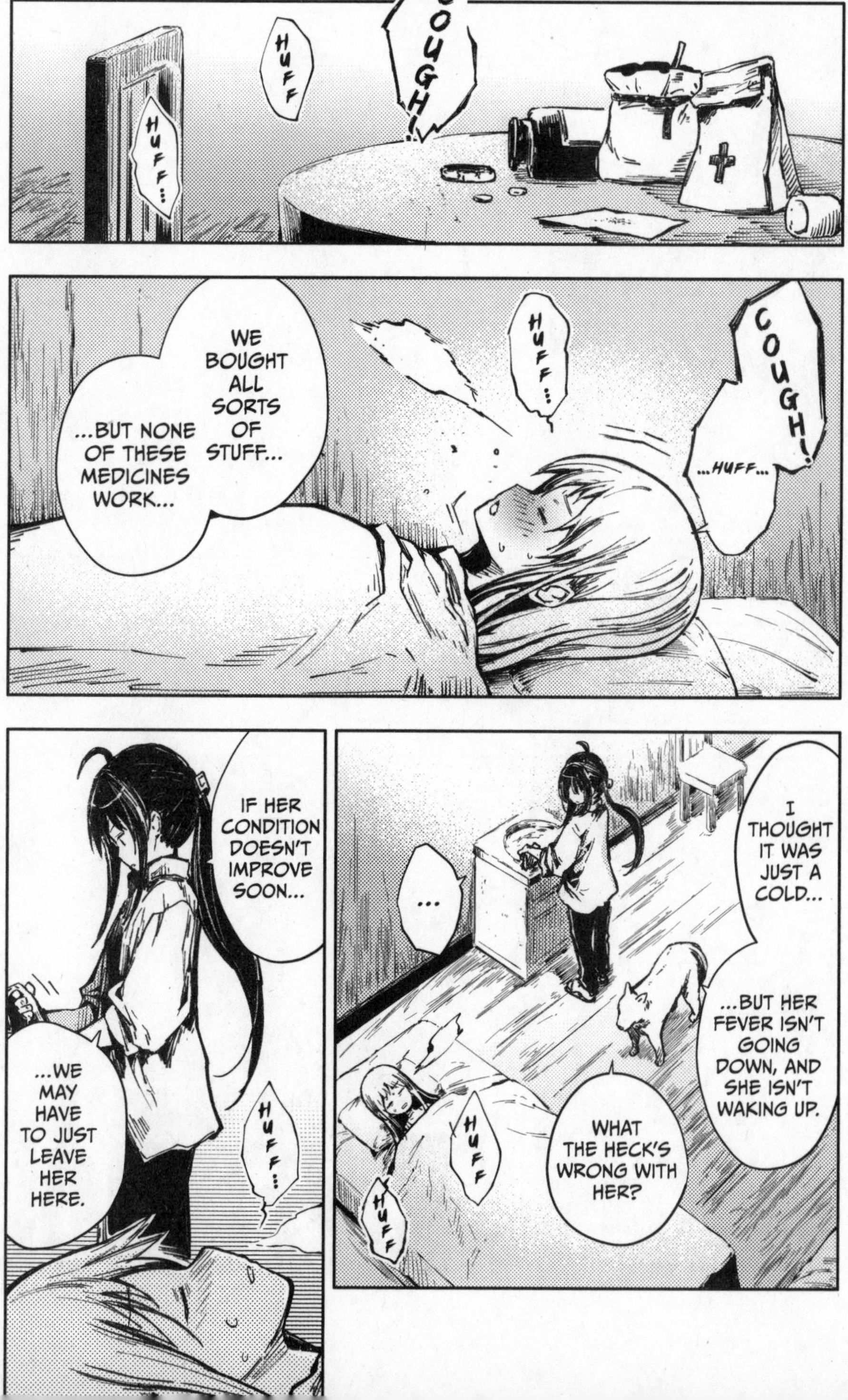
COUGH!
HUFF
HUFF...
COUGH!
...HUFF...
HUFF...
WE BOUGHT ALL SORTS OF STUFF...
...BUT NONE OF THESE MEDICINES WORK...
I THOUGHT IT WAS JUST A COLD...
...BUT HER FEVER ISN'T GOING DOWN, AND SHE ISN'T WAKING UP.
...
WHAT THE HECK'S WRONG WITH HER?
HUFF
HUFF
IF HER CONDITION DOESN'T IMPROVE SOON...
...WE MAY HAVE TO JUST LEAVE HER HERE.
HUFF...

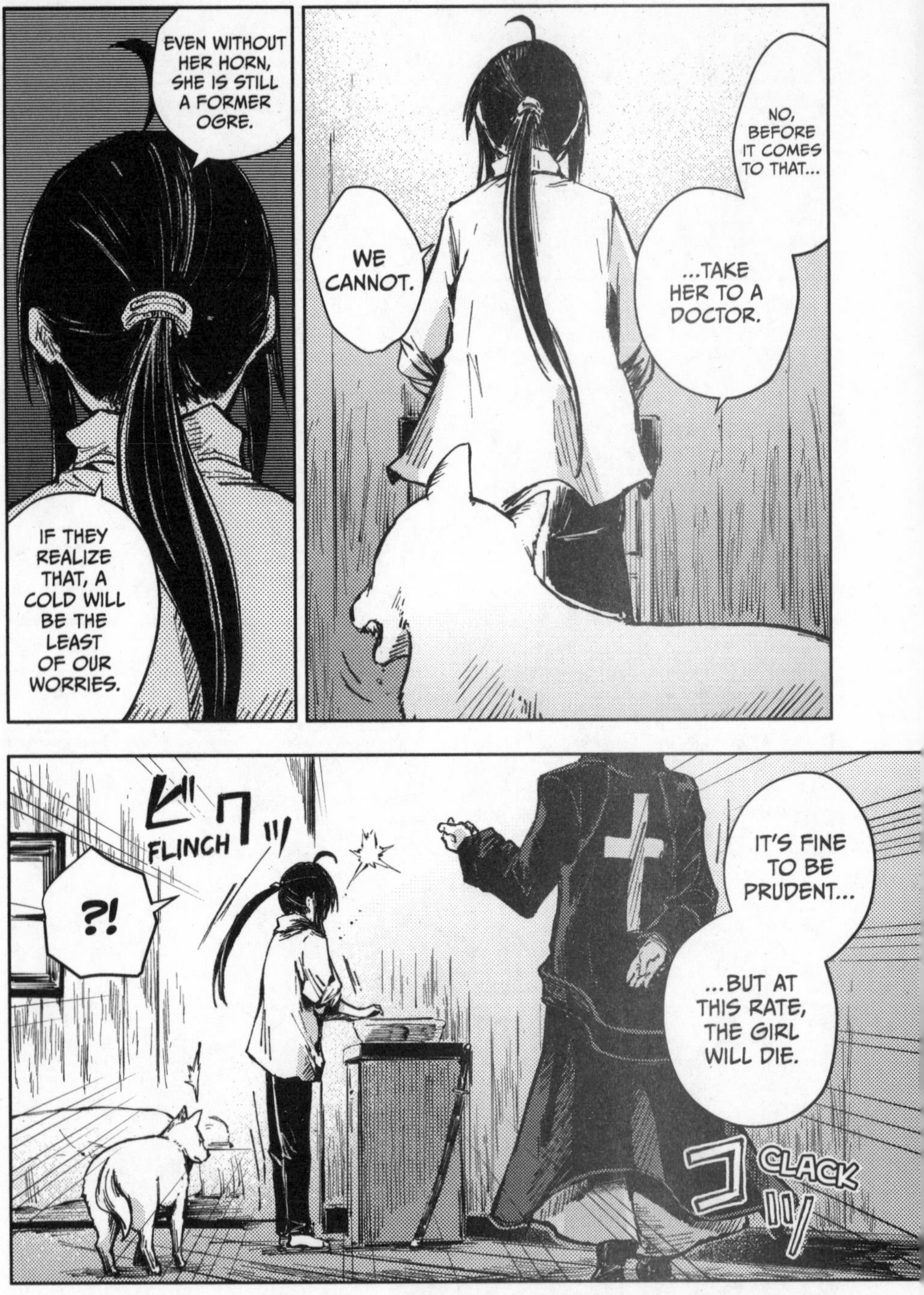
NO, BEFORE IT COMES TO THAT...
...TAKE HER TO A DOCTOR.
WE CANNOT.
EVEN WITHOUT HER HORN, SHE IS STILL A FORMER OGRE.
IF THEY REALIZE THAT, A COLD WILL BE THE LEAST OF OUR WORRIES.
IT'S FINE TO BE PRUDENT...
...BUT AT THIS RATE, THE GIRL WILL DIE.
CLACK
FLINCH
?!

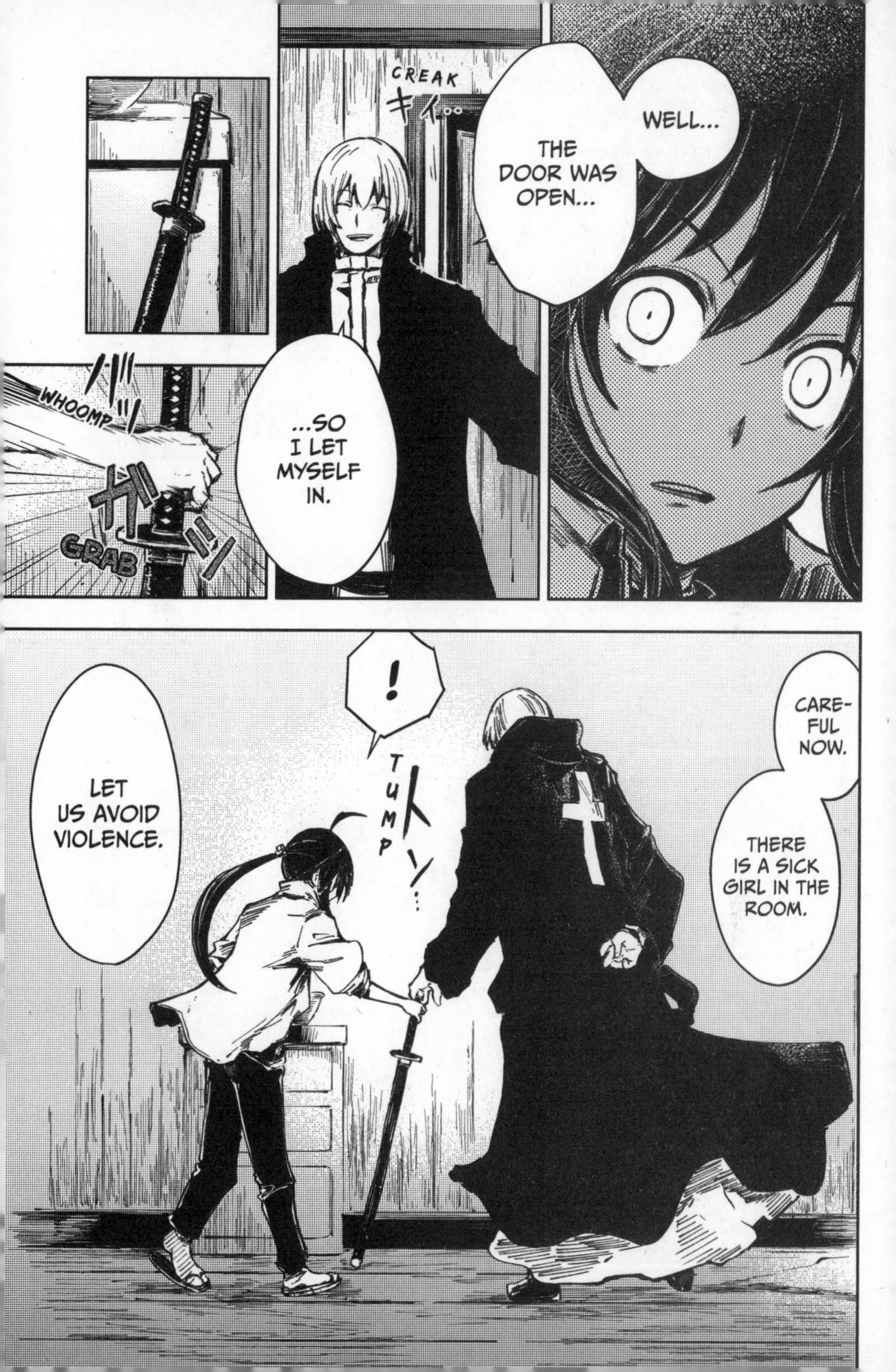
WELL...
THE DOOR WAS OPEN...
CREAK
...SO I LET MYSELF IN.
WHOOMP
GRAB
CARE-FUL NOW.
THERE IS A SICK GIRL IN THE ROOM.
!
TUMP
LET US AVOID VIOLENCE.

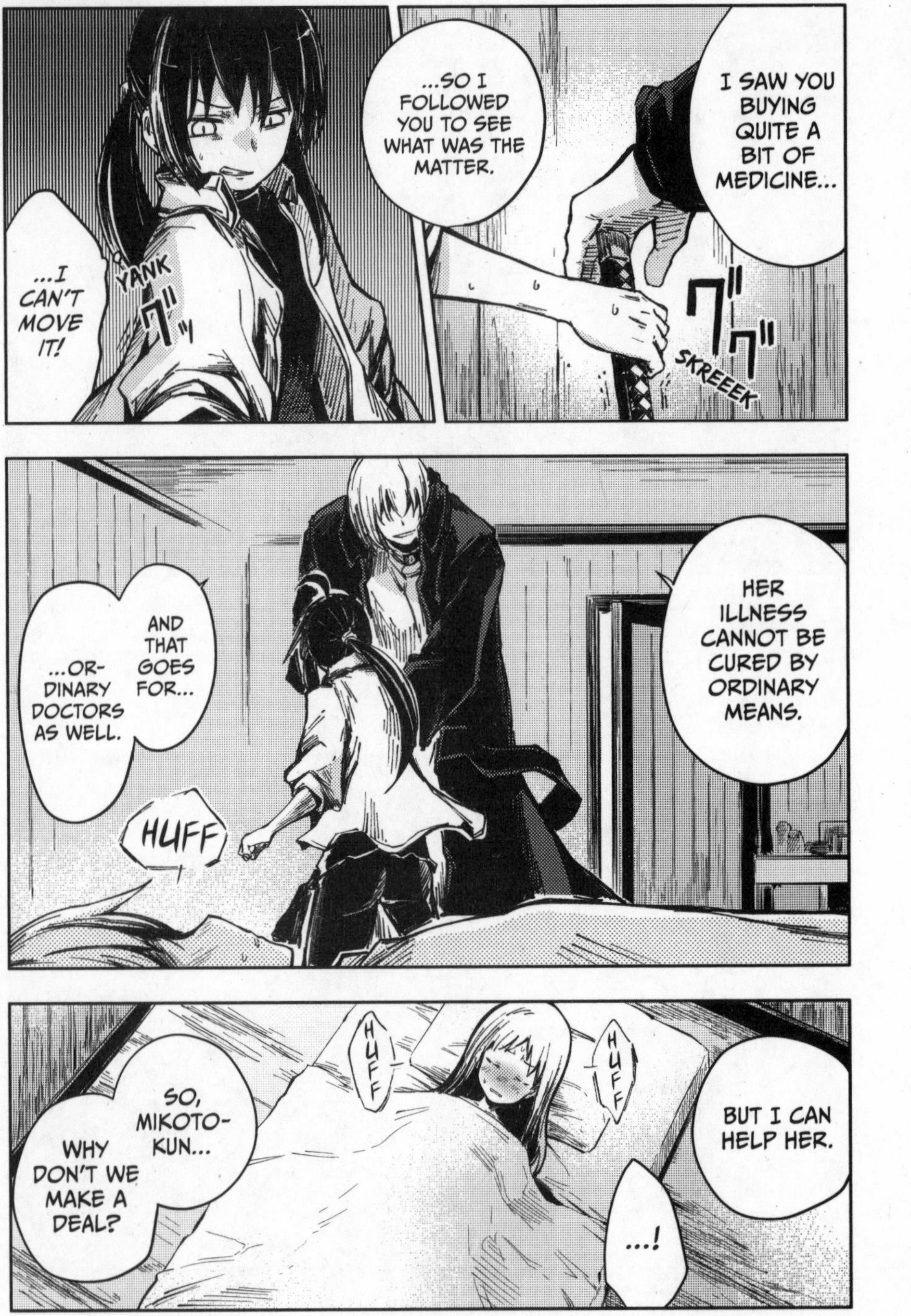

I SAW YOU BUYING QUITE A BIT OF MEDICINE...
...SO I FOLLOWED YOU TO SEE WHAT WAS THE MATTER.
ググ
SKREEEK
YANK
グッ
...I CAN'T MOVE IT!
HER ILLNESS CANNOT BE CURED BY ORDINARY MEANS.
AND THAT GOES FOR...
...OR-DINARY DOCTORS AS WELL.
HUFF
BUT I CAN HELP HER.
HUFF
...!
HUFF
SO, MIKOTO-KUN...
WHY DON'T WE MAKE A DEAL?

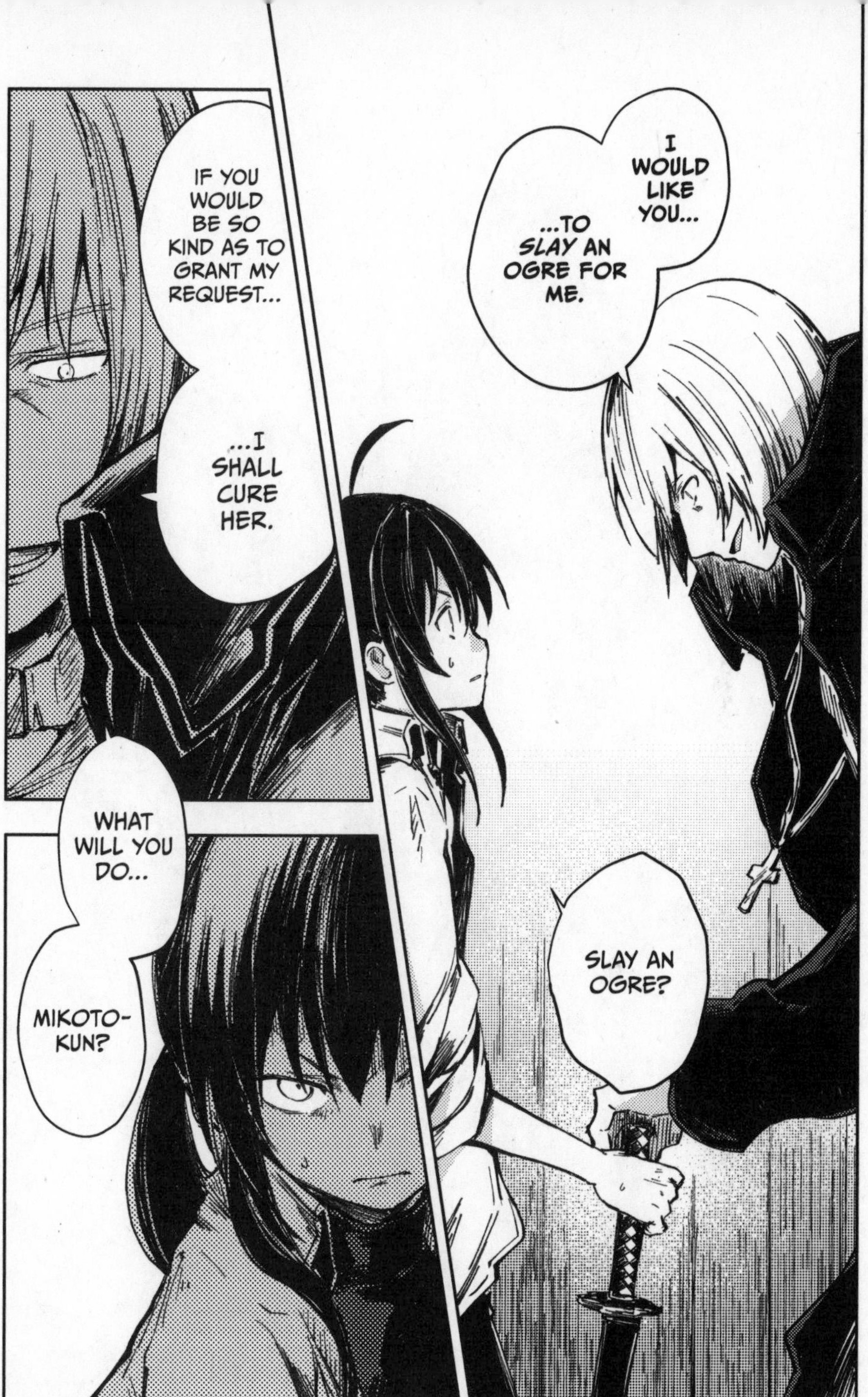
I WOULD LIKE YOU...
...TO SLAY AN OGRE FOR ME.
SLAY AN OGRE?
IF YOU WOULD BE SO KIND AS TO GRANT MY REQUEST...
...I SHALL CURE HER.
WHAT WILL YOU DO...
MIKOTO-KUN?

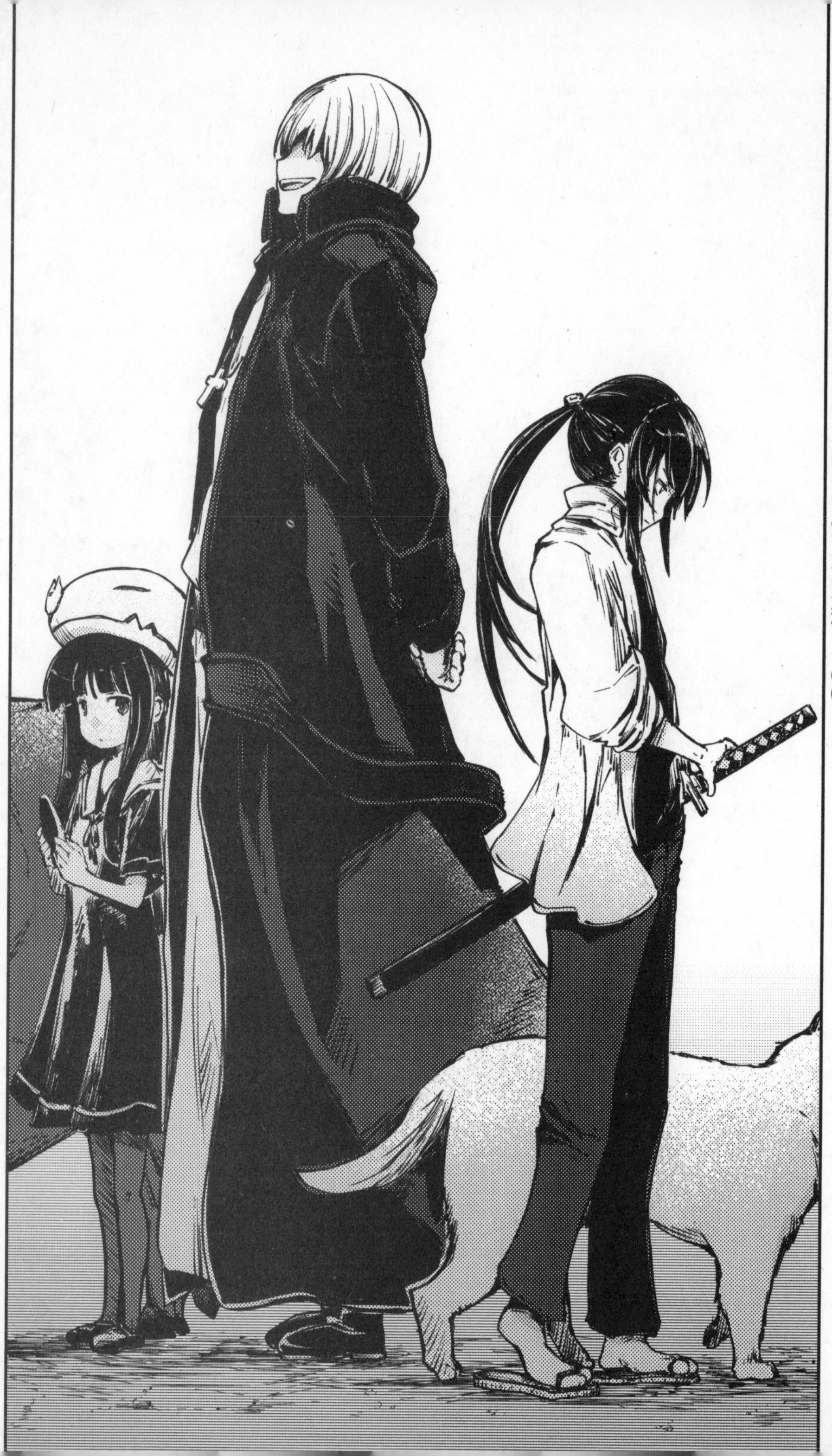

CHAPTER 26: HEART OF A PEACH AND HEART OF A MAN

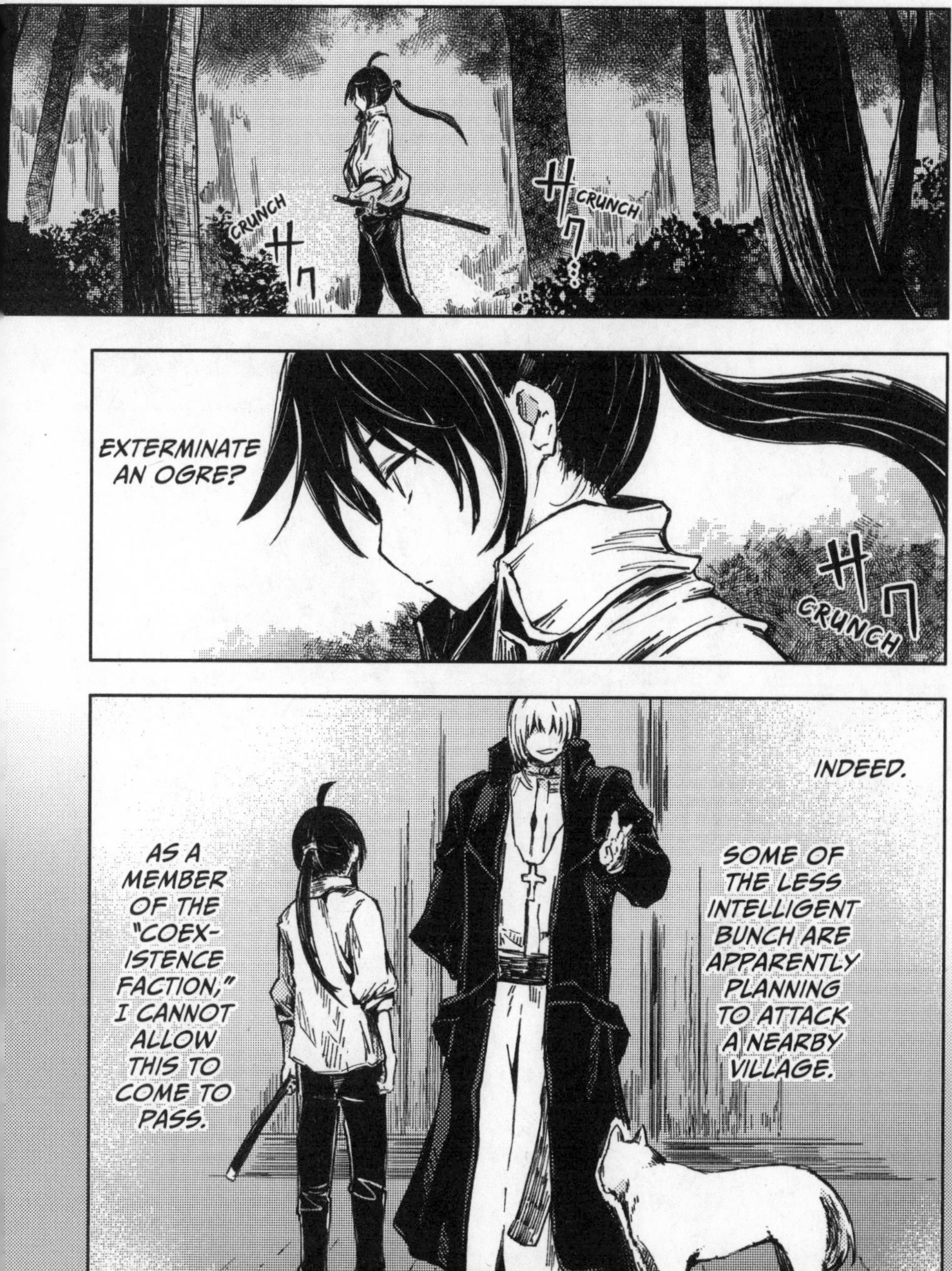

サク
CRUNCH
CRUNCH
サク
EXTERMINATE AN OGRE?
サク
CRUNCH
INDEED.
SOME OF THE LESS INTELLIGENT BUNCH ARE APPARENTLY PLANNING TO ATTACK A NEARBY VILLAGE.
AS A MEMBER OF THE "COEX-ISTENCE FACTION," I CANNOT ALLOW THIS TO COME TO PASS.

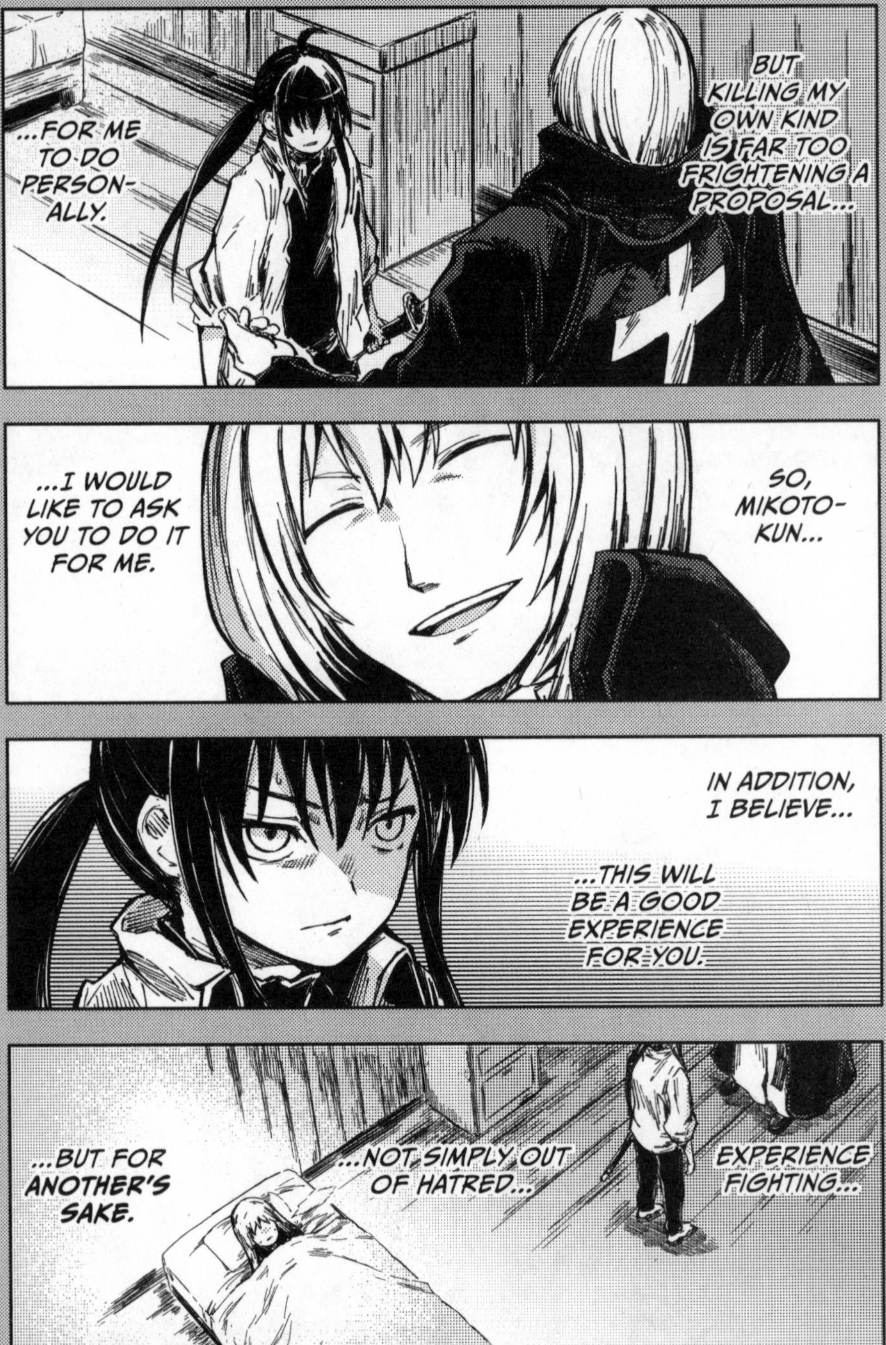
BUT KILLING MY OWN KIND IS FAR TOO FRIGHTENING A PROPOSAL...
...FOR ME TO DO PERSON-ALLY.
SO, MIKOTO-KUN...
...I WOULD LIKE TO ASK YOU TO DO IT FOR ME.
IN ADDITION, I BELIEVE...
...THIS WILL BE A GOOD EXPERIENCE FOR YOU.
EXPERIENCE FIGHTING...
...NOT SIMPLY OUT OF HATRED...
...BUT FOR ANOTHER'S SAKE.

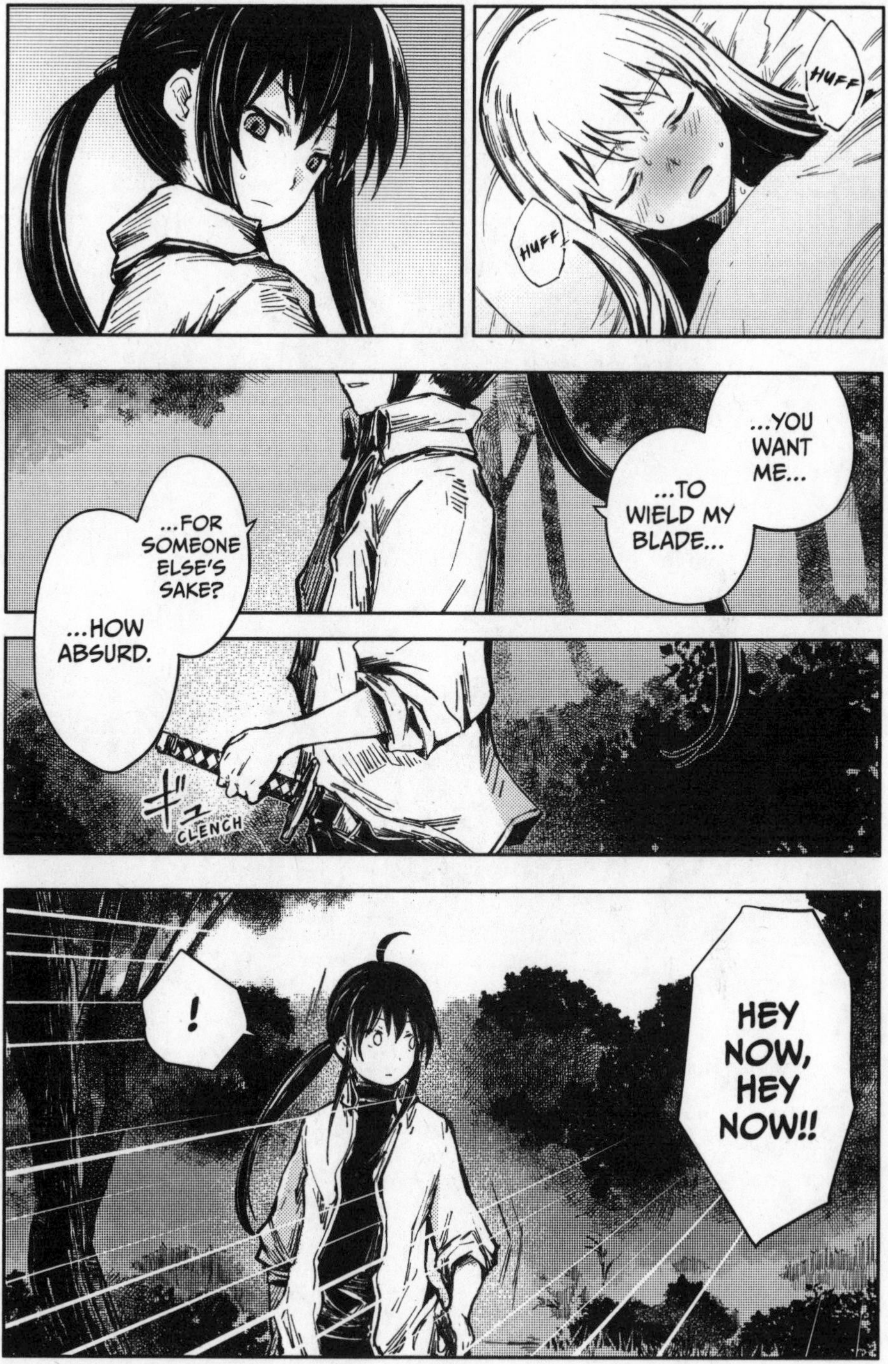
HUFF
HUFF
...YOU WANT ME...
...TO WIELD MY BLADE...
...FOR SOMEONE ELSE'S SAKE?
...HOW ABSURD.
ギュ
CLENCH
HEY NOW, HEY NOW!!
!

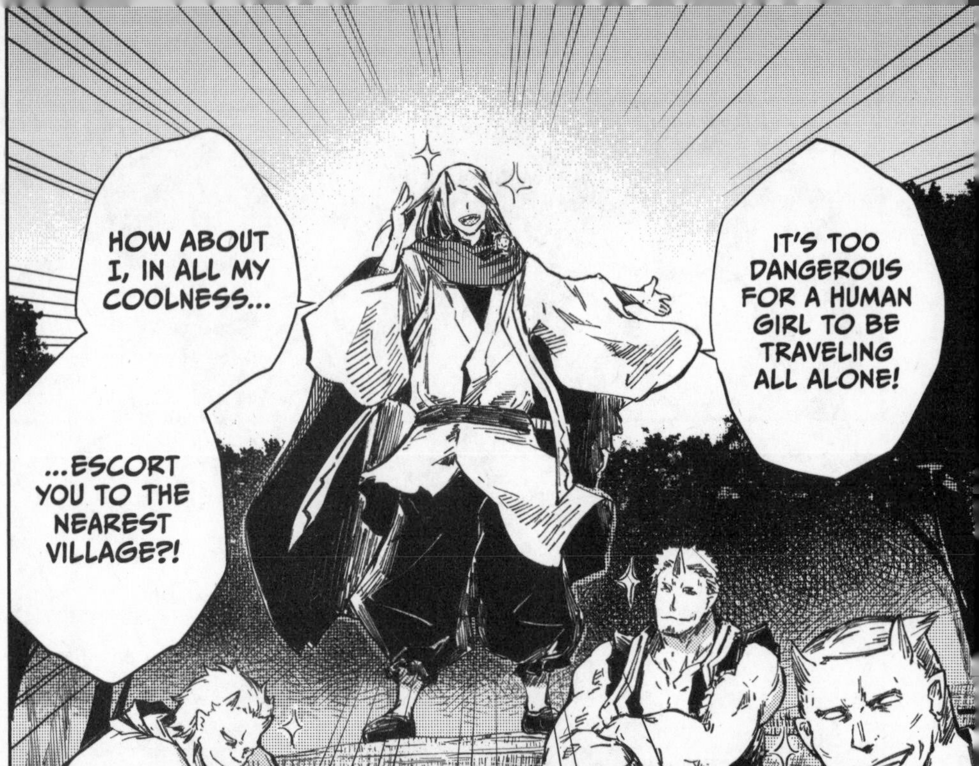
IT'S TOO DANGEROUS FOR A HUMAN GIRL TO BE TRAVELING ALL ALONE!
HOW ABOUT I, IN ALL MY COOLNESS...
...ESCORT YOU TO THE NEAREST VILLAGE?!
BWOOOM

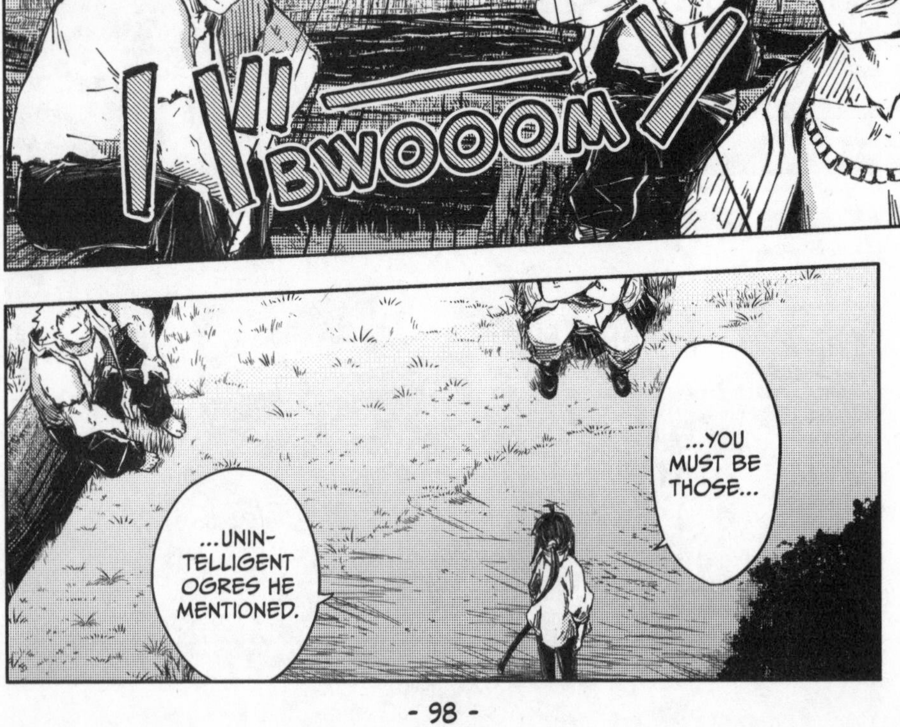
...YOU MUST BE THOSE...
...UNIN-TELLIGENT OGRES HE MENTIONED.

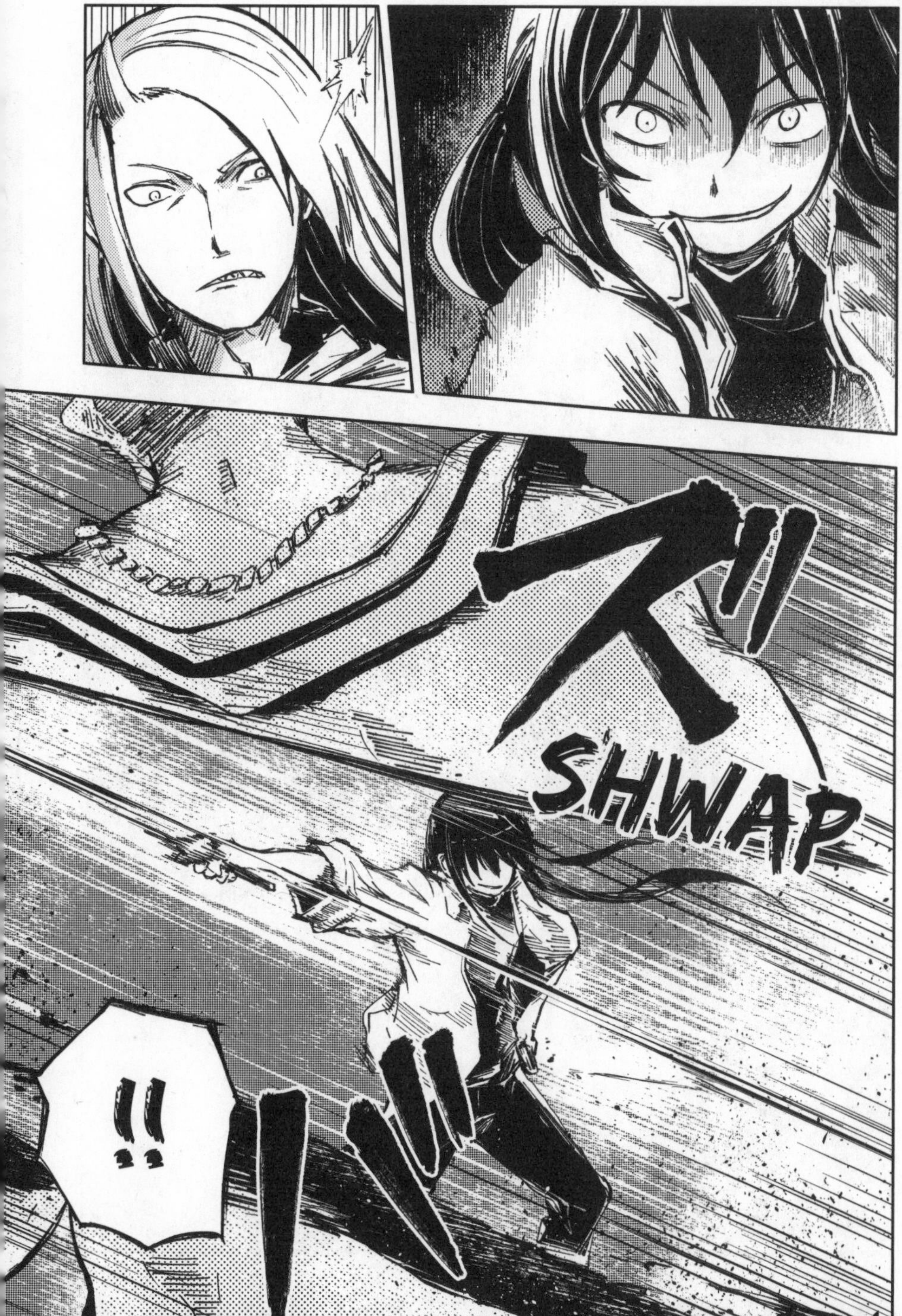

SHWAP
!!

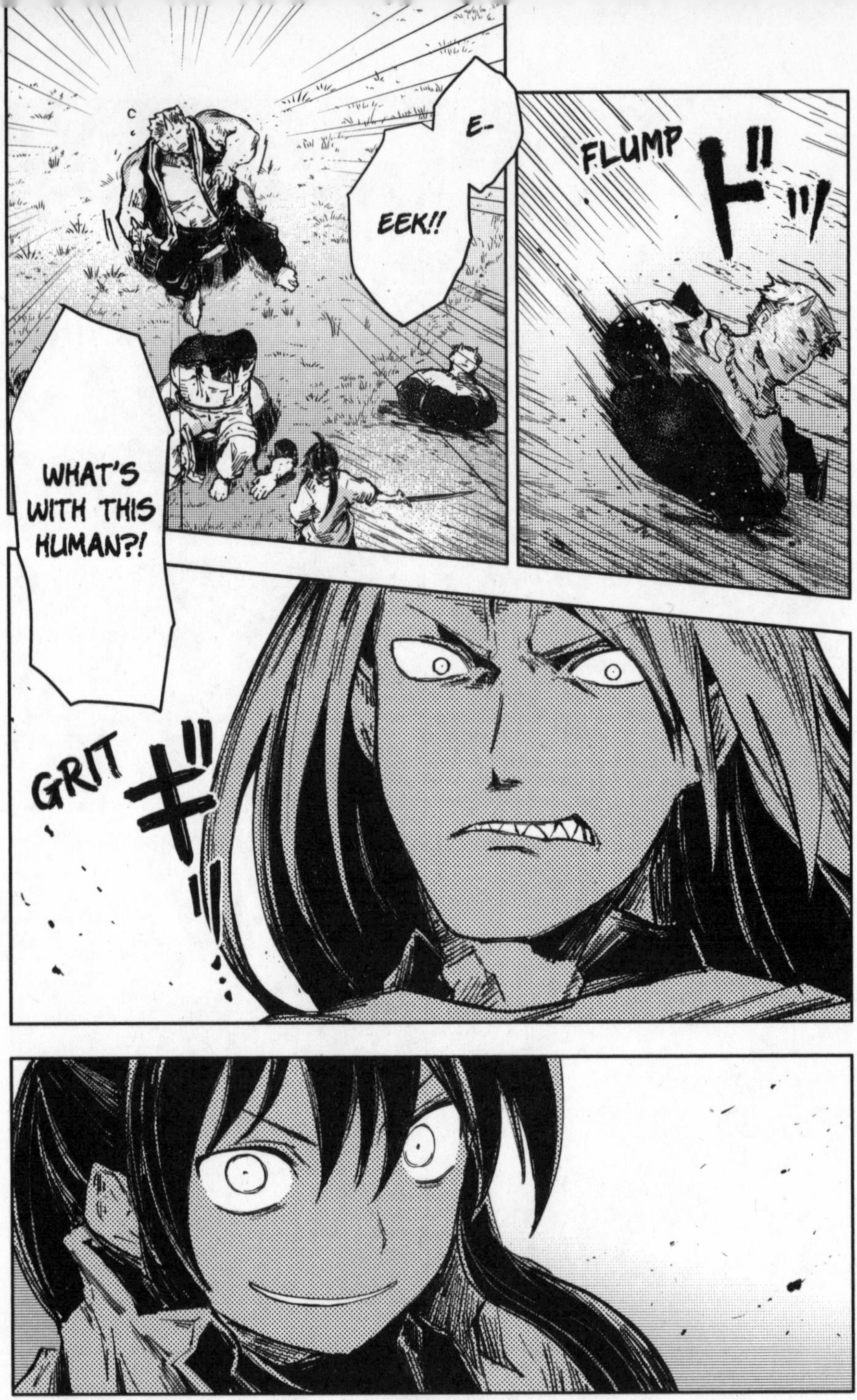
FLUMP
ドッ
E-
EEK!!
WHAT'S WITH THIS HUMAN?!
GRIT
ギ

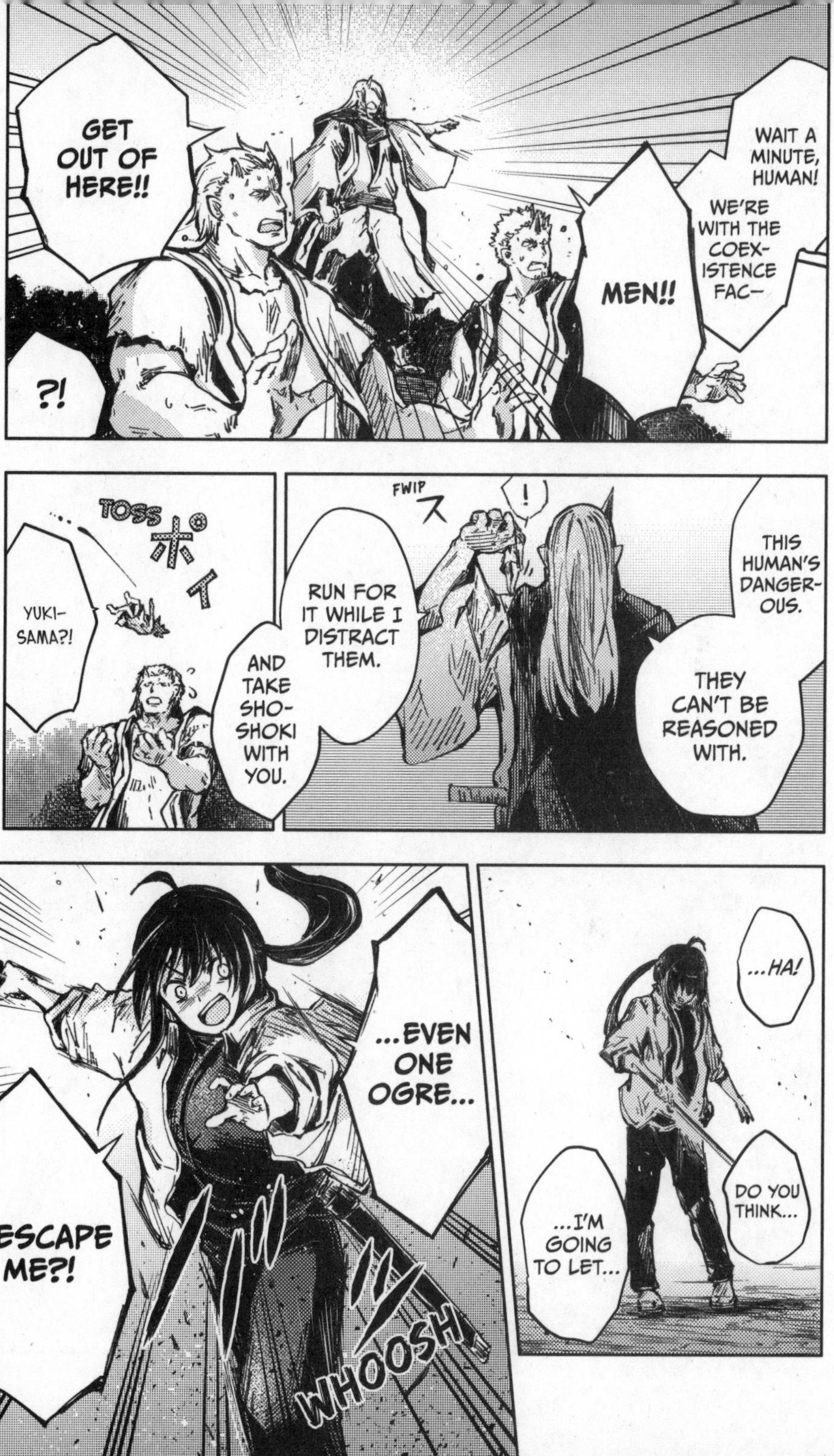

WAIT A MINUTE, HUMAN!
WE'RE WITH THE COEXISTENCE FAC—
MEN!!
GET OUT OF HERE!!
?!
!
FWIP ス
THIS HUMAN'S DANGEROUS.
THEY CAN'T BE REASONED WITH.
RUN FOR IT WHILE I DISTRACT THEM.
AND TAKE SHOSHOKI WITH YOU.
TOSS ポイ
...
YUKI-SAMA?!
...HA!
DO YOU THINK...
...I'M GOING TO LET...
...EVEN ONE OGRE...
...ESCAPE ME?!
WHOOSH

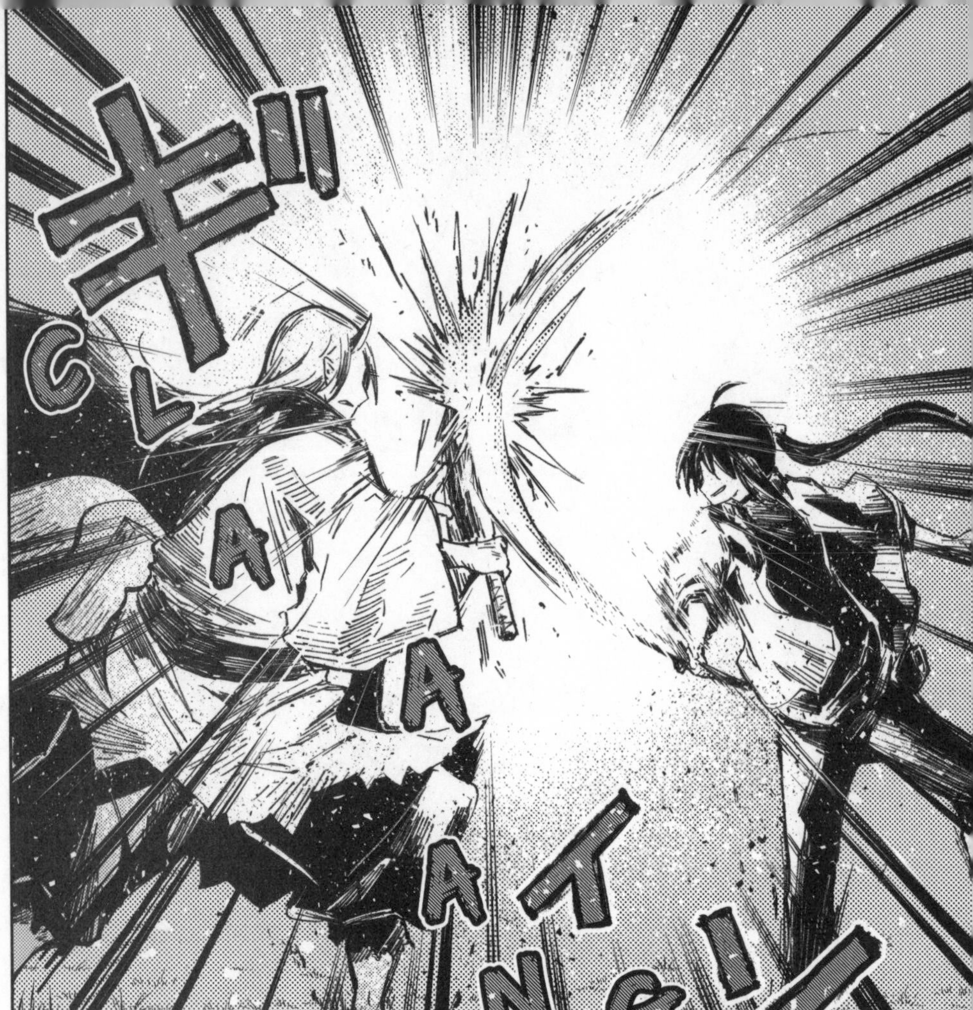
CLAAANG

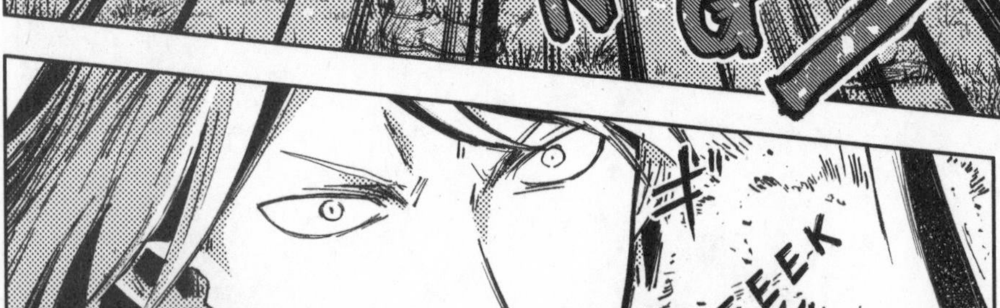
SKREEEEEK

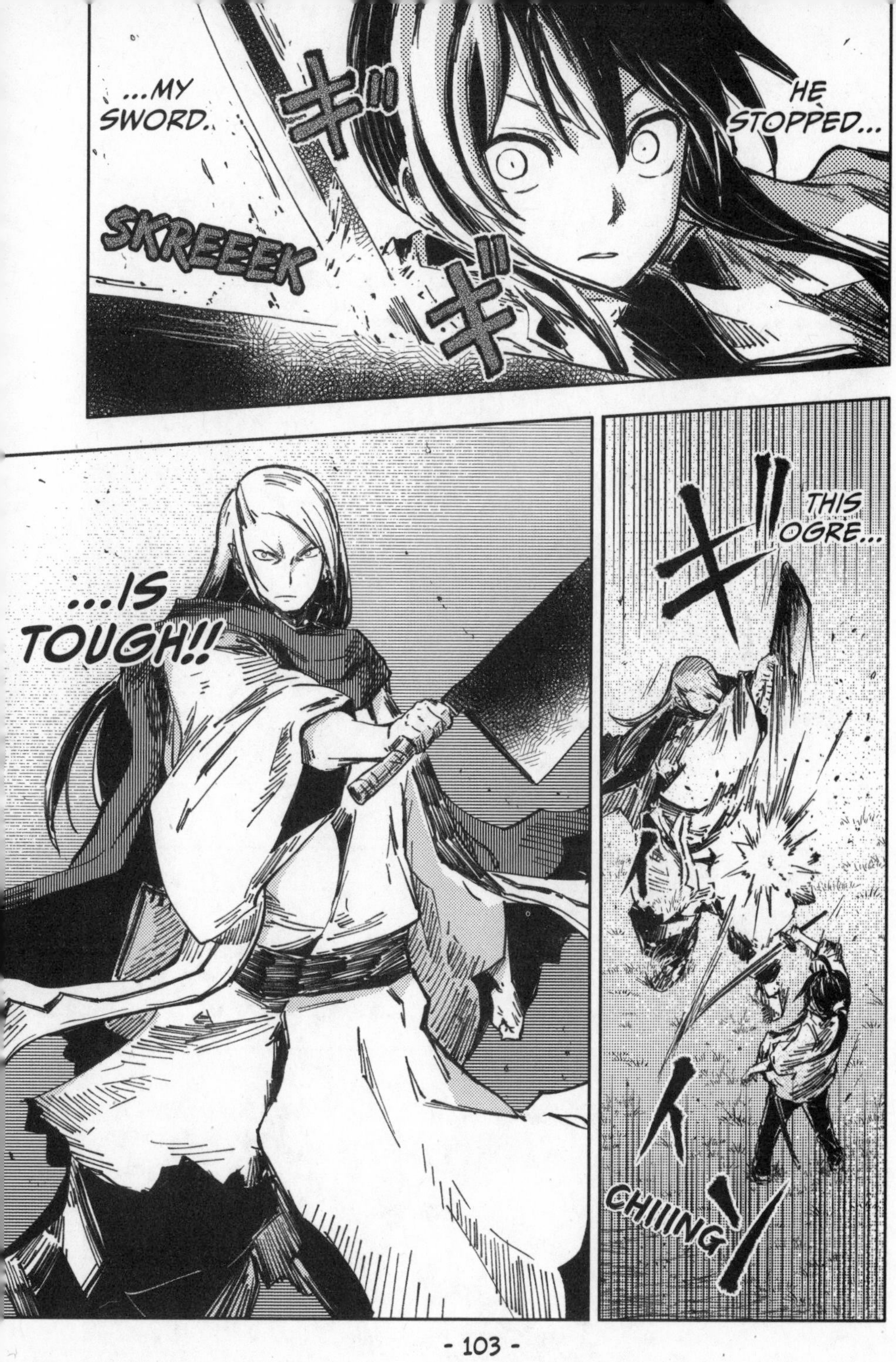
HE STOPPED...
...MY SWORD.
SKREEEK
THIS OGRE...
CHIIING
...IS TOUGH!!

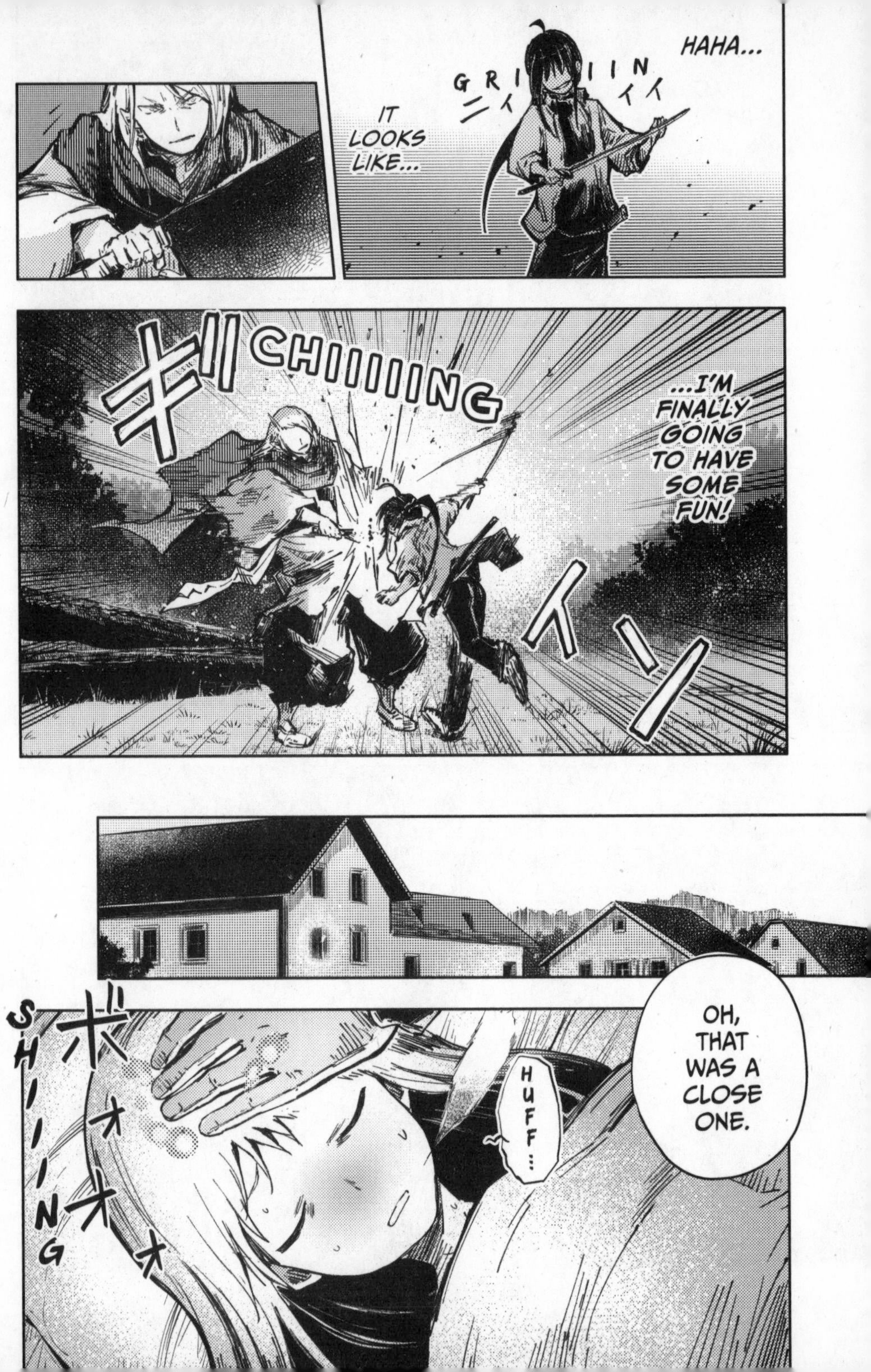
HAHA...
GRIIIN
IT LOOKS LIKE...
CHIIIIIING
...I'M FINALLY GOING TO HAVE SOME FUN!
OH, THAT WAS A CLOSE ONE.
HUFF...
SHIIIING

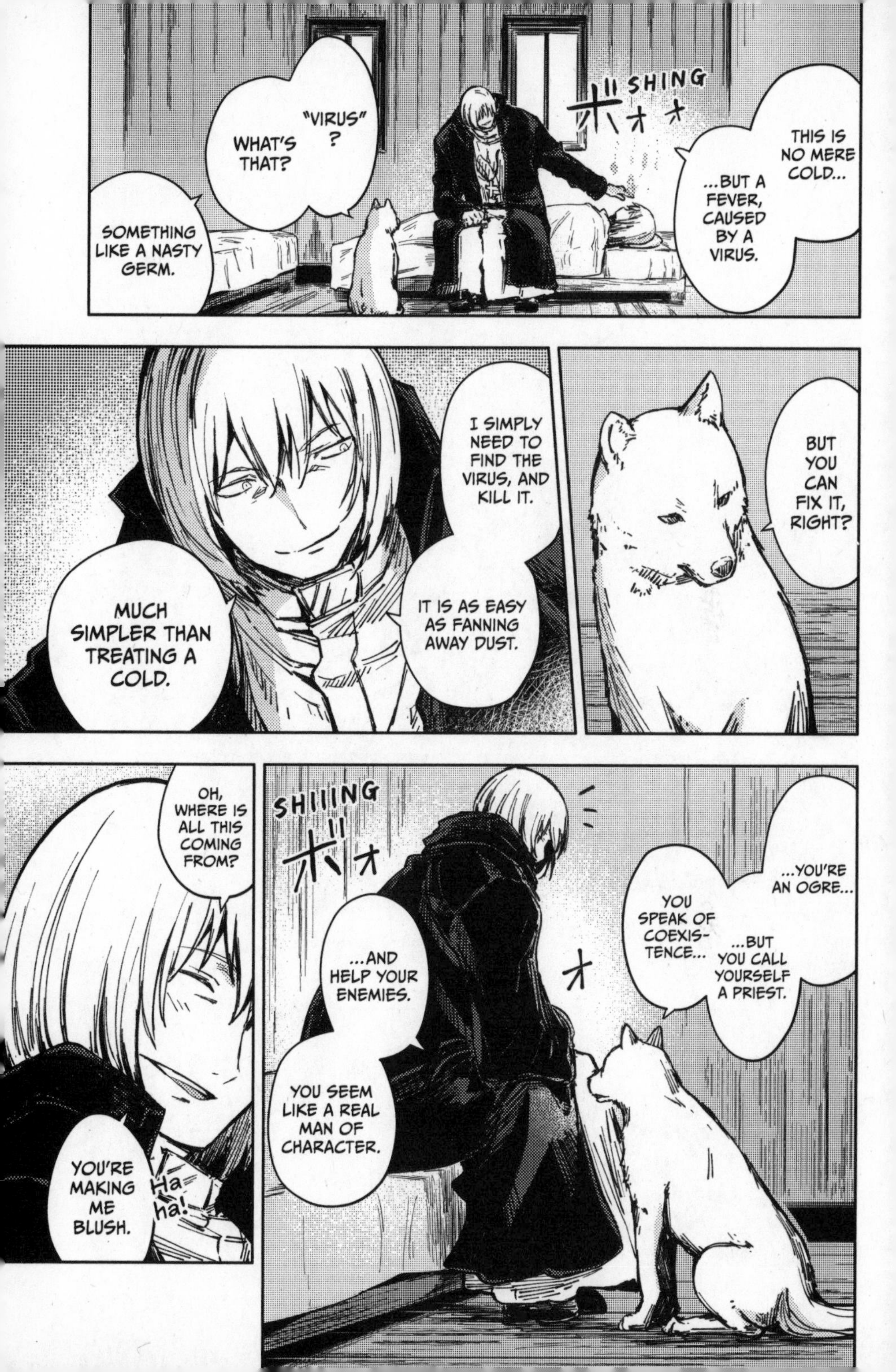
THIS IS NO MERE COLD...
...BUT A FEVER, CAUSED BY A VIRUS.
SHING
ボォォ
"VIRUS"?
WHAT'S THAT?
SOMETHING LIKE A NASTY GERM.
BUT YOU CAN FIX IT, RIGHT?
I SIMPLY NEED TO FIND THE VIRUS, AND KILL IT.
IT IS AS EASY AS FANNING AWAY DUST.
MUCH SIMPLER THAN TREATING A COLD.
...YOU'RE AN OGRE...
...BUT YOU CALL YOURSELF A PRIEST.
YOU SPEAK OF COEXIS-TENCE...
...AND HELP YOUR ENEMIES.
SHIIING
ボォ
オ
YOU SEEM LIKE A REAL MAN OF CHARACTER.
OH, WHERE IS ALL THIS COMING FROM?
YOU'RE MAKING ME BLUSH.
Ha ha!

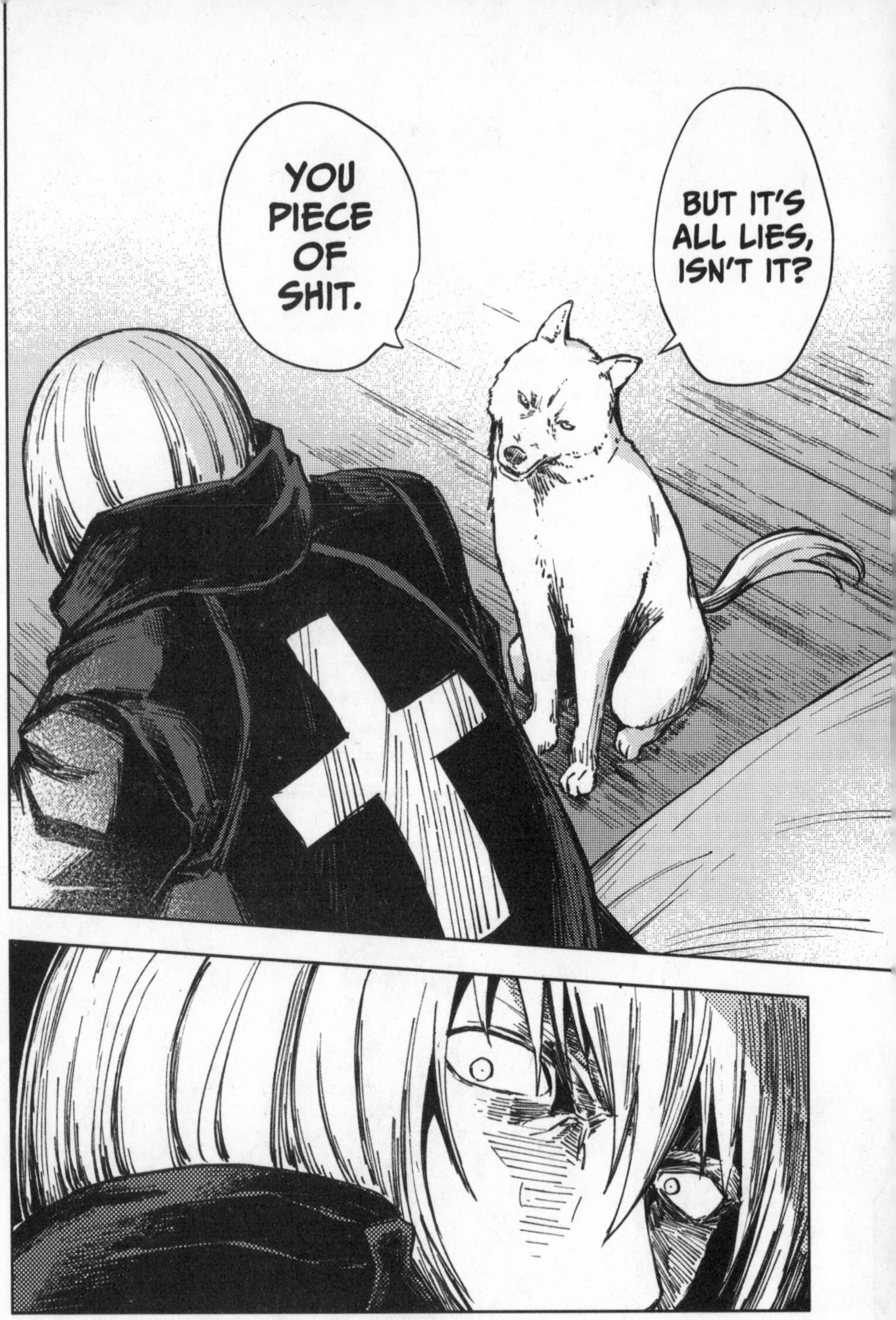
BUT IT'S ALL LIES, ISN'T IT?
YOU PIECE OF SHIT.

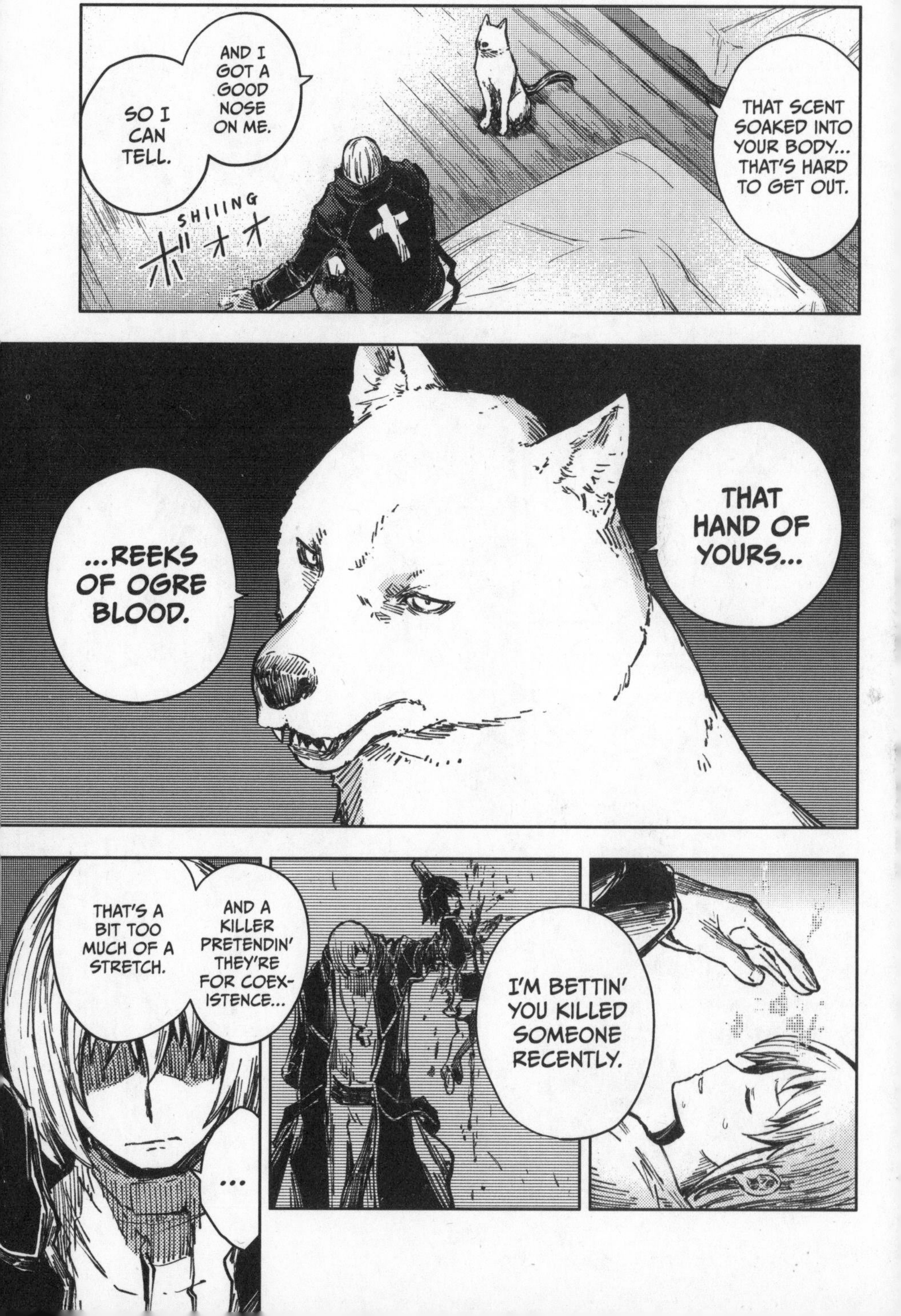

THAT SCENT SOAKED INTO YOUR BODY... THAT'S HARD TO GET OUT.
AND I GOT A GOOD NOSE ON ME.
SO I CAN TELL.
SHIIING
THAT HAND OF YOURS...
...REEKS OF OGRE BLOOD.
I'M BETTIN' YOU KILLED SOMEONE RECENTLY.
AND A KILLER PRETENDIN' THEY'RE FOR COEXISTENCE...
THAT'S A BIT TOO MUCH OF A STRETCH.
...

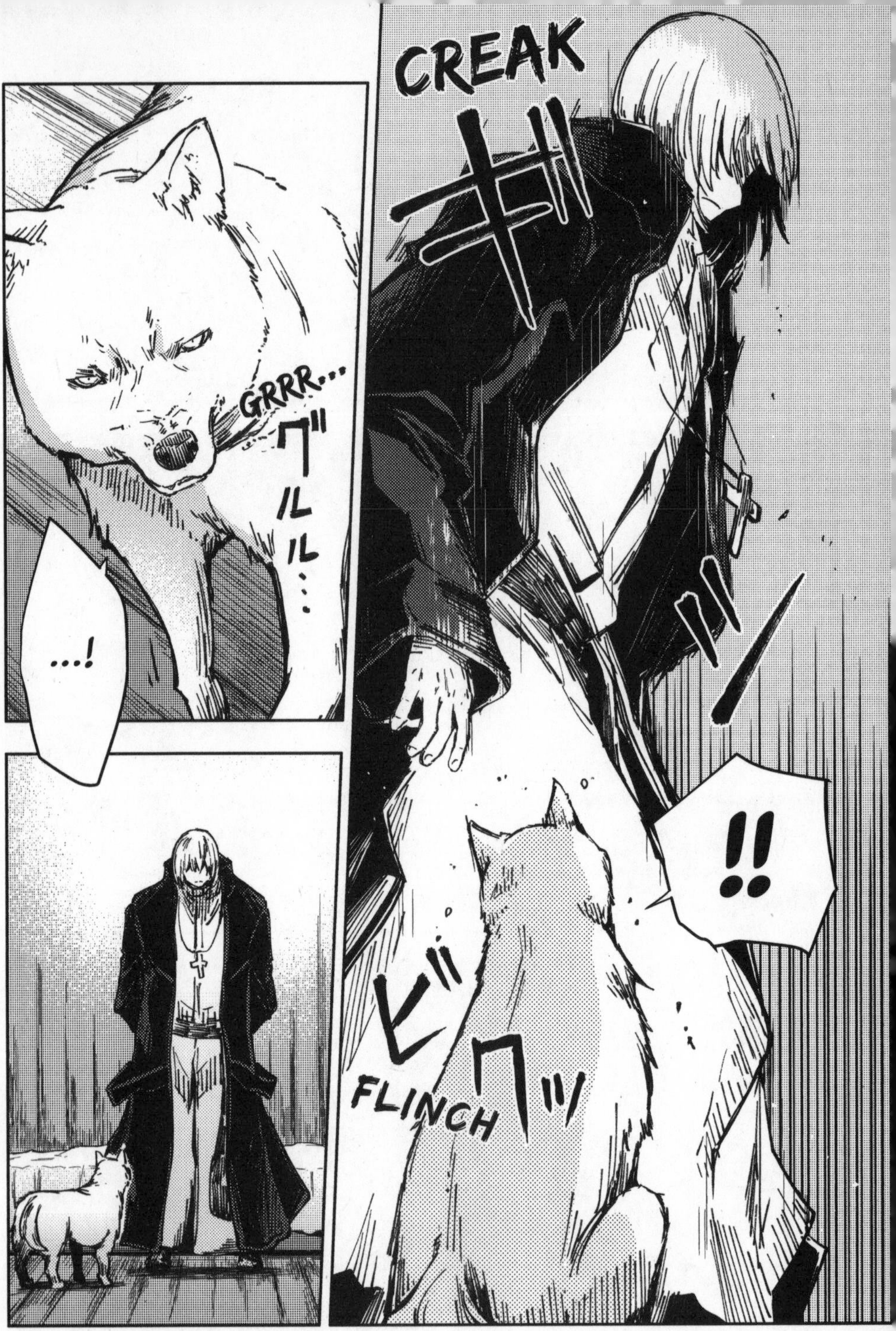
CREAK
ギッ
!!
FLINCH
ビクッ
GRRR...
グルル…
...!

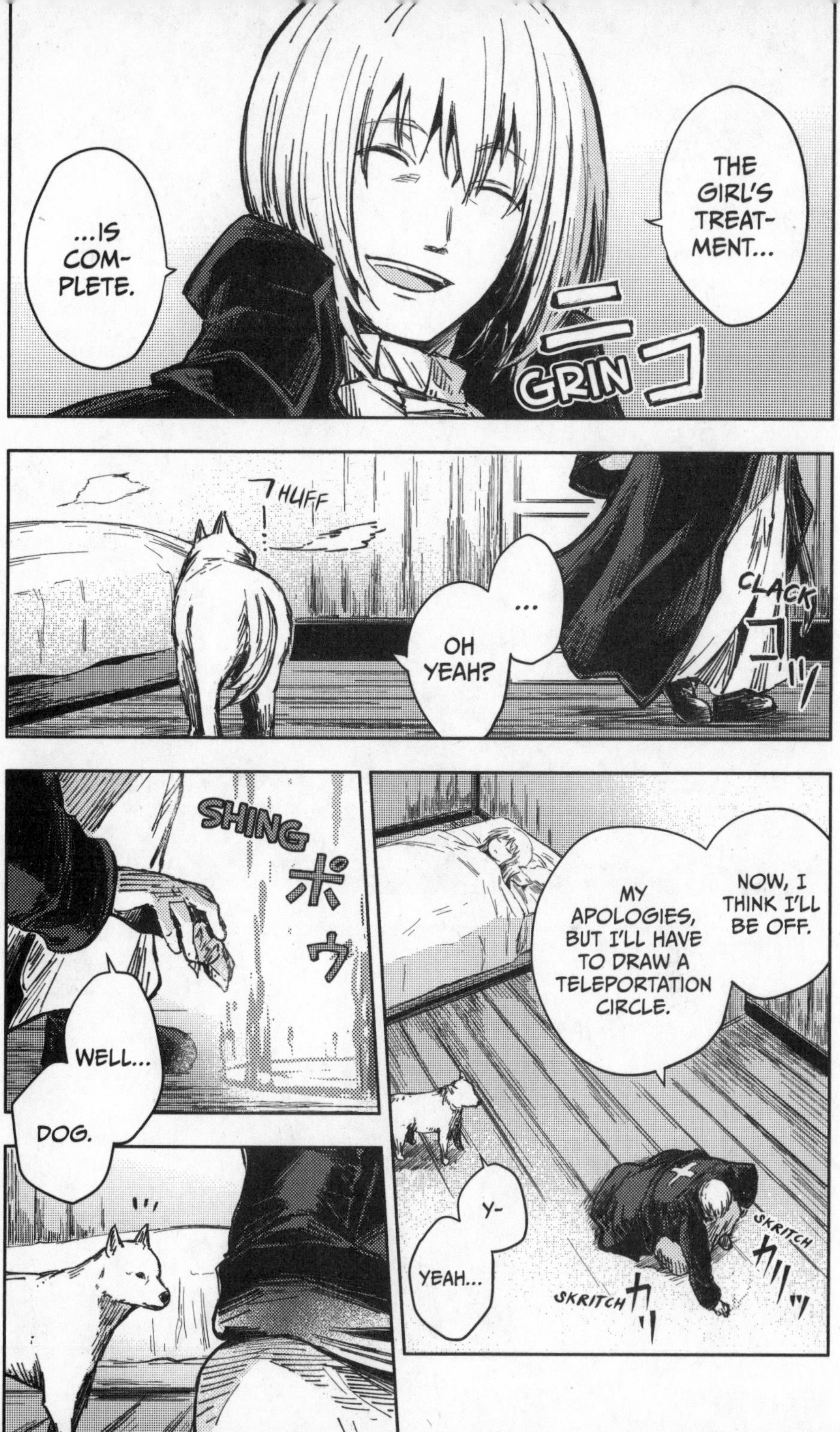
THE GIRL'S TREATMENT...
...IS COMPLETE.
GRIN ニコ
CLACK コツ
... OH YEAH?
HUFF
NOW, I THINK I'LL BE OFF.
MY APOLOGIES, BUT I'LL HAVE TO DRAW A TELEPORTATION CIRCLE.
SKRITCH カリッ
SKRITCH カリ
Y- YEAH...
SHING ポウ
WELL...
DOG.

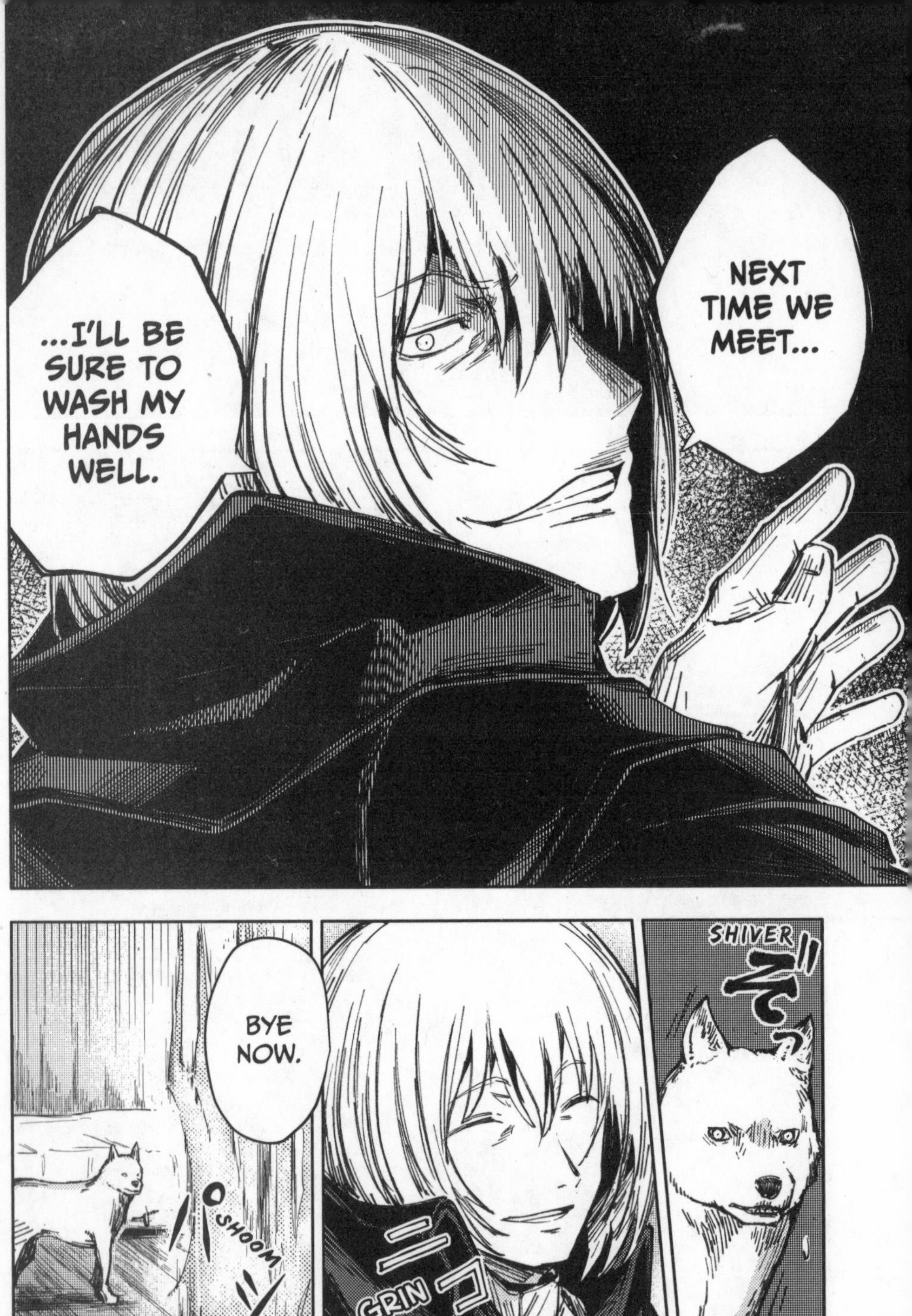
NEXT TIME WE MEET...
...I'LL BE SURE TO WASH MY HANDS WELL.
SHIVER
GRIN
BYE NOW.
SHOOM

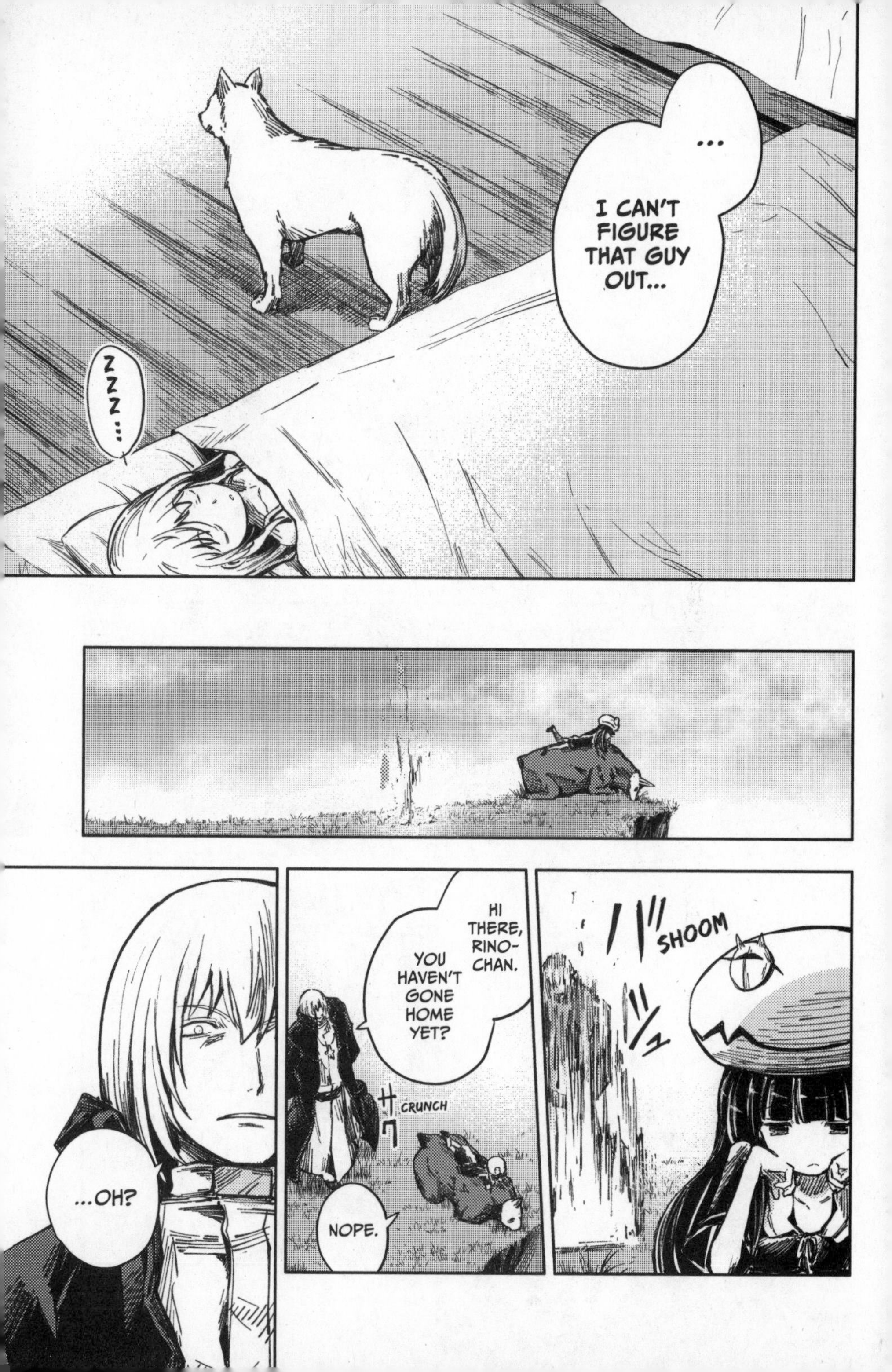
...
I CAN'T FIGURE THAT GUY OUT...
ZZZ...
SHOOM
HI THERE, RINO-CHAN.
YOU HAVEN'T GONE HOME YET?
CRUNCH
NOPE.
...OH?

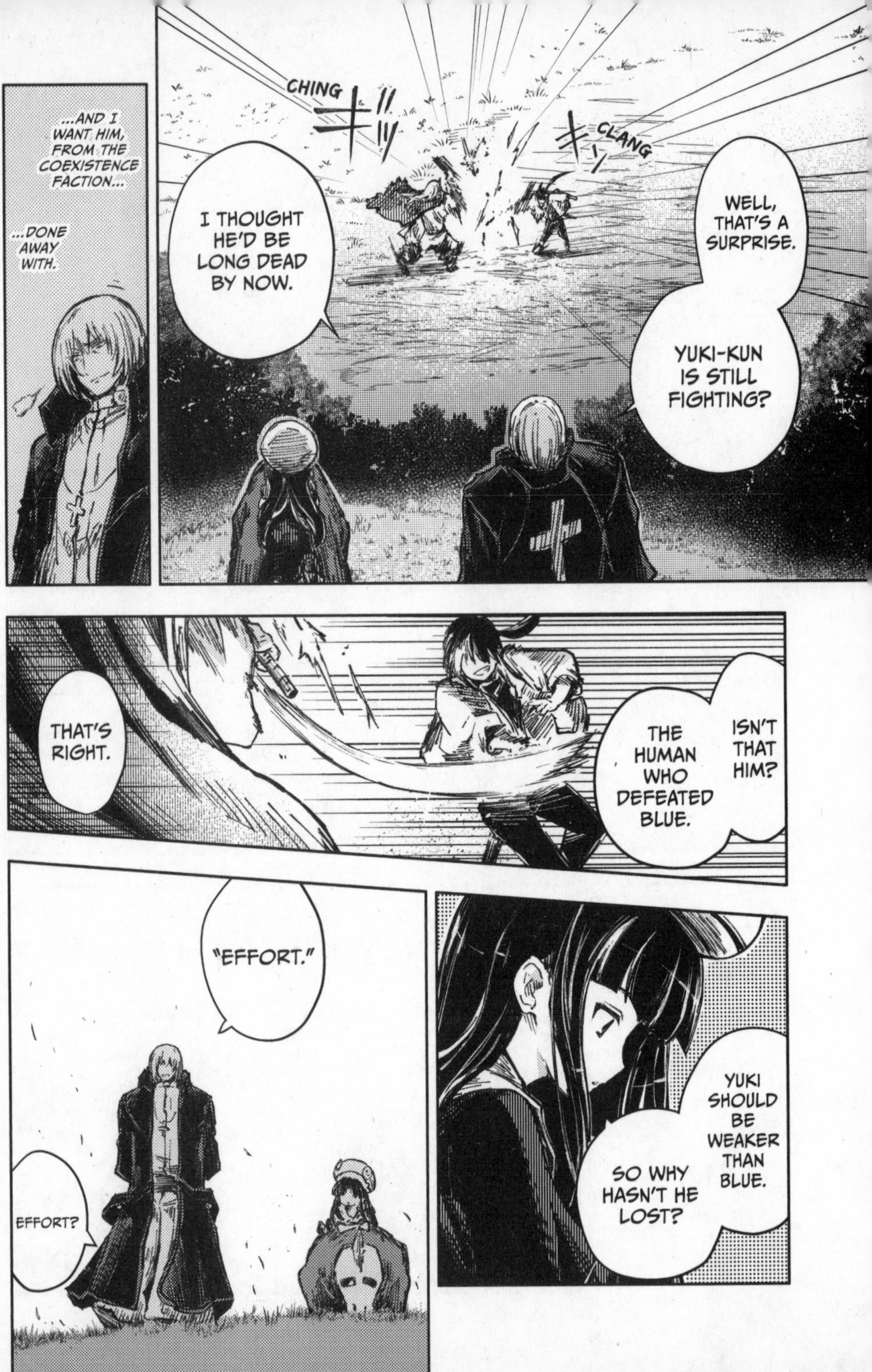
CLANG
CHING
WELL, THAT'S A SURPRISE.
YUKI-KUN IS STILL FIGHTING?
I THOUGHT HE'D BE LONG DEAD BY NOW.
...AND I WANT HIM, FROM THE COEXISTENCE FACTION...
...DONE AWAY WITH.
ISN'T THAT HIM?
THE HUMAN WHO DEFEATED BLUE.
THAT'S RIGHT.
YUKI SHOULD BE WEAKER THAN BLUE.
SO WHY HASN'T HE LOST?
"EFFORT."
EFFORT?

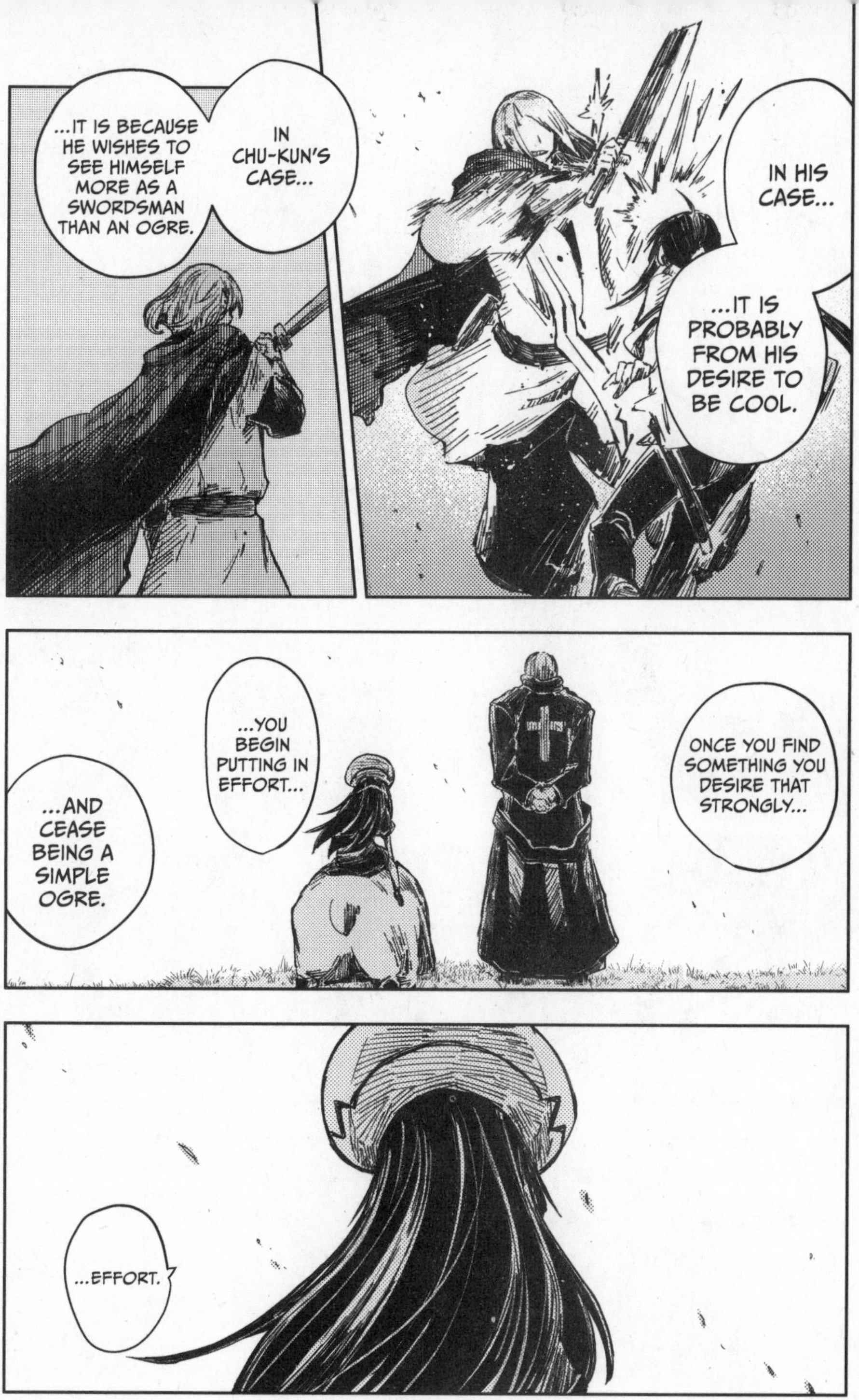
IN HIS CASE...
...IT IS PROBABLY FROM HIS DESIRE TO BE COOL.
IN CHU-KUN'S CASE...
...IT IS BECAUSE HE WISHES TO SEE HIMSELF MORE AS A SWORDSMAN THAN AN OGRE.
ONCE YOU FIND SOMETHING YOU DESIRE THAT STRONGLY...
...YOU BEGIN PUTTING IN EFFORT...
...AND CEASE BEING A SIMPLE OGRE.
...EFFORT.

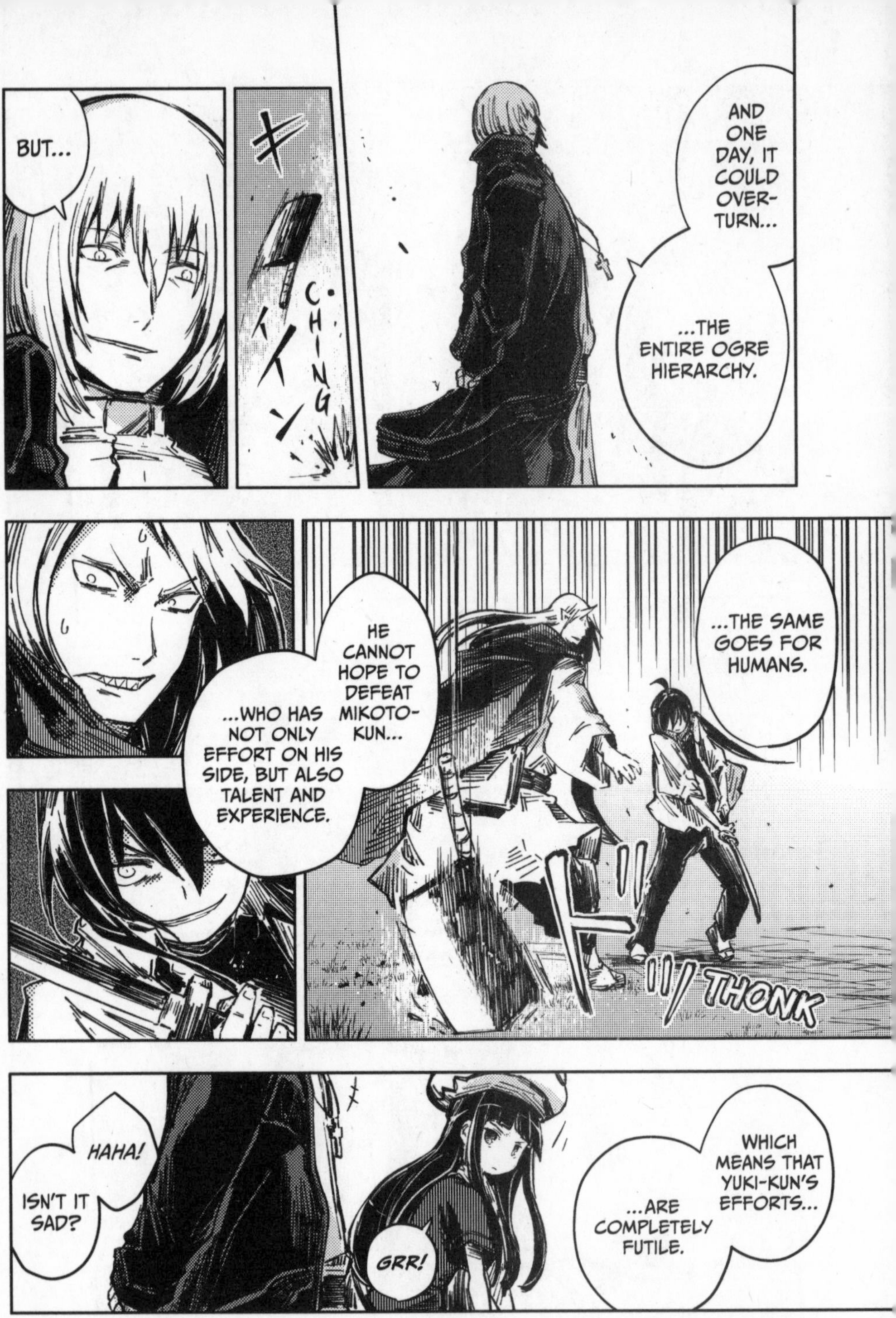
AND ONE DAY, IT COULD OVER-TURN...
...THE ENTIRE OGRE HIERARCHY.
CHING
BUT...
...THE SAME GOES FOR HUMANS.
HE CANNOT HOPE TO DEFEAT MIKOTO-KUN...
...WHO HAS NOT ONLY EFFORT ON HIS SIDE, BUT ALSO TALENT AND EXPERIENCE.
THONK
WHICH MEANS THAT YUKI-KUN'S EFFORTS...
...ARE COMPLETELY FUTILE.
GRR!
HAHA!
ISN'T IT SAD?

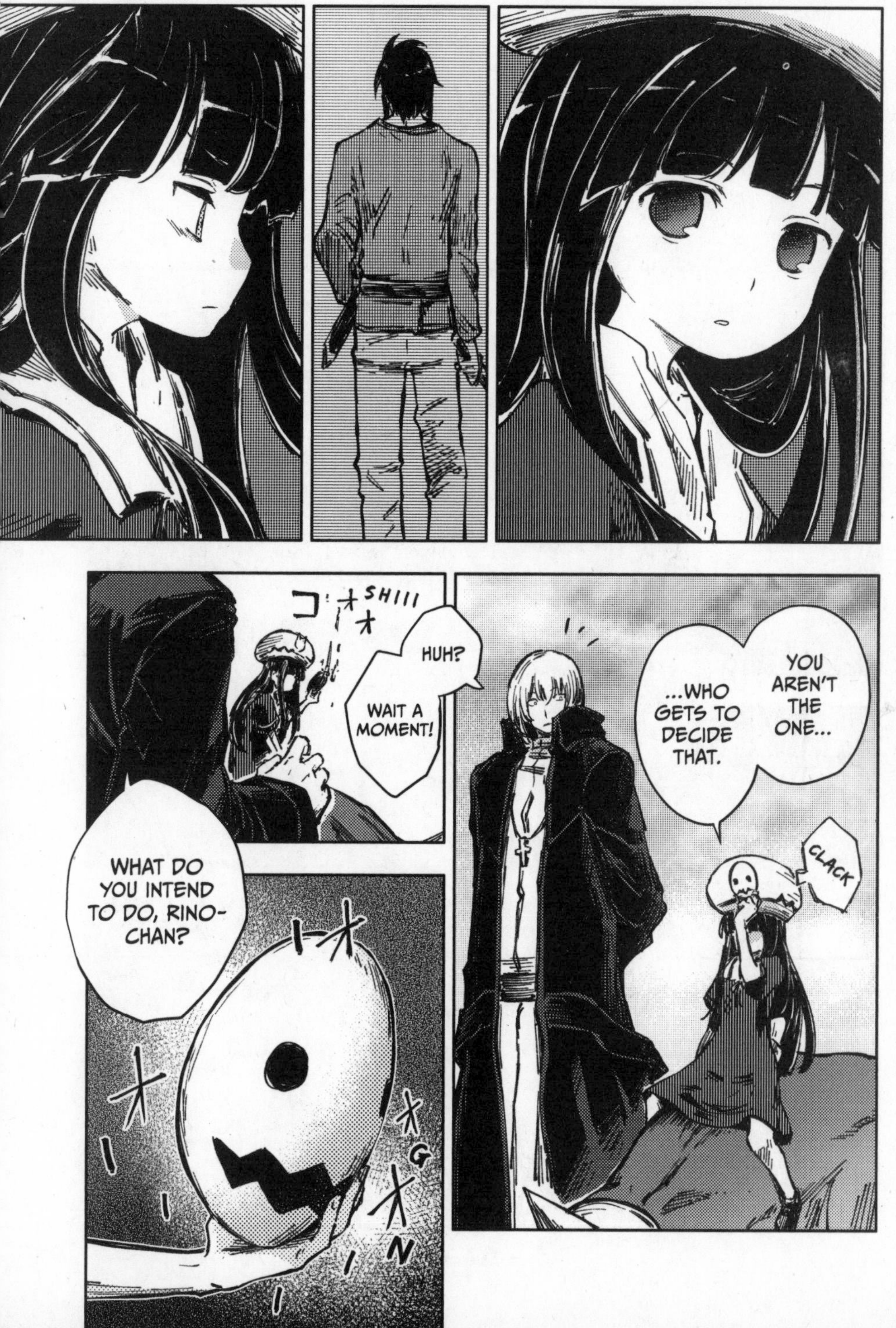
YOU AREN'T THE ONE...
...WHO GETS TO DECIDE THAT.
CLACK
SHIIII
HUH?
WAIT A MOMENT!
WHAT DO YOU INTEND TO DO, RINO-CHAN?

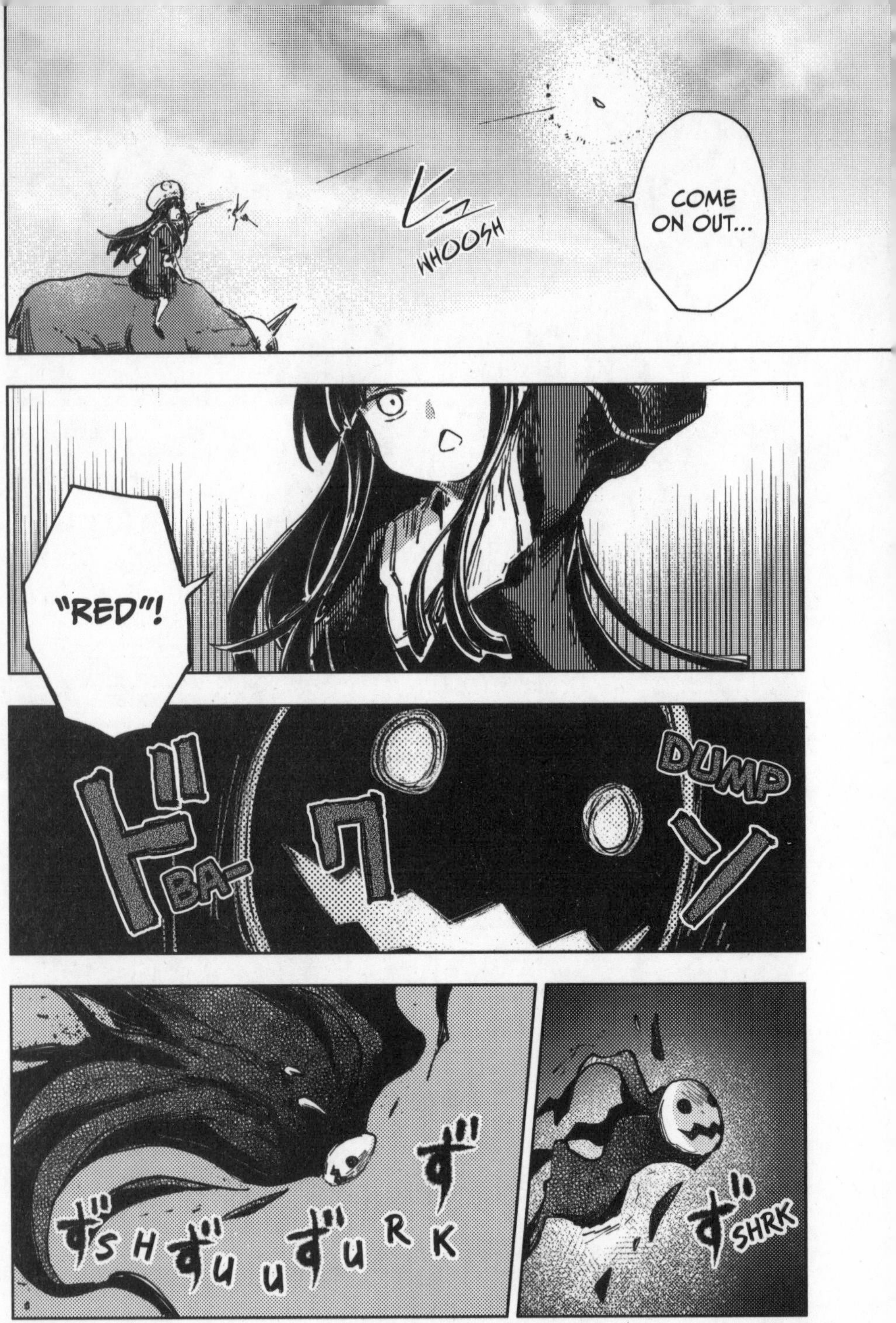
COME ON OUT...
ヒュ
WHOOSH
"RED"!
DUMP
ドクン
BA-
ず
SHRK
ずずずず
SHUUURK

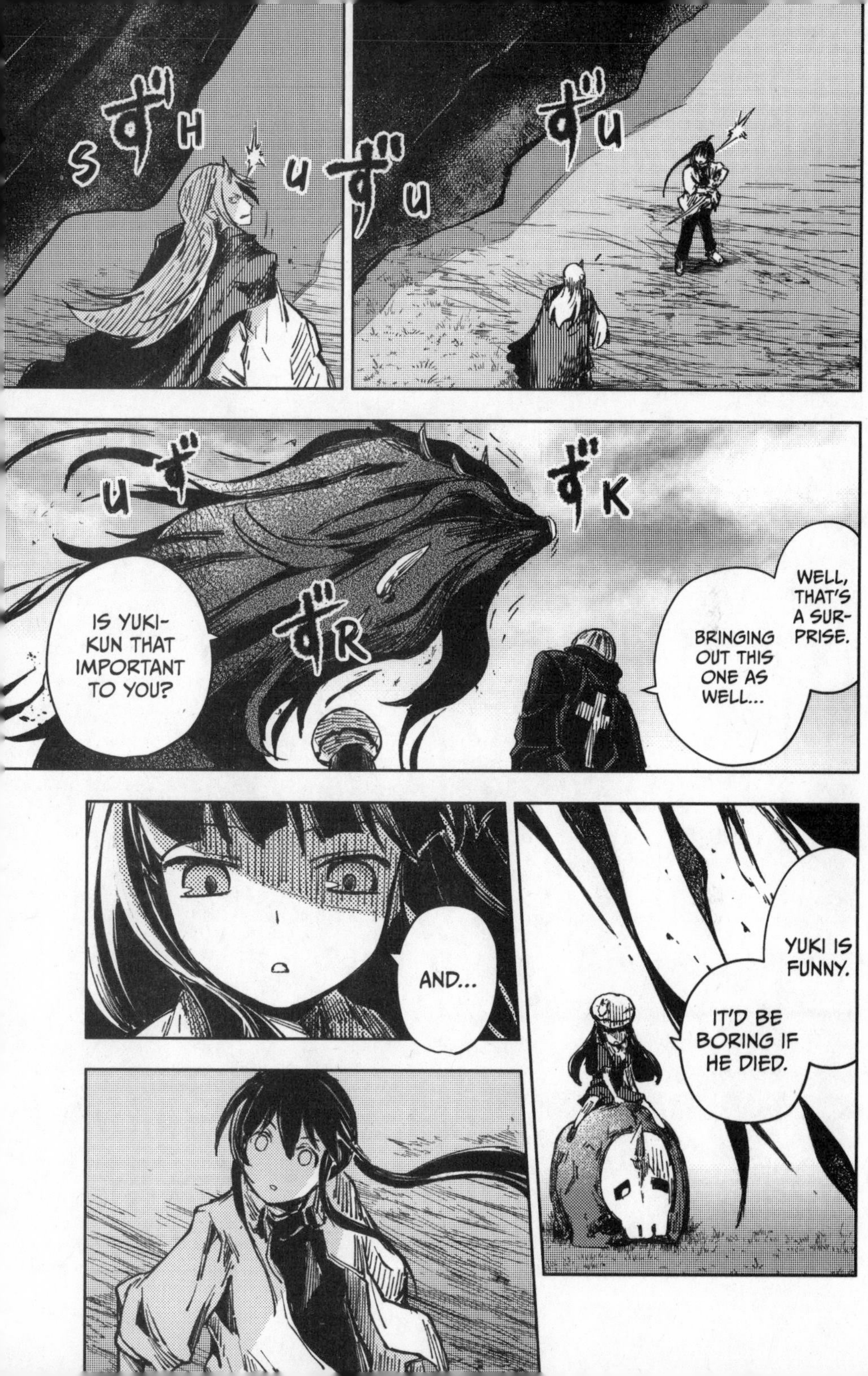

ずu
sずH
uずu
ずK
WELL, THAT'S A SURPRISE.
BRINGING OUT THIS ONE AS WELL...
uず
ずR
IS YUKI-KUN THAT IMPORTANT TO YOU?
YUKI IS FUNNY.
IT'D BE BORING IF HE DIED.
AND...

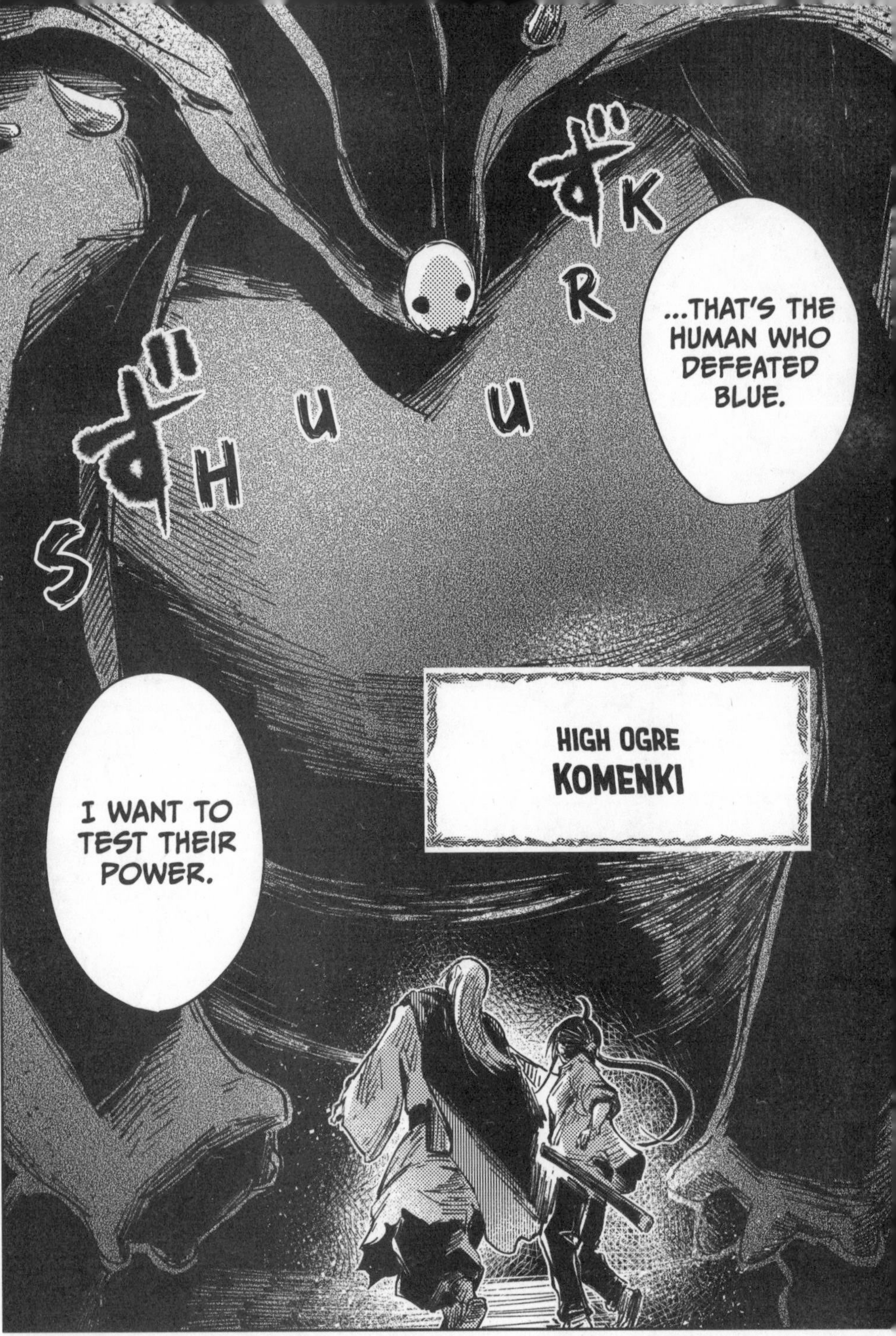
...THAT'S THE HUMAN WHO DEFEATED BLUE.
SHUURK
HIGH OGRE KOMENKI
I WANT TO TEST THEIR POWER.

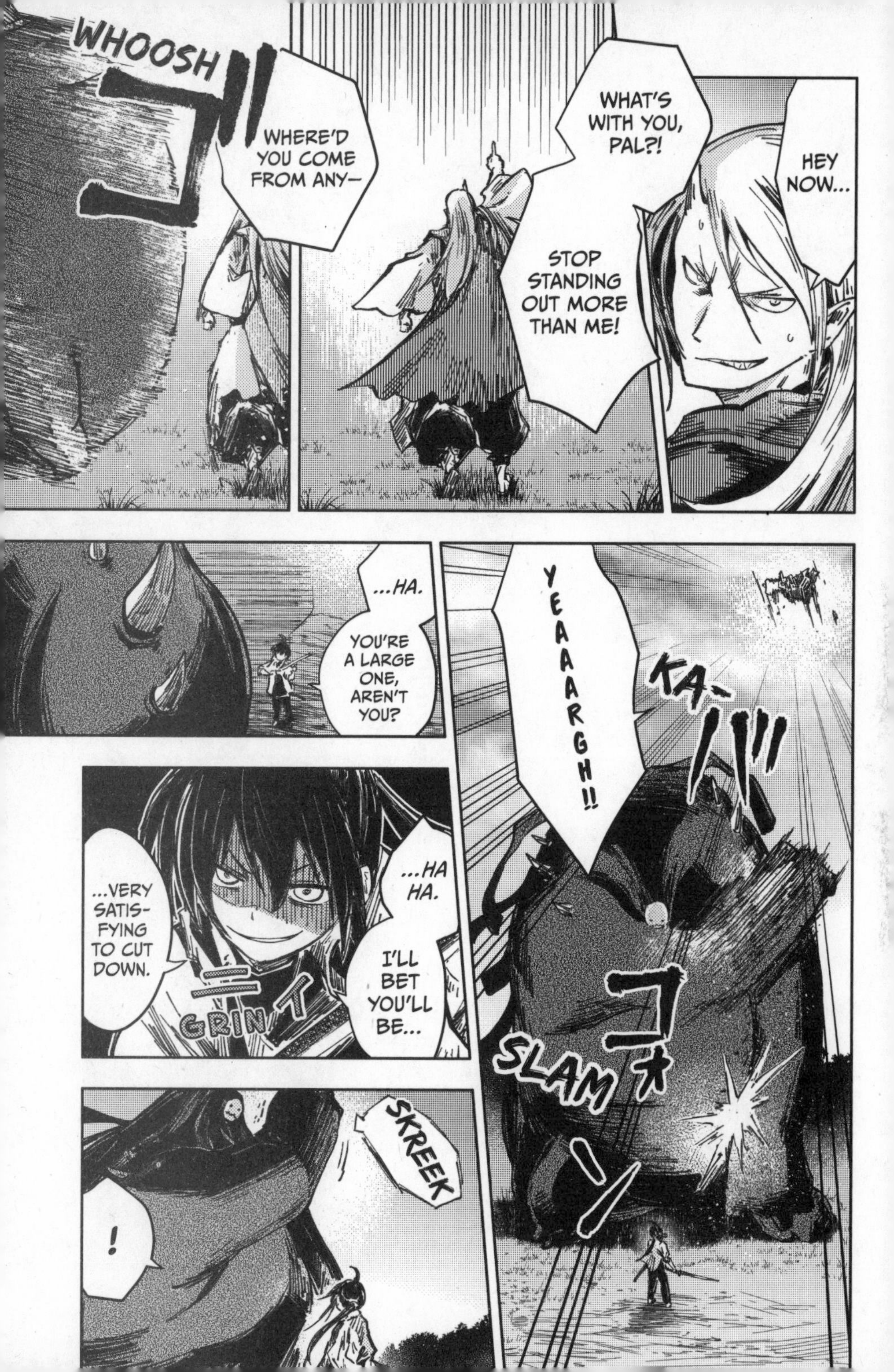
HEY NOW...
WHAT'S WITH YOU, PAL?!
STOP STANDING OUT MORE THAN ME!
WHERE'D YOU COME FROM ANY—
WHOOSH
YEAAARGH!!
KA-
SLAM
...HA.
YOU'RE A LARGE ONE, AREN'T YOU?
...HA HA.
I'LL BET YOU'LL BE...
...VERY SATIS-FYING TO CUT DOWN.
GRIN
SKREEK
!

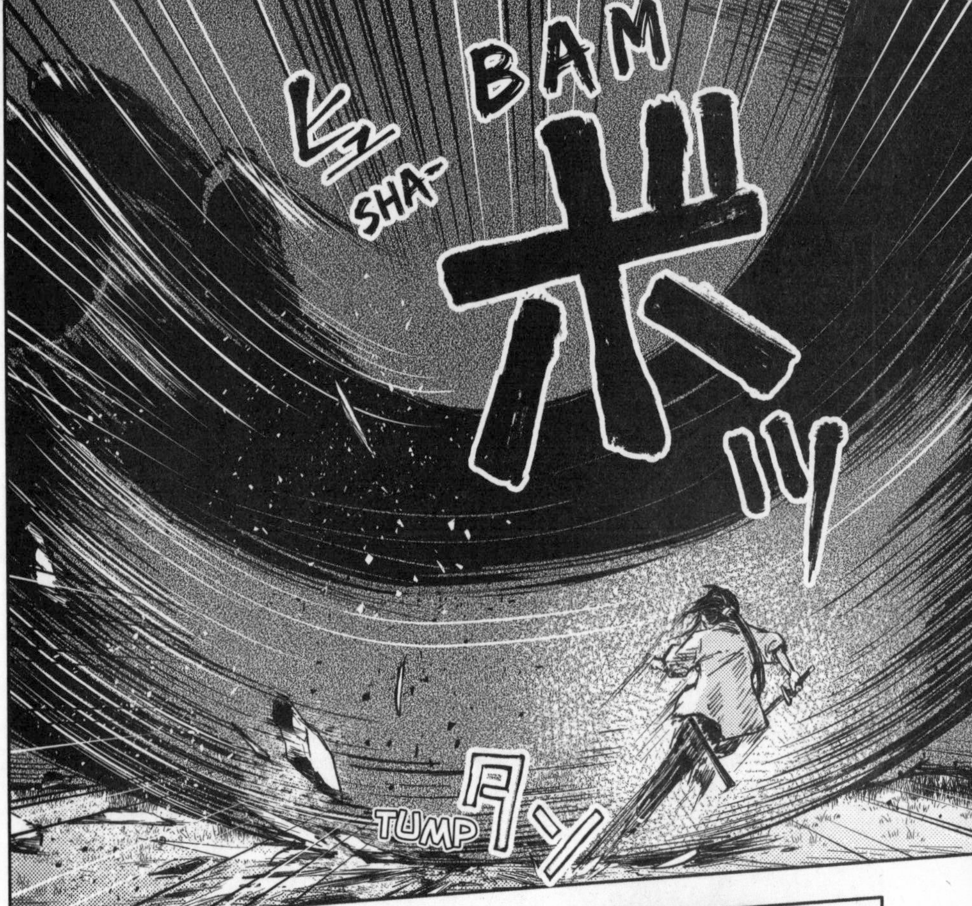
SHA-
BAM
TUMP
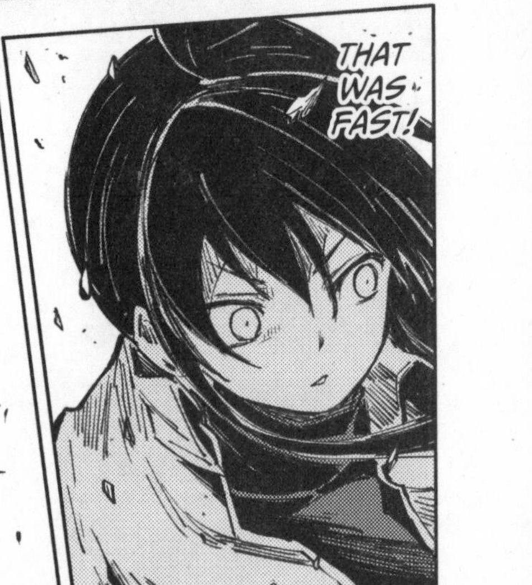
THAT WAS FAST!
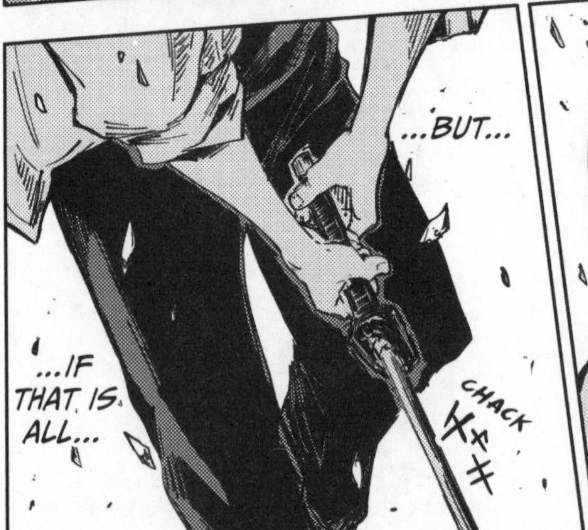
...BUT...
...IF THAT IS ALL...
CHACK

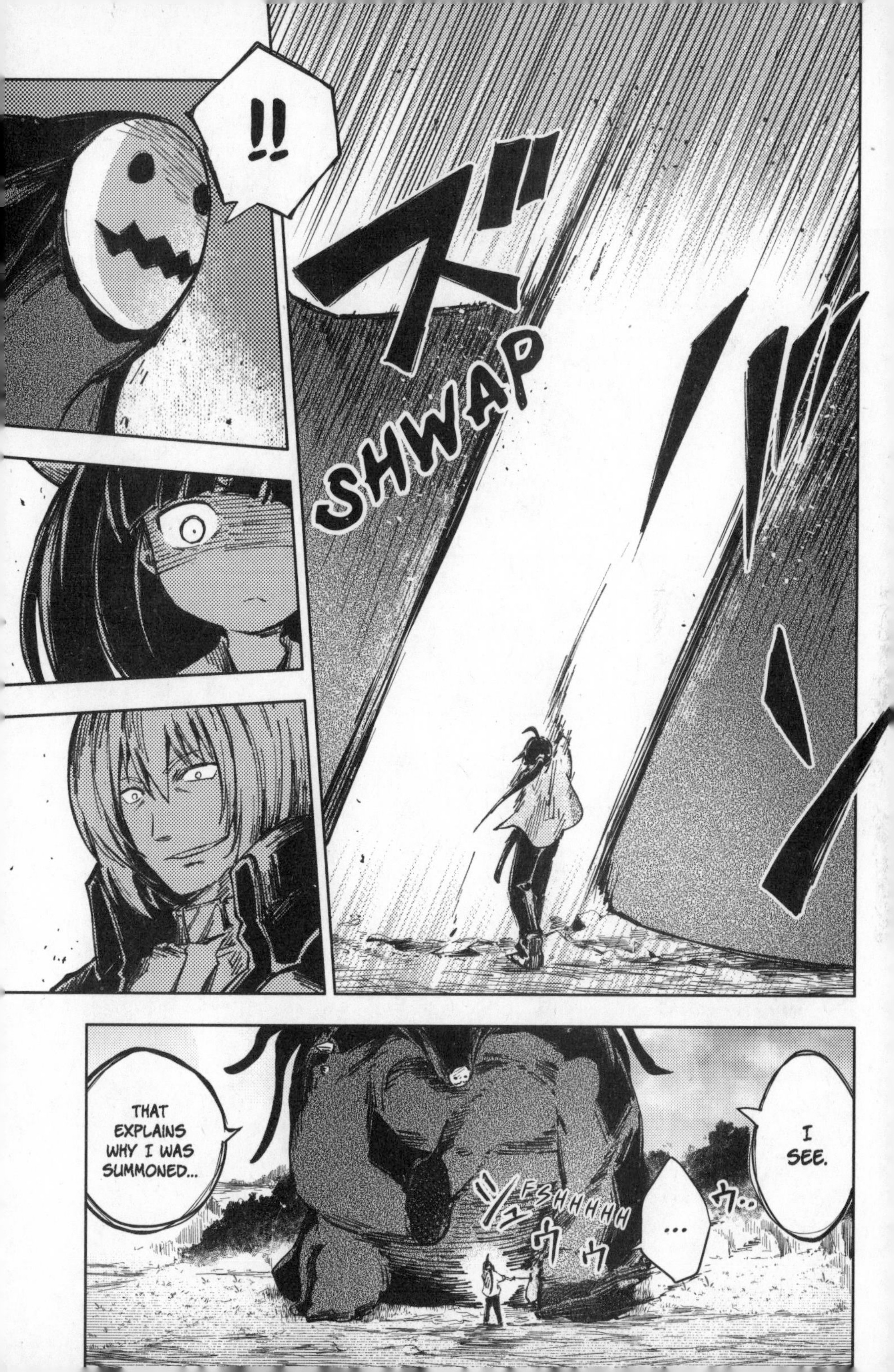

ズ
SHWAP
!!
I SEE.
ウ..
...
シュ FSHHHHH ウウ
THAT EXPLAINS WHY I WAS SUMMONED...

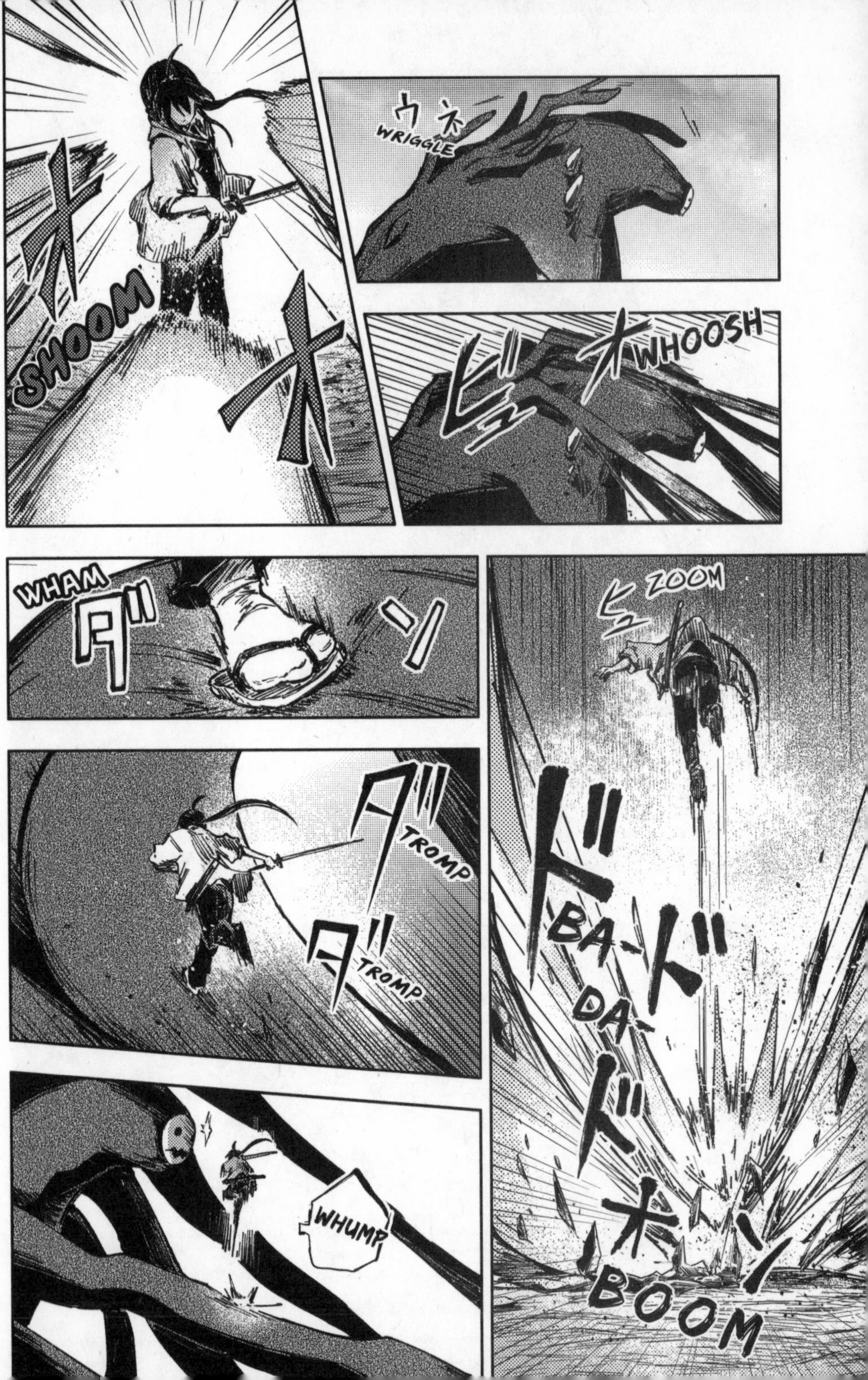

ウネ
WRIGGLE
WHOOSH
SHOOM
ZOOM
BA-DA-BOOM
WHAM
TROMP
TROMP
WHUMP

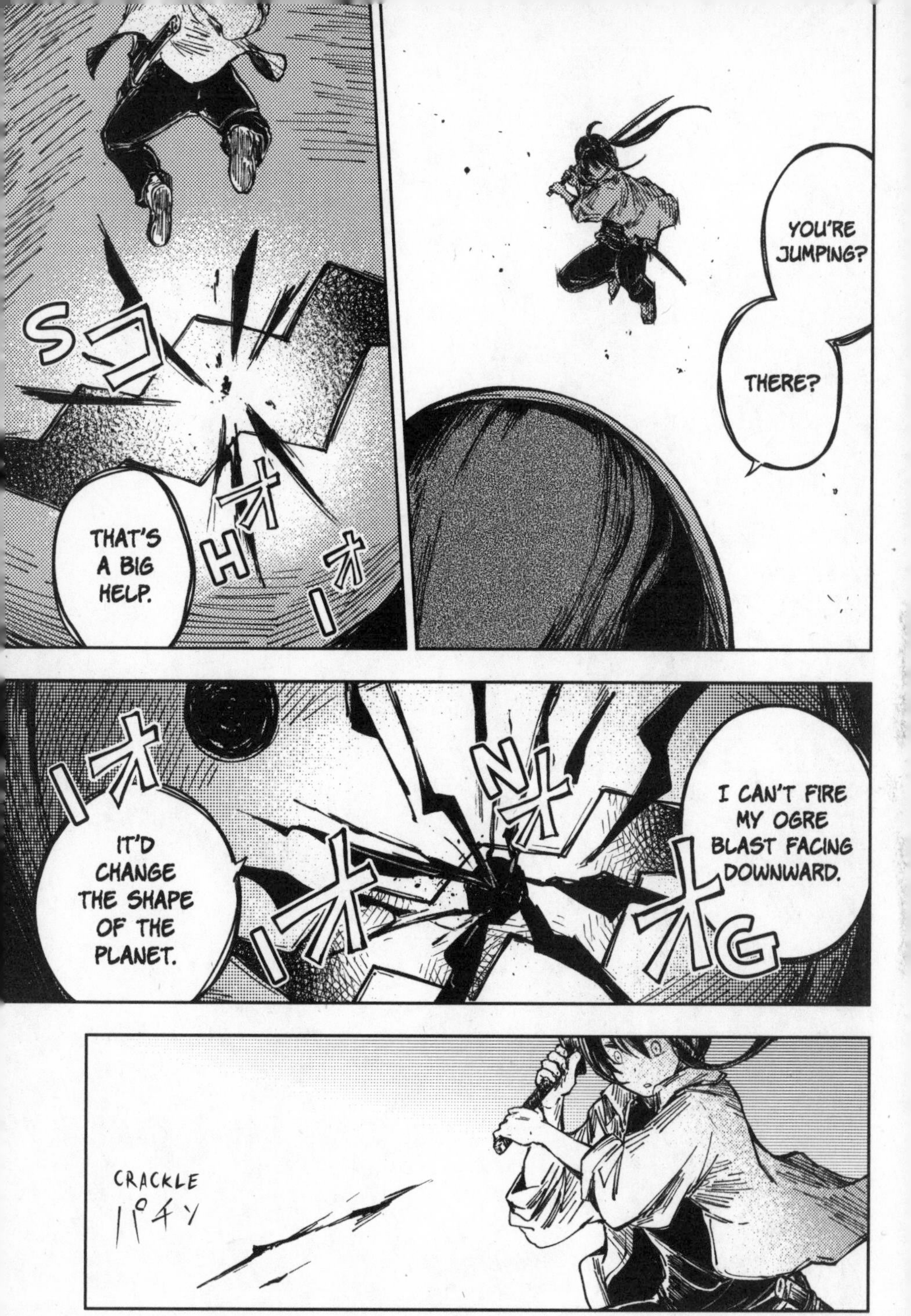

YOU'RE JUMPING?
THERE?
S
THAT'S A BIG HELP.
H
I
I CAN'T FIRE MY OGRE BLAST FACING DOWNWARD.
N
G
IT'D CHANGE THE SHAPE OF THE PLANET.
CRACKLE
パチッ

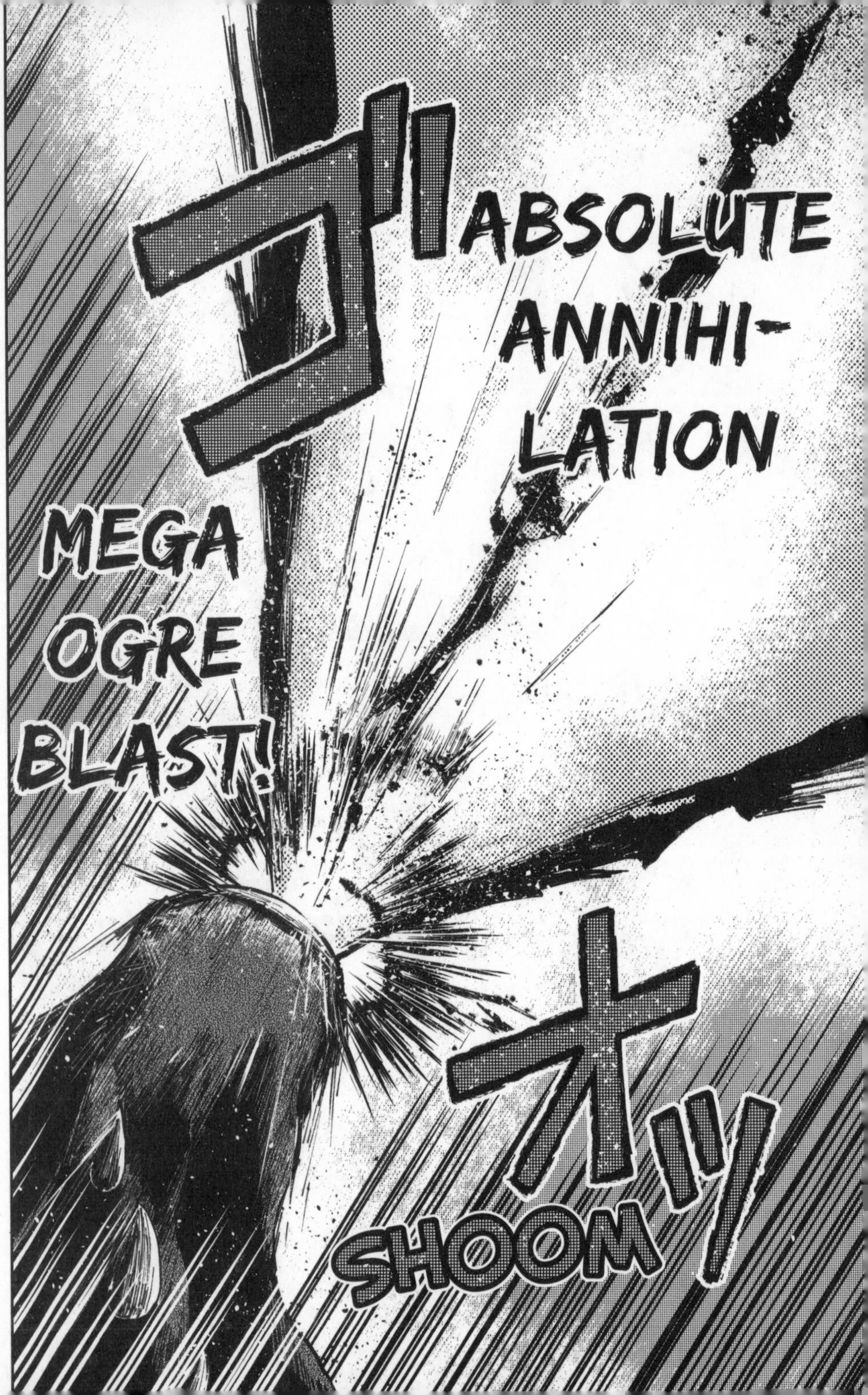
ABSOLUTE ANNIHI-LATION
MEGA OGRE BLAST!
SHOOM

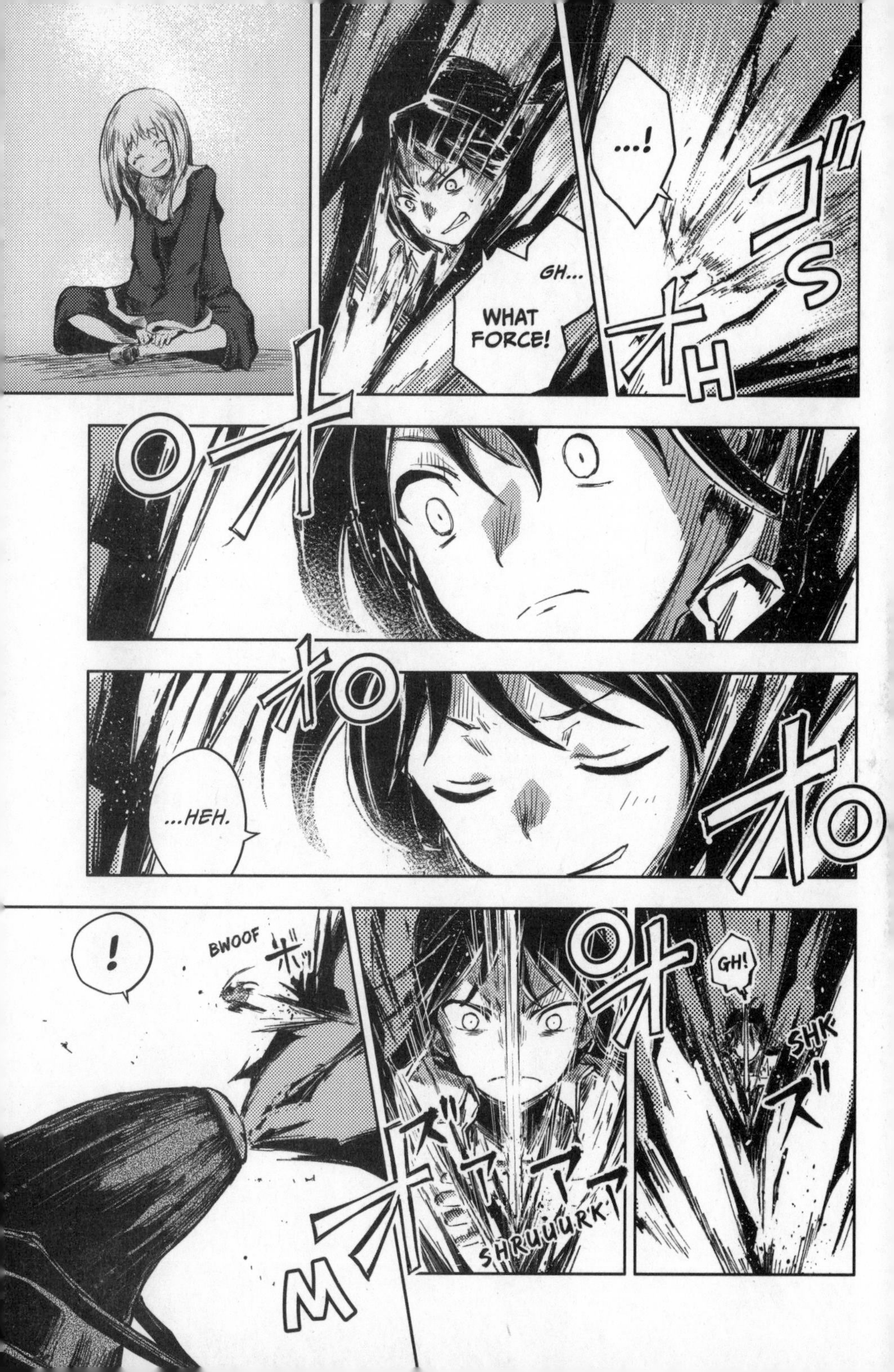

...!
ゴ
S
GH...
WHAT FORCE!
オ
H
オ
オ
...HEH.
オ
GH!
SHK
ズ
ズァァァ
SHRUUUURK
オ
M
!
BWOOF
ボッ

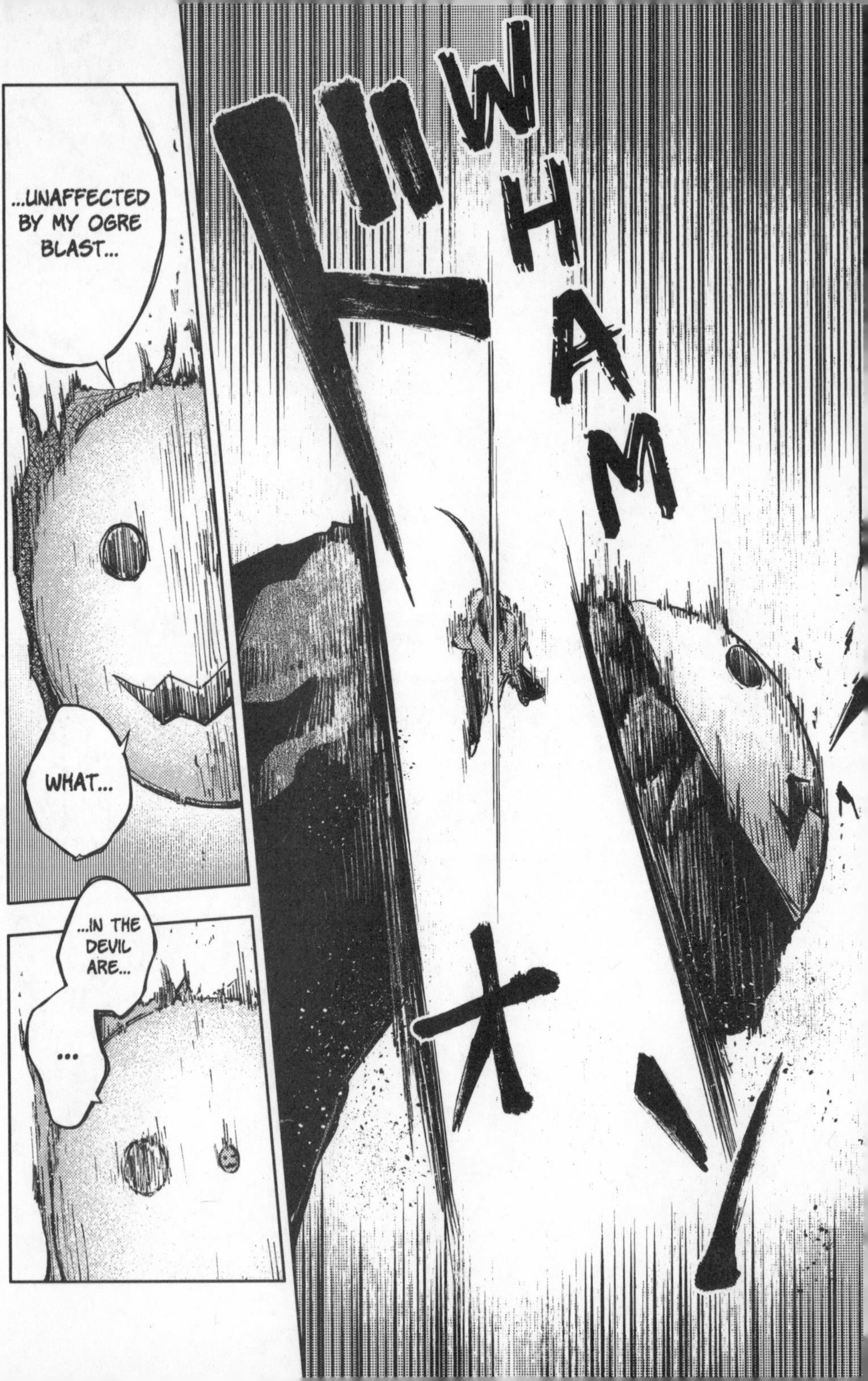
WHAM
...UNAFFECTED BY MY OGRE BLAST...
WHAT...
...IN THE DEVIL ARE...
...

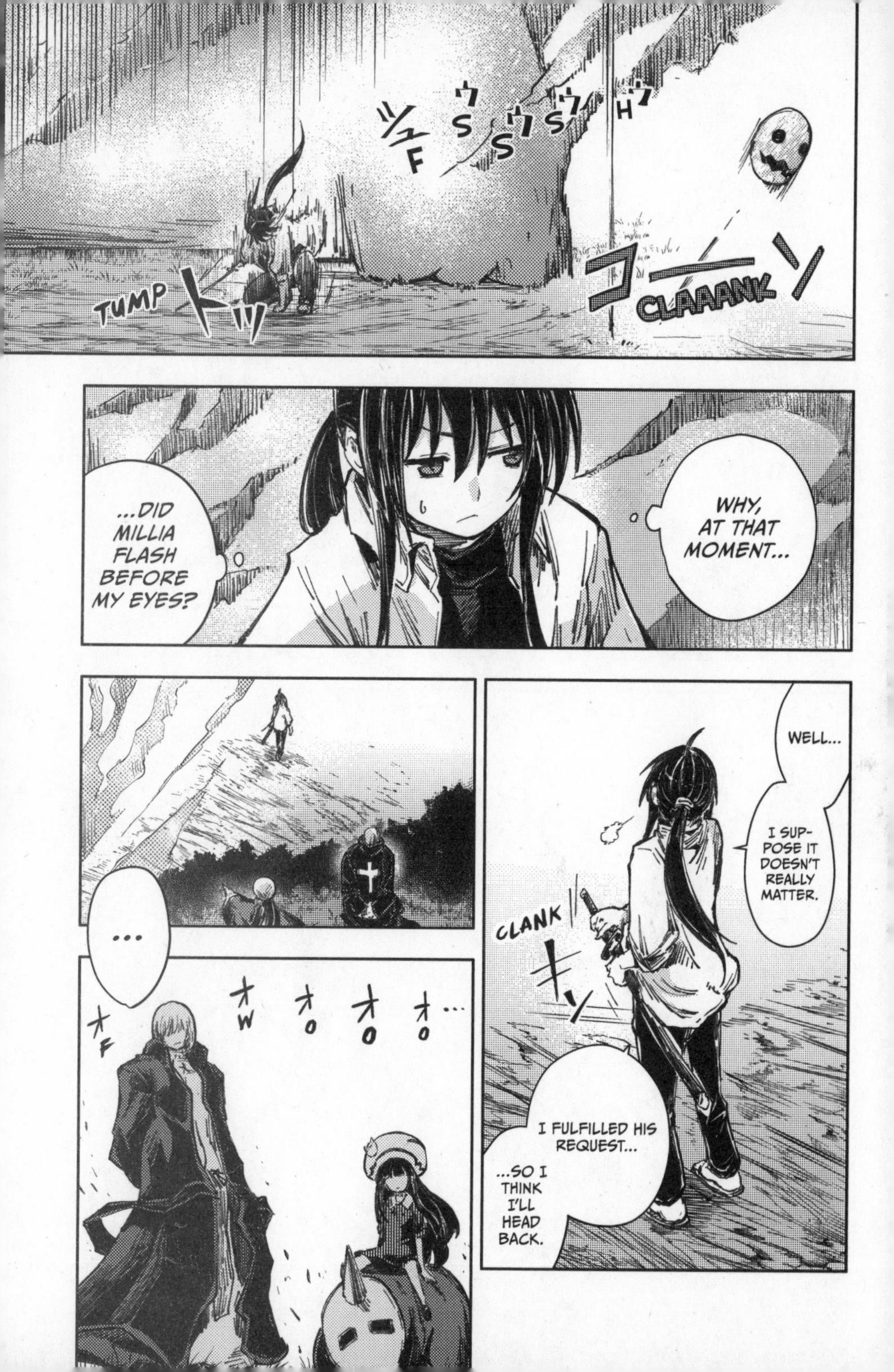

FSSSH
CLAAANK
TUMP
WHY, AT THAT MOMENT...
...DID MILLIA FLASH BEFORE MY EYES?
WELL...
I SUPPOSE IT DOESN'T REALLY MATTER.
CLANK
I FULFILLED HIS REQUEST...
...SO I THINK I'LL HEAD BACK.
...
FWOOO...

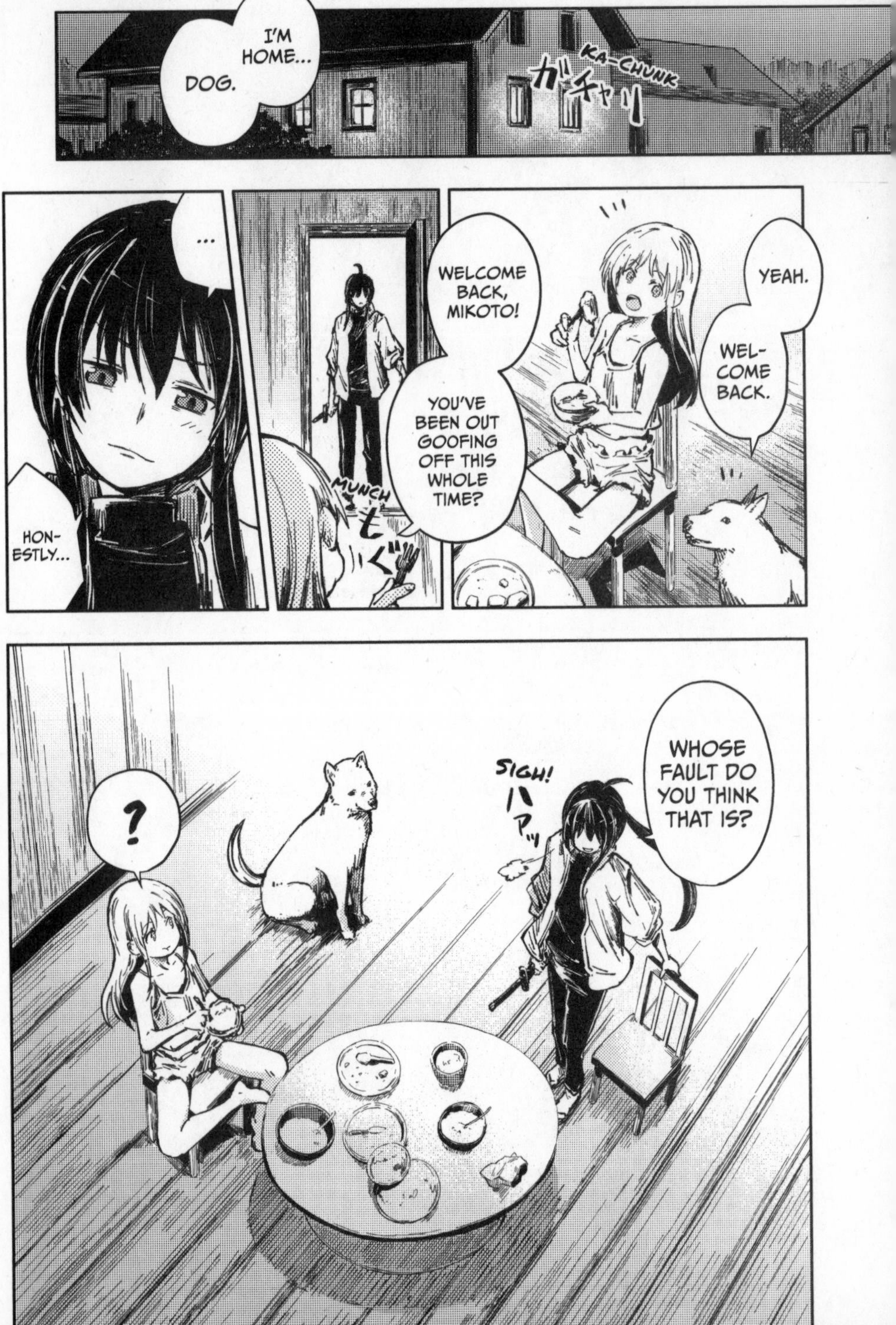
KA-CHUNK
ガチャリ
I'M HOME... DOG.
YEAH.
WEL-COME BACK.
WELCOME BACK, MIKOTO!
YOU'VE BEEN OUT GOOFING OFF THIS WHOLE TIME?
MUNCH
もぐ
...
HON-ESTLY...
WHOSE FAULT DO YOU THINK THAT IS?
SIGH!
ハアッ
?

Good
job.

Ahhhh,
he's so
scary!

PEACH BOY
RIVERSIDE

Chapter 27: Harefolk and Harefolk

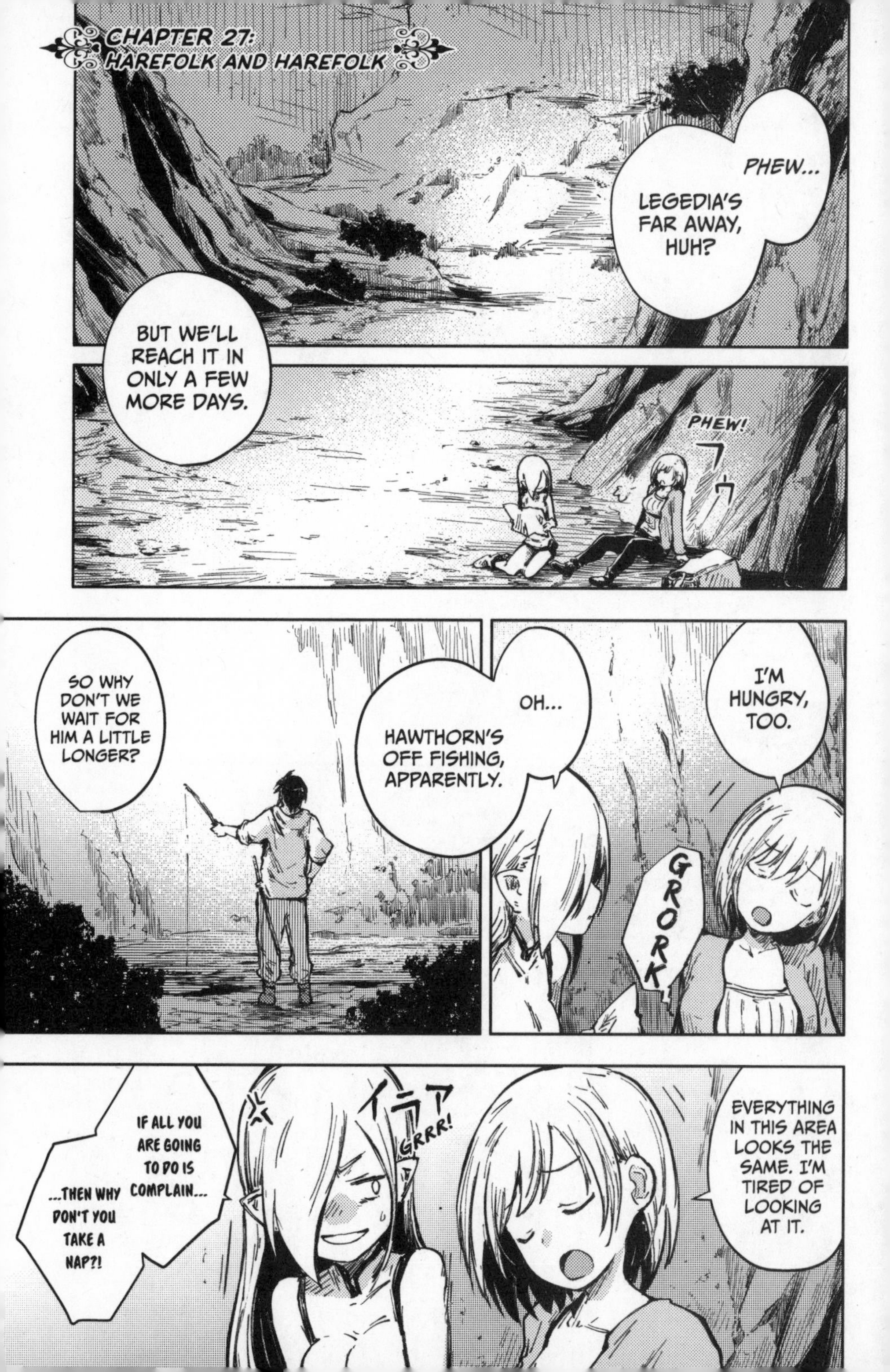
PHEW...
LEGEDIA'S FAR AWAY, HUH?
BUT WE'LL REACH IT IN ONLY A FEW MORE DAYS.
PHEW!
I'M HUNGRY, TOO.
GRORK
OH...
HAWTHORN'S OFF FISHING, APPARENTLY.
SO WHY DON'T WE WAIT FOR HIM A LITTLE LONGER?
EVERYTHING IN THIS AREA LOOKS THE SAME. I'M TIRED OF LOOKING AT IT.
GRRR!
IF ALL YOU ARE GOING TO DO IS COMPLAIN...
...THEN WHY DON'T YOU TAKE A NAP?!

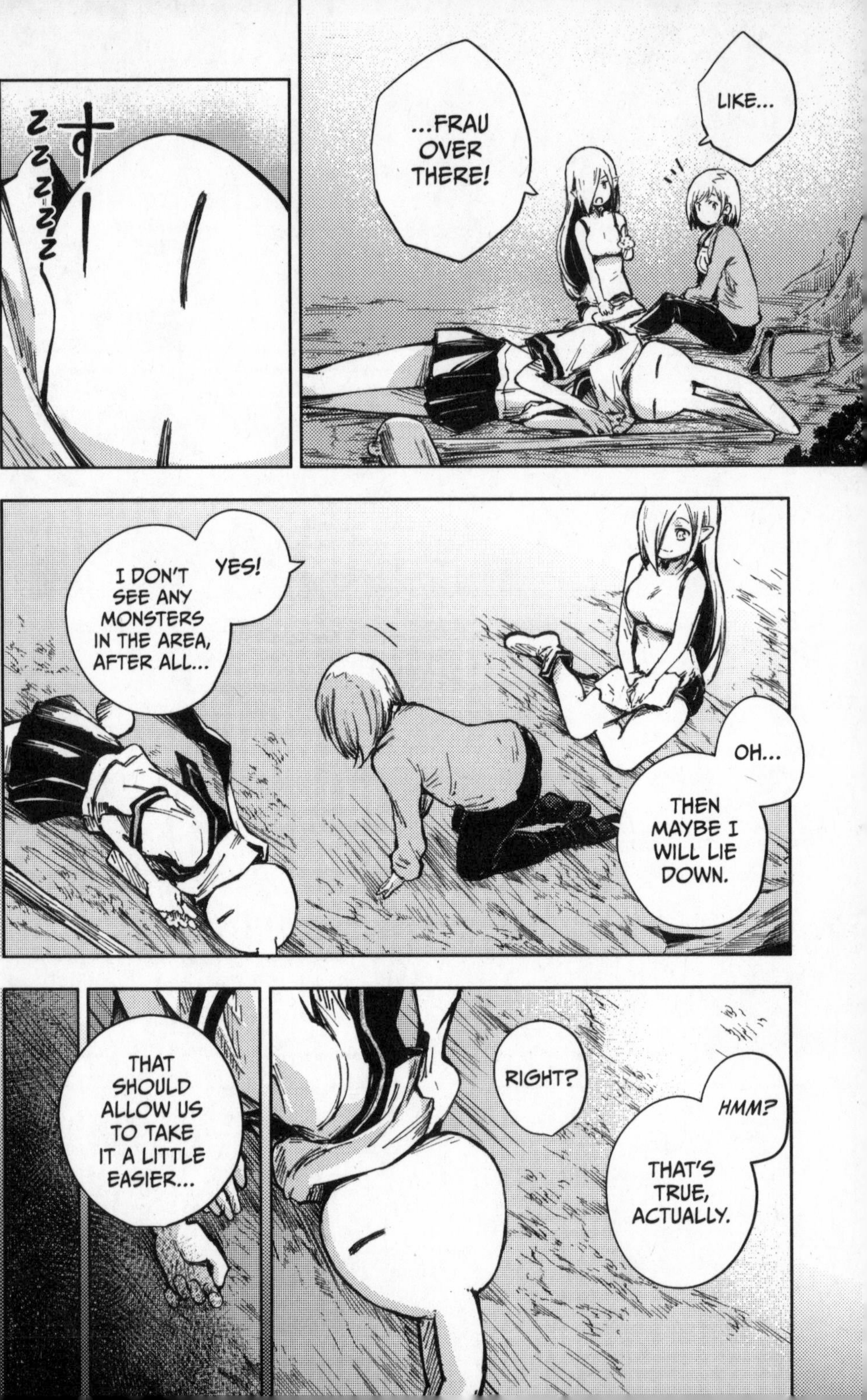
LIKE...
...FRAU OVER THERE!
すー
ZZZZZ
YES!
I DON'T SEE ANY MONSTERS IN THE AREA, AFTER ALL...
OH...
THEN MAYBE I WILL LIE DOWN.
RIGHT?
HMM?
THAT'S TRUE, ACTUALLY.
THAT SHOULD ALLOW US TO TAKE IT A LITTLE EASIER...

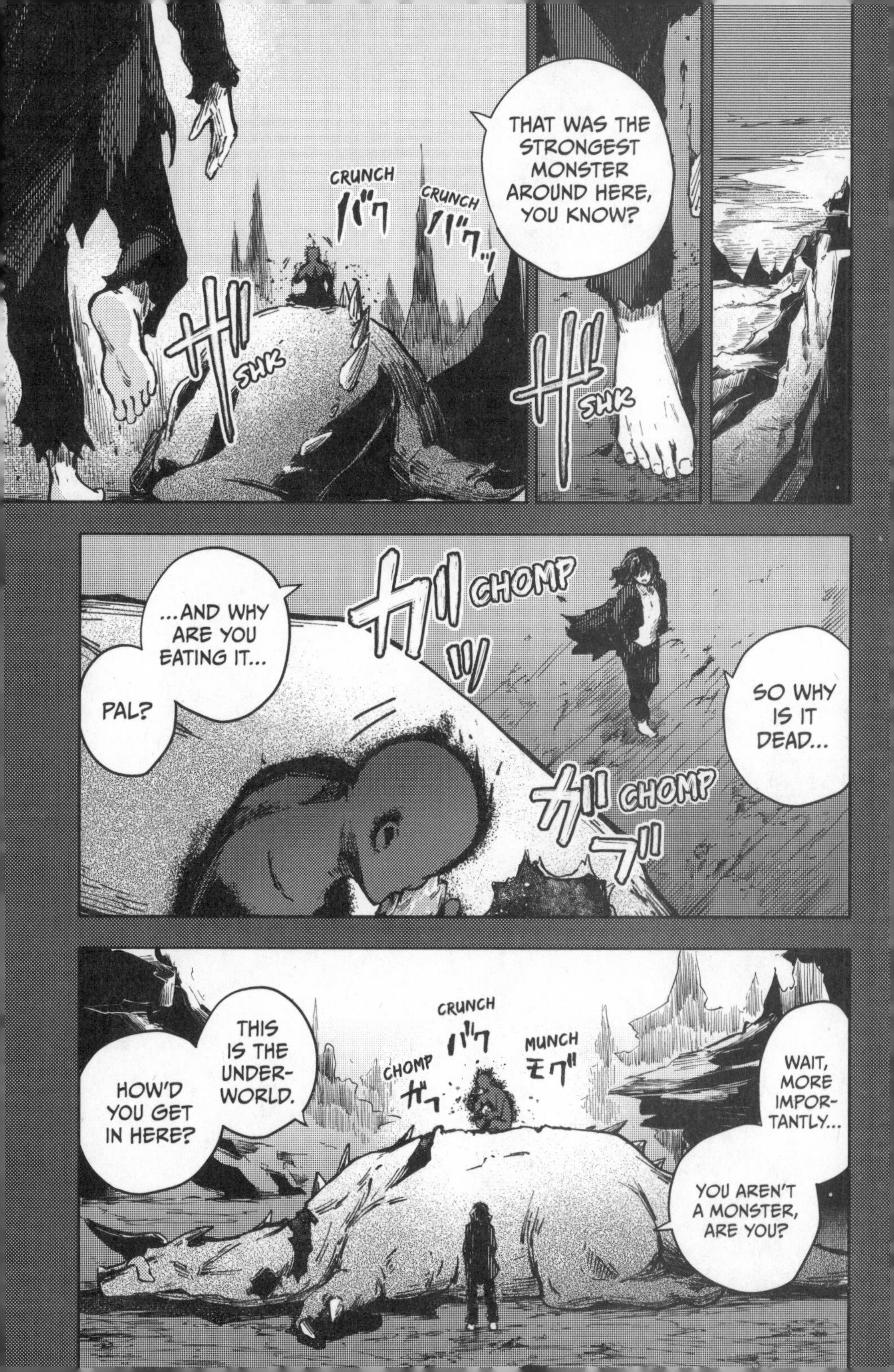

THAT WAS THE STRONGEST MONSTER AROUND HERE, YOU KNOW?
ザッ SHK
CRUNCH バク
CRUNCH バクッ
ザッ SHK
SO WHY IS IT DEAD...
ガリッ CHOMP
...AND WHY ARE YOU EATING IT...
PAL?
ガリッ CHOMP
WAIT, MORE IMPORTANTLY...
YOU AREN'T A MONSTER, ARE YOU?
MUNCH モグ
CRUNCH バク
CHOMP ガブ
THIS IS THE UNDERWORLD.
HOW'D YOU GET IN HERE?

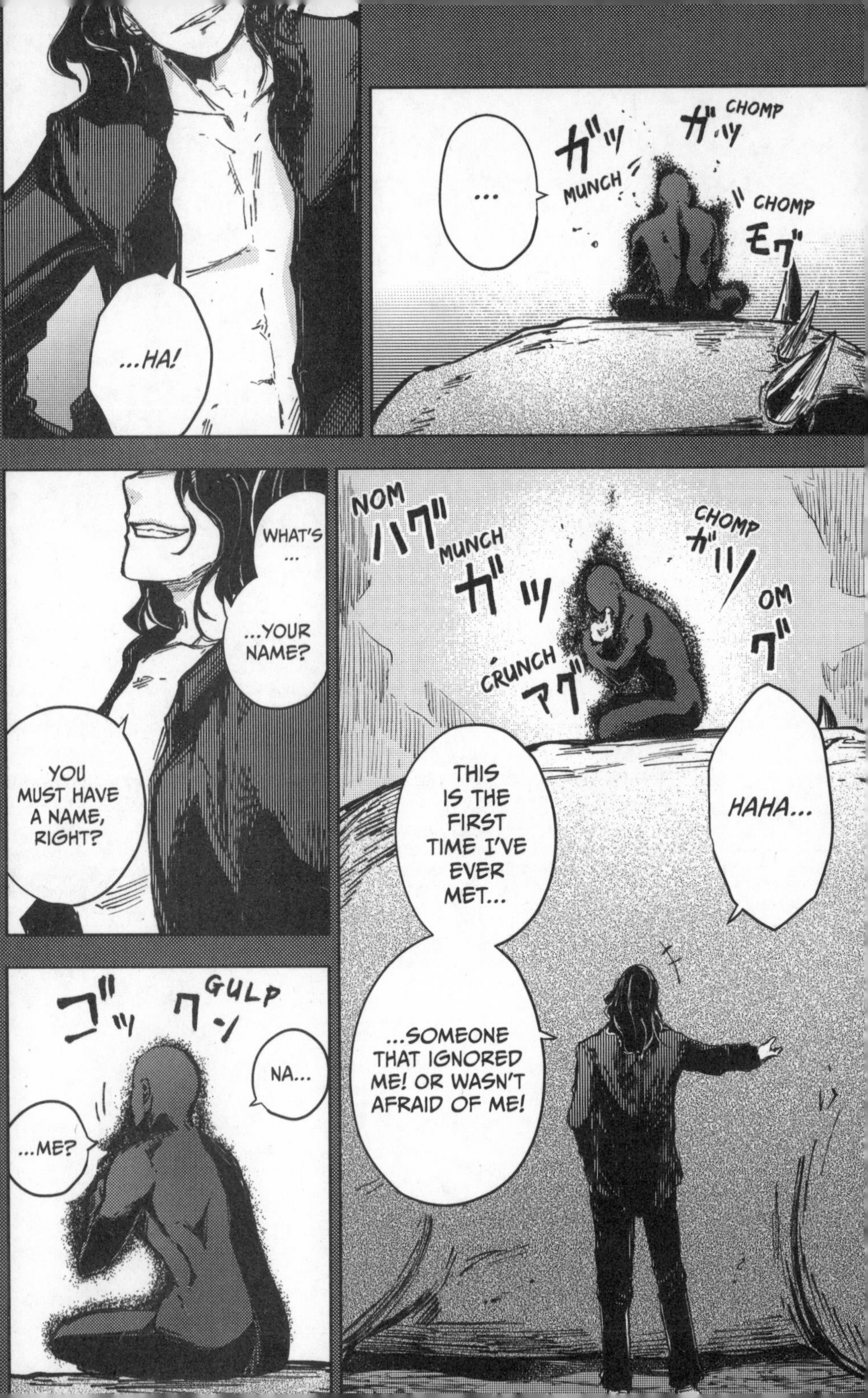

ガッ
CHOMP
ガッ
MUNCH
CHOMP
モグ
...
...HA!
NOM
ハグ
MUNCH
ガッ
CHOMP
ガリッ
OM
グ
CRUNCH
アグ
HAHA...
THIS IS THE FIRST TIME I'VE EVER MET...
...SOMEONE THAT IGNORED ME! OR WASN'T AFRAID OF ME!
WHAT'S ...
...YOUR NAME?
YOU MUST HAVE A NAME, RIGHT?
ゴッ
GULP
クン
NA...
...ME?

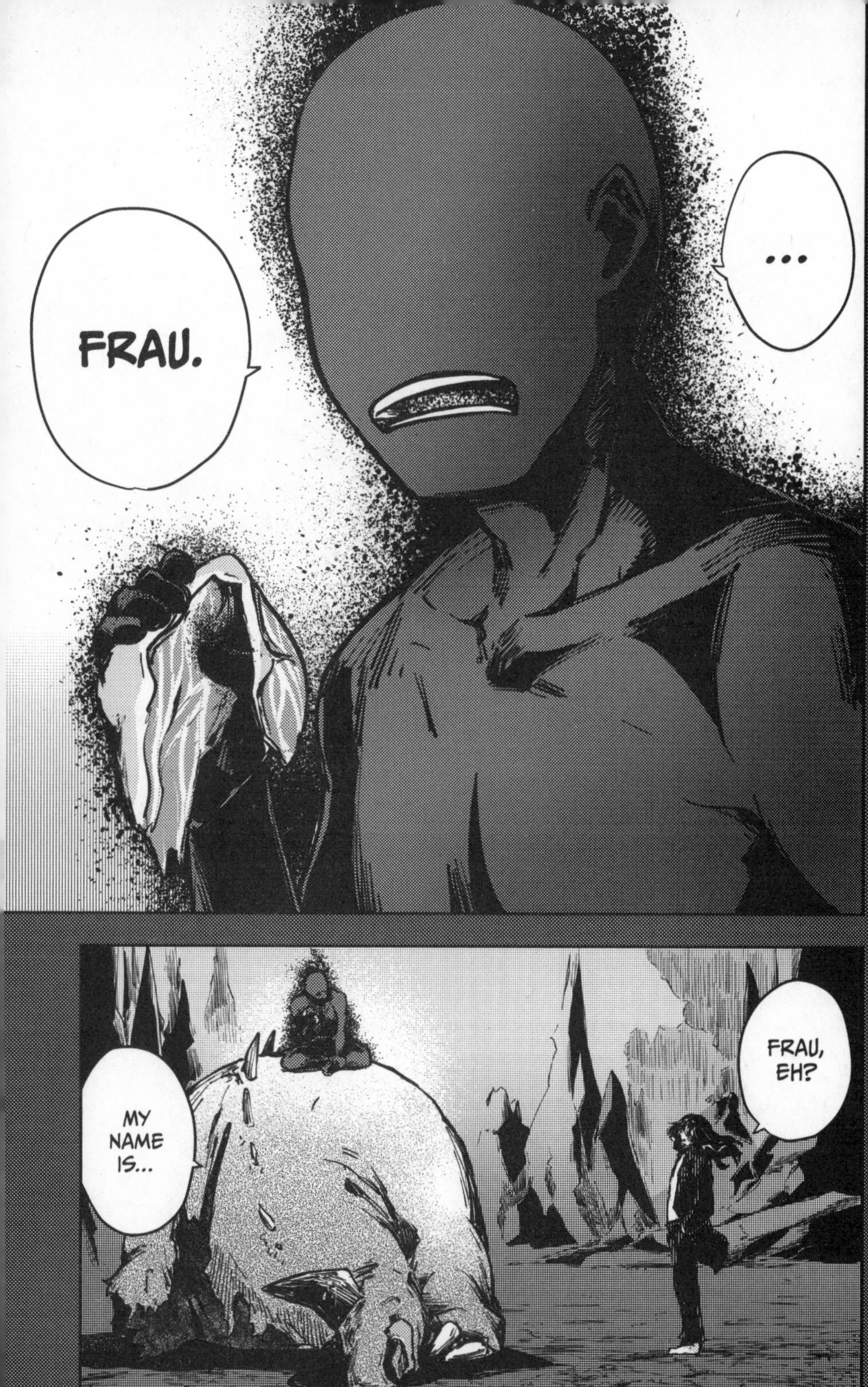
...
FRAU.
FRAU, EH?
MY NAME IS...

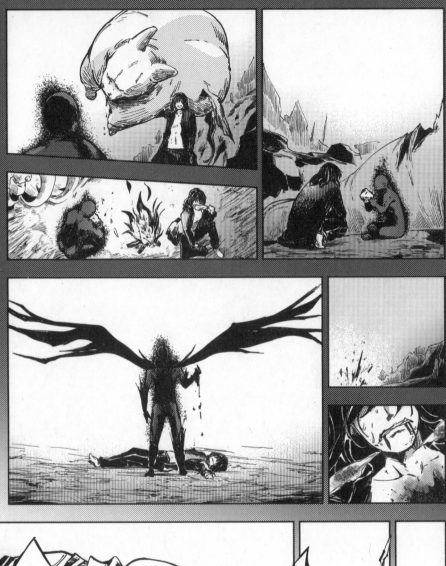

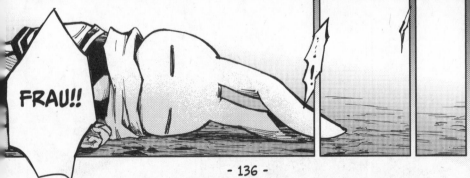

FRAU!!

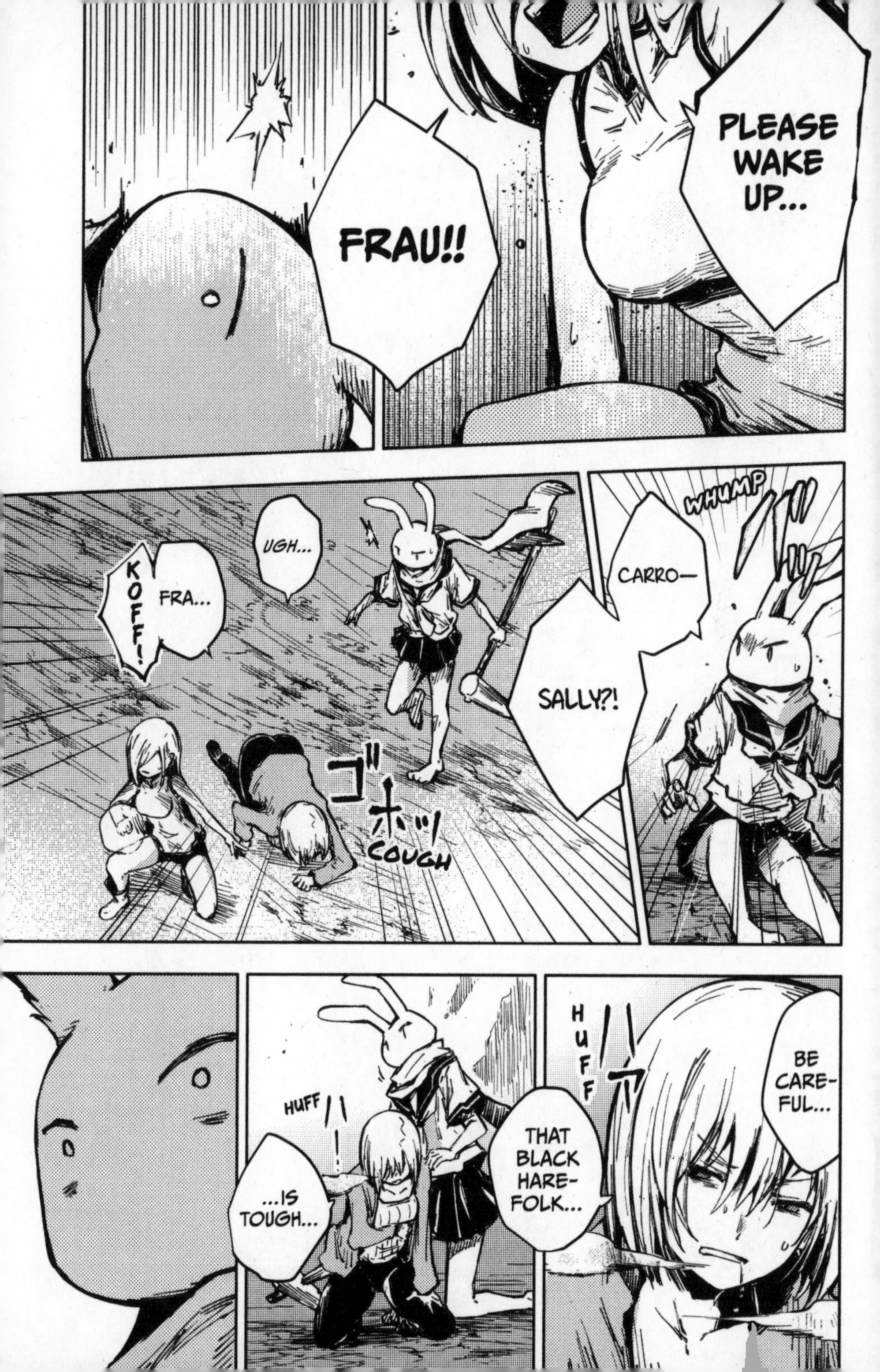
PLEASE WAKE UP...
FRAU!!
WHUMP
CARRO—
SALLY?!
UGH...
FRA...
KOFF!
ゴホッ
COUGH
HUFF
BE CARE-FUL...
THAT BLACK HARE-FOLK...
HUFF
...IS TOUGH...

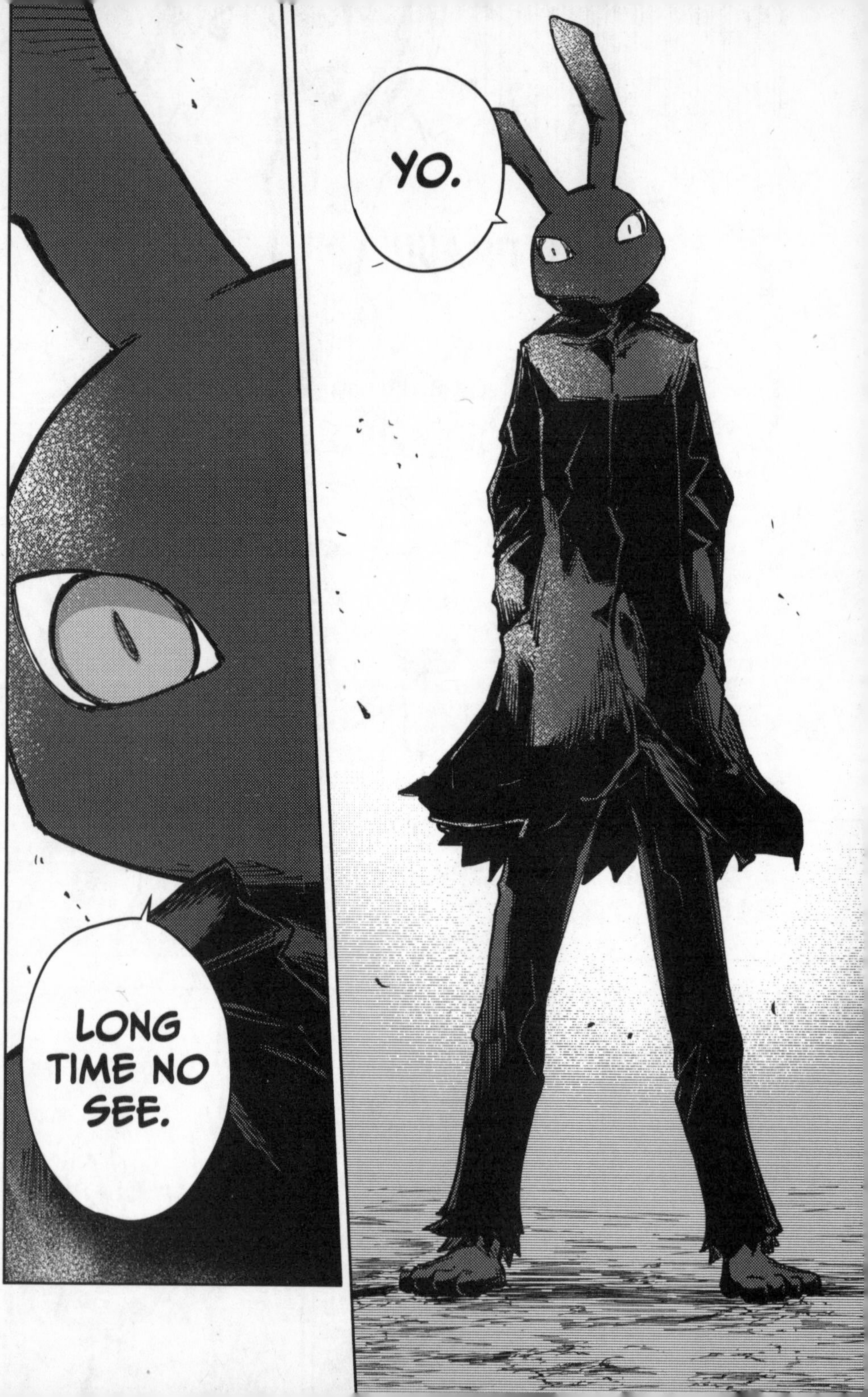
YO.
LONG TIME NO SEE.

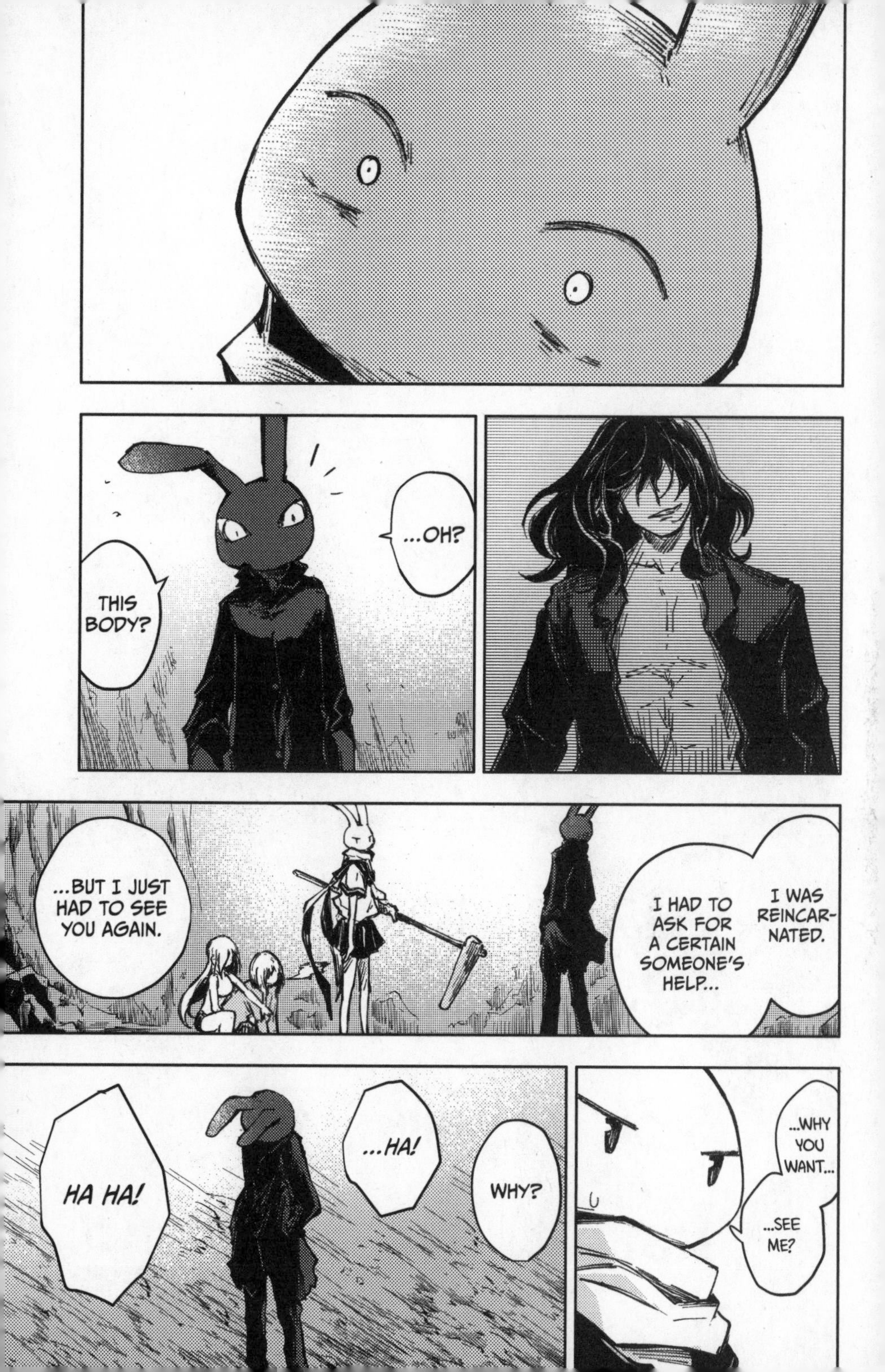
...OH?
THIS BODY?
I WAS REINCAR-NATED.
I HAD TO ASK FOR A CERTAIN SOMEONE'S HELP...
...BUT I JUST HAD TO SEE YOU AGAIN.
...WHY YOU WANT...
...SEE ME?
WHY?
...HA!
HA HA!

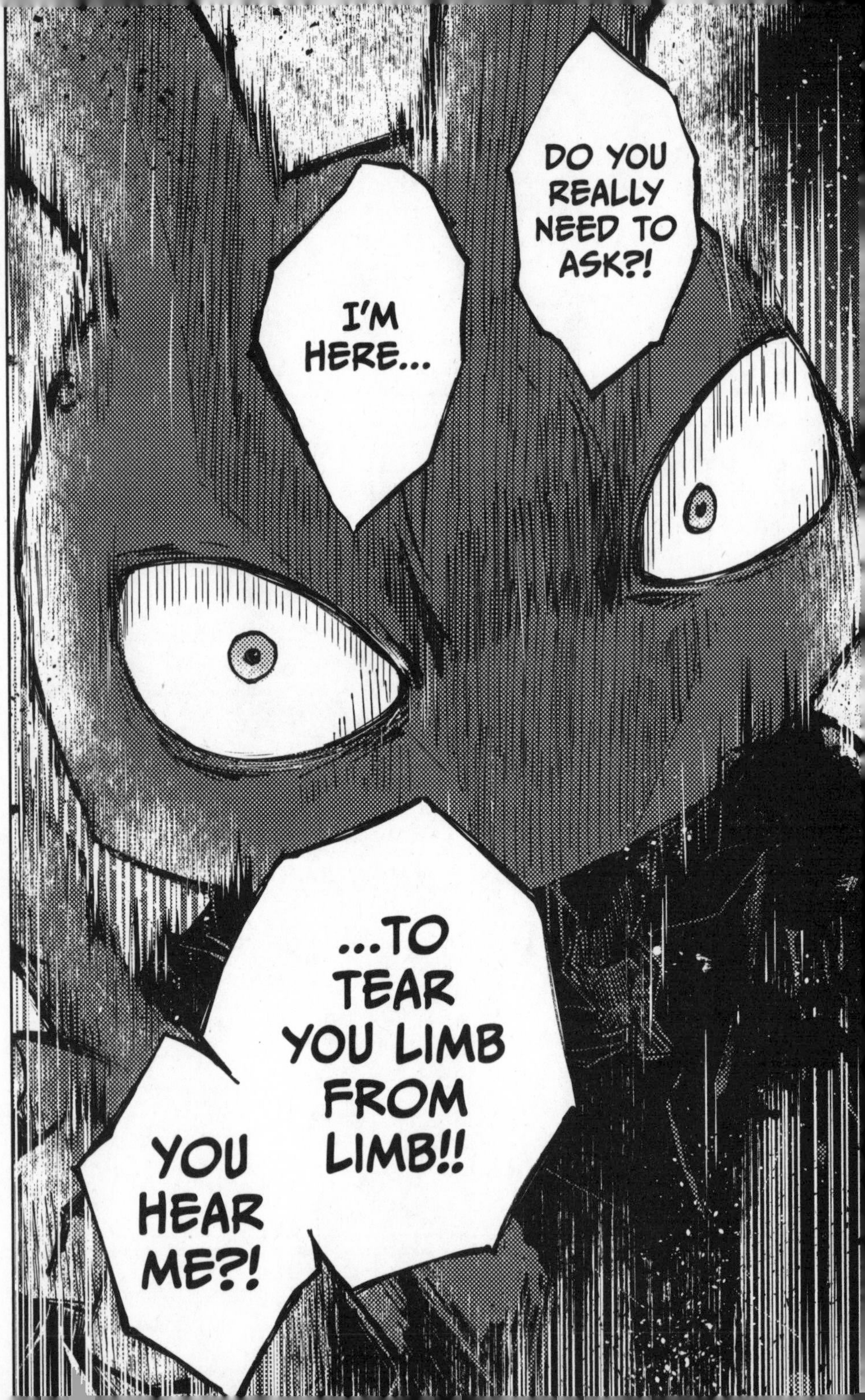
DO YOU REALLY NEED TO ASK?!
I'M HERE...
...TO TEAR YOU LIMB FROM LIMB!!
YOU HEAR ME?!

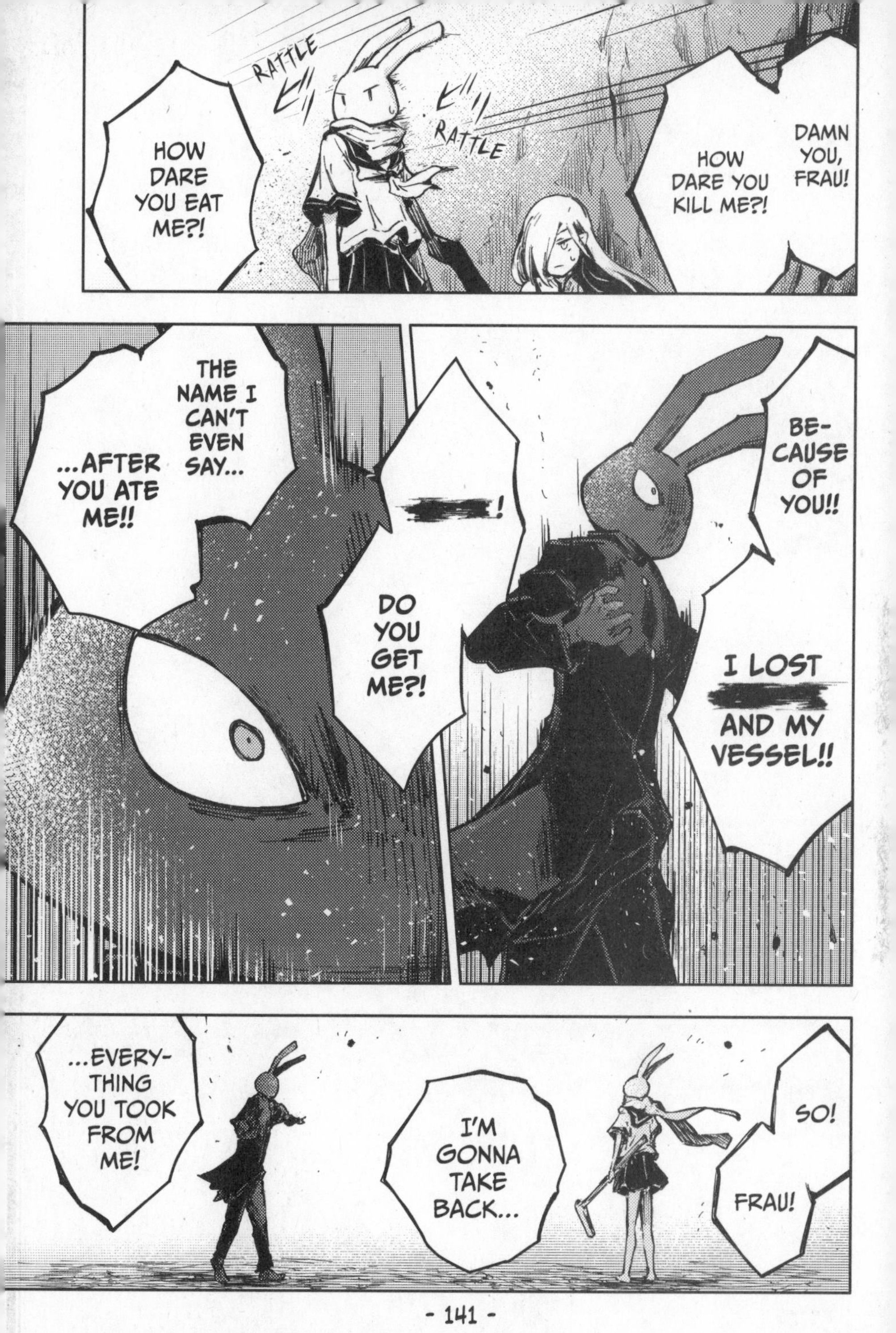
DAMN YOU, FRAU!
HOW DARE YOU KILL ME?!
RATTLE
RATTLE
HOW DARE YOU EAT ME?!
BE-CAUSE OF YOU!!
[redacted]!
I LOST [redacted] AND MY VESSEL!!
DO YOU GET ME?!
THE NAME I CAN'T EVEN SAY...
...AFTER YOU ATE ME!!
SO! FRAU!
I'M GONNA TAKE BACK...
...EVERY-THING YOU TOOK FROM ME!

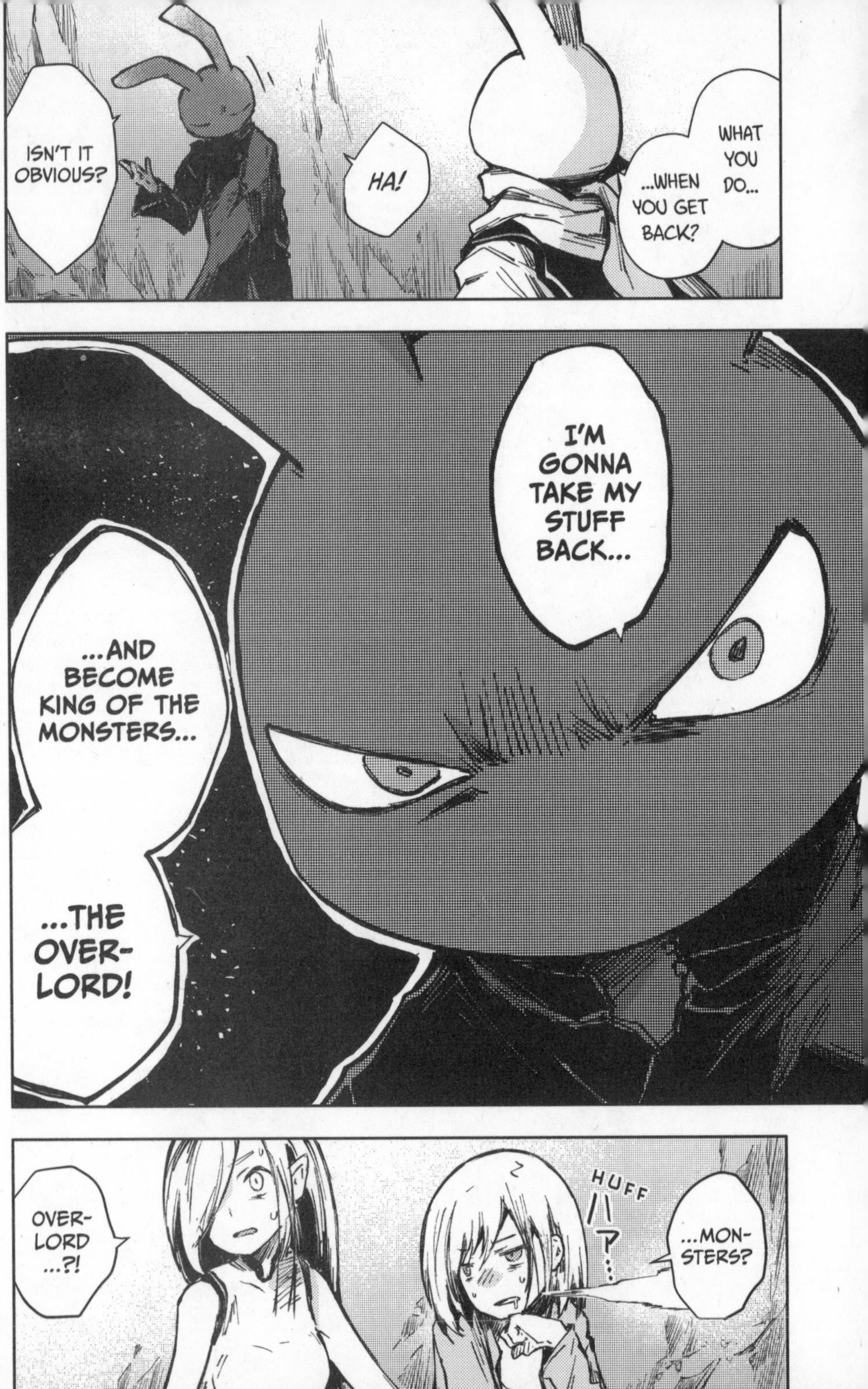
WHAT YOU DO... ...WHEN YOU GET BACK?
HA!
ISN'T IT OBVIOUS?
I'M GONNA TAKE MY STUFF BACK...
...AND BECOME KING OF THE MONSTERS...
...THE OVER-LORD!
...MON-STERS?
HUFF
OVER-LORD ...?!

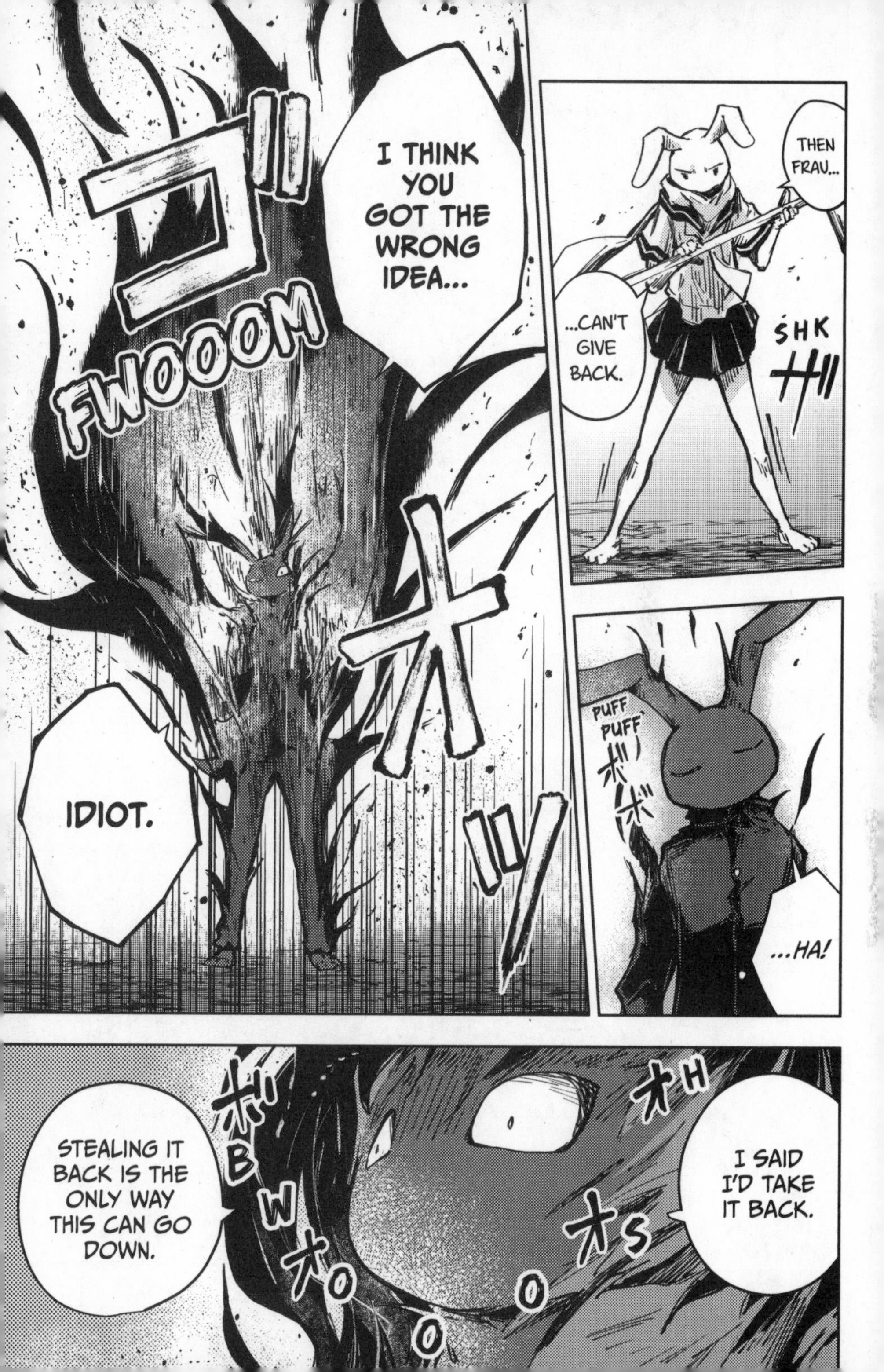
THEN FRAU...
...CAN'T GIVE BACK.
SHK
PUFF PUFF
...HA!
I THINK YOU GOT THE WRONG IDEA...
FWOOOM
IDIOT.
I SAID I'D TAKE IT BACK.
BWOOOSH
STEALING IT BACK IS THE ONLY WAY THIS CAN GO DOWN.

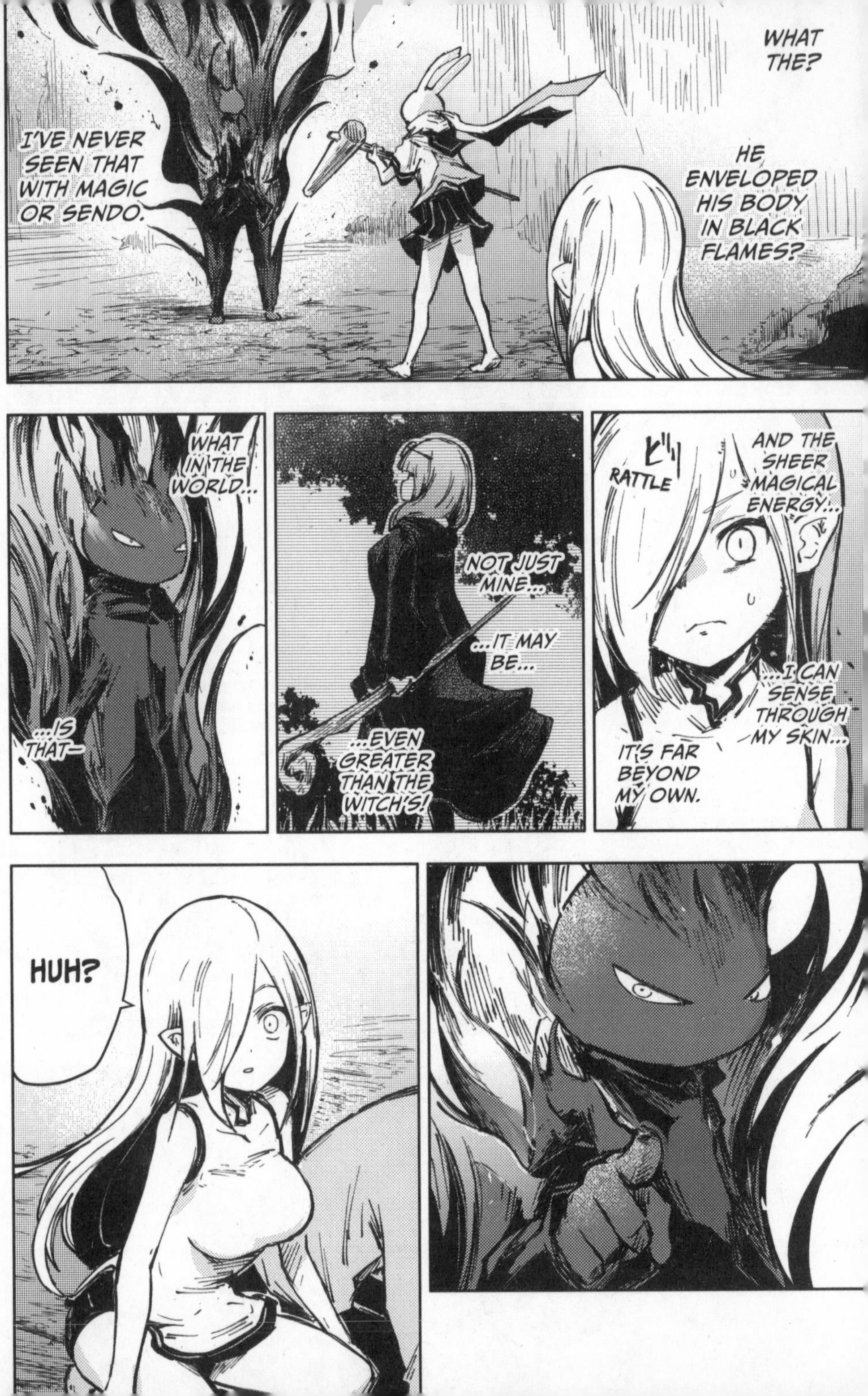
WHAT THE?
HE ENVELOPED HIS BODY IN BLACK FLAMES?
I'VE NEVER SEEN THAT WITH MAGIC OR SENDO.
RATTLE
AND THE SHEER MAGICAL ENERGY...
...I CAN SENSE THROUGH MY SKIN...
IT'S FAR BEYOND MY OWN.
NOT JUST MINE...
...IT MAY BE...
...EVEN GREATER THAN THE WITCH'S!
WHAT IN THE WORLD...
...IS THAT—
HUH?

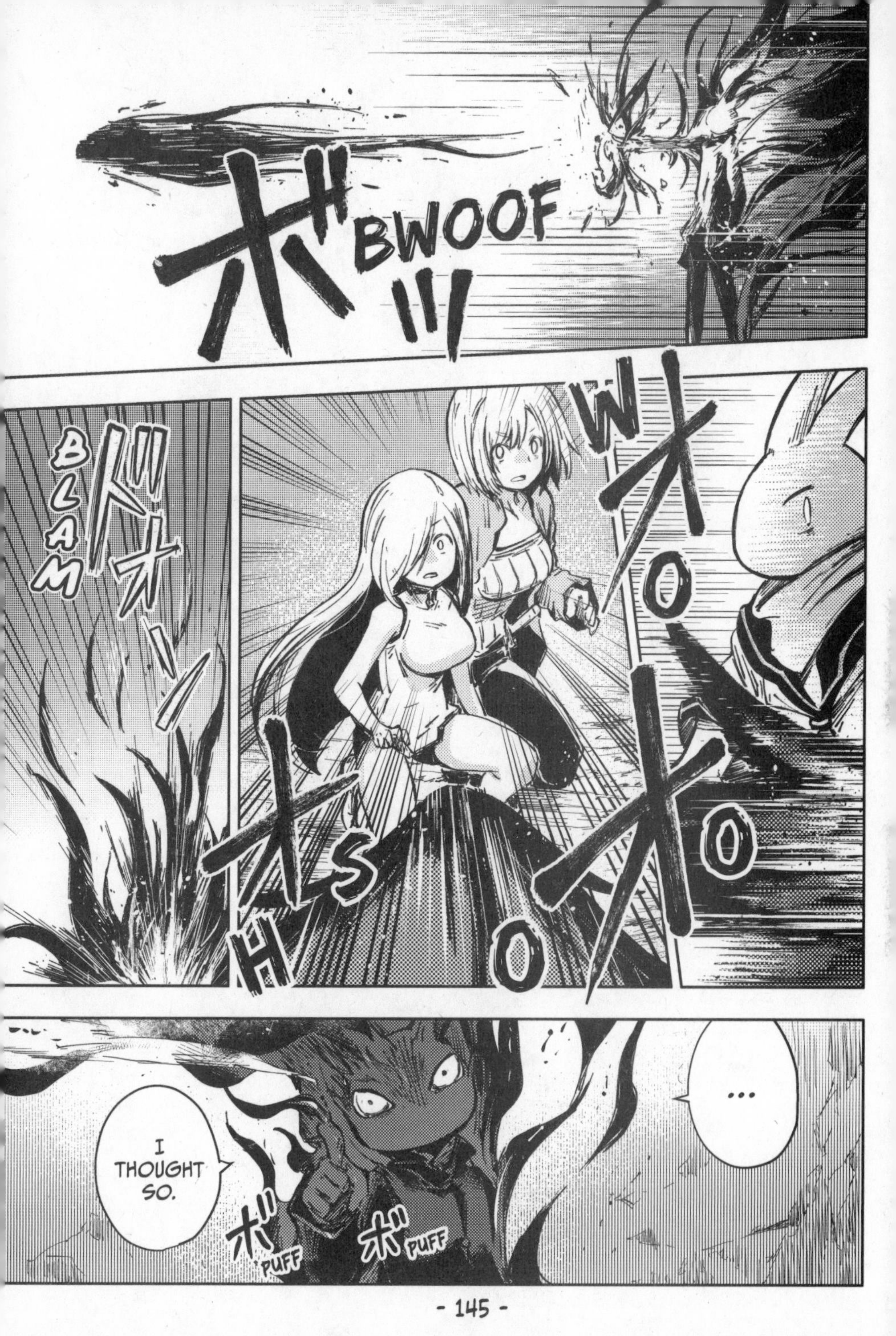

ボッ
BWOOF
WOOOSH
ドォーン
BLAM
...
I THOUGHT SO.
ボ
PUFF
ボ
PUFF

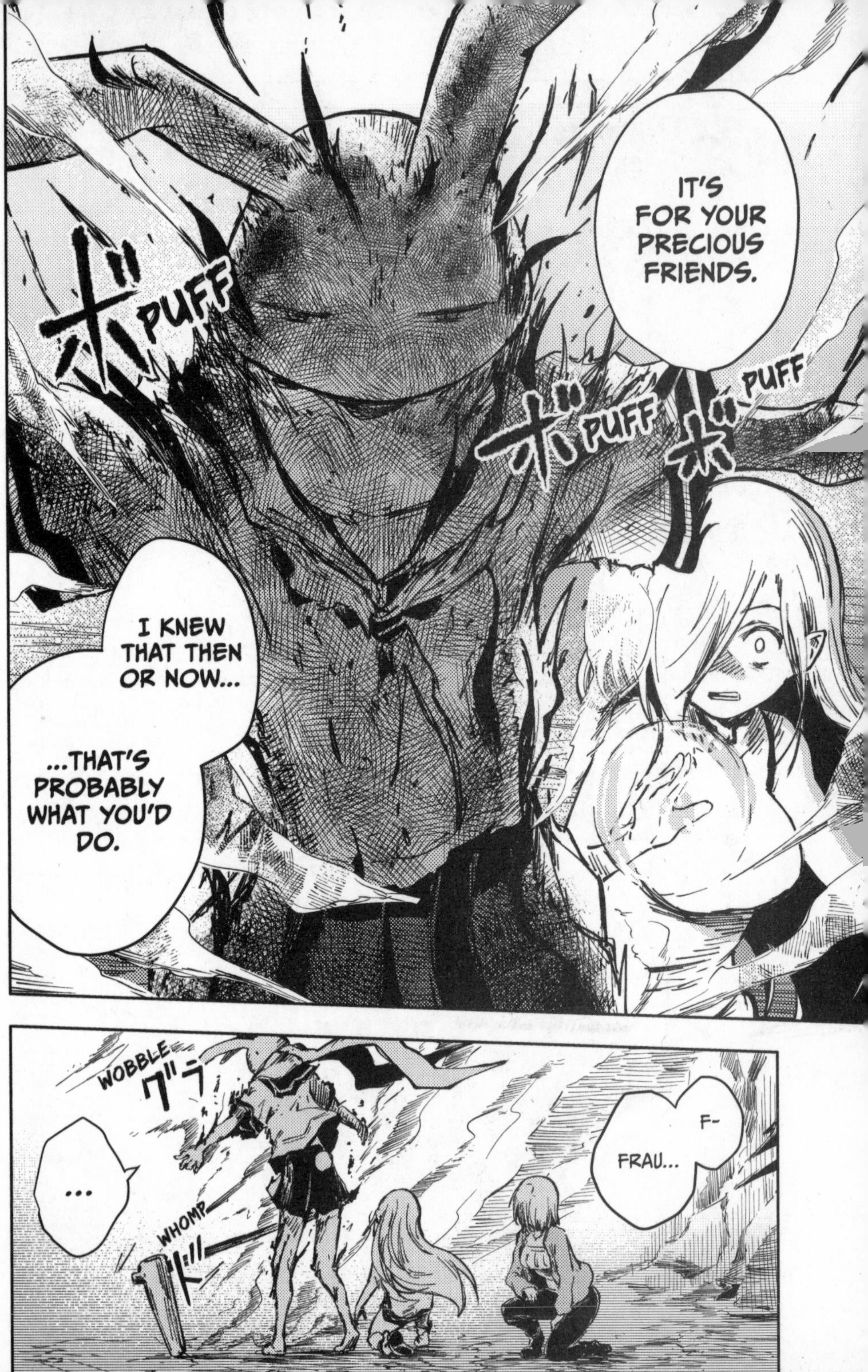
IT'S FOR YOUR PRECIOUS FRIENDS.
PUFF
PUFF
PUFF
PUFF
I KNEW THAT THEN OR NOW...
...THAT'S PROBABLY WHAT YOU'D DO.
F- FRAU...
WOBBLE
...
WHOMP

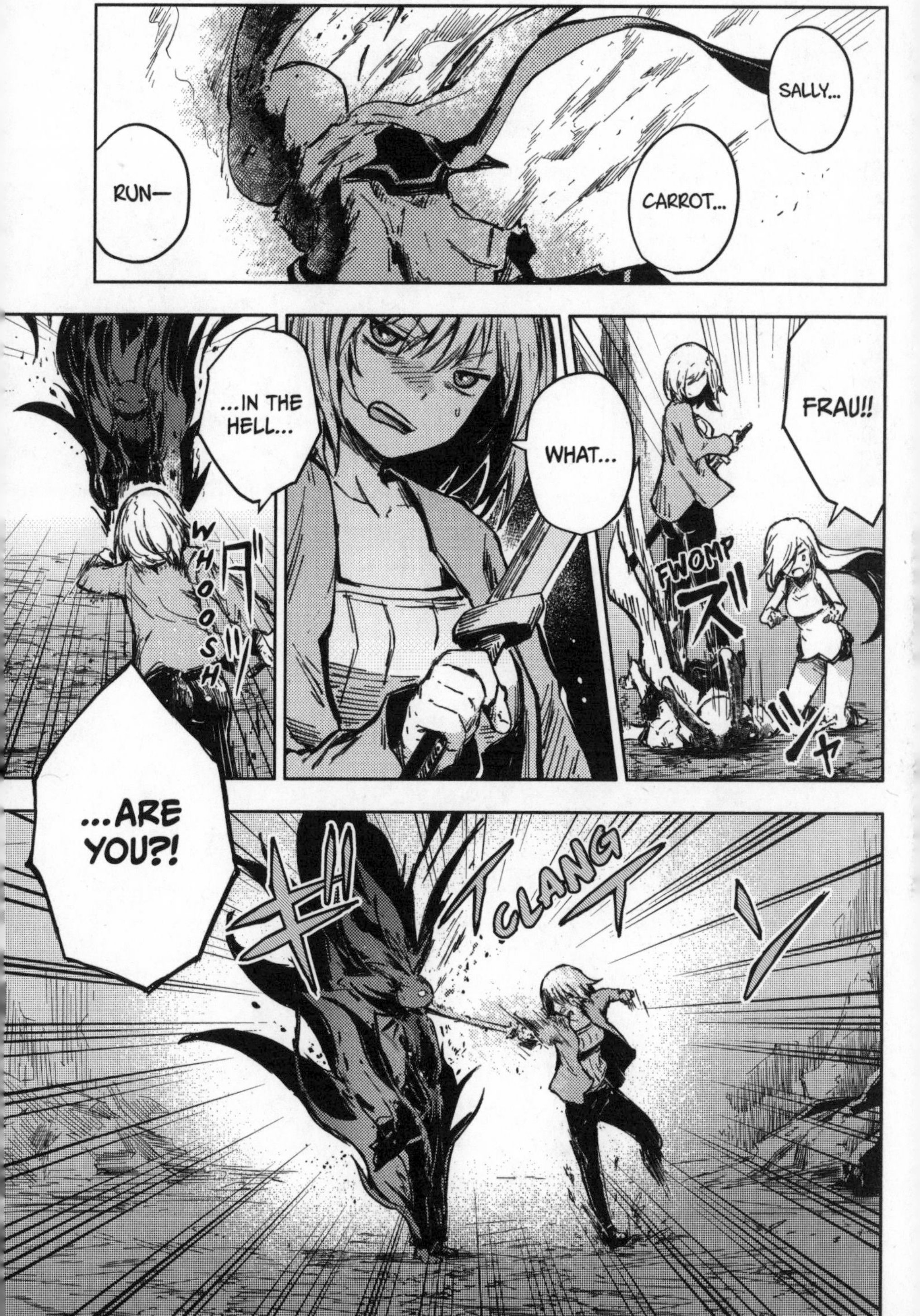
SALLY...
CARROT...
RUN—
FRAU!!
FWOMP
ズ
WHAT...
...IN THE HELL...
WHOOSH
...ARE YOU?!
CLANG

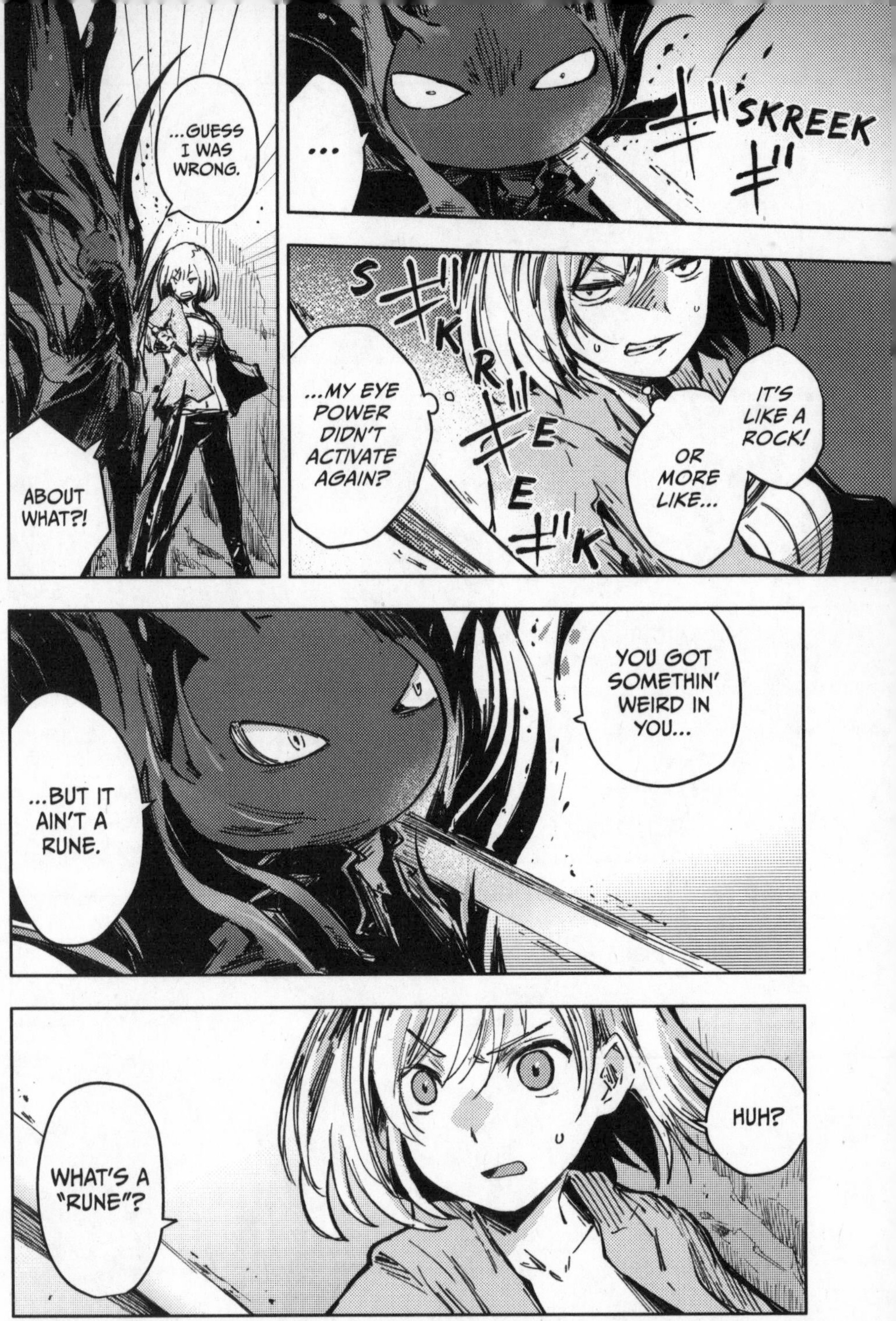
...
SKREEK
IT'S LIKE A ROCK!
OR MORE LIKE...
SKREEK
...MY EYE POWER DIDN'T ACTIVATE AGAIN?
...GUESS I WAS WRONG.
ABOUT WHAT?!
YOU GOT SOMETHIN' WEIRD IN YOU...
...BUT IT AIN'T A RUNE.
HUH?
WHAT'S A "RUNE"?

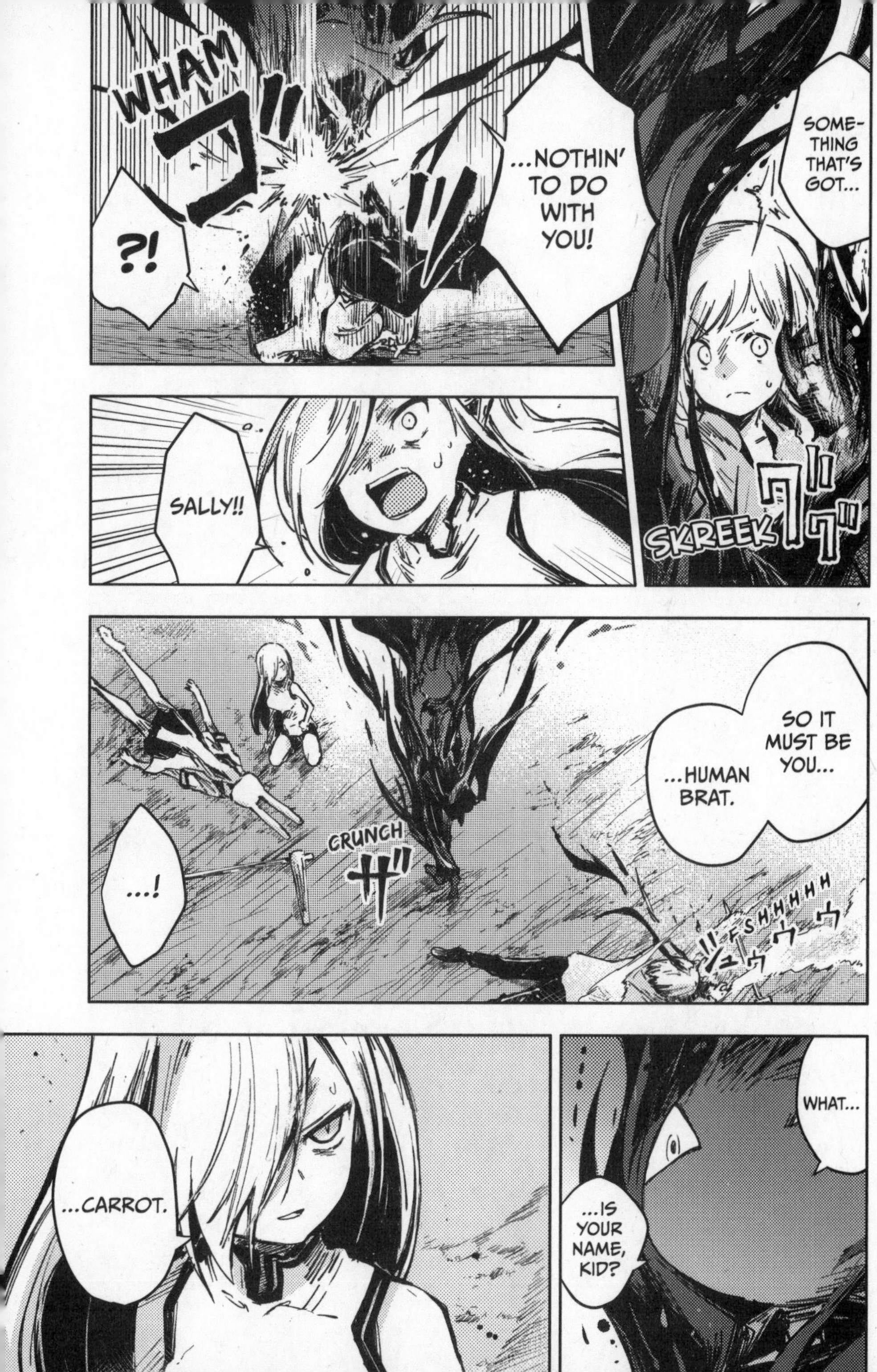
SOMETHING THAT'S GOT...
SKREEK
...NOTHIN' TO DO WITH YOU!
WHAM
?!
SALLY!!
SO IT MUST BE YOU...
...HUMAN BRAT.
FSHHHHHH
CRUNCH
...!
WHAT...
...IS YOUR NAME, KID?
...CARROT.

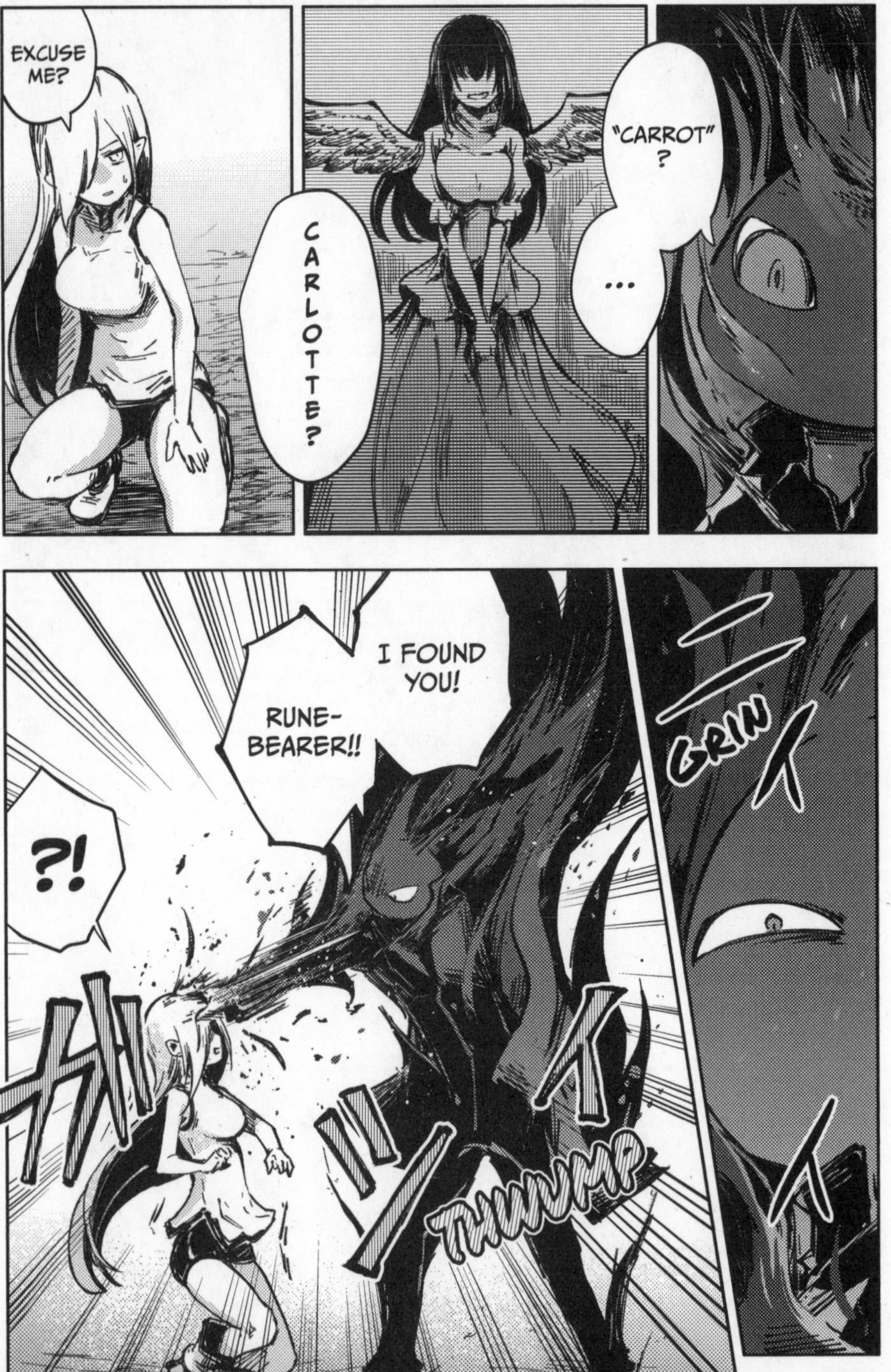
"CARROT"?
...
CARLOTTE?
EXCUSE ME?
GRIN
I FOUND YOU!
RUNE-BEARER!!
?!
THWUMP

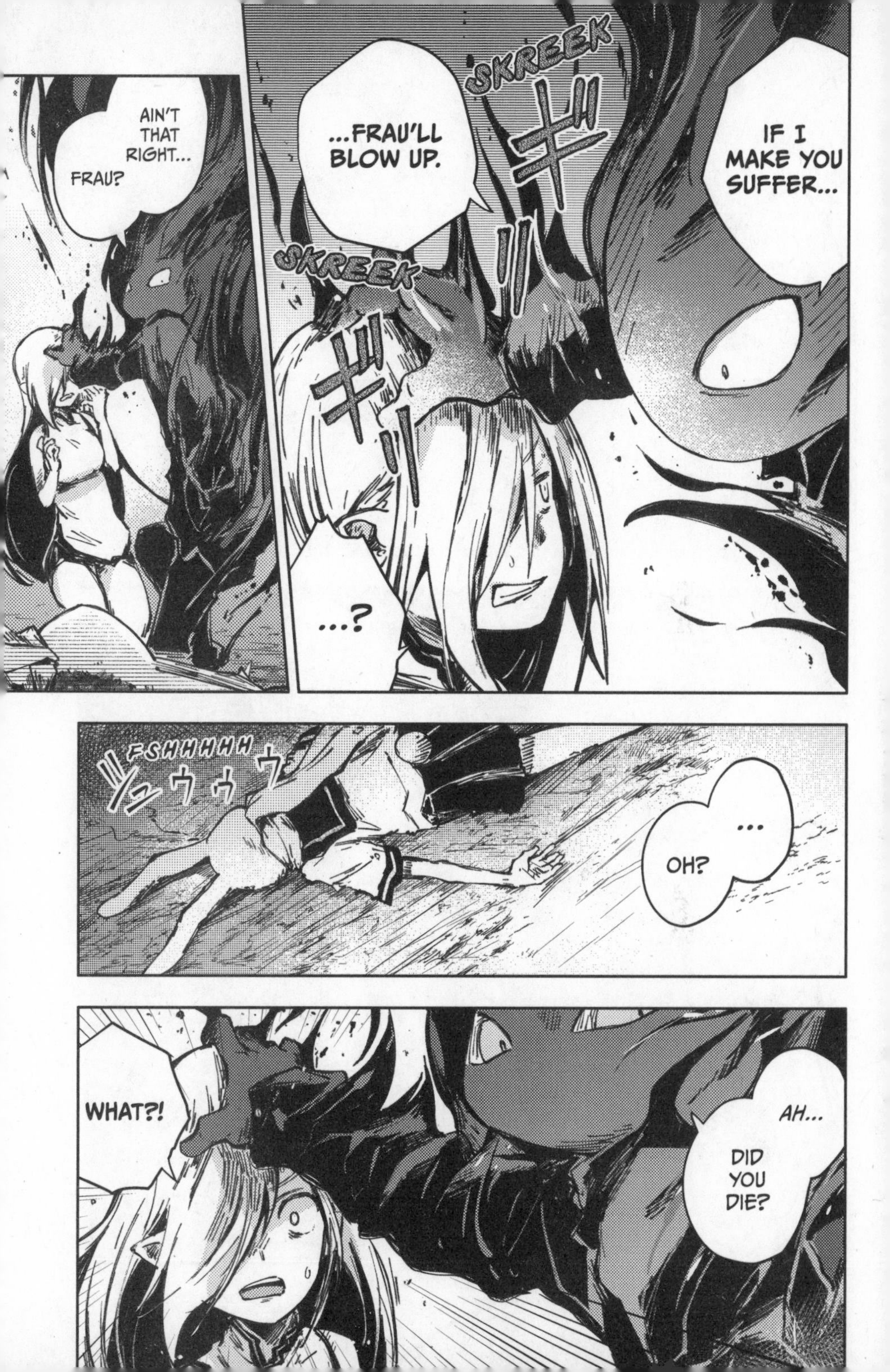

IF I MAKE YOU SUFFER...
SKREEK
SKREEK
...FRAU'LL BLOW UP.
...?
AIN'T THAT RIGHT... FRAU?
FSHHHHH
... OH?
AH... DID YOU DIE?
WHAT?!

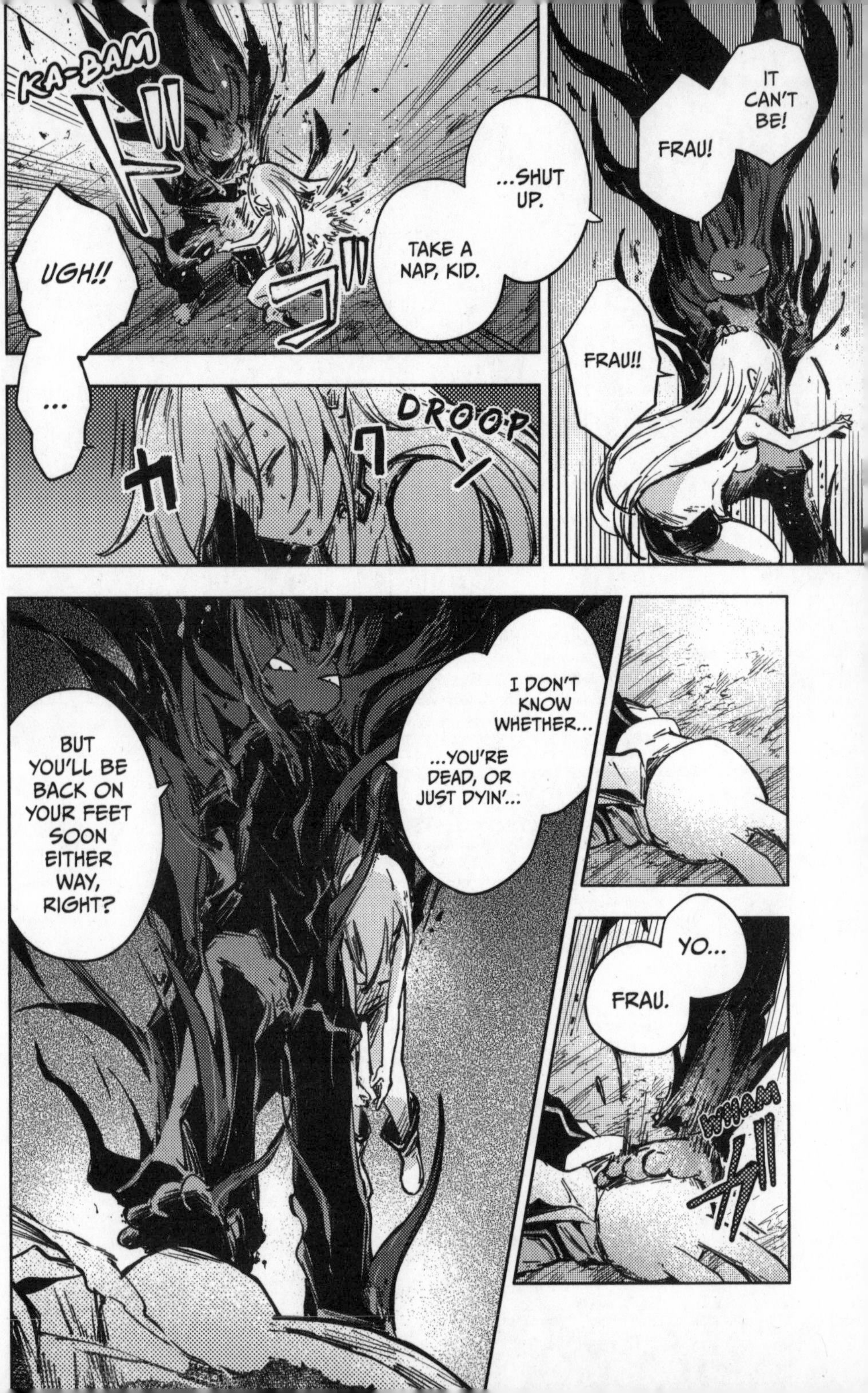
IT CAN'T BE!
FRAU!
FRAU!!
...SHUT UP.
TAKE A NAP, KID.
KA-BAM
UGH!!
...
DROOP
YO...
FRAU.
WHAM
I DON'T KNOW WHETHER...
...YOU'RE DEAD, OR JUST DYIN'...
BUT YOU'LL BE BACK ON YOUR FEET SOON EITHER WAY, RIGHT?

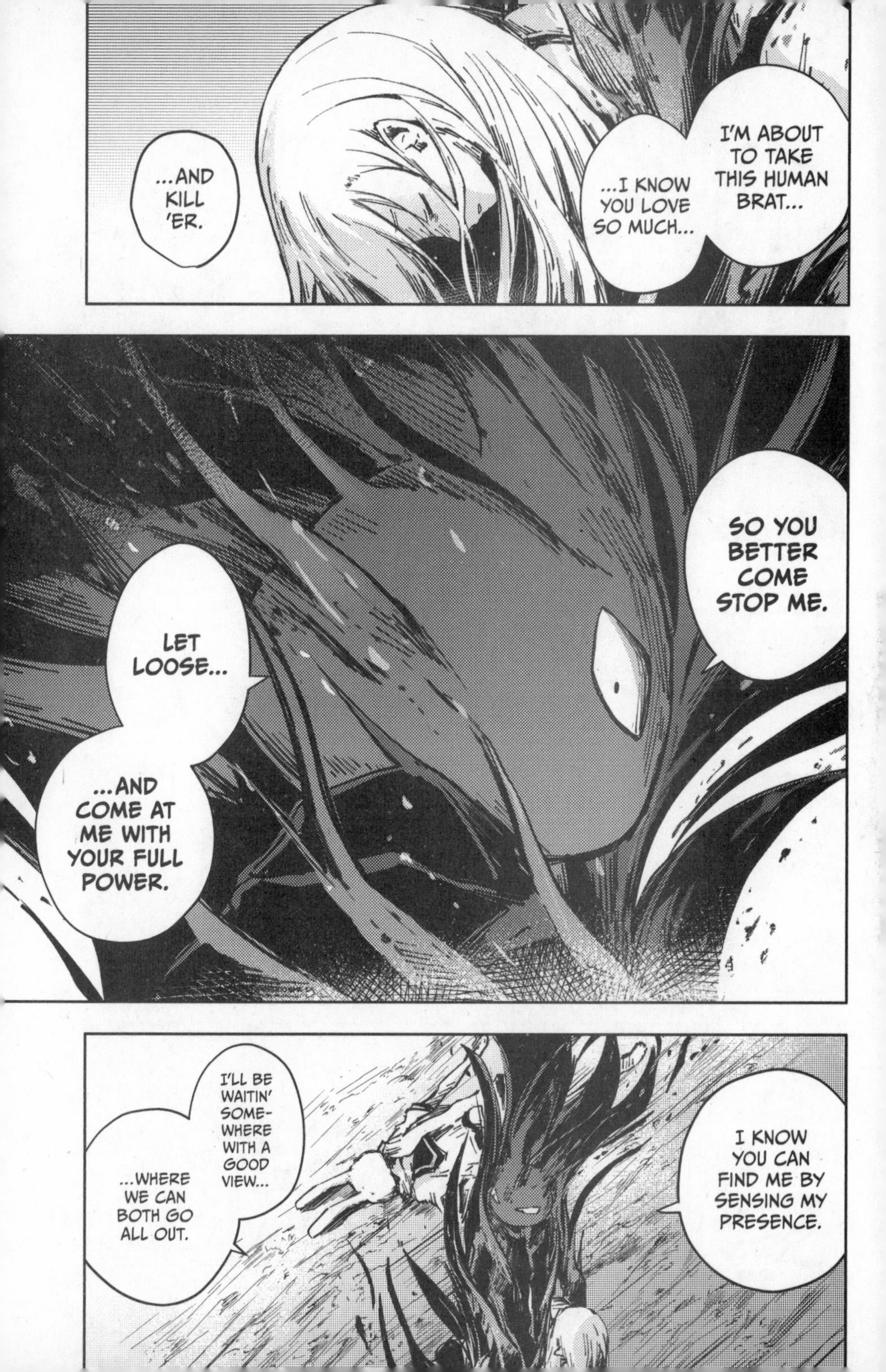
I'M ABOUT TO TAKE THIS HUMAN BRAT...
...I KNOW YOU LOVE SO MUCH...
...AND KILL 'ER.
SO YOU BETTER COME STOP ME.
LET LOOSE...
...AND COME AT ME WITH YOUR FULL POWER.
I KNOW YOU CAN FIND ME BY SENSING MY PRESENCE.
I'LL BE WAITIN' SOME-WHERE WITH A GOOD VIEW...
...WHERE WE CAN BOTH GO ALL OUT.

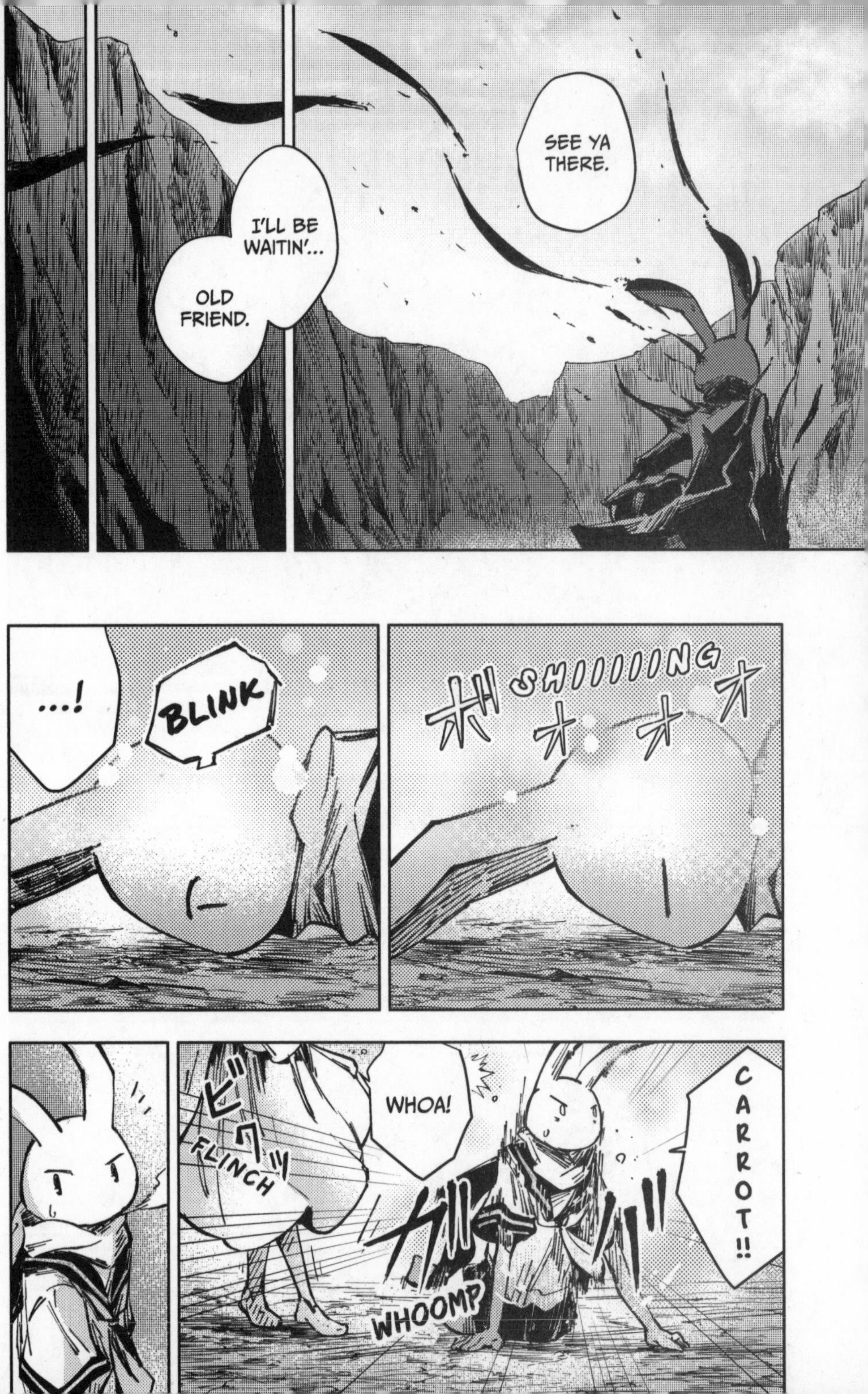
SEE YA THERE.
I'LL BE WAITIN'...
OLD FRIEND.
SHIIIIIING
BLINK
...!
CARROT!!
WHOA!
FLINCH
WHOOMP

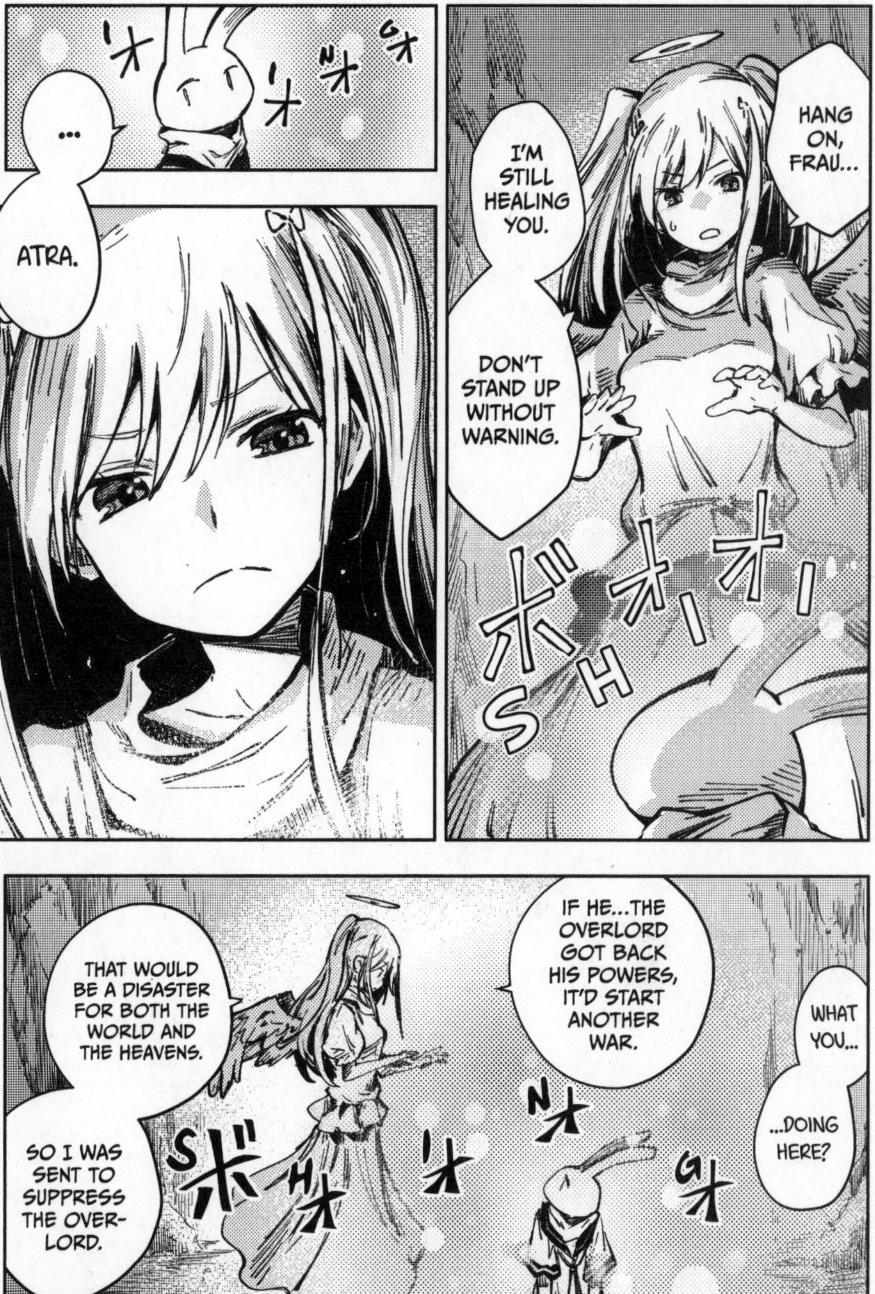
HANG ON, FRAU...
I'M STILL HEALING YOU.
DON'T STAND UP WITHOUT WARNING.
SHI
...
ATRA.
WHAT YOU...
...DOING HERE?
IF HE...THE OVERLORD GOT BACK HIS POWERS, IT'D START ANOTHER WAR.
THAT WOULD BE A DISASTER FOR BOTH THE WORLD AND THE HEAVENS.
SO I WAS SENT TO SUPPRESS THE OVER-LORD.

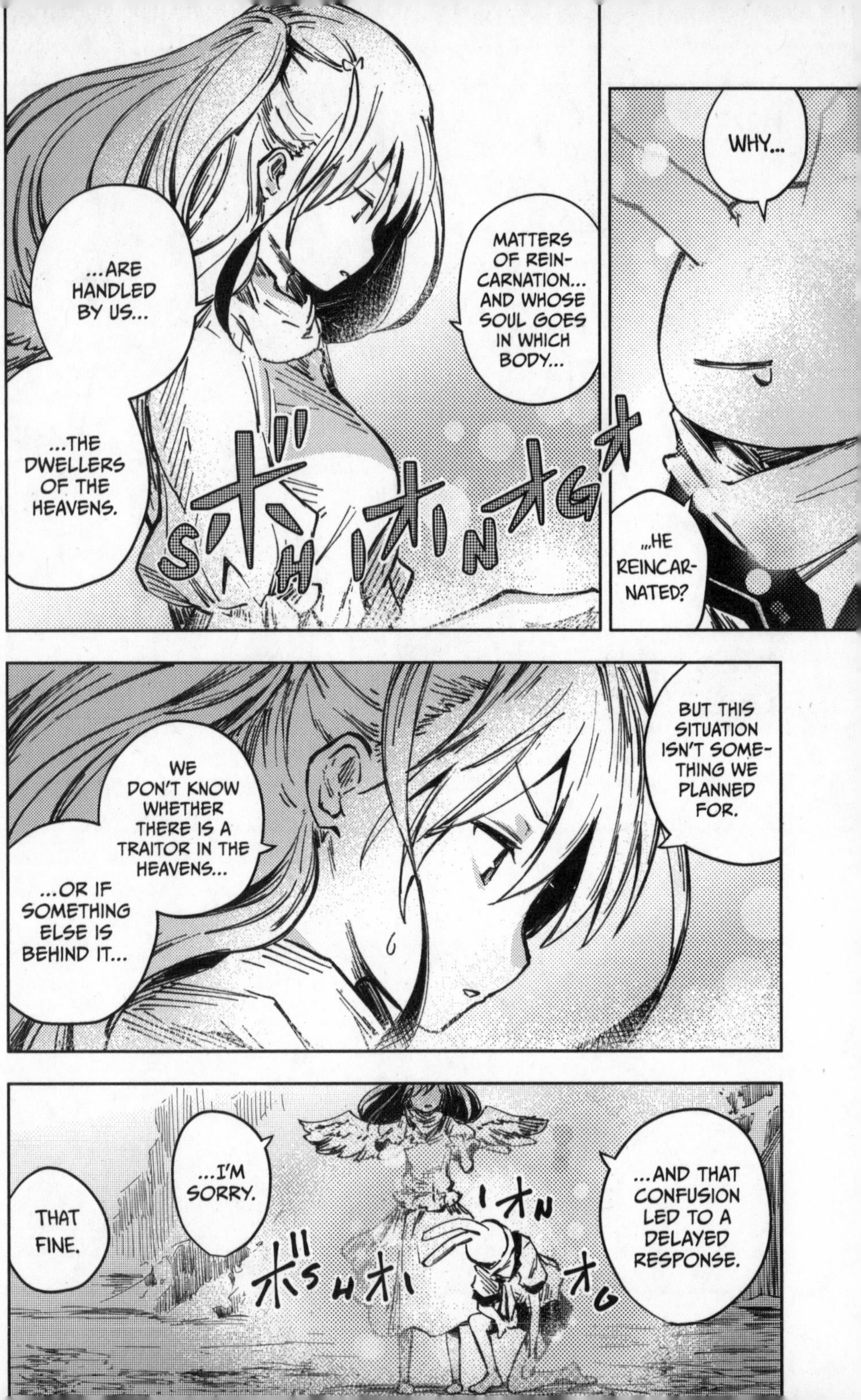
WHY...
...HE REINCARNATED?
MATTERS OF REINCARNATION... AND WHOSE SOUL GOES IN WHICH BODY...
...ARE HANDLED BY US...
SHING
...THE DWELLERS OF THE HEAVENS.
BUT THIS SITUATION ISN'T SOMETHING WE PLANNED FOR.
WE DON'T KNOW WHETHER THERE IS A TRAITOR IN THE HEAVENS...
...OR IF SOMETHING ELSE IS BEHIND IT...
...AND THAT CONFUSION LED TO A DELAYED RESPONSE.
SHING
...I'M SORRY.
THAT FINE.

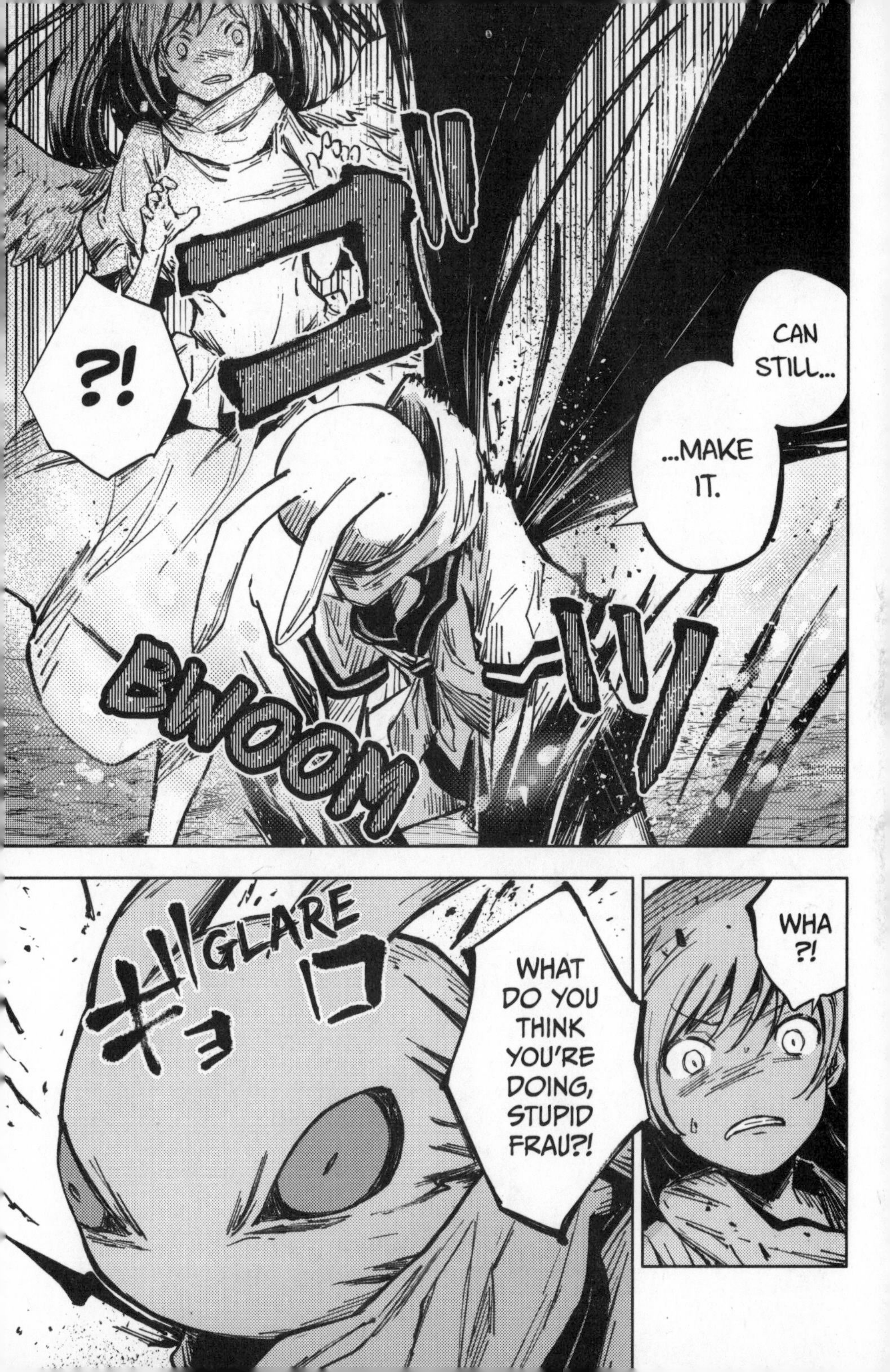
CAN STILL...
...MAKE IT.
?!
BWOOM
WHA ?!
WHAT DO YOU THINK YOU'RE DOING, STUPID FRAU?!
GLARE

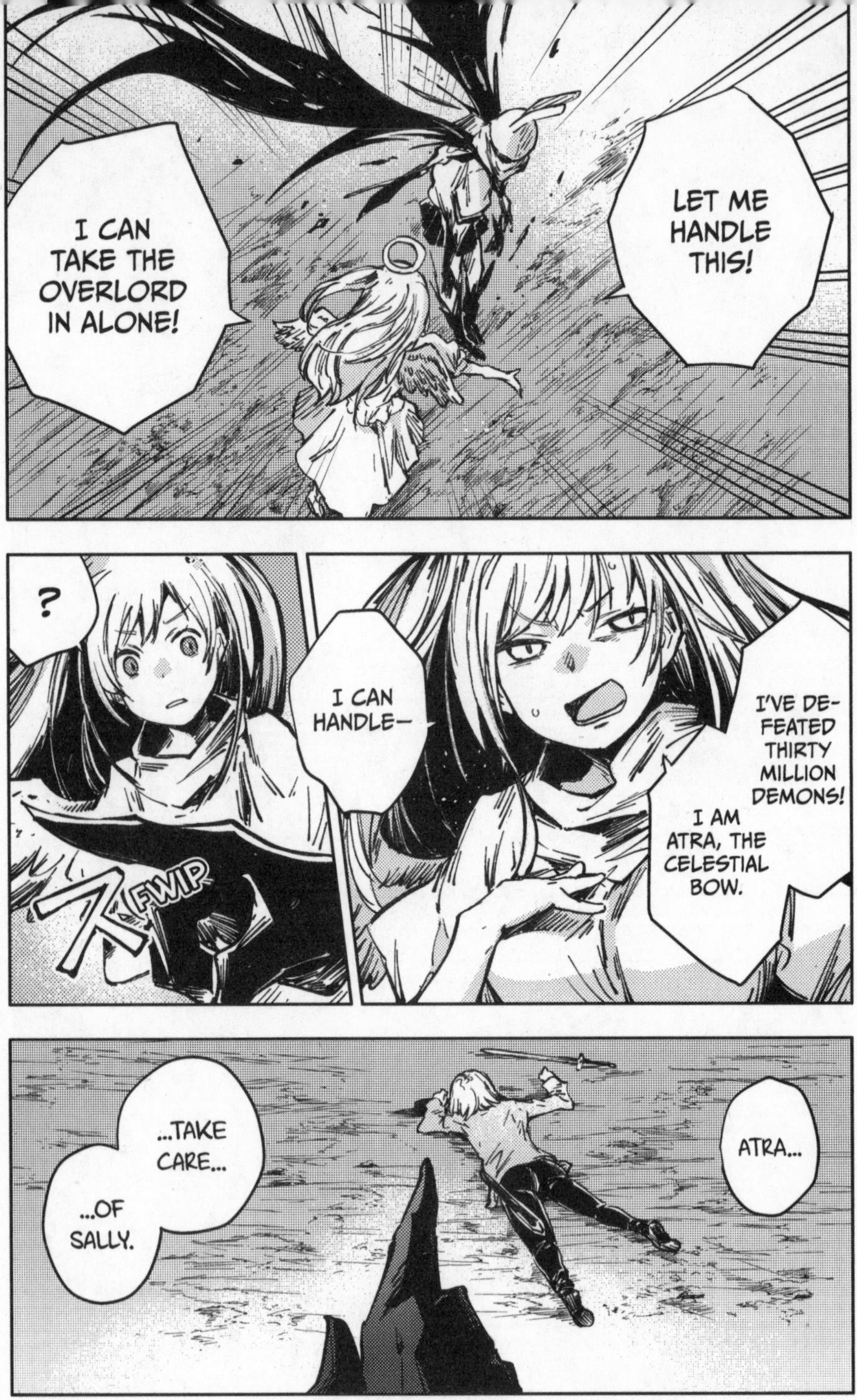
LET ME HANDLE THIS!
I CAN TAKE THE OVERLORD IN ALONE!
I'VE DEFEATED THIRTY MILLION DEMONS!
I AM ATRA, THE CELESTIAL BOW.
I CAN HANDLE—
?
FWIP
ATRA...
...TAKE CARE...
...OF SALLY.

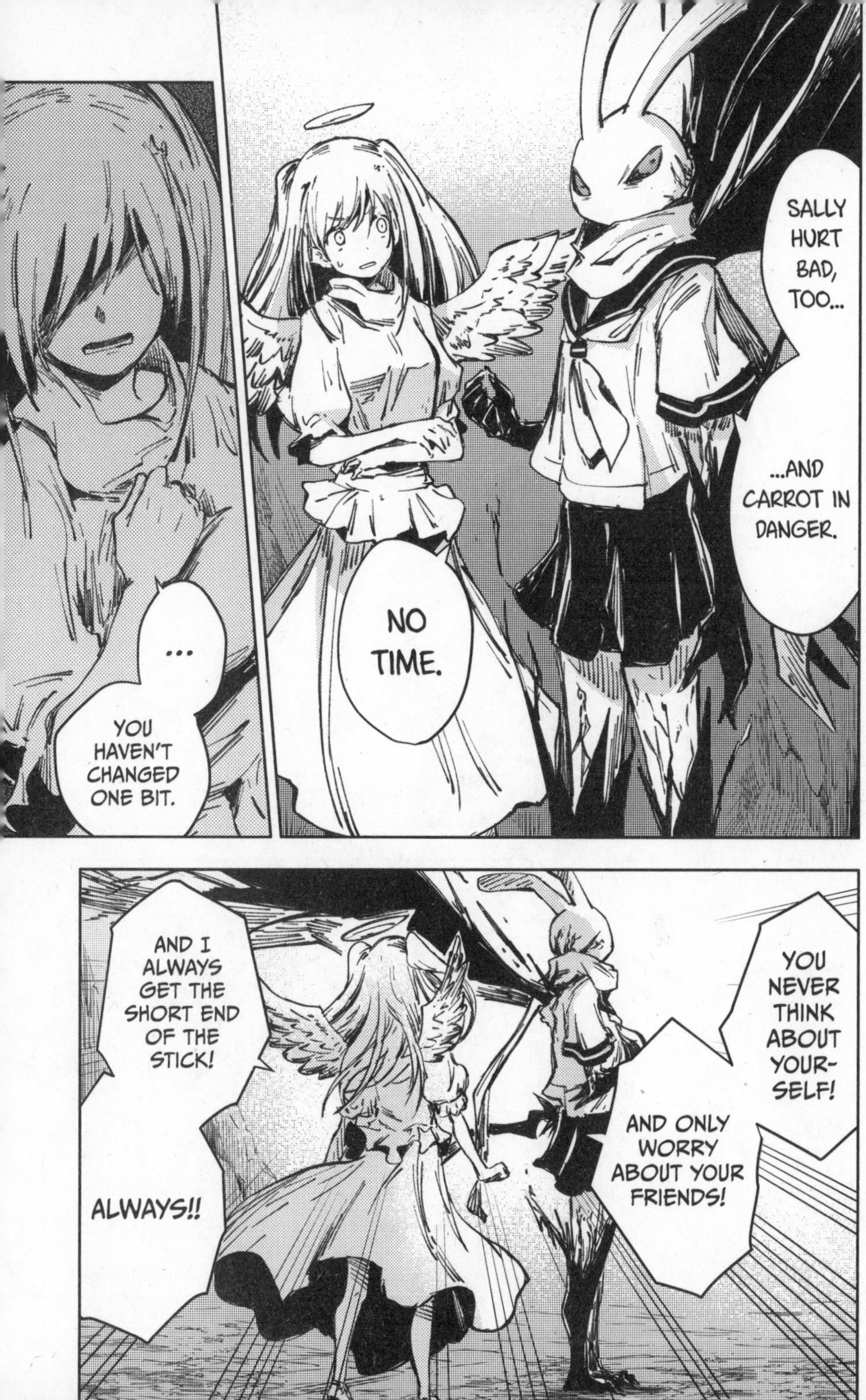
SALLY HURT BAD, TOO...
...AND CARROT IN DANGER.
NO TIME.
...
YOU HAVEN'T CHANGED ONE BIT.
YOU NEVER THINK ABOUT YOUR-SELF!
AND ONLY WORRY ABOUT YOUR FRIENDS!
AND I ALWAYS GET THE SHORT END OF THE STICK!
ALWAYS!!

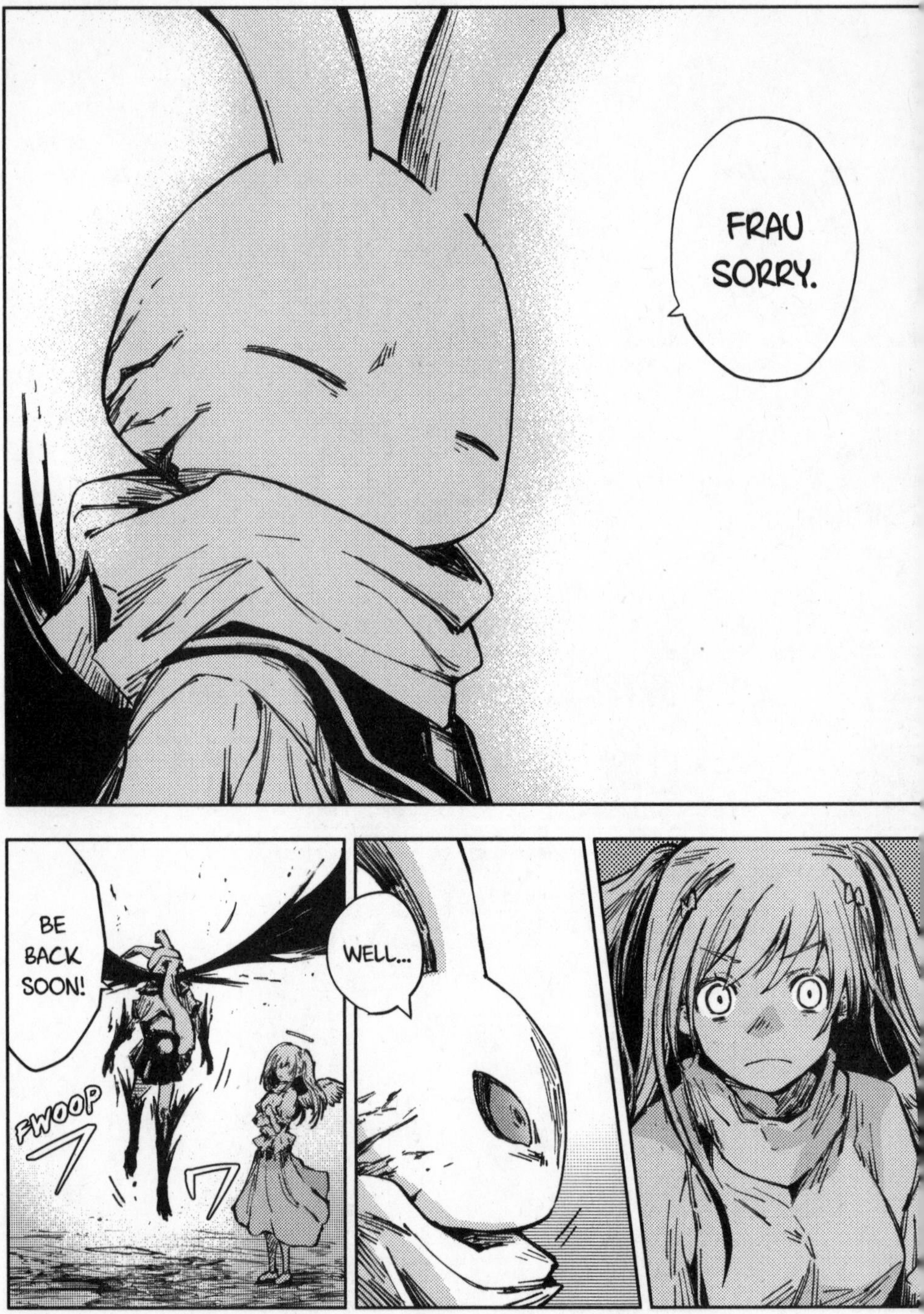
FRAU SORRY.
WELL...
BE BACK SOON!
FWOOP

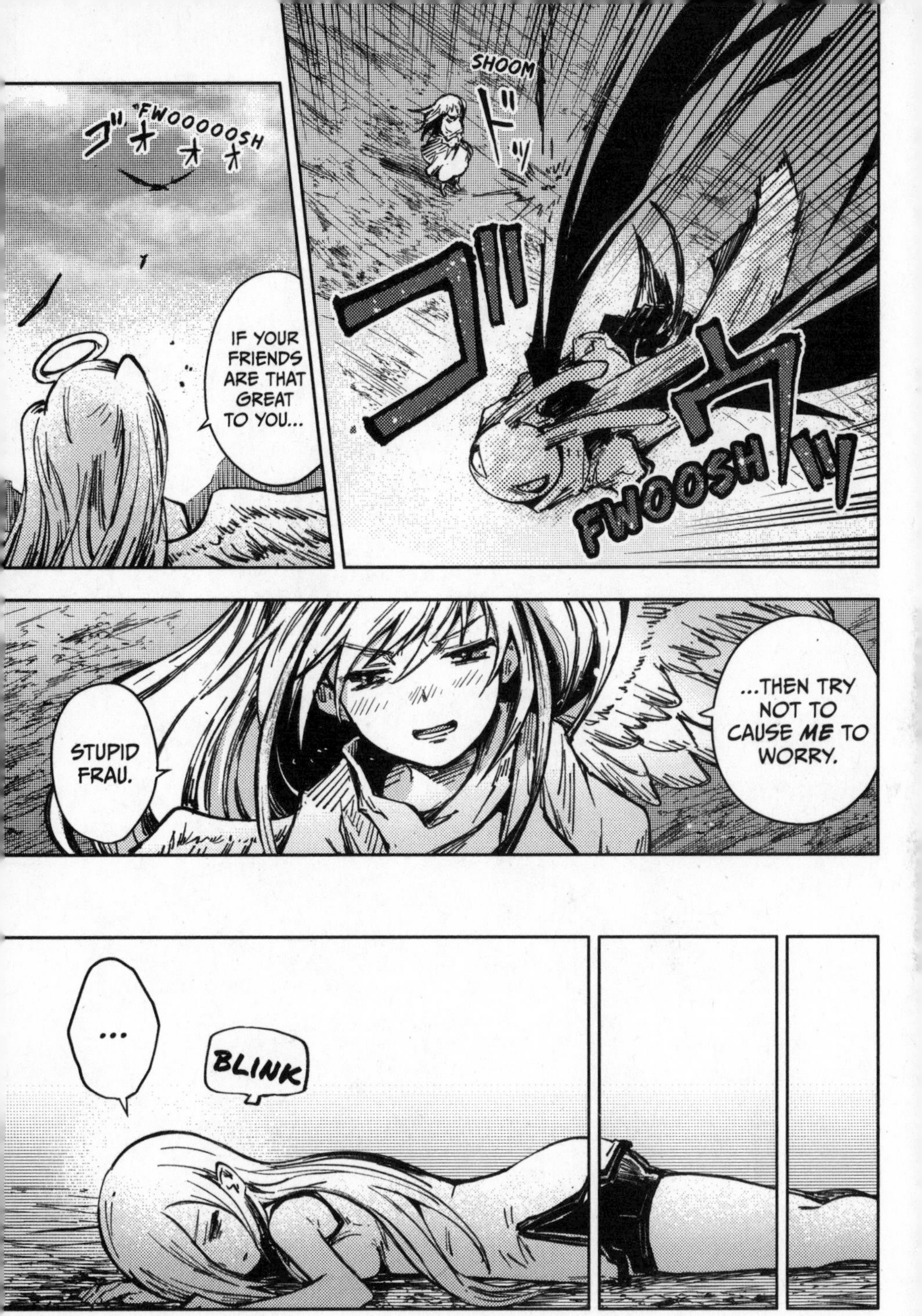

ドッ
SHOOM
ゴウッ
FWOOSH!!!
ゴォォォ
FWOOOOOOSH
IF YOUR FRIENDS ARE THAT GREAT TO YOU...
...THEN TRY NOT TO CAUSE *ME* TO WORRY.
STUPID FRAU.
...
BLINK

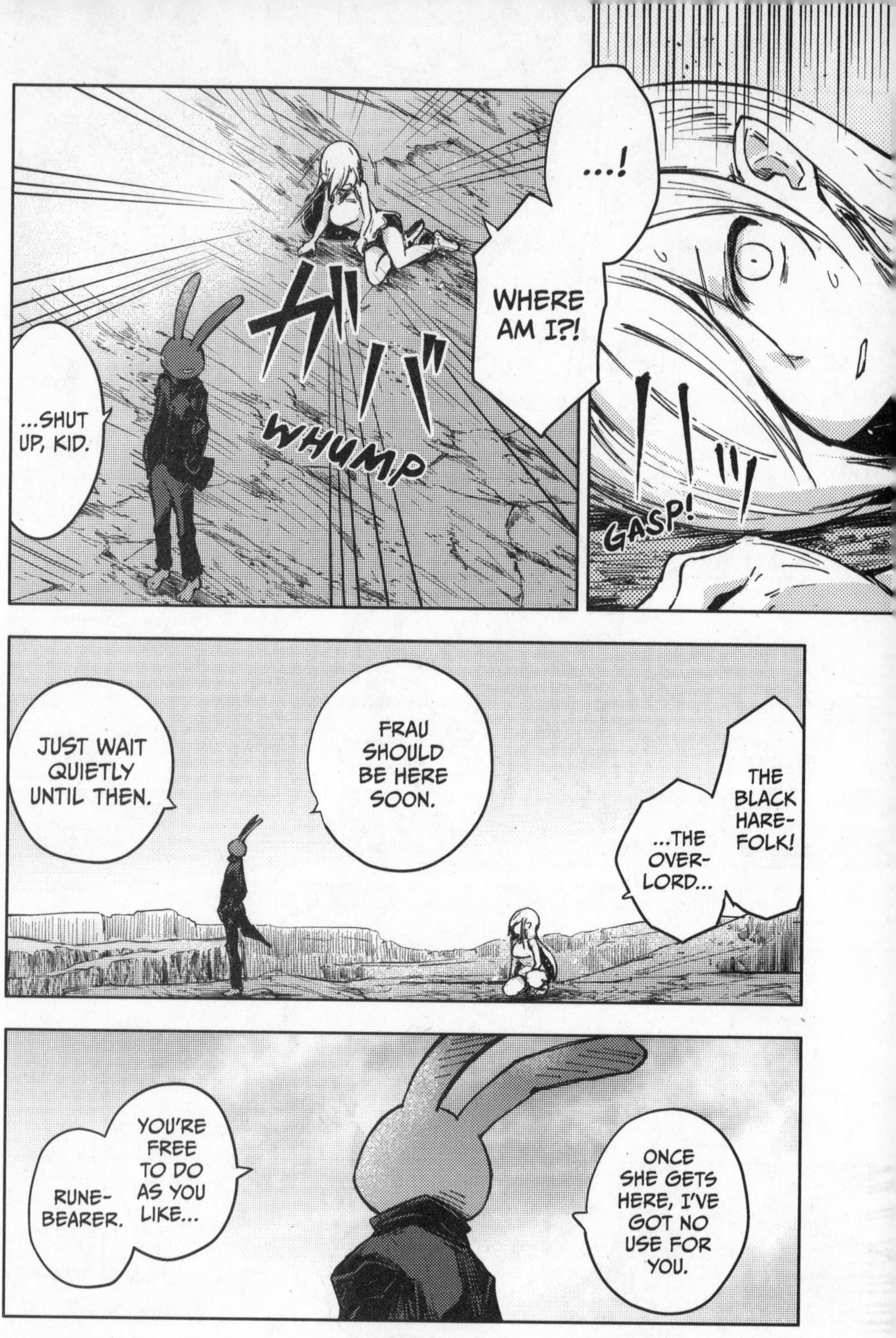
...!
WHERE AM I?!
GASP!
ガバ
WHUMP
...SHUT UP, KID.
THE BLACK HARE-FOLK!
...THE OVERLORD...
FRAU SHOULD BE HERE SOON.
JUST WAIT QUIETLY UNTIL THEN.
ONCE SHE GETS HERE, I'VE GOT NO USE FOR YOU.
YOU'RE FREE TO DO AS YOU LIKE...
RUNE-BEARER.

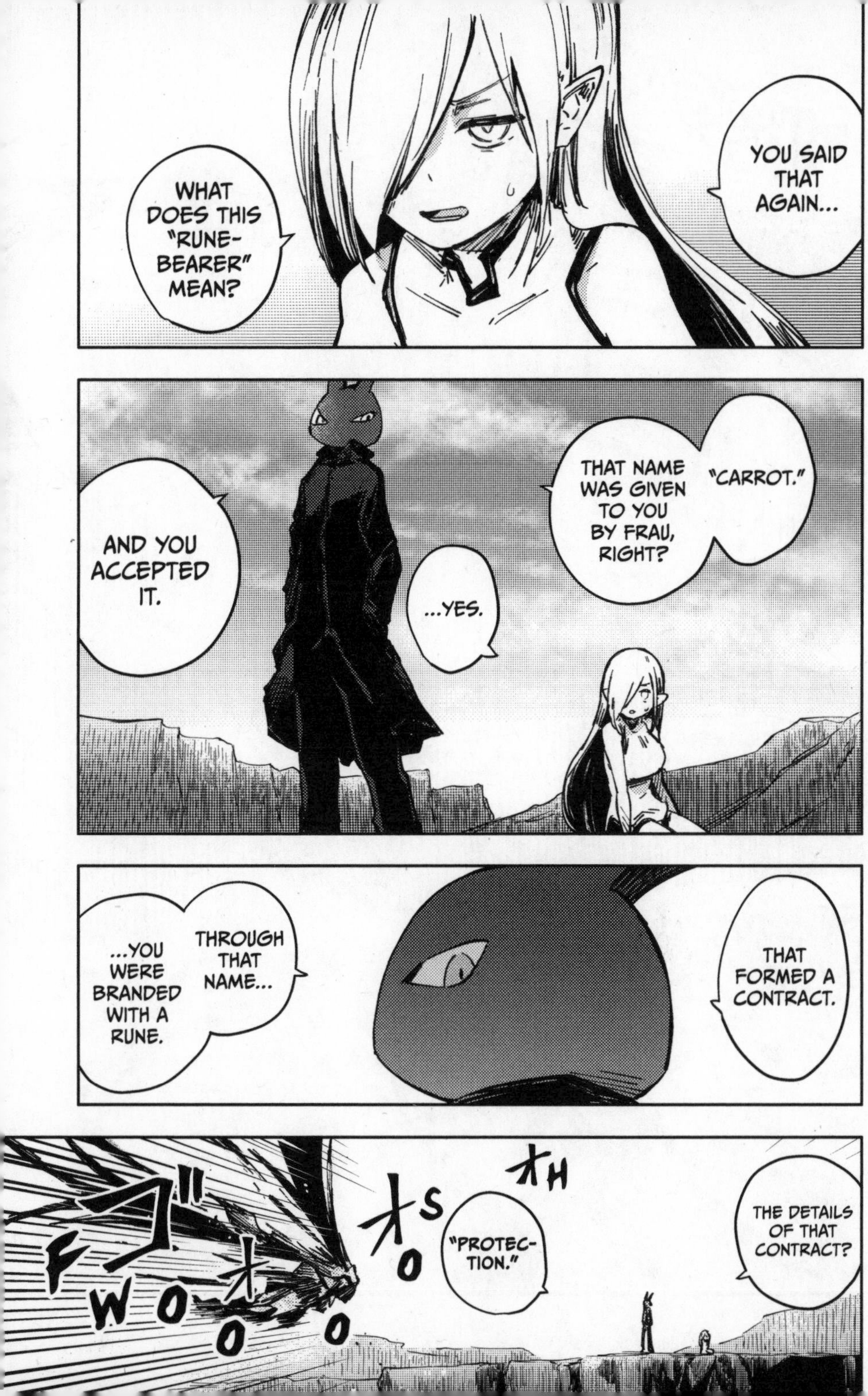
YOU SAID THAT AGAIN...
WHAT DOES THIS "RUNE-BEARER" MEAN?
"CARROT."
THAT NAME WAS GIVEN TO YOU BY FRAU, RIGHT?
...YES.
AND YOU ACCEPTED IT.
THAT FORMED A CONTRACT.
THROUGH THAT NAME...
...YOU WERE BRANDED WITH A RUNE.
THE DETAILS OF THAT CONTRACT?
"PROTECTION."
FWOOOOSH

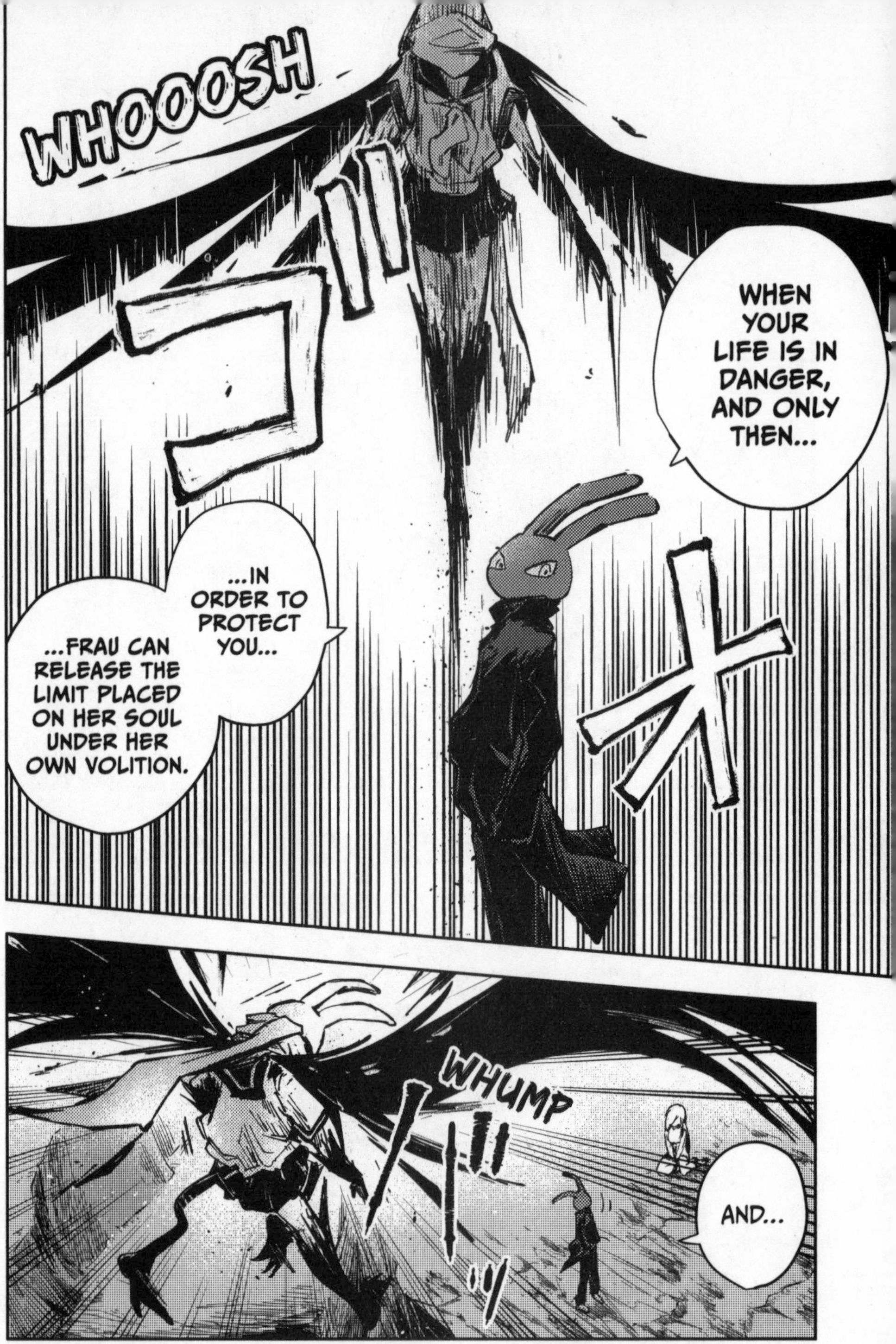
WHOOOSH
WHEN YOUR LIFE IS IN DANGER, AND ONLY THEN...
...IN ORDER TO PROTECT YOU...
...FRAU CAN RELEASE THE LIMIT PLACED ON HER SOUL UNDER HER OWN VOLITION.
AND...
WHUMP

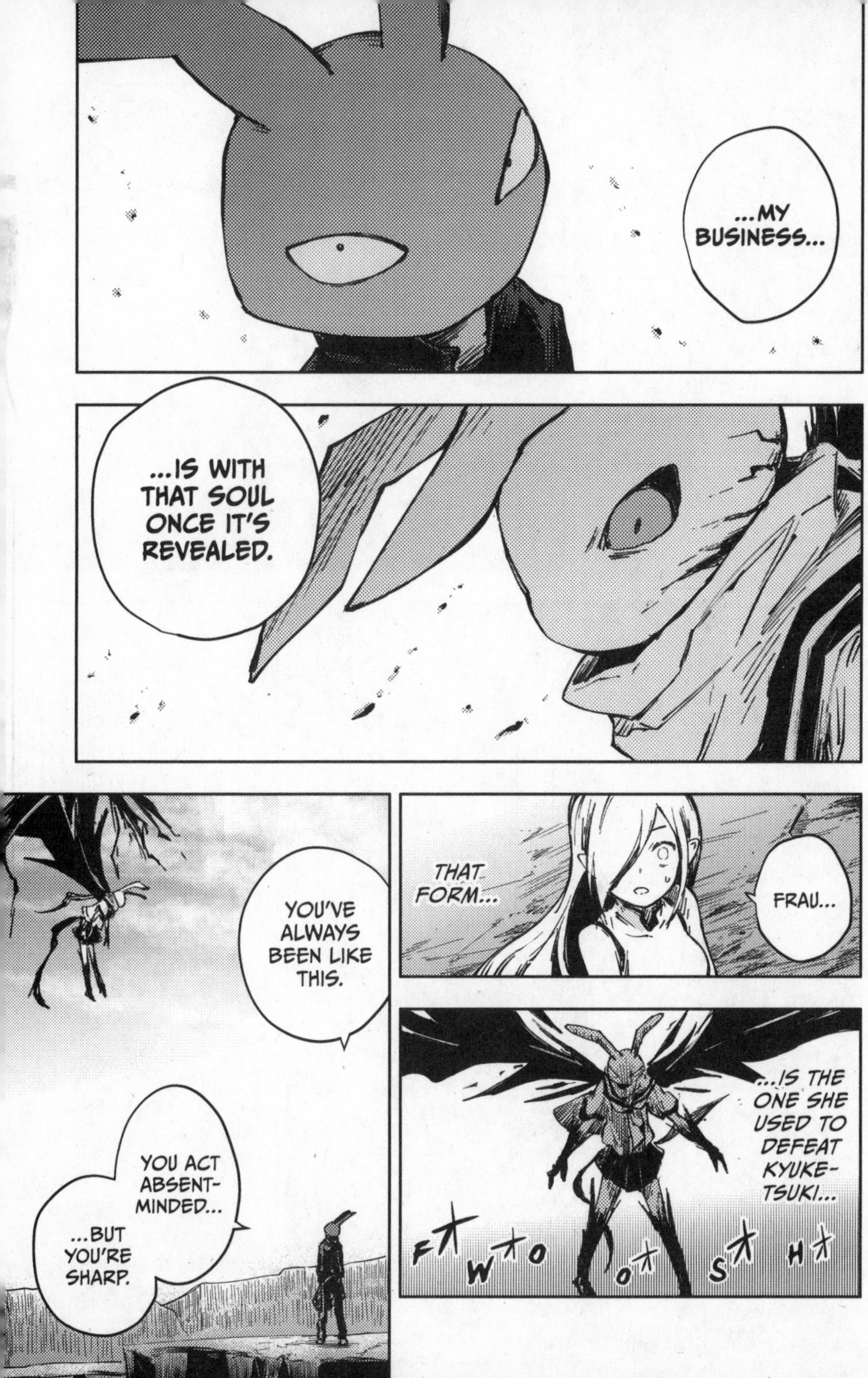
...MY BUSINESS...
...IS WITH THAT SOUL ONCE IT'S REVEALED.
FRAU...
THAT FORM...
...IS THE ONE SHE USED TO DEFEAT KYUKE-TSUKI...
FWOOSH
YOU'VE ALWAYS BEEN LIKE THIS.
YOU ACT ABSENT-MINDED...
...BUT YOU'RE SHARP.

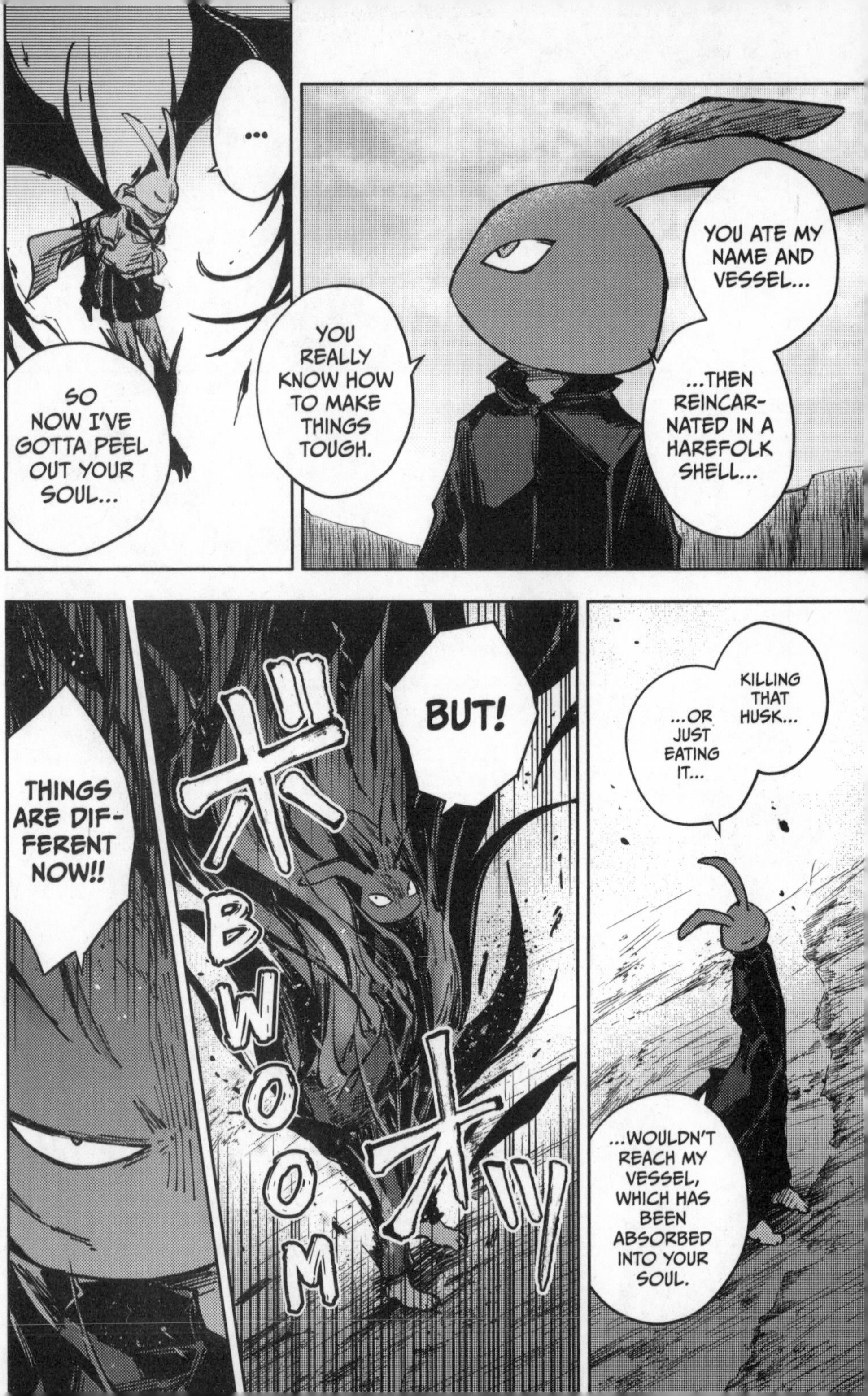
YOU ATE MY NAME AND VESSEL...
...THEN REINCARNATED IN A HAREFOLK SHELL...
YOU REALLY KNOW HOW TO MAKE THINGS TOUGH.
...
SO NOW I'VE GOTTA PEEL OUT YOUR SOUL...
KILLING THAT HUSK...
...OR JUST EATING IT...
...WOULDN'T REACH MY VESSEL, WHICH HAS BEEN ABSORBED INTO YOUR SOUL.
BUT!
BWOOOM
THINGS ARE DIFFERENT NOW!!

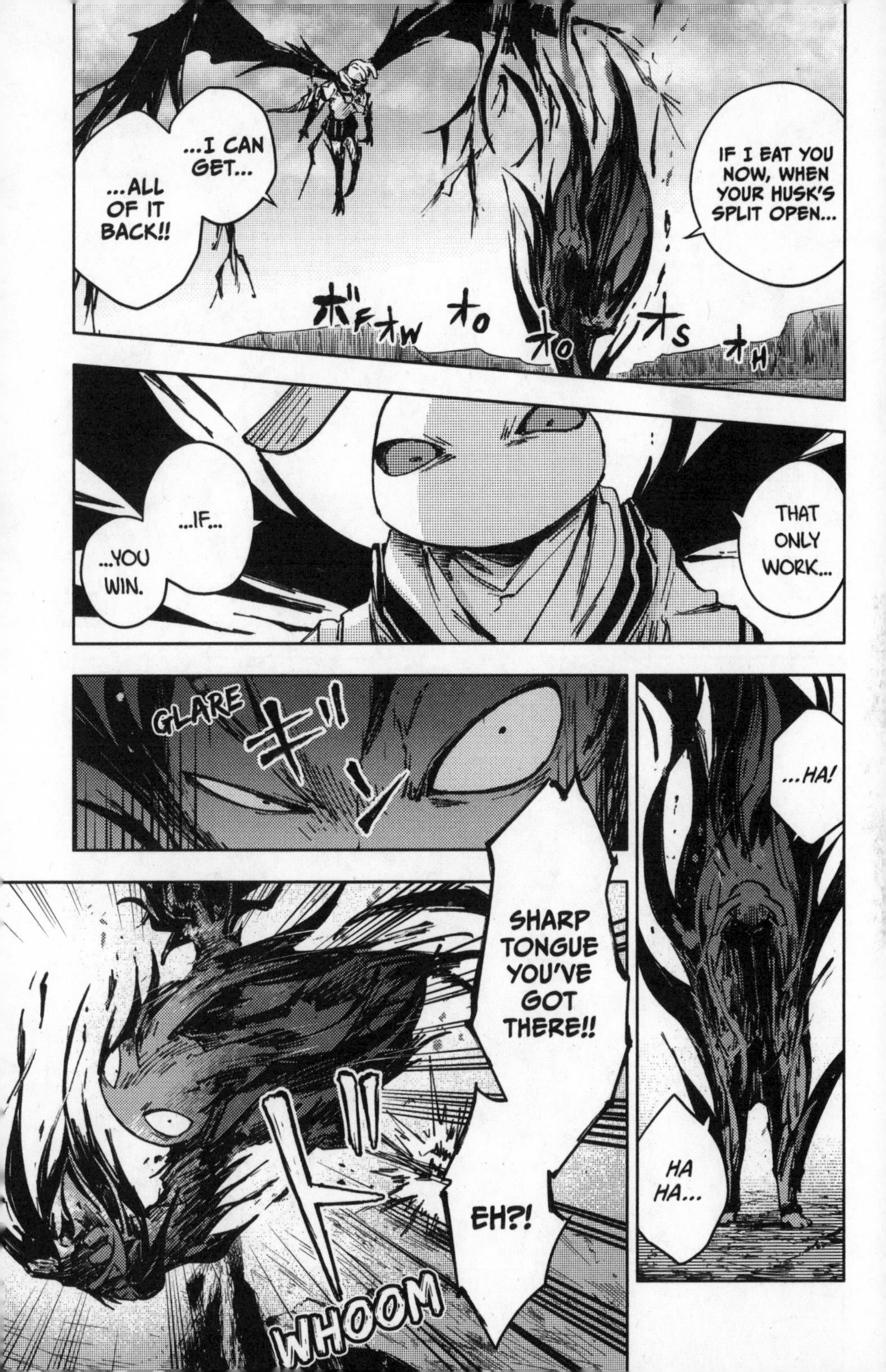
IF I EAT YOU NOW, WHEN YOUR HUSK'S SPLIT OPEN...
...I CAN GET...
...ALL OF IT BACK!!
FWOOSH
THAT ONLY WORK...
...IF...
...YOU WIN.
...HA!
HA HA...
GLARE
SHARP TONGUE YOU'VE GOT THERE!!
EH?!
WHOOM

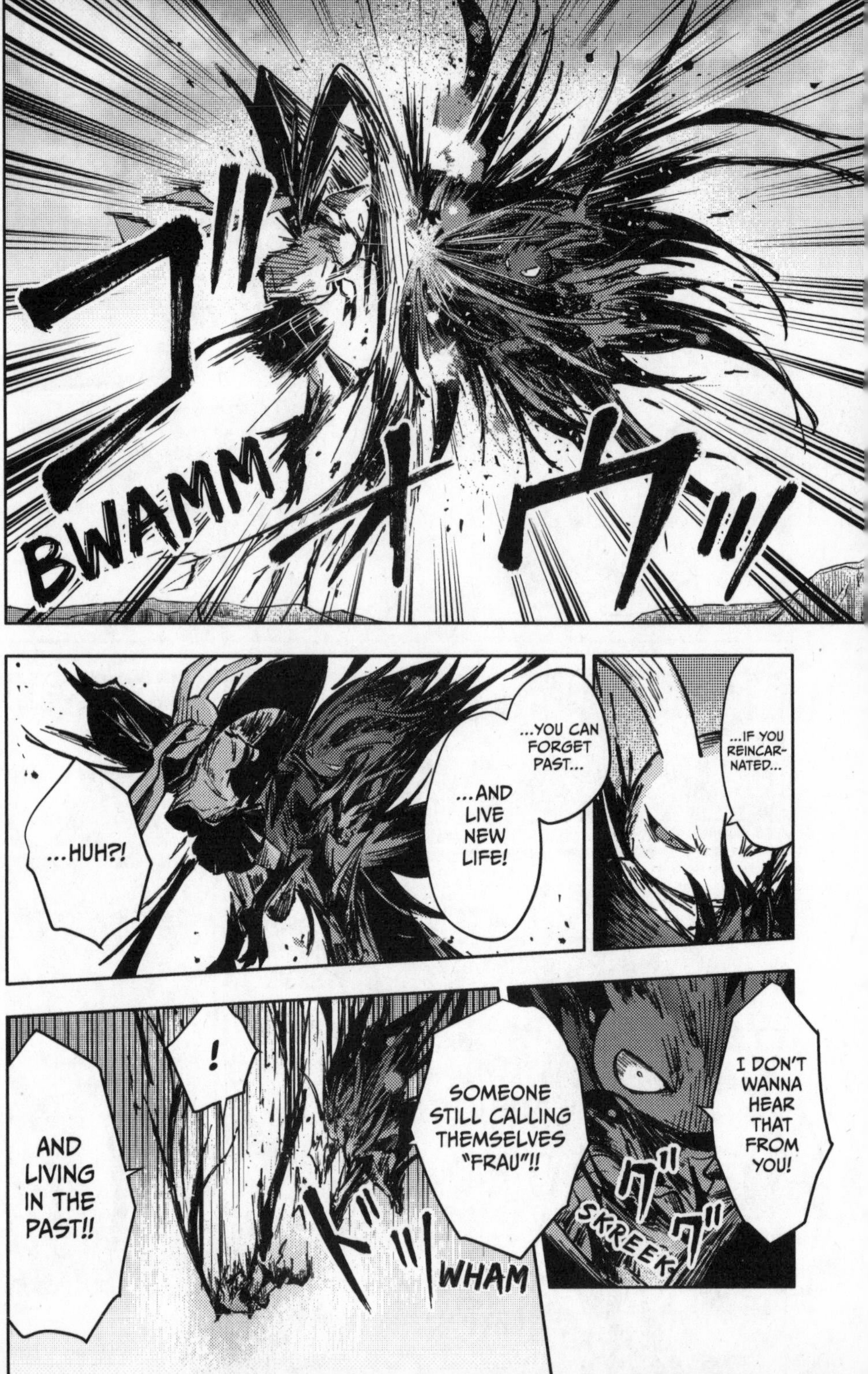
BWAMM
...IF YOU REINCAR-NATED...
...YOU CAN FORGET PAST...
...AND LIVE NEW LIFE!
...HUH?!
I DON'T WANNA HEAR THAT FROM YOU!
SKREEK
SOMEONE STILL CALLING THEMSELVES "FRAU"!!
!
AND LIVING IN THE PAST!!
WHAM

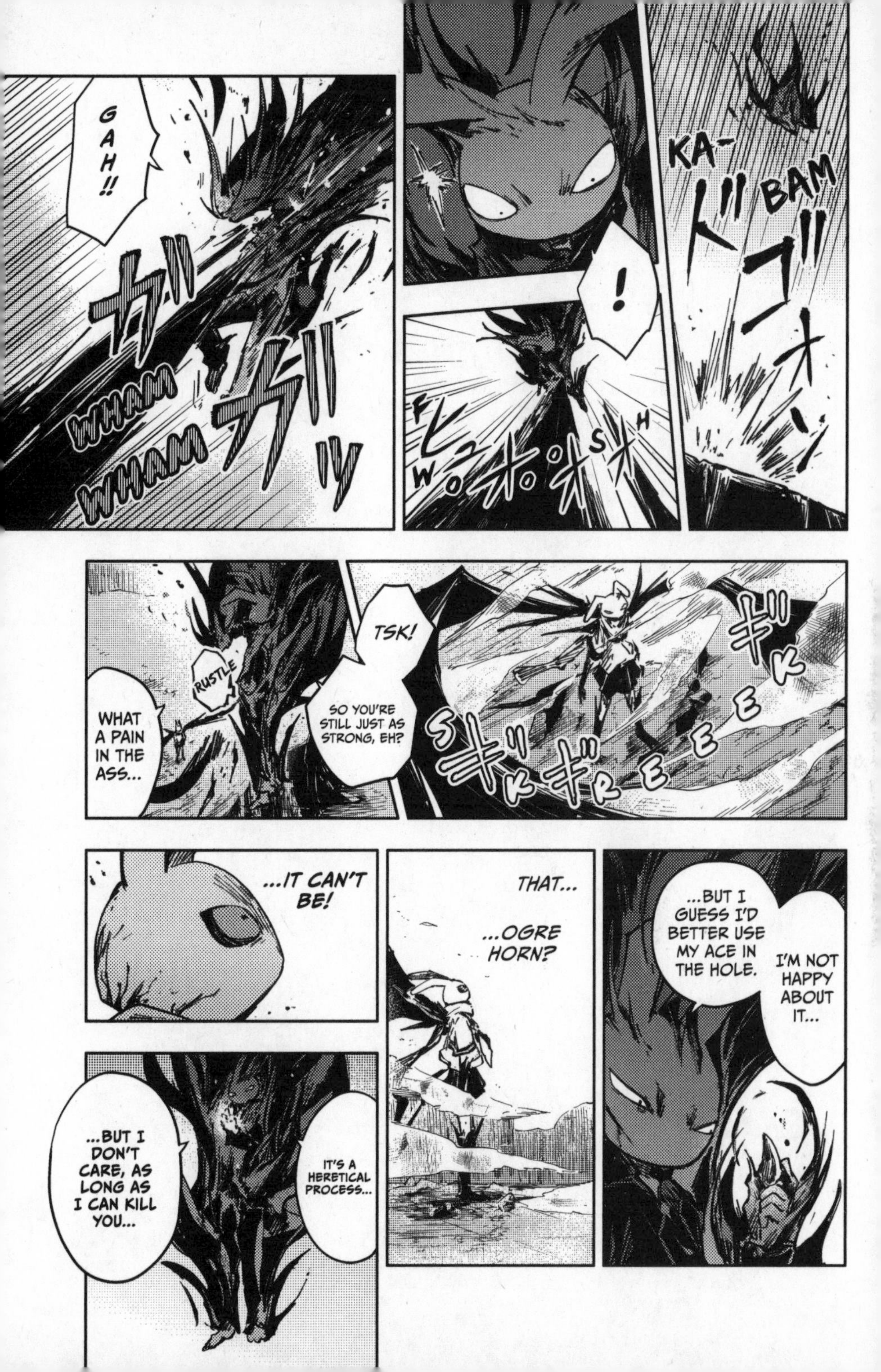
KA-BAM
!
FWOOSH
GAH!!
WHAM
WHAM
TSK!
SO YOU'RE STILL JUST AS STRONG, EH?
SKREEEEK
RUSTLE
WHAT A PAIN IN THE ASS...
I'M NOT HAPPY ABOUT IT...
...BUT I GUESS I'D BETTER USE MY ACE IN THE HOLE.
THAT...
...OGRE HORN?
...IT CAN'T BE!
IT'S A HERETICAL PROCESS...
...BUT I DON'T CARE, AS LONG AS I CAN KILL YOU...

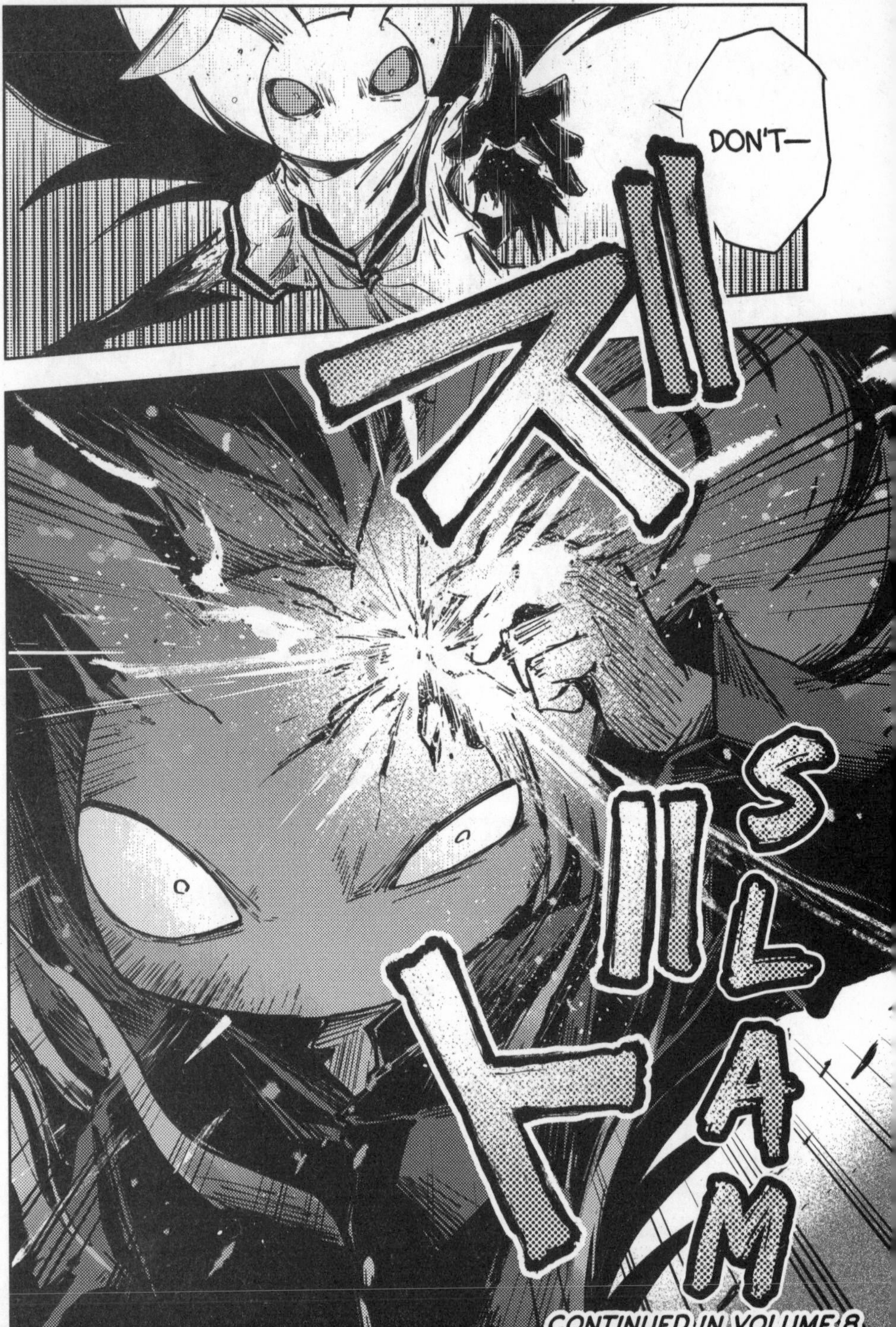
DON'T—
SLAM
CONTINUED IN VOLUME 8

EW...

...that way?

Y-You use our horns...

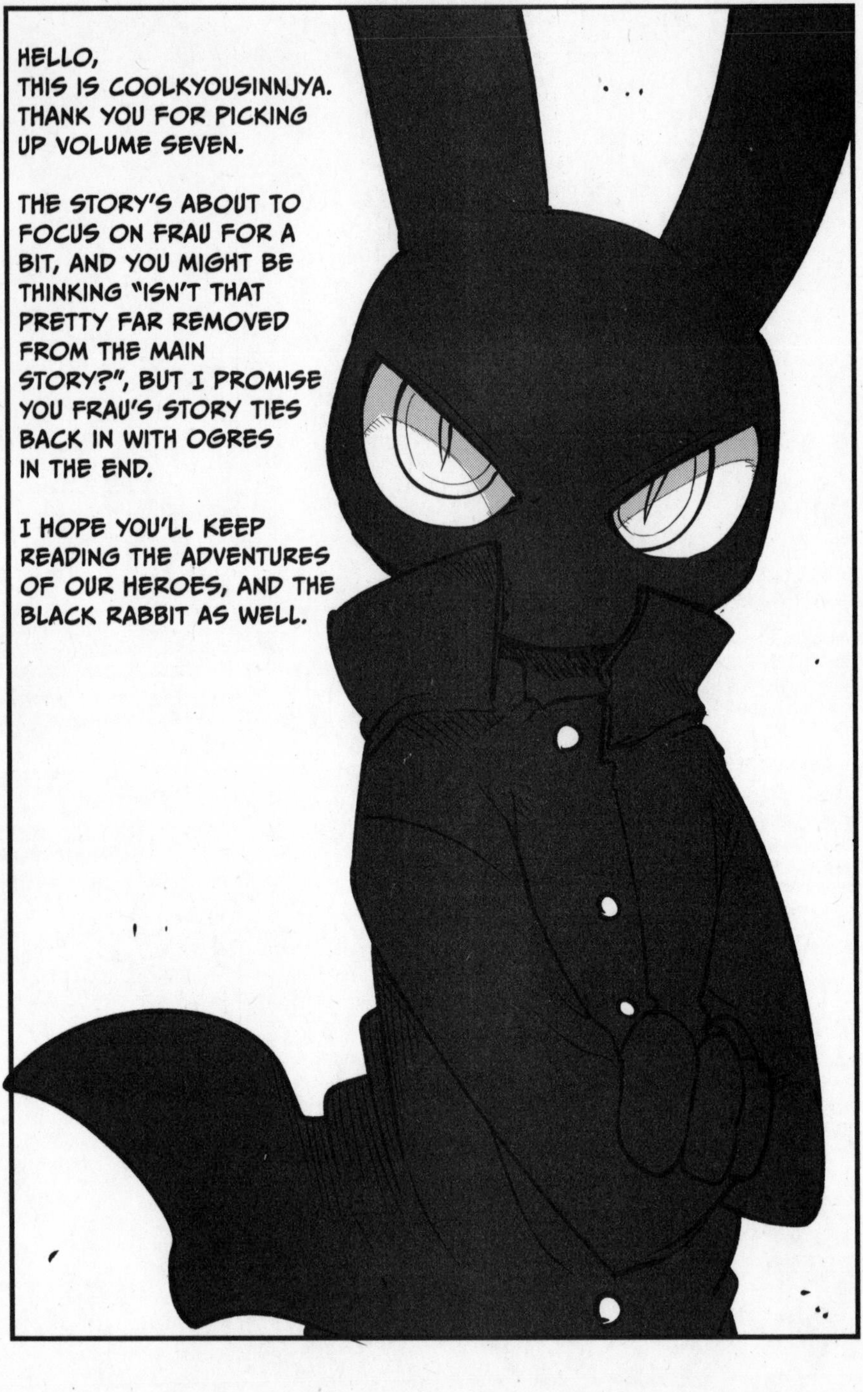
HELLO,
THIS IS COOLKYOUSINNJYA. THANK YOU FOR PICKING UP VOLUME SEVEN.
THE STORY'S ABOUT TO FOCUS ON FRAU FOR A BIT, AND YOU MIGHT BE THINKING "ISN'T THAT PRETTY FAR REMOVED FROM THE MAIN STORY?", BUT I PROMISE YOU FRAU'S STORY TIES BACK IN WITH OGRES IN THE END.
I HOPE YOU'LL KEEP READING THE ADVENTURES OF OUR HEROES, AND THE BLACK RABBIT AS WELL.
. . .

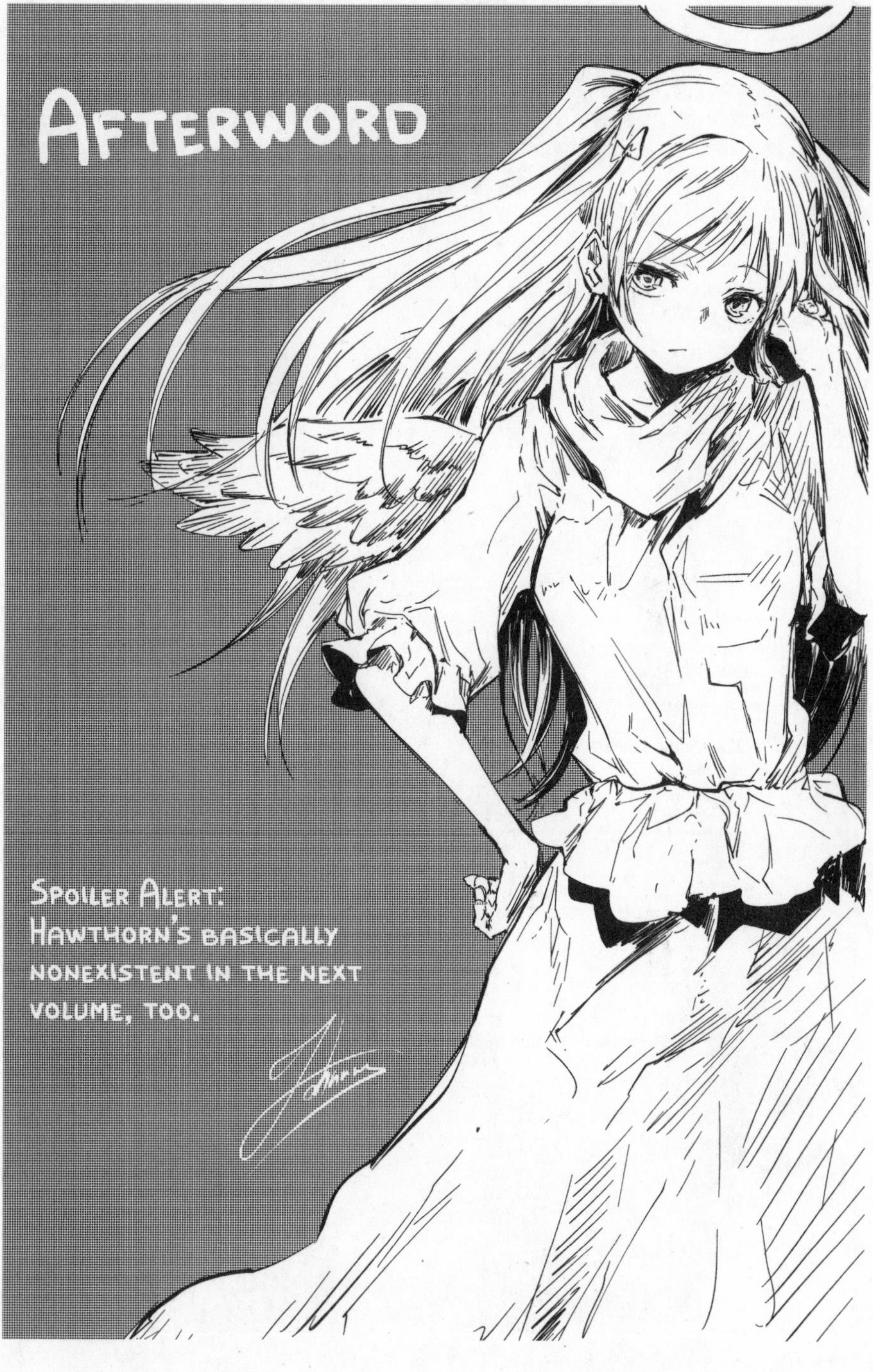
AFTERWORD
SPOILER ALERT:
HAWTHORN'S BASICALLY
NONEXISTENT IN THE NEXT
VOLUME, TOO.

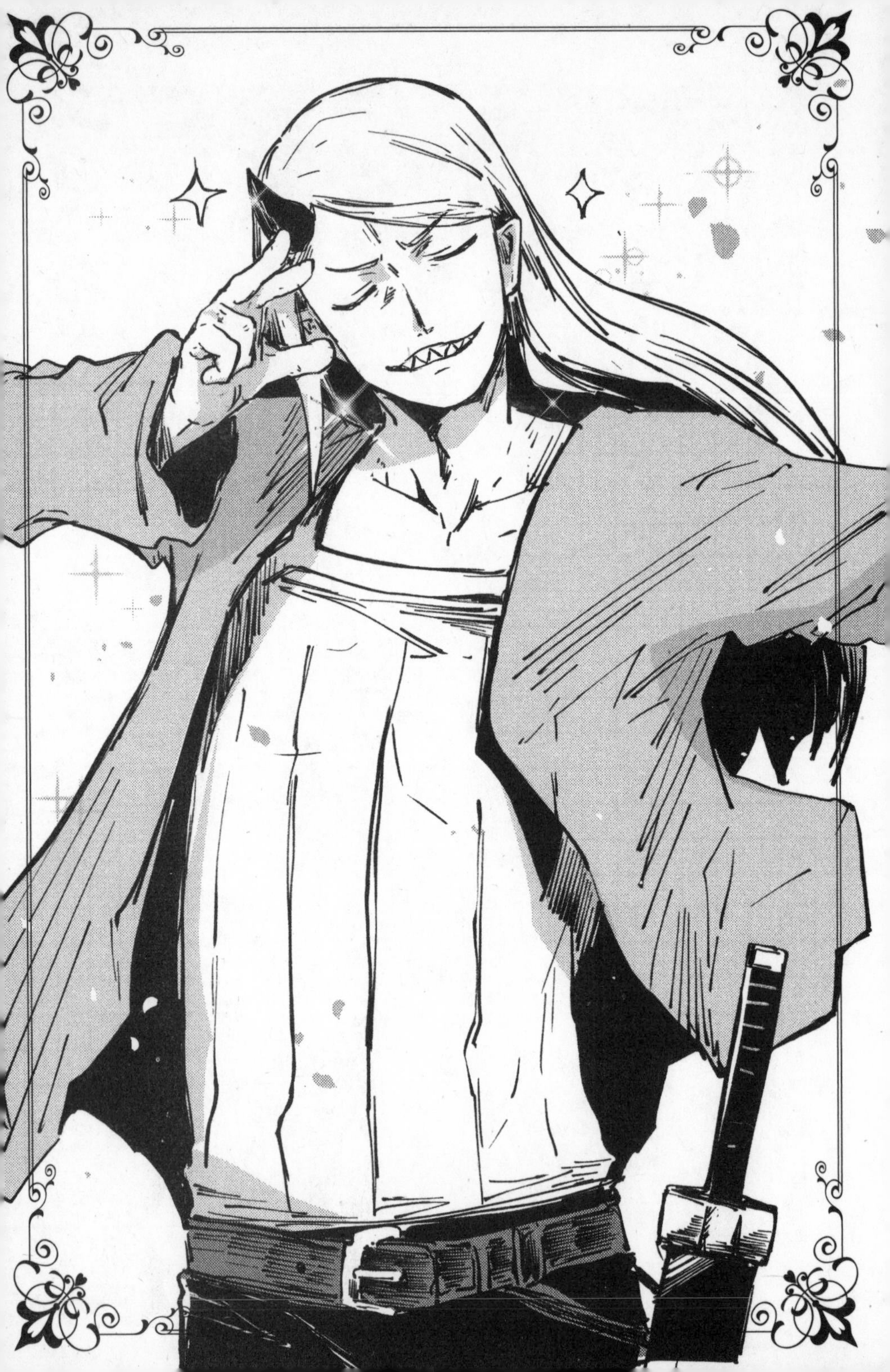

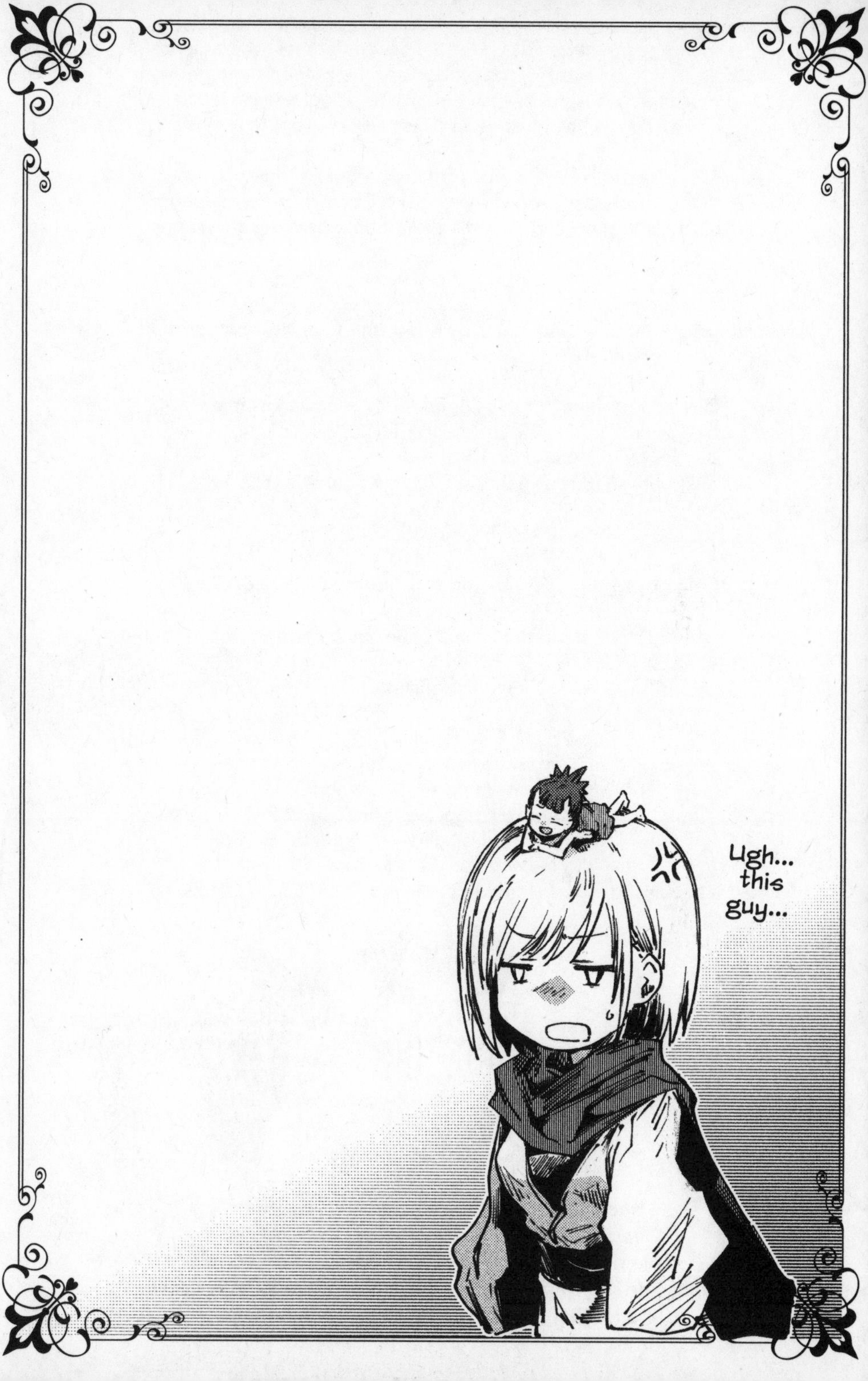
Ugh... this guy...

A Kodansha Comics Trade Paperback Original
Peach Boy Riverside 7 copyright © 2020 Coolkyousinnjya/Johanne
English translation copyright © 2022 Coolkyousinnjya/Johanne

Published in the United States by Kodansha Comics, an imprint of Kodansha USA Publishing, LLC, New York.

Publication rights for this English edition arranged through Kodansha Ltd., Tokyo.

First published in Japan in 2020 by Kodansha Ltd., Tokyo.

ISBN 978-1-64651-345-1

Original cover design by Tadashi Hisamochi (hive&co.,ltd.)

Printed in the United States of America.

www.kodansha.us

1st Printing
Translation: Steven LeCroy
Lettering: Andrew Copeland
Additional Lettering: Belynda Ungurath
Editing: Thalia Sutton, Maggie Le
YKS Services LLC/SKY Japan, Inc.
Kodansha Comics edition cover design by Adam Del Re

Publisher: Kiichiro Sugawara

Director of publishing services: Ben Applegate
Director of publishing operations: Dave Barrett
Associate director of publishing operations: Stephen Pakula
Publishing services managing editors: Alanna Ruse, Madison Salters
Production managers: Emi Lotto, Angela Zurlo
Logo and character art ©Kodansha USA Publishing, LLC